THE SZEKLER NATION AND MEDIEVAL HUNGARY

THE SZEKLER NATION AND MEDIEVAL HUNGARY

Politics, Law and Identity on the Frontier

Nathalie Kálnoky

Translated from the French by
Farkas Kálnoky

BLOOMSBURY ACADEMIC
LONDON • NEW YORK • OXFORD • NEW DELHI • SYDNEY

BLOOMSBURY ACADEMIC
Bloomsbury Publishing Plc
50 Bedford Square, London, WC1B 3DP, UK
1385 Broadway, New York, NY 10018, USA
29 Earlsfort Terrace, Dublin 2, Ireland

BLOOMSBURY, BLOOMSBURY ACADEMIC and the Diana logo
are trademarks of Bloomsbury Publishing Plc

First published in Great Britain 2020
Paperback edition published 2021

Copyright © Nathalie Kálnoky, 2020

English Translation Copyright © Farkas Kálnoky, 2020

Nathalie Kálnoky has asserted her right under the Copyright, Designs and
Patents Act, 1988, to be identified as Author of this work.

Cover design: Terry Woodley
Cover image: Chronicon Pictum, Hungarian Illuminated Chronicle (Képes Krónika),
Széchényi Hungarian National Library, Budapest

All rights reserved. No part of this publication may be reproduced or transmitted in
any form or by any means, electronic or mechanical, including photocopying,
recording, or any information storage or retrieval system, without
prior permission in writing from the publishers.

Bloomsbury Publishing Plc does not have any control over, or responsibility for,
any third-party websites referred to or in this book. All internet addresses given
in this book were correct at the time of going to press. The author and publisher
regret any inconvenience caused if addresses have changed or sites have ceased
to exist, but can accept no responsibility for any such changes.

A catalogue record for this book is available from the British Library.

A catalog record for this book is available from the Library of Congress.

ISBN: HB: 978-1-7883-1482-4
       PB: 978-1-3502-4534-1
       ePDF: 978-1-7867-3632-1
       eBook: 978-1-7867-2626-1

Typeset by Integra Software Services Pvt. Ltd.

To find out more about our authors and books visit www.bloomsbury.com
and sign up for our newsletters.

CONTENTS

List of Maps	ix
List of Tables	x
List of Illustrations	xi
Translator's Preface	xiii
Preamble	xvii
INTRODUCTION	1
The Sources	6
Utilization of the Sources	8
The Studies	9

Part I
THE STRUCTURES OF THE SZEKLER COMMUNITY (THIRTEENTH–FIFTEENTH CENTURIES) — 11

Chapter I
ON THE ORIGINS OF THE MILITARY AUXILIARY PEOPLE AND THEIR SETTLING IN THE SZEKLERLAND — 13

I. *'Privileged nobles, descendants of the Scythians'* – The Origins of the Szeklers	13
A. The Theories on the Origin of the Szeklers	14
1. The Tradition since the Earliest Chronicles: Attila and Scythia	14
2. The Onset of Critical Analysis: Functionalism, Etymology and Totemism	15
3. Archaeology and the Theory of the Double Conquest	16
4. The Khazaro-Kavar Theory in the Light of Byzantine Sources	16
B. Szekler Origins and Szekler Law	18
II. *'Skilled in the art of war'* – The Military Role of the Szeklers	19
A. The Hungarian Confederation at the Time of the Conquest (Ninth–Tenth Centuries)	20
1. A Military-Political Confederation	20
2. Power Shared	21
3. Military Functions, Lineages and the Sharing of Property	21
B. The Szeklers' Place in the Hungarian Military Organization under the Árpád Dynasty (Tenth–Thirteenth Centuries)	22
1. The Structures of the New Kingdom	22
2. Just One of Several Auxiliary Peoples	23
C. From Privilege to Integration: The Auxiliary Peoples and the Szekler Exception	24
III. Migration toward the Szeklerland	25
A. From Moson to the *Altland,* Stopover at Telegd	25

B. The Transylvanian Particularism 28
　　　　1. The Voivode of Transylvania 28
　　　　2. The Assembly of the Three Nations 29
　　　　　　The Absence of the Romanians from the Institutions 29
　　　　3. The Saxon Community 31
　　C. From the *Altland* to the Szeklerland 33
　　　　1. The Three Stages of Settlement 33
　　　　2. The Three Ecclesiastic Circumscriptions 35
　　　　3. The *tres genera Siculorum* in the Military Organization ... 36

Chapter II
THE NOBLE SZEKLER NATION: A PRIVILEGED COMMUNITY 39
　I. *'Privileged Nobles'* 39
　　A. A Collective Privilege 39
　　　　1. The Notion of Privilege 40
　　　　2. The Particularism of the Szekler Community's Privilege ... 40
　　B. Personal Military Obligation 42
　　　　1. The Szekler Military Structure 42
　　　　2. The Reforms of King Matthias 46
　　　　　　An Indispensable Military Adaptation … 46
　　　　　　… which Confirms the Traditions of the Szekler
　　　　　　Community 47
　　　　3. The Statutory Tax Exemption and the Gift of the Branded Oxen 49
　II. The Organization of the Szeklerland 50
　　A. The Place of the Church 50
　　　　Problems of Historiography 50
　　　　1. Church History and Szekler Society 51
　　　　　　Paganism, Occidental and Oriental Christianities and
　　　　　　Reformation 51
　　　　　　Ecclesiastic Organization 52
　　　　2. Privileges in Conflict – Conflicting Privileges 54
　　　　　　Privileged Ecclesiastic Enclaves in the Szeklerland 54
　　　　　　Conflicts of Jurisdictional Competence 55
　　B. The Royal Free Towns 57
　　C. The Szeklerland, its Seats and Clans 60
　　　　1. The Szeklerland Divided into Seats 60
　　　　　　The Particularism of the Seat of Aranyos 61
　　　　　　The Sub-Seats 61
　　　　　　The Villages 63
　　　　　　The 'tízes' and the Village 63
　　　　2. A Structure of Clans 65

Part II
CUSTOMARY LAW, AS PRACTISED – AND RECORDED
(FIFTEENTH–SIXTEENTH CENTURIES) 69
Royal Authority, Oligarchy and the Nobility 69
The Ottoman Menace 70

Chapter III
THE RECORDING OF CUSTOMARY LAW 73
From Common Use to Codified Procedure 73
I. Conflicts within the Community (1466–1473) 75
   A. 1466, Zabola, Confirmation of the Free Status of the Common
      Szeklers 75
   B. 1473, the Three Military Strata 75
II. The Affirmation of the Szekler Community (1493–1514) 76
   A. 1493, Solidarity against the Voivode 76
   B. 1499, Royal Confirmation of the Szekler Community's Privileges 77
   C. 1503, the 'Concordat' between the Diocese of Transylvania
      and the Szekler Community 77
   D. 1505 and 1506, the 'Constitutions' of Udvarhely and Agyagfalva 78
      Rearguard Action? 78
      … or Golden Age? 79
   E. The Consecration: 1514, *Opus Tripartitum, Pars* III, *Titulus* IV 79
III. 1555: Codification in Detail 81

Chapter IV
THE PRACTICE OF LAW: LEGAL PROCEDURE IN THE SZEKLERLAND 83
Procedure and Jurisdictions 83
Applicable Law: Territoriality versus Individuality 83
I. The Echelons of Jurisdiction and the Steps of a Legal Procedure 84
      Military-Judiciary Structure 85
   A. Local Jurisdictions Applying Szekler Law 86
      'Decarchal Jurisdictions', Village Judges and Arbitrators 87
   B. The Jurisdictions of the Seats 90
   C. Procedural Steps 90
      1. Steps in the Conduct of a Trial 90
         Rights of Appeal 92
         Execution of Judgements 95
      2. The Holding of Judiciary Assemblies 102
         Judiciary Assemblies in the Székely Archives 103
         Frequency of Assemblies 103
II. The Judged and the Judges 108
   A. The Community, Juries, Seat Judges, Captains and Judges of
      the Crown Council: What these Terms Signify 108
   B. *'Universitas Siculorum'* 109
   C. *'Iurati Assessores'* 109
   D. The Szekler Tribunal 110
      1. Who Was the Crown Judge? 111
      2. The Judge of the Seat (*iudex terrestris*) 112
      3. The Captain 113
III. The Paradox of the Primipilate 113
   A. The Principles of Eligibility to the Dignities of Judge and Captain 113
      1. From Land that Comes with the Function … 114
      2. … to Land as a Condition for Access to the Function 114

3. The Number of Dignitaries by Seat	116
B. The Case of the Seat of Maros in the Early Sixteenth Century	118
1. The Sharing out of Dignities between the Clans	122
2. Sharing in, and Concentration of, Clan Rights by Families	122
3. Presence of Clans and Primipilates in the Villages	129

Chapter V
LAND OWNERSHIP   133
  I. Prohibition of Royal Donations and Confiscations in the Szeklerland   134
    A. Hungarian Families and Szekler Land   134
    B. Szekler Families and Royal Donations of Land Adjoining the Szeklerland.   135
  II. Alienation of Land Property   137
    A. The Categories of Szekler Land: Acquest and Inheritance   137
    B. The Types of Alienation: Mortgaging and Sale in Perpetuity (*perpetua proprietas*)   138
    C. Conditions for Alienation of Inheritances: Kinship Rights   139
  III. Rules of Inheritance   142
    A. The Testament   143
    B. Custom: Division and Orderly Succession   146
      1. Codified Rules of Division   147
        The Status of the Widow   148
        The Rights of Collaterals   150
        The Question of the Dowry   151
      2. Successoral Order: 'Women's Rights' and the Kindred   153
        Successions by Women   153
      3. Rules Deduced from Practice   157
  IV. The Right of Confiscation before 1562   158
    A. The Underlying Principles   158
    B. The Practice   159
    C. The Decision of 1562   161

BY WAY OF CONCLUSION   167

  Glossary   173
  Documents   178
  Chronology   182
  Names of the Cities of Transylvania Quoted in this Study   187
  List of Szekler Villages   187
  Abbreviations   202
  Sources   203
  Notes   206
  Bibliography   226
  English Bibliography Supplement   232
  Index   236

MAPS

1. Hungary, Yesterday and Today — 3
2. The Kingdom of Hungary at the End of the Middle Ages (Fifteenth Century) — 3
3. Hungary after the Battle of Mohács — 5
4. Szekler Migrations and Establishment in the Szeklerland — 26
5. The Szeklerland (Seats and Royal Free Towns) and the Royal Fortresses — 44
6. Twenty Villages of the Seat of Maros with Primipilates (Late Fifteenth Century) — 130

TABLES

1	Establishment of Saxon Seats – German (Hungarian) Names	32
2	Displacement and Settlement in the Seats of Kézdi, Sepsi and Orbai	34
3	Szekler Migrations to their Permanent Seats	35
4	The *tres genera Siculorum* and the other Ternary Divisions	37
5	Szeklers Mobilized by Cardinal Point and Command	45
6	Monastic Orders in the Szekler Seats of the Archdeaconry of Telegd	55
7	Royal Free Towns in the Szeklerland	58
8	The Changes of the Status of Sepsiszentgyörgy as Royal Free Town	59
9	Sub-Seats in the Szeklerland	62
10	Villages in the Szeklerland by Number of Families (1614)	64
11	The Six Tribes and Twenty-four Clans of the Seat of Maros	65
12	Details on Clans Mentioned	66
13	Echelons of Jurisdiction Applicable to a Szekler	86
14	Overview of Penalties Incurred	100
15	Penalties Incurred for Court Costs	107
16	Composition of a Judiciary Assembly in the Szeklerland	108
17	Dignitaries per Seat (1506)	117
18	Breakdown of Dignitaries by Seat and Sub-Seat	117
19	Distribution of Dignities by Seat and Family	118
A.	The Six Tribes and Twenty-four Clans of the Seat of Maros	118
B.	The Sequential Order of Rotation for the Dignities of Captain and Judge	119
C.	The Families Occupying the Dignities	120
D.	Clan Rights to Dignities Borne by Families	123
E.	The Six Principal Families Bearing Dignities in the Seat of Maros (1499–1514)	125
F.	Rotation of Dignities	126
G.	Rotation of Dignities within the Six Most Frequently Cited Families	128
G.1	Rotation of Dignities within Families, by Clan	129

Genealogical Tables

1	Diagrams of the Rules of Successoral Devolution	162
2	The Gyerőfi Succession	164
3	The Madarasi Successions	165
4	The Szentkirályi Succession	166
5	The Successions of Barlabássi, Szentgyörgyi and Káli	166

ILLUSTRATIONS

1 Hungarian Illuminated Chronicle, Chronica de Gestis Hungarorum, Dercsenyi, Dezsö (ed.), Budapest, 1968 — 1
2 Balás, Gábor. A székelyek nyomában (*On the Track of the Szeklers*), Budapest, 1984, p. 269 — 18
3 Light Cavalryman in King Matthias' Time, Illustration from 'Weisskunig' (Der weisse König – The White King), a prose chronicle of the fifteenth century, first published in 1775, in Sádvári, György and Somogyi, Győző. Nagy huszárkönyv (*The Great Book of Hussars*), Budapest, 1999, p. 22 — 46
4 Light Cavalryman in King Matthias' Time – the curved sabre is characteristic of the light cavalry — 47
5 The Medieval Church of Zabola Fortification fourteenth–fifteenth century Reconstitution, Gyöngyössy, János. Székely templomerődök (*Szekler Fortified Churches*), Csíkszereda, 1999, p. 82 — 54

TRANSLATOR'S PREFACE

> 'If a Szekler hangs the Szekler flag on a public building, I will string him up alongside.'
> Mihai Tudose, Romanian Prime Minister,
> Bucharest, 1 November 2018.

After 1,000 years in Transylvania and 100 in Romania, the Szeklers have defiantly preserved their sense of identity, which, in everyday life, is manifested by their flag and their perseverance in the use of the Hungarian language. The language, a Uralic island in an Indo-European sea, has a rich but hermetic vocabulary, in which nouns have thirty cases – only seventeen in daily use. It is a barrier difficult for outsiders to breach. In their new environment in Romania, it is the Szeklers who surmounted the obstacle, adding the Romanians' language to their own, but their equally rich cultural and institutional heritage, represented by their flag, lives on and seems to irritate. It is seen to embody the Szeklers' individuality within their broader Hungarian heritage in Romania.

The kingdom of Hungary was founded about the year 1000 around two seminal principles. One, the pagan Grand Prince Géza (AD 940–997) had embraced the Latin rite of Christianity, while the Greek rite, centred on Constantinople, was still present in Transylvania. Two, in his admonition to his son and successor Emeric, Hungary' first crowned King, Stephen, affirmed: '... *nam unius lingue uniusque moris regnum imbecile et fragile est*' (for a Kingdom with [only] one language and one custom is weak and fragile).

The first of these principles allowed Hungary to affirm its place in Europe's occidental Christianity and avoid sharing the short-lived fate of earlier arrivals like the Huns and Avars. The kingdom soon flourished at the eastern frontier of Latin Christianity.

In line with the second, King Stephen's precept, it played host to a number of populations, Pechenegs, Cumans, Iasians – and Szeklers. Order was consolidated in the kingdom by firmly assigning the newcomers places to settle and functions to fulfil. The Pechenegs, erstwhile eastern enemies, were installed to the west, the Cumans and Iasians in the centre around the king and the Szeklers as border guards along the frontiers, essentially in the southeastern corner of the kingdom, in Transylvania.

The nascent kingdom felt strengthened by this diversity in its ranks and granted the different communities collective privileges for their service. The existence of a special juridical status for different, not necessarily ethnic groupings in the Hungarian kingdom ensured their loyalty and standing. With their integration, the maturing kingdom came to resemble its western neighbours and the privileged communities faded, merged and eventually let their identity wane.

All but one. Assigned by the king to guard the Eastern frontier of the kingdom, the Szeklers adapted their structures and customs from their time in the Steppes to their new environment in a Western European kingdom. In so doing, they achieved institutional autonomy within a modern state and cemented their sense of historical individuality. They, in turn, applied King Stephen's admonition of gaining strength through the assimilation of ethnic diversity within their ranks, as is shown by the toponymic curiosities in the Szeklerland. These sometimes called into question the Szeklers' ethnic authenticity. Slavic place names jostle with Armenian, Cuman, Pecheneg, Iasian and Vlach villages on a map of the Szeklerland. And, while their neighbours are tempted to pride themselves on ethnic purity, the Szeklers' pride is in their system of laws and self-governance. The acceptance by ethnic communities of the Szeklers' obligations and rights constituted their integration.

In today's post-Marxian idiom, the Szeklers' 'privilege' reeks of undeserved advantages enjoyed by a socially superior class over the common man. In France, the 'Bretons' privilege', accorded and confirmed by the French kings related not to creature comfort but to their right to determine their own destiny with a parliament and judiciary rules of their own. It was summarily abolished by the French revolution, with the death knell of *Liberté, égalité*. (*Fraternité* was yet to be invented and never codified.) The Bretons' identity survives, however. Their black-and-white flag is ever present on French bumper stickers; their folklore joins that of their Celtic cousins in popular festivals with Irish, Scottish, Galician and Asturian participants. But then, Breton identity does not test that of France.

In medieval Szekler society, *liberté* meant to have no subservience to any lord between them and the king and to move about freely; *égalité* was the right of all to vote at assemblies and to elect officials and judges. *Fraternité* was a day-to-day practice, though occasionally giving way to vociferous altercations – which ended up before their elected judges and gave rich subject matter for this study to deal with.

To quote the Szekler author Áron Tamási: 'The world was created for everyone to have someplace to call his home.' Wistful sentiment for a lifelong migrant to proclaim. Born in Hungarian Transylvania, in the Szeklerland, he emigrated to the United States in 1923 when Transylvania became part of Romania, returned to Transylvania three years later and moved to Hungary in 1944, where he died. His writings breathe the folklore of his origins. His perception is evident for Szeklers, for whom 'home' refers to their land in Transylvania but equally to their identity: the framework of tradition, laws and customs carried over from their place in the Steppes. Its presence is a spice that helped define bearing, attitude in all manner of situations wherever Szeklers found themselves. An American source refers to it as 'their extreme superiority complexes' (cf. László Kürti, *The Remote Borderland*).

True, they are still conscious of their status as 'original nobles', *Uradel* in German, nobles already on arrival in the Pannonian basin, as cavalrymen. This was seamlessly confirmed by the king's assignment as guards of the Eastern border.

Anachronism aside, it is tempting to liken the preamble 'we the inhabitants of' in statutes voted by Szekler communities to the all-important 'we the people' in more recent charters. They voted of a common accord the sets of laws under which they agreed to live. A formal variant to the more casual accumulation of customary or common laws observed elsewhere. Hence the original, French edition of this work, titled '*Les Constitutions et Privilèges de la Noble Nation Sicule*' put the first word in the plural. It was a PhD thesis where this contextual accuracy was natural in the academic world. Nevertheless, lay readers of the first drafts of the English translation invariably suggested the term be put in the singular, no doubt with the constitution of the United States of America in mind. Still, the 'we the people' of the preambles, with the voting of constitutions by the entire population is a measure of the precocity of the Szekler system of laws and institutions, in the very first years of the sixteenth century.

But is this democracy?

The American Constitution dates from 1787; the French was adopted in 1791, by constituent assemblies in the name of the people. England perseveres without a written constitution, the rule of law based essentially on judicial precedent, supplemented by legislation. They are readily recognized as archetypes of modern, representative democracy.

No doubt some English would wince at being told that theirs is a tribal system, but common-law systems do reach back beyond the onset of written documentation. In fact they are an essential part of democracy itself; they take us back to our origins, to before the Normans for the English and the Steppes of Central Asia for the Szeklers. Organizational discipline was a necessity, for a warrior had to be able to rely on the horseman riding alongside (cf. Karol Modzelewski, *L'Europe des Barbares*).

Democracy in Europe is thought of as Greek, but in fact it concerns the Germanic cultures, the Slavs and the Scandinavians among others. In the Caucasus, archaeologists have found traces from the tenth century of the Grand Council of the Ossets, which survived until the eighteenth century, when it was forced to call on the Russian Empire for help.

To various degrees Europe's primeval cultures shared principles and structures that today constitute the ideals represented by the term 'democracy': individual freedom, societal and legal equality of all to enact rules and elect dignitaries, and a status that defined their relation to higher authority.

This volume deals equally with the internal structures of the Szekler community and their adaptation to ambient events to ensure their survival. But this study allows us to look beyond the Szekler question, beyond Transylvania, Hungary and to historical minorities everywhere.

The compilation of laws and case histories presented here shows how a society under customary law may respond to structural and economic changes by resistance or adaptation, while conserving its cohesion. In the embrace of its conventions and customs it evolves through changes that often may surprise to the point of an apparent paradox, 'legal fiction' in an evolution we encounter elsewhere, at different periods. We see here what the anthropologist Lévi-Strauss calls 'cold societies'; societies that devote the bulk of their energy to the conservation of their ancestral customs. Readers interested in the fate of minorities will find fundamental elements to evaluate different scientific analytical approaches. Here it is history of law, supported by the methodological instruments of juridical anthropology.

In these few pages with tables, a glossary, chronologies and the evocation of situation after situation, the author hopes to have presented as precise a picture as possible of the importance of the Szeklers' juridical history of their identity. Based on their ancient system of laws and innate sense of justice, the Szeklers' cohesion tends to thrive, not crumble, in the face of outside hostility perceived as unjust.

Farkas Kálnoky

The author and her translator owe a debt of thanks to all those who have shown active interest in the making of this work. Among them especially Stephen Pálffy.

PREAMBLE

'About the Scythians of Transylvania, whom we call Székelys'[1]

Furthermore there live in Transylvania privileged nobles,[2] descendants of the Scythian people when they first entered Pannonia, whom we commonly call Székelys[3] in our current language. Skilled in the art of war, they observe different laws and customs, and share out their possessions and functions among their tribes and clans in the manner of the ancients. […/…] Their laws in cases of dispute amongst themselves being so different and practiced only amongst themselves, there is no need to dwell on them more amply here.

István Werbőczy,
Opus Tripartitum,
Pars III, Titulus IV
(1514)

INTRODUCTION

Figure 1. Hungarian Illuminated Chronicle, Chronica de Gestis Hungarorum, Dercsenyi, Dezso (ed.), Budapest, 1968.

A hundred years after their arrival in the Pannonian basin (896), the Hungarians linked their fate to that of the West with the coronation of King Stephen I (1000). While this ritual was the symbolic expression of their political choice of the occidental Christian model, it did not mask the persistence of diversity within the new kingdom. The very first miniature illustrating the Hungarian Illuminated Chronicle[1] (Figure 1 and cover) is painstakingly spot-on in its observation, depicting the king of Hungary in the fourteenth century in the presence of Hungarian barons, in occidental dress on his right, and the dignitaries of the auxiliary peoples, in oriental attire on his left. This variety of costumes, which the illuminator shows in purposeful detail, presents the diversity of Hungarian society that constituted the medieval Hungarian kingdom.

The realm of Hungary was fashioned from this diversity, as witness St. Stephen's warning of 'the fragility of a state where but one language is spoken and one single custom is observed',[2] and the Golden Bull of 1222, often compared to the *Magna Carta* of England. In this political compromise, the king recognizes the nobility's privileges and political power collectively. When, in 1351, Louis of Anjou (Louis the Great, the Hungarian king represented in the opening miniature) confirmed the Golden Bull, the entire nobility, from the greatest families to the royal *servientes*, was once again recognized as equal (*una eademque nobilitas*), notwithstanding the reality that the exercise of power was the domain of a few pre-eminent families.

The six barons in occidental attire, and an air somewhat less than affable, on the right of the throne and the five dignitaries on the left are considered to be one and equal in nobility. The five men to the left of the king are to the East and the barons are to the West, the direction that seems to engage the king's attention. Less concerned with the appearances of Italian elegance in vogue at the time, the dignitaries in oriental attire are shown in an attitude of loyalty, as manifested by the personage nearest the throne, who raises his hand, palm outward, toward the king. The eleven personages around the king at the middle of the fourteenth century, whatever their military role or armament (from armour with a helmet and long, straight sword to a mace and curved sabre) illustrate by their heterogeneity and number the collective nobility of the kingdom of Hungary.

Judging by the red attire – red was perpetuated as the colour of its military uniforms – the Szekler community is represented among the oriental-style dignitaries by the man with the curved sabre, the third in the first row and therefore the one farthest to the east, to the left of the king. At the time these illuminations were composed, the Pechenegs (no doubt represented by the person with a raised hand) and the Cumans (the man in yellow dress armed with a mace) enjoyed, like the Szeklers, collective privileges due to their military role; thus the positioning of the three men in the illumination would correspond to their geographic localization on a map of the Hungarian kingdom. At that time, the Pechenegs were the king's bodyguards, the Cumans were settled between the Danube and the Tisza, while the Szeklers were charged with the defence of the eastern border, in Transylvania. Who, then, are the men in the second row? One of them, bearded and of occidental allure, could well represent the Germans, who had been settled in the kingdom since the end of the eleventh century. He wears a helmet because these settlers were also accorded their privileges in exchange for military service, though by the middle of the fourteenth century, when the illumination was painted, their military role was waning and these western settlers were increasingly active in the development of towns and commerce. In this context they were still privileged but of a secondary standing, and though the privileges for free towns were in the process of evolution during the fourteenth century, they did not yet enjoy the prestige attached to military service. Finally, the other personage, discretely placed behind the three military peoples and flanking the western settlers, could well be seen to represent the Iasian community or, more generally, symbolize the various oriental, non-military communities present in the kingdom.

Now let us take another look at the barons affecting western style, similarly placed in two ranks. The six are more closely spaced, as if in closed ranks; those nearest to the throne in the first row wield their swords in a somewhat unseemly fashion. Relations between the king and the nobles of Hungary were often tense, the result of swing-wing alliances where internal dissensions or solidarity fluctuated with the circumstances, for or against the central authority of the Crown.

The history of the Hungarian kingdom, with its remarkable success in its first centuries, saw its monarchy entrenched firmly in the face of a recalcitrant aristocracy. This can be explained, as in the opening illumination of the Hungarian Chronicle, by its astute balancing between the feudal aristocracy characteristic of its time and the persistence, sometimes with the active support of the monarch's political will, of the military tribalism of a sizeable group of auxiliary peoples of diverse origins. Centralizing institutions patterned after Carolingian models and implanted with the help of the Church were used, and judiciously nurtured, to deal with the magnates, who were a persistent threat to the Crown. At the same time the perpetuation of the clannic traditions of the auxiliary peoples (traditions rooted in Hungarian history) contributed to the structuring of this evolution.

Map 1. Hungary: Yesterday and Today

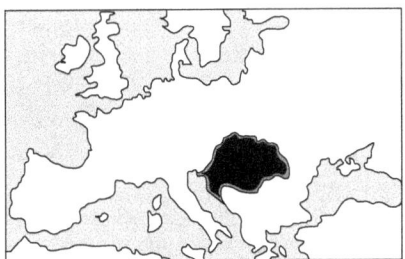

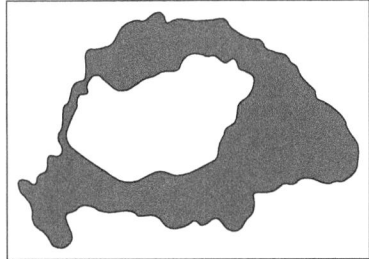

Hungary in the fourteenth century

In white: Hungary today

Map 2. The Kingdom of Hungary at the End of the Middle Ages (Fifteenth Century)

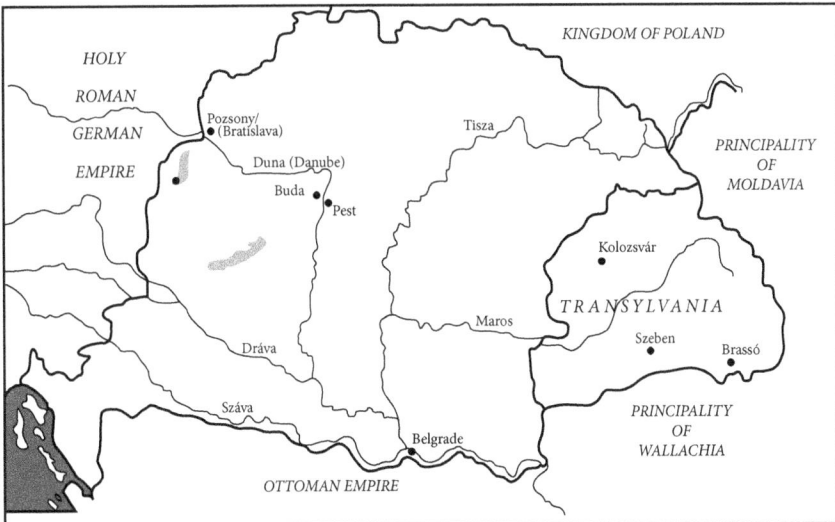

The Szekler community, a constituent part of the Hungarian kingdom, is an instructive example of the evolution of Central-European history, which the West has started to rediscover in recent years. The kingdom succeeded in respecting the multi-ethnic nature of its society while adopting the occidental model for the forming of a State. Thanks in turn to their political pragmatism, the Szeklers, from the thirteenth century onwards, ruled a territory of their own in Transylvania – the Szeklerland (*Székelyföld, Terra Siculorum*) – where they lived in observance of their own customs.

The aim of this study is to present these customs and the structures of which they were initially the expression, and later, as the need for recourse to writing became pressing, the guarantors.

The history of medieval Szekler law is the history of a system of laws founded on tradition for its rules and autonomy for its practice. The influence of Hungarian history did not manifest itself in the exercise of Szekler law until relatively late. On the contrary, certain aspects of the customs of the Szekler community are often described as mirroring what must have prevailed in a Hungarian society composed of clans, before their settling and the promulgation of the laws of St. Stephen.

History of law is in itself a double discipline. Presenting a study of the customary law of a community within medieval Hungary requires a choice to be made of the historical aspects needed to situate an elaboration of the system of laws. Those aspects of Hungarian history that are needed to understand the evolution of Szekler customary law will be presented as and when they affect the analysis of the Szekler community and its legal customs i.e.:

Part I, Chapter 1:	Military Institutions in the Tenth Century
	The Auxiliary Peoples
	St. Stephen's Laws Concerning Property
	The Place of the Church
	The Institutions of Transylvania
Part II, Introduction	The Estates and the Ottoman Menace

At this point the reader will merely find the division into the key periods that are used in Hungarian historiography, and an enumeration of the essential phases of medieval Hungary conventionally used.

Prior to the arrival of the Hungarians, the Carpathian basin had been crossed and occupied by numerous peoples. At the end of the ninth century, this region to the east of the Ostmark was not unoccupied, but no lasting political structure was established there. Great Moravia, which disappeared under the assault of the Hungarians in 905, had its centre of gravity slightly to the northwest. In the space of one century (AD 895–1000), the Hungarians evolved from plundering semi-nomads and pagans – like most of those who had preceded them – to become sedentary subjects of their kingdom and Christians.

The period preceding the arrival of the Hungarians in the Carpathian basin is generally dealt with in the first two chapters of Hungarian history books: the history of the territory and that of the Hungarian people settling it (often referred to as proto-Hungarians). Next we find the Middle Ages, starting with the Conquest (*Honfoglalás*). In western historiography and west of the river Leitha, the arrival of the Hungarians in the Carpathian basin is less often associated with the term 'conquest' or 'land-taking'. It is customarily viewed as a series of recurring incursions or invasions. In this study, the term 'Conquest' is used for what the Hungarians more peacefully call '*honfoglalás*' or 'land-taking'. In the English language 'Conquest' has come to be associated with the Normans in 1066, while the term 'land-taking' (*Landnahme, Landnáma*),[3] paradoxically enough, recalls Viking conquests.

The Middle Ages in Hungary are generally divided into two major periods. The first – the Árpád age – covers four centuries (895–1301), from the Conquest to the last male descendant of the conquering Árpád dynasty. The second (1301–1526) ends with the disastrous defeat by the Turks at the battle of Mohács, after which the Hungarian kingdom was divided into three political entities: the Ottoman pashalik in the middle, framed by two Christian kingdoms; the Habsburgs to the west; and to the east the Szapolya, whose territory (the province of Transylvania and the *Partium*) became the internationally recognized principality of Transylvania after the treaty of Speyer in 1570.

Map 3. Hungary after the Battle of Mohács

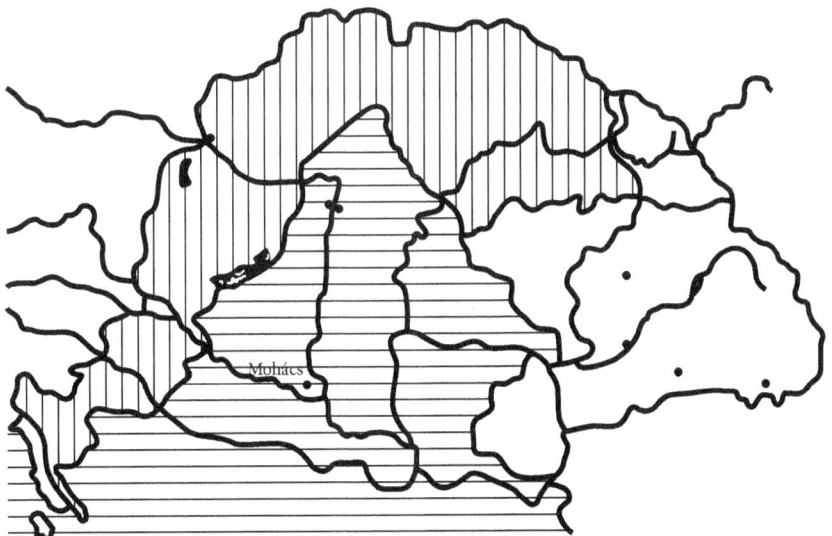

| horizontal hatching: Turkish-occupied territory |
| vertical hatching: Habsburg domination |
| white: Transylvania and the attached '*Partium*' |

The borders of the '*Partium*' were continually modified between 1545 and 1664. The contours here are as they appear in the History of Hungary published by Miklós Molnár.[4]

The two medieval periods are in turn subdivided into the reigns of the sovereigns. Following the end of the Árpád dynasty, only one more Hungarian ascended the throne (Matthias Hunyadi, commonly known as 'Corvinus'). According to the French historian Jean Bérenger,[5] 'the absence of well-defined successoral rules like the "Salic law" […/∴] facilitating the transmission of the (Hungarian) crown to foreign dynasties by election or marriage to a legitimate heir' explains the later formation of the Habsburg empire in central Europe. The majority of the foreign kings ruling this elective monarchy bore other crowns besides that of St. Stephen, the Holy Crown, which dates from the end of the eleventh century, the national symbol of Greater Hungary, today placed in the parliament in Budapest. They bore the crown of Poland: Louis of Anjou, Wladislas I Jagiello (III as king of Poland); the crown of Bohemia: Sigismund of Luxembourg, Albert V of Habsburg, Ladislas V of Habsburg, Wladislas II, and Louis Jagiello. Sigismund of Luxembourg was also emperor of the Holy Roman Empire.

No doubt this plurality of states – and of the institutions inherent in each of them – under the authority of a single sovereign crowned king of Hungary, favoured the preservation of the Szeklers' autonomous judicial system. It was not until the breaking up of Hungary, following the defeat at Mohács, that the royal authority exercised by the Szapolyas over a diminished kingdom adopted repressive measures against the juridical autonomy and privileges of the Szekler people.

There is no date in history that signals a full stop; history encompasses currents of movement within the stream of time, within which the study of history needs to evolve around markers – instants of pause – in its narration. The study of law benefits from more solidly posed points of reference, signposts of persisting customs, movement flagged by laws newly decreed and statutes newly legislated, around which its day-to-day practice is articulated, its deviations, refusals and abandons phrased. In the domain of Szekler law, the Middle Ages end in 1562 with the decree of King John II Szapolya that overthrows the established order of their system of justice – for a time.

From the thirteenth to the sixteenth century, within a kingdom that had espoused Roman Christianity and Occidental values, the Szekler community remained faithful in its structures to a more ancient system of organization. This particularism found its expression not in language, religious belief or folklore – which in any case would not have survived without undergoing ulterior recompositions – but in an ancestral system of oral law buttressed by a progressive commitment to written form.

The Sources

Any enquiry – judicial or historical – is limited and conditioned in its progress by the availability of evidence and testimony. The reconstitution of the juridical rules of the medieval Szekler community is assembled from documents that have survived in archives. Such evidence is necessarily fragmentary: some normative matters were never committed to writing; some documents have since disappeared. Does it follow therefore that our sources are partial? No doubt, if our aim were painstakingly to portray day-to-day life in the Szekler-Land in the Middle Ages. Not at all, if our aim is to trace the evolution of its society, the 'horizontal' structuring of the community, embedded as it was in a strictly 'vertical' seignorial regime. Inevitably, the judicial decisions issuing from confrontations opposing the contrary interests of these two forms of society were committed to writing and, in spite of the vicissitudes of the passage of time, the documentation that has been conserved is sufficiently abundant and varied to allow us to perceive the most significant situations.

In 1818, the principal documents of Szekler law – still in force at that time – were published with royal and imperial affirmation. The original version of the present study derived its title from the publication: 'Constitutions and Privileges of the Noble Szekler Nation',[6] published by Mihály Székely de Killyén in 1818. From the end of the eighteenth century onwards, studies of the history of the Szeklers appear, documents are copied and published. However, the motives of these historians do not always measure up to the standards of scientific objectivity observed in more recent years. For one thing, Szekler law was not yet a subject of historiography and certain forgeries – since identified as such – were fashioned for the express purpose of lending weight to a particular argument before a court of law. One well-known example is the 'Szekler Chronicle of Csík', supposedly written in 1533 and miraculously discovered in 1796. The forger, Zsigmond Sándor, a brilliant student of law, invented a fantastic story around the arrival of the Szeklers in Transylvania, as proof of his family's rights in a lawsuit against the Apor family.[7] Other authors proved remarkably creative and imaginative in compiling 'copies' of ancient documents. Their motives are less obviously self-serving. The literary ambition of authoring a pleasing and coherent historical narrative seems to have prevailed over any fastidious obsession with mere fact.

During the second half of the nineteenth century, the study of Szekler history was revived as the science of historiography evolved and as, in 1848, the institutions of Hungary and Transylvania were merged.

The *Székely Archives* – in Hungarian: *Székely Oklevéltár*, abbreviated to 'SzOkl' in the following, '*Székely Archives*' with initial capital letters and in italics refers to these publications – were published in seven volumes between 1872 and 1898. An additional tome, often referred to as 'volume VIII' was published in Budapest in 1934 (see 'Abbreviations' and 'Sources'). This collection of more than 1,800 documents dating from 1219 to 1776 was assembled from several sources. The records of the Chapter of the Episcopal See of Transylvania at Gyulafehérvár and the Convent of Kolozsmonostor are the principal sources for the period under examination. Unless the context dictates otherwise, Transylvanian place names are given in Hungarian, the spoken language of the Szeklers. A table of correspondence in Romanian and German appears in the Annex. In addition, the compilers obtained access to a number of family archives and documents emanating from Szekler, Transylvanian and Hungarian institutions (legal decisions, minutes of Transylvanian assemblies and royal writs). Over eight hundred documents concern the Szeklers during the period up to 1562.

There is nothing specifically Hungarian about the development of the royal chancellery. A permanent institution by the end of the twelfth century, the royal chancellery, to quote the Hungarian historian György Györffy, evolved under the impulse of the papal curia, the imperial chancellery and the royal chancellery of France and, by and large, in parallel with those of Bohemia and Poland. Like their European models and those of their neighbours, the Hungarian chancellery was an institution of the *curia regis*.[8]

On the other hand, the ecclesiastic *locus credibilis* (place of authentication), as an institution for the recording of both private documents and royal charters, is specific to Hungary. It indicates the role of the Church in the formation and organization of the kingdom's institutions. From the middle of the twelfth century and all the way to 1874, 'certain ecclesiastic communities – monasteries, secular chapters – were authorized to establish charters with their proper seal, at the demand of private persons, by royal command, or judicial order.[9] Witnesses (*pro testimonium fidedignum*) as well as notaries or emissaries of these *loca credibilia*, were solicited 'for the pledging of estates as security, for the division of lands and in issues involving inheritance […/…] etc. in order to provide an authentic writ that was valid before all authorities.'[10]

As the number of *loca credibilia* increased at the end of the thirteenth century until, in 1351, the lesser convents' capacitations were revoked. The network thereafter encompassed about forty sites and included, for Transylvania, the chapter of Gyulafehérvár and the convent of Kolozsmonostor.

Utilization of the Sources

With source documents for this study spread across numerous volumes, a first pass at sequencing the documents was necessary. Several years had intervened between the publication of the volumes and in numerous instances documents dated the same year – or relating to the same dispute – would be spread across two or more volumes. The creation of a computer file with the date, the publication references,[11] the sources and the translation of the Hungarian compilers' abstracts heading the Latin text, provided significant advantages. The chronological sequencing once established, this voluminous file became both the material base and the tool for the development of this study.

With the fall of the Iron Curtain the publication of compilations of archives started again in Hungary, in about 1990. Besides the – invaluable – re-editions of books first published around the turn of the nineteenth to twentieth century that contain the integral original texts, among them the work of Imre Szentpétery (SRH) with the text of the medieval chronicles, several collections appeared from which the material needed to round out the 'base file' could be culled. Among these were the registers of the convent of Kolozsmonostor (Kmk), the archives of Transylvania (EOkm) and, somewhat less complete, the archives of the Angevin period (AOkm) and those of the reign of King Sisgismund (details on these publications can be found in the annex under 'Abbreviations' and 'Sources'). These publications have the merit of more advanced historiographic methodology (thematic indices and attentiveness to forgeries in particular) but they do not reproduce the integral, original Latin texts. Their abstracts tend to reflect the preoccupation of the compiler and not always those of the original documents – themselves on occasion influenced by the interests of their transcribers and their epoch. Meticulous perusal of my 'base file' brought these obstacles to light (if the compilers never missed a family name, consistent terminology regarding titles and functions was not their foremost aim, for example) rendering indispensable a return to the source, the examination of the Latin texts, but the newer publications lacked these. Where the history of the Szeklers is concerned, however, a cross-check between the thematic indices and the referenced Latin source materials (almost always contained in the *Székely Archives*) soon revealed that the essence of the medieval, Latin documentation that concerns the Szeklers is recorded verbatim in the *Székely Archives*.

In 1983, the publication of the *Székely Archives, New Series* was undertaken under the direction of Lajos Demény (SzOkl új). This series, containing extensive hitherto unpublished material, combines modern historiographic tools (in particular excellent indexing) with complete texts, starting from 1569. Volume IV contains all the military registers from 1575 to 1627, which proved indispensable in validating the outcome of certain earlier litigations, within the period under study. With all its newly published documents, this series has the merit of completing the *Székely Archives*, but, regrettably for this study, the inconvenience of falling outside of the Middle Ages.

The Studies

The bibliography of works dealing with the Szeklers is badly unbalanced. The question of the Szeklers' origin – which, it is true, cannot be left unaddressed – is the subject of a multitude of learned studies in Hungary; in fact the majority of bibliographic references concern theories on this problem. In works on Hungarian history, the Szeklers are never totally absent, but the attention they receive is limited. They are more present in histories of Transylvania, but here they fall victim to a common syndrome: the aim to move on and hasten to the arrival of the epoch of the independent Principality of Transylvania (end of the sixteenth to the beginning of the eighteenth centuries). The attention devoted to the history of the Szeklers in the Middle Ages is thus found to be remarkably hasty.

Hence, whilst most works of history seem to take Werbőczy at his word (there is no need to deal with them more amply here), others are entirely devoted to the subject of the Szeklers. In 1927, L. Szádeczky-Kardoss (the compiler of volumes III to VII of the *Székely Archives*) published a synthetic study of the Szeklers that remains a work of reference to this day.[12] A number of historians, Transylvanians for the most part, have also published works on the Szeklers since the 1970s.[13] Few deal with Szekler law, however, and all cover the period after 1562. The scarcity of studies dealing with medieval Szekler law is evident from a glance at the reference notes.

Closer attention is paid to medieval Szekler law in works on the history of Transylvanian law.[14] But once again, the period of the Middle Ages, when Transylvania was but a province of the greater Hungarian kingdom, is not dwelt on, any more than it is in other works on the history of Transylvania.

In 1980, we find the posthumous publication of an article by a Szekler jurist, Gy. Bodor, which recapitulates his work on the structures of Szekler society before 1562.[15] Regrettably never completed, Bodor's work aimed at the same period and subject matter as the present study. Finally, the work to which my own study is the most indebted is Gy. Bónis' history of law, published in 1942.[16] The only, modest, reservation I would formulate on this tome is that it examines Szekler law essentially under the aspects of private law. This point of view – broadly inspired by positive juridicism in general – does not adequately reflect the notion the medieval Szeklers had of their customs and neglects a double pertinence, that of their institutions (which go beyond the notion of private law) as factors in the evolution of their laws and that of the recording of their laws as a factor of protection for their institutions.

Whilst the Szeklers are always accorded a few lines in history books and their special character is given due credit, their mention is most often in reference to the quest of origins. This said, it is common knowledge that other peoples, whose origins are more clearly differentiated from those of the Hungarians, populated the Hungarian kingdom of the Middle Ages, living there initially under their own, distinct customs, only to gradually be assimilated and merged into the structures of the kingdom. The Szeklers alone (the colonists arriving from the West follow a course of their own) managed to maintain their communal autonomy. They realized their own assimilation of their proper legal procedures in the Middle Ages, putting legal formalisms at the service of their own institutions. This is a sufficiently documented historical example of a separate legal system not integrated in that of a state – itself embedded in Roman-Christian Europe – to merit closer scrutiny.

What better way to open a study on the medieval customs of the Szeklers than to do so in the company of István Werbőczy, the renowned jurist of the early sixteenth century? He seems to have seized the essentials: the origin of the Szeklers, their military aptitude, and their tribal customs so distinct – in the eyes of this urbane man of the Renaissance – from those of the kingdom of Hungary. In dealing with them more amply here – the only point of discord with István Werbőczy – we will adopt his reasoning, follow his evocation of the subject faithfully, step-by-step. The origins of these *Scythians of Transylvania*, their status of *privileged nobles* and their *skills in the art of war* will constitute Part I. Part II will delve into *the distinct laws and customs* and analyse *the sharing out of property and functions between the tribes and clans* by dealing with the recording of these customs, the persistence of the tribal organization in the rules governing procedure, as well as the role of kinship in matters of land ownership, in the face of a society of Estates emerging in Hungary. The study will close with the legal upheaval caused by the royal edict of 1562, under the changed political conditions following the catastrophic defeat of the Hungarians at Mohács.

Part I

THE STRUCTURES OF THE SZEKLER COMMUNITY (THIRTEENTH–FIFTEENTH CENTURIES)

Besides the unavoidable theories about the origins of the Szeklers, we should consider their military role in the tenth to twelfth centuries, their migration to Transylvania, the land that was to be theirs, and the first indications about their tribal structures described in data about this period.

By the end of the thirteenth century, the Szekler community was a structured society established in its territory, the Szeklerland, and in its military function, that of guarding the eastern frontier. These two factors – territorial and functional – characteristic of the Szekler community, were complemented by a third: their possession of collective privileges, structured along tribal lines.

What is the origin of this '*sharing out of property and offices among tribes and kinships*' that Werbőczy noted?

Chapter I

ON THE ORIGINS OF THE MILITARY AUXILIARY PEOPLE AND THEIR SETTLING IN THE SZEKLERLAND

Within the principal object of this study, the analysis of the medieval customs of the Szeklers of Transylvania, a brief digression in time and space is in order, far away from Transylvania, at a time when Western Europe is already in the Middle Ages but which is still 'medieval' for the kingdom of Hungary. Our interest encompasses the question of institutions – military structures, those of the state (i.e. organization of a kingdom), and territorial and ecclesiastic organization – before properly considering questions of law and legal systems.

There are practically no data of a strictly juridical nature on the Szekler community prior to its establishment in the *Székelyföld* (Szeklerland) of Transylvania. This said, there are certain aspects of the still unresolved question of their origin, of their military function and their peregrinations across the kingdom of Hungary towards what was to become the Szeklerland that suggest a ternary structure, ethnic or military-territorial in nature, which would persist, without really merging with the tribal structure that was to determine the organization of the Szekler community of Transylvania, until the middle of the sixteenth century.

I. 'Privileged nobles, descendants of the Scythians' – *The Origins of the Szeklers*

Without anticipating a final and irrefutable resolution of this question, it seems more than likely that the Szeklers – at least part of them – descend from the Kavar tribes, allied to the Hungarians several decades before the Conquest. As a point of view shared by the majority of historians who have delved into the question, it helps, but serves only to shift the venue: who are the Kavars and who are the Hungarians?

This sort of designation – like those for the 'Bulgarians', the 'Turks', or the 'Huns' – is misleadingly simple and certainly should not be used with any implication of 'ethnic purity'. Rather, we are dealing with federative structures motivated essentially by military expediency: tribal membership came by birth, but it could just as well be obtained by integration. Membership by integration entailed acceptance of the established tribal order. Such integration, however, did not necessarily carry with it a renunciation of divergent civil traditions (as opposed, say, to the military), provided they could be accommodated, or even adopted, by the order in force. Thus, in the case of the Szeklers, internal structures that could serve to improve the efficacious execution of military functions assigned by the leaders of the host federation could readily be accommodated.

But why would Werbőczy, like his contemporaries of the beginning of the sixteenth century, consider the Szeklers to be descendants of the Scythians? And would such an ancestry in the opinion of the time have distinguished them from that of the Hungarians?

The very first Hungarian chronicles identify the Hungarians with the 'Scythians', one more designation the definition of which is left largely in the realm of speculation. This Scythian ancestry, culled by the medieval Hungarian writers from occidental sources (themselves relying on Byzantine sources), was further embellished by assertions of a Hunno-Hungarian kinship, drawn from the same occidental sources, which blandly amalgamated Huns, Avars and Hungarians. The Hunno-Hungarian kinship theory has its ardent followers to this day.

A. *The Theories on the Origin of the Szeklers*

1. The Tradition since the Earliest Chronicles: Attila and Scythia The earliest *Gesta Hungarorum*, now lost but referred to in the *Gesta Hungarorum* of the notary Anonymus around 1200 and in those of Simon Kézai around 1280, claim Hunor and Magor, sons of the Scythian kings Gog and Magog, as the ancestors of the Hungarians. With the same aim of legitimizing the powers in place by tracing them back to ancient times, the Hunno-Hungarian kinship is evoked in these chronicles. The Illuminated Chronicle of Vienna (*Chronicon Pictum*) of the mid-fourteenth century in turn cites the Chronicle of Simon Kézai.

The *Gesta Hungarorum* – written at the beginning of the thirteenth century by the notary Anonymus, identified as 'Master P', no doubt the provost of the archdiocese of Esztergom and notary of king Béla III – recount the glorious land-taking Conquest and early Hungarian history in the manner characteristic for the period. According to Gy. Györffy[1] this account of the past is a reconstruction, reflecting the interests of the nobility in a position of power at the time it was written.

One notes the effort to trace back ancestries, even to kings mentioned in the Bible, no doubt under the influence of the Church – but, curious irony, we find the lineage Gog and Magog, not the most reputable of ancestors in the Judeo-Christian tradition! Not so long before, prayers were still imploring '*de sagittis Hungarorum libera nos Domine*'. The *Gesta* also enlist Attila, whose grandeur was painted in diabolic hues, perpetuated in the surname 'the scourge of God'. Along the way, references to Scythia are interspersed.

It is in this context that the Szeklers are presented as being one of the peoples of the king Attila,[2] already conscious of an identity of their own and, 'calling themselves Szeklers',[3] who, after the death of Attila (this point is not mentioned by the notary Anonymus, but by Simon Kézai[4]) joined his son Csaba – the legendary ancestor of Árpád – and were already in the Pannonian basin to welcome the arriving Hungarians as the long-awaited relatives for its (re-)conquest.

During the second half of the nineteenth century, B. Orbán, in his writings on the Szeklerland, is of the opinion that 'the theory that the Szeklers are survivors of Attila's Huns has attained the dignity of an historical fact'.[5] Ch. d'Eszláry agreed in 1958, when he said that: 'The Szeklers' conviction that they are a very ancient population of Hungary, settled there before the conquest of the Carpathian basin by the Hungarians themselves and descending from Attila, could not have become so engrained without some basis in fact.'[6]

2. The Onset of Critical Analysis: Functionalism, Etymology and Totemism Starting in the eighteenth century, doubts arose around this traditional concept. The accumulation of tenuous terms, epochs, peoples and historically dubious conceptions, produced a variety of speculative theories.

A document[7] cited in the *Székely Archives* is viewed with disdain by K. Szabó for the functionalist interpretation made of it by one of his predecessors. This royal privilege accorded to the Szekler community of Vág (in the region of Pozsony/Bratislava, Pressburg in German, in Slovakia today) leads Gy. Fejér, a historian of the first half of the nineteenth century, to construct a theory that resolves the question of the Szeklers' origin. According to him, the term 'Székely' (*Siculus*) refers to the function of frontier guard and has nothing to do with ethnic considerations. K. Szabó notes this hypothesis in a footnote only to refute it vehemently. He points out that the charters granting collective royal privileges always designate the exact ethnic entity concerned: Pechenegs, Cumans, etc., never just the function performed or the service rendered that merit the granting of a privilege.

A number of hypotheses have been proposed – and refuted – based on the name 'Székely' (*Siculus*). In the interest of benefiting from linguistic competence, reference is made here to the synthesis of interpretations published by Bernard Le Calloc'h:[8] *Székely* derived from *szék* (*sedes,* seat); from *sikil* (meaning 'runaway' in Turk); or from a tribe named *yikil*, from 'sikil' ('pure' in Tchagatâi), but for the linguists it seems obvious that these hypotheses are unfounded.[9] According to I. Bóna[10] the first mention of the name dates from 1092, in the form of *Scicul/Scichul*:

> King Béla II's authenticated charter from around 1131, confirmed king Ladislas I's grant of the right to transport salt of 1092 [.../...]. The twenty-four names copied from the charter of 1092 support the Transylvanian origin of the salt transporters. It is in this charter that the word *Scicul/Scichul*, which is the oldest form of the designation '*Székely*' first appears.

It should be noted that the word appears here as a proper name. During the thirteenth to fourteenth centuries, we find more than a dozen spellings. Zoltán Kordé[11] lists the forms: *Zakuli, Zekuli, Zekeli, Siculi, Syculi, Sycli, Sjcli, Scecul, Scekel, Zecul, Dzsikil, Eszekel*. Starting in the fifteenth century, we find essentially the Latin spelling *Siculus*, while the Hungarian orthography remains more unstable; we find *Zekely* in the registers of the early seventeenth century[12] alongside the present spelling *Székely*. The etymology of this name is still disputed.

Linguistics and ethnology have converged on a 'Turkic' term, *sikül* or *säkül*, interpreted to mean 'horse with white hoofs', which would make the name Székely a derivative of the totem animal.[13]

3. Archaeology and the Theory of the Double Conquest The theory referred to as that of the 'Double Conquest' was developed by Gy. László on the basis of archaeological data and references in the chronicles to a people said to have already been present in order to welcome Árpád on his arrival in the Carpathian basin at the end of the ninth century. From these indications, Gy. László concludes that peoples related to the Hungarians had arrived well before Árpád – with Attila or with the Avars around 670.

Gy. Györffy discussed in 1965 how his theory implicates the Szeklers; 'nevertheless we need to point out that the question of the origin of the Szeklers is still unresolved and there are some who think that the notary Anonymus mentions the Szeklers as Attila's people because they had preceded the Hungarians on this territory by several centuries and had lived before that in the Avar Empire.'[14] In a note he points out: 'This opinion is shared by Gy. László.'

L. Makkai similarly refers to this theory on the origin of the Szeklers, only to refute it, from a linguistic point of view.[15]

Despite the demise of Gy. László in June 1998, and continuing scepticism, the theory of the double conquest has not been abandoned completely. It came to light again in connection with recent archaeological discoveries in the southern Hungarian county of Somogy.[16]

4. The Khazaro-Kavar Theory in the Light of Byzantine Sources But for now, back to the Steppes. Between the seventh and ninth centuries the empire of the Khazars – these 'civilized Turks' (René Grousset) – dominates the peoples of the region, the Hungarians among them. Without going into details that might lead us to stray too far from the Transylvanian Szeklers of the thirteenth to fifteenth centuries, let us just establish that, in the course of the ninth century, one of the groups of the Khazar empire, the Kavars, rebelled against the Khazar leadership – maybe as a result of the latter's conversion to Judaism. Defeated, the Kavars joined up with the Hungarians, who at that time were an auxiliary people within the Khazar empire, and the Hungarians and Kavars acquainted themselves with each others' languages. Composed of three groups (γενεάις), this dissident faction ('kabar' is said to mean 'rebel') of the Khazar empire went on to participate in the conquest of the Pannonian basin.[17]

In 1927,[18] L. Szádeczky-Kardoss dealt with the Kavar origin of the Szeklers, pointing out that references to the *tres genera Siculorum* appear very early (1339)[19] in the *Székely Archives*, which cannot but evoke the tripartite composition of the Kavar tribe. Thus, the ancestors of the Szeklers appear to have arrived with the Hungarians at the time of the land-taking Conquest.

In 1941,[20] Gy. Györffy explored the hypothesis of a multi-ethnic origin for the Szeklers, envisaging the possible integration of Avar descendants into the Szekler community, affirming as almost certain the integration of the Pechenegs into the community, and evoking the structure of Turkic and Bulgarian nomad societies that were characterized by the ready absorption of alien elements. But Gy. Györffy never ventures to assert a definitive conclusion. By 1965, he has adopted the Khazaro-Kavar theory: 'In our opinion, the Székelys belong to the Khazaro-Kavar tribes, preceding the seven Hungarian tribes in the Land-taking by no more than a year.'[21] For Ch. d'Eszláry,[22] the theory is interesting, but not sufficiently well-founded.

In 1946, L. Makkai chose not to commit himself.

> As for the origin of the Székelys and their settling in Transylvania, there are two opposing theories. Certain historians maintain that originally the Székelys were a Hungarian tribe, or at least Onoguro-Bulgarian, closely akin to the Hungarians and led by the Avars (confused in the public mind of the time [Middle Ages] with the Huns) to the Carpathian basin, where they lived continuously until the Land-Taking by the Árpádians [cf. the theory of the double conquest]. Contrary to this hypothesis, most Hungarian linguists believe that the ethnic Székely tribe, of Turkic origin and culture, fused with the Hungarians in southern Russia and was already completely assimilated when they arrived together in the Carpathian basin at the same time as the other Hungarian tribes, i.e. at the end of the ninth century.[23]

In 1992, still basing his reasoning on linguistics, he arrives at the conclusion:

> The most plausible [view] is that the Székelys, or at least the group that was given this designation, are descendants of the Kavar tribe mentioned by the Byzantine Emperor Constantine, a tribe that rose up against the Khazars and joined up with the Hungarians before the conquest of the Carpathian basin. This tribe was still bilingual around 950: it used its own Turkic language, whilst also replacing it gradually by the Finno-Ugrian language of the Hungarians.

Today's research centres on the composition of this Kavar federation. According to Z. Kordé, one should look beyond this artificial designation for the precise denomination of the three tribes comprising the so-called 'Kavar' population. One of them could well be *Äskäl*, the name of one of the Bulgarian tribes along the Volga, where certain linguists surmise the origin of the name 'Székely':

> In my opinion, the Székelys (that is to say the *Äskäls*) were the lead tribe of the Kavars. […/…] In the Hungarian chronicles we do not find the name *Kavar*, for this was an artificial designation. As a rule, tribes that joined carried their own names initially, later adopting the name of the lead tribe, in this case that of the Szeklers. […/…] This hypothesis could help explain a somewhat mysterious phenomenon. The Kavars disappear from the sources starting with the tenth century and the Szeklers appear early in the twelfth. It seems likely that the Kavars were dispersed along the frontiers during the reign of St. Stephen (1000–1038), or later in the course of the eleventh century.[24]

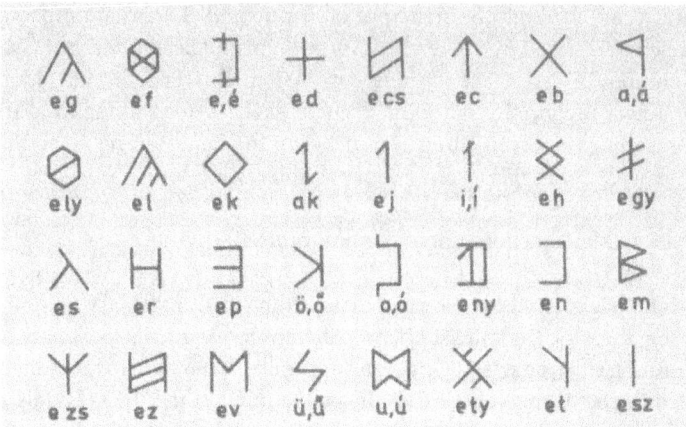

Figure 2. Balás, Gábor. *A székelyek nyomában* (*On the Track of the Szeklers*), Budapest, 1984, p. 269.

The majority of historians and linguists agree today on a Turkic-speaking origin for the Szeklers, as witness the enduring use of a Turkic runic writing (see Figure 2[25]). However, all linguistic considerations indicate that the Szeklers spoke Hungarian, and in fact their alphabet does contain specific runes for phonemes that are strictly Hungarian. For L. Makkai 'this (the passage from Turkic to Hungarian) could hardly have happened in their present area of habitation, on the southeast extremity of the territory where Hungarian was spoken'.[26]

Which supports the Kavar theory. On the other hand, some contrary arguments are worth noting: For one thing, it is not known what languages the peoples led by Attila spoke and for certain authors a Turkic language cannot be excluded;[27] what is more, the Szeklers were not settled on the southeast fringe of Hungary until around 1220–1230. This leaves room for the hypothesis that their acculturation could have happened between the late ninth and early thirteenth centuries, and for continued speculation on the timing of the Szeklers' arrival.

B. Szekler Origins and Szekler Law

The point in common between the theories on the origin of the Szeklers is that they all refer to tribal structures (Turkic or Hungarian). A large number of legal documents draw on tribal structure, claims based on ethnic distinctness are few and of a later date. The insistence on a tribal structure, a common trait of semi-nomadic peoples, does not of itself favour one or the other of the theories. This said, the similarities between early Hungarian law in force prior to the legal system of King Stephen I, and Szekler law are numerous: the participation of the entire community in the framing of rules ('for in earlier days a law became a law only after the community had decided it, when the elders had concluded with the entire population'),[28] the distinction between a military and a judiciary authority, and tribal ownership of land. Szekler law is sometimes seen, by Ch. d'Eszláry and Gy. Bónis for instance, as a throwback to ancestral Hungarian law.

The reference to *'the era of Greater Scythia'* in a document from 1506[29] indicates that the Szekler community was made to affirm its place within the Hungarian nation and its loyalty to the king of Hungary. The conviction of a Scythian descent was nurtured not only by the Szekler community, it was just as much a part of collective Hungarian imagination. Is it to be interpreted as the persisting memory of a distant past or attributed to the assimilation of affirmations in the thirteenth century chronicles? In the context of the tensions of the time it is not unreasonable to see this recall of the Szeklers' ancestral presence (regardless of any ethnic distinctness) as political rather than historical.

No doubt the study of Szekler law will never be the decisive factor in resolving the riddle of the origin of this people. None of the theories accepted today use arguments that are openly contradicted by the juridical documents. We must not attach too much weight to the similarity between ancestral Hungarian law and Szekler law either, as we find comparable practices with other peoples of the Steppes, as we shall see later, when we examine the status of other auxiliary peoples: the Pechenegs, Cumans and Iasians.

The complex sophistication of the rules governing access to the office of judge or captain, as documented in the sixteenth century, indicates that the status of being Szekler is not derived directly from ethnic membership, but rather from acceptance of the military (and social) rules of the community. The interlaced notions of 'tribe' and 'clan' – which recall military structures – as well as the notions of lineage and kinship – stemming from ties of consanguinity and alliances – can all be seen as political and juridical notions rather than strictly ethnic considerations. The Szeklers, given the imperatives of their military mission, could well have favoured the enrolling in their ranks of groups of diverse origins.

The meticulous care taken in defining the process of taking turns in acceding to dignities certainly appears more appropriate for a multi-ethnic community than for a homogeneous group in which the role and the place of everyone is firmly embedded in ancestral tradition. The Szekler tribal system, the diverse references to which are certainly very ancient, must have been redefined and formalized starting in the eleventh century, when the community was consolidated and then settled in the Szeklerland. The need of going to battle side by side, of having to trust the man on the horse hard by, certainly helped the Szeklers maintain the principle of individual liberty and develop a tribal system that seems astonishingly modern in ensuring alternating access to the diarchic positions of authority; military and judicial. Such a system is most likely to imply a need for negotiation between groups of different origins and the status of *siculitas* appears as a form of citizenship.

II. 'Skilled in the art of war' – The Military Role of the Szeklers

The term 'military auxiliary people' used to define the place of the Szeklers, Pechenegs and Cumans within the Hungarian military organization expresses distinctive functional and ethnic characteristics. The expression *military auxiliaries* is used in Hungarian historiography to refer to peoples of foreign origin who played an important military role on the side of the Hungarians.[30] The Szeklers insisted on either or both aspects of this distinction always with the same aim: safeguarding their privileges within the monarchy and ensuring the integrity of their internal structures.

The military role of the Szeklers is claimed as ancestral. It is the fundament of the privileged status the Szekler community enjoyed collectively. Based on the Hungarian military structures of the time of the Conquest, only the Szeklers among the diverse auxiliary peoples were able to conserve their status in the face of numerous reorganizations in the Hungarian kingdom.

A. *The Hungarian Confederation at the Time of the Conquest (Ninth–Tenth Centuries)*

The composition of Árpád's army, its hierarchical structure and the principles governing the sharing of property closely resemble the structures of the Szekler community in the Middle Ages.

1. A Military-Political Confederation I. Zimonyi[31] recalls: 'The Khazar Empire had a determining role in the forming of the Hungarian people'. To be more precise, in its hierarchical organization, with the diarchic principle. Comparing the internal structures of the Hungarian people before the year 1000 and the Szeklers of the Middle Ages, we find a great number of points in common. Gy. Kristó[32] lingers on the *nomad* and *pagan* aspects in characterizing Hungarian society before the year 1000, characteristics which the Szeklers abandoned at about the same pace as the Hungarians. The essential difference for the period under analysis is the tribal structure conserved by the Szeklers and its corollary: the individual juridical liberty of all within the tribe.

The organization of the conquering Árpádian army with its confederation of tribes comprises ethnic complexities the subtleties of which historians, aided by archaeology and linguistics,[33] are still attempting to untangle.

It is difficult to give a concise outline of the organization of the so-called 'Hungarian people' prior to the conquest: the sources are fragmentary and often contradictory, and the analyses come to divergent conclusions. Two points – which, in turn, raise more questions than they answer – appear to have been settled: for one, the heterogeneity of the peoples composing the semi-nomad organizations commonly referred to under deceptively simple denominations: Khazars, Bulgars, Hungarians and the like; also, particularly concerning the Hungarians, the multitude of chiefs leading these tribes before the arrival of Árpád, suggesting a federative, rather than ethnic structure.

Should we be speaking of 'Magyars' or 'Hungarians' in referring to the tribes entering the Carpathian basin with Árpád? To Hungarians, the question is moot: 'Hungarian' is '*magyar*' in Hungary; 'Hungary' is '*Magyarország*' and so on. Most historiography[34] traditionally uses the term 'Magyar' to refer to the Hungarians before their assumption of a sedentary lifestyle in Hungary. Gy. Györffy, on the contrary believes that it is 'more correct to use the designation *Hungarian, Ungar, hongrois*, which covers a broader range from an ethnic point of view than the term

Magyar designating the common people having conserved the Finno-Ugrian language'.[35]

M. Molnár[36] circumvents the issue by speaking of 'proto-Hungarians' for the period preceding their arrival in Pannonia. The term *magyar* tends to refer back to the 'pre-Conquest' period, but also to the Finno-Ugrian language, while the term 'Hungarian' is most likely derived from the word 'Onogur' (or 'Onogunur' or 'Onoghur') designating a Turkic-Bulgarian people supposed to have had military control over the Magyars of the ninth century. The contemporary sources enumerate seven Hungarian tribes[37] and an eighth, the Kavar tribe (itself a confederation of three tribes).

2. Power Shared These tribes, which in turn encompassed over a hundred clans, had at their head a principal, religious chieftain (*kende* or *kündü*) and a military chieftain (*gyula*). A third dignity (*horka*) is mentioned by certain authors[38] as supreme judge, but as a rule this function was exercised by the *gyula*. A council of tribal chiefs participated in the palavers that preceded military operations. Árpád appears to have been the principal chief initially, cumulating the two functions later, after the death of the military chief Kurszán (or Kúsál) in 904. Of particular interest in this organization is the tradition of power-sharing between a sovereign (the term *kende* disappears in the late tenth century, to be supplanted by that of 'Duke' or 'Grand Prince') and a second chief. This distinction between military and judicial power-holders is conserved in the Szekler community's offices of captain and of judge, which can never be vested jointly in the same person.

3. Military Functions, Lineages and the Sharing of Property The '*sharing out of offices and property between the tribes and clans*' in the Szekler community mentioned by Werbőczy was the Hungarians' system at the time of the Conquest. Ch. D'Eszláry says: 'We find the same relations of property ownership in the Szekler community as with the Hungarians [of the time of the Conquest]. It is characteristic that the common ownership of land was still in force in some parts of the Szeklerland as late as in the nineteenth century'.[39] Then, property was attributed according to strategic needs and the proceeds from military campaigns. The military hierarchy was organized along tribal lines and private property did not come under legal protection until the early eleventh century. With the assumption of a sedentary lifestyle and the need for the imposition of the king's will, the pre-eminence of the military function in the Hungarian tribal organization lost its significance. But, given the Szeklers' role as guards of the eastern frontier, the military function maintained its priority and, even after settling, Szekler society conserved the principle of collective, community property.

With the Szeklers, as with the Hungarians of the ninth to tenth centuries, land was the property of the clan, held in common. Under such a system, land ownership was disposed between entities, but these could, at any moment, decide to leave the central federation. Consequently, with the formation of the Hungarian kingdom, reforms favouring individual ownership were enacted by King Stephen I, with the aim of concentrating power in the person of the monarch, the sole purveyor of donations.

B. The Szeklers' Place in the Hungarian Military Organization under the Árpád Dynasty (Tenth-Thirteenth Centuries)

Let us consider the evolution of Hungarian society as it affected the auxiliary peoples, all of them privileged communities, amongst which the status of the Szeklers was nothing exceptional. But, it becomes unique by its persistence when, from the end of the thirteenth century, the Szeklers and their military role appear exclusively within the confines of Transylvania.

1. The Structures of the New Kingdom During the first three centuries of the Hungarian kingdom – the reign of the Árpád dynasty – the evolving monarchy turned to the Church of Rome, relying on this attachment to affirm its independence from its Germanic and Byzantine neighbours and to consolidate and centralize its internal organization. The first crowned king, Stephen I, successor to his father the Grand Prince Géza, organized the kingdom along occidental lines by counties (*comitatus, vármegye*). There were territories protected by a fortified place that served as a residence for a royal agent, the *comes*. In the course of two centuries, the monarchy increasingly asserted itself, especially under the long reigns of Stephen I (997–1038), then Ladislas I (1077–1095) and Coloman the Learned (1095–1116). But the question of the succession in this elective monarchy was always difficult to resolve, giving the more powerful nobles the opportunity to recover land, gain military force and challenge royal authority.

The political strategy of the Árpád dynasty consisted in the recognition and protection of individual, private property in place of the ancestral system of clan-held collective ownership, the very concept of which was a threat to royal centralism. This approach was put in practice through confiscations *manu militaris* and redistributions – partly to the Church's benefit – and the promulgation of laws governing property ownership which broke with ancestral custom. The principle of private property is defined in Article 6 of King Stephen's first Book of Laws: 'By virtue of our royal authority, we have decided that everyone shall be free to dispose of his possessions between his wife, his sons and his daughters or to donate them to the Church and those dispositions may not be challenged even after his death.'[40]

This initial affirmation of individual rights is reiterated and refined in the second Book of Laws (II, § 2): 'We have decided […/…] that everyone shall dispose freely of his own (inherited) possessions and royal donations during his life and after his death and that his sons shall inherit with the same rights of property.'[41]

These new dispositions were not imposed on the auxiliary peoples. The royal will was essentially aimed at the powerful families capable of challenging it directly, while it manifested a federative and tolerant attitude toward the allied peoples.

Other peoples from the Steppes – the Pechenegs and Cumans – appeared at the eastern frontier. The attitude of the Árpádian kings toward these warrior peoples – converting them from pillaging enemies to military auxiliaries of the kingdom – is seen by Gy. Bónis and Ch. d'Eszláry as an astute policy to ensure a stable kingdom by assigning a place to these peoples without interfering with their customs. Gy. Bónis speaks of an 'intelligent and purposeful policy of dispersion and integration'.[42] In Ch. d'Eszláry's opinion, it was through this construction of a political entity that the Hungarians were able to establish their State.[43] Though the Crown granted them privileges similar to those of the Szeklers, these peoples did not succeed in maintaining their juridical autonomy.

2. Just One of Several Auxiliary Peoples The earliest documents referring to the Szeklers' feats of war always mention them alongside other peoples: Pechenegs when evoking battles of the twelfth century,[44] and thereafter, still Pechenegs, but also Saxons, Cumans and Vlachs in the early thirteenth century in Transylvania.[45] As mentioned, comparable privileges to those of the Szeklers' were accorded the Pechenegs and Cumans within the framework of the Hungarian army, but in their case not lastingly, for their military elite soon arrogated the privileges to themselves exclusively, to the detriment of the many.

While Pechenegs and Cumans are mentioned several times as enemies of the Hungarians, not always as allies, the Kavars and Szeklers always appear as allies. The history of each of these peoples could fill volumes, but in the present study we will examine only the points in common between Pechenegs, Cumans, Iasians and Szeklers within the Hungarian kingdom.

The Pechenegs, a Turkic people of the Steppes, are first mentioned as having been the cause of the Magyars' arrival in Europe. Presented as 'one of the major preoccupations of Byzantine diplomacy' by L. Musset,[46] they were reduced to 'efficient but rebellious auxiliaries' following their defeats at the hands of the Byzantine Empire (1091 and 1122). A. Pálóczi Horváth compares their military organization to that of the Szeklers. He adds, however, that, if the first written documents confirming their status do evoke their collective liberty (*libertas Bissenorum*) in return for their military service (up to the mid-fourteenth century), the class of military chiefs very soon arrogated land and titles to themselves and reduced the class of free soldiers to servitude. The author does not bring up documents mentioning Pecheneg autonomy dated later than 1495 and concludes his chapter with their assimilation.[47]

The presence of Pechenegs is documented very early in the Szeklerland,[48] where they are referred to as freemen. In fact, one of the Szekler clans – i.e. an entity integral to the structure of the Szekler community – carries the name of 'Besenyő' (Pecheneg),[49] thus probably conserving the memory of a local alliance between the two auxiliary peoples. Such an alliance presupposes, in the Szeklerland as elsewhere in Hungary, the assimilation of the Pechenegs into the ambient structure. The presence of Pecheneg elements is also attested by the name of the village of Besenyő in the Seat of Sepsi (mentioned in the Papal Registers of 1332–1337)[50] and the place called 'Besenyőfalva' (Pecheneg village), near Patakfalva, in the Seat of Udvarhely, no longer extant by the time of the military conscription registers of the sixteenth century.[51]

The Cumans, another people of shifting fortunes arriving from Asia, spoke a Turkic dialect. We find them in 1091 allied with Byzantium against the Pechenegs, and in 1122 at the head of a coalition that includes the Pechenegs in a lost battle against the Byzantine Empire. Next, they turn up pillaging in Hungary, but in the early thirteenth century, before the devastating Mongol invasion, the heir apparent, the later King Béla IV organized the defence of the southeastern frontier by integrating Cumania (southeast of Transylvania) into the realm. This integration was interrupted by the Mongol assault of 1239–1241,[52] when the Cuman population was dispersed, in part to central Hungary, the rest leaving with the Mongols of the Golden Horde toward the north of the Black Sea.

The internal organization of the Cumans within the Hungarian realm, essentially between the Danube and the Tisza, is presented by A. Pálóczi Horváth[53] as similar to that of the Pechenegs and Szeklers. It comprised a noble class (*principales*) who were called *beg* or *bey* and served as the military commanders (*capitanei*) and elected judges (*judices*) for each clan. This stratification of dignities in the hands of a minority seems more elitist than any that the Szekler structures would ever permit and rapidly led to the servitude of the common soldiers, while the elite merged with the Hungarian nobility.

It is worth pointing out, however, that whenever the Cuman communities were allied with the so-called Iasian (*Iazones* or *As, Jazyges, Jász*) – according to A. Pálóczi Horváth the identification with the Sarmatian Iasians is erroneous[54] – communities east of Buda (between the Danube and the Tisza), the assimilation was much less rapid. The first written reference to this Iasian people, who spoke a Persian dialect and adhered not to shamanism but to a religion along dualistic concepts not practising magic, dates from the early fourteenth century.[55] The origin of the Iasians is at least as disputed as that of the Szeklers, as is the timing of their arrival in Hungary. Be that as it may, even if their exemption from paying taxes was abolished by the fifteenth century, the administration of the Iasian and Cuman territories was not integrated into the royal counties until the end of the sixteenth century;[56] what is more, reference to an 'Iasian-Cuman' status persists until 1848, a status under which the rules of inheritance of ancestral property – in favour of male or, in their absence, female descendants – exclude the possibility of any contrary testamentary disposition. This aspect, which gives precedence to lineage in the possession of land, evidently calls to mind the Szekler system.

C. From Privilege to Integration: The Auxiliary Peoples and the Szekler Exception

At the time of the Conquest, the organization of Hungary's armed force was based on a logic of lineages, of consanguinity or of alliances, but, gradually, new hierarchies evolved around strictly military criteria. In the course of the first centuries of the kingdom, the interests of functionality prevailed over those of kinship, as King Stephen I and his successors proceeded to break the hold of the tribal chiefs and established a new structure in which the monarch was the protector and sole dispenser of privilege.

The military elite of the auxiliary peoples gradually neglected the community-related aspects of its functions and became integrated into the military nobility of the Hungarian realm. It was at about the time when the Pecheneg and Cuman internal structures dissolved, leading to integration into Hungarian society, that references to clan structure first appear in the *Székely Archives* as the core of their military organization.

No doubt, the fact that the Szekler community's privileged status survived much longer than that of other military auxiliaries stems in part from its remote position at the eastern frontier, but it also benefitted from the particular structure within Transylvania (similarly due to its remoteness): the fact of having the Saxon settlers (themselves fiercely attached to their privileges) as neighbours. Moreover, their own, internal juridical structure of individual liberty and collective dispositions concerning ownership of land and bestowal of dignities, more deeply engrained in the Szekler community than had been the case with the Pechenegs and Cumans, served to conserve the former's status.

A similar persistence of privileged status can be observed with the German settlers of the Szepes region (in the north-east of medieval Hungary, today the north-east of Slovakia). In their case, as with the Saxons of Transylvania, military obligations quickly lost their significance and their privileges, formally accorded and confirmed by the Crown, were derived from their contributions to economic development (essentially mining, crafts and markets).

As for the 'Iaso-Cumans', the persistence of their status seems to be due to a strong internal juridical structure and is in this sense comparable to the perpetuation of Szekler customs. On the other hand, the military obligation of these communities was less exacting and the presence of a dualist religion was a factor of historical differentiation.

In spite of speaking the same language as the Hungarians and, like them, adhering to Roman Christianity, the Szeklers were not absorbed into the new-born kingdom, their privileges (i.e. private laws (*privata lex*)) being derived from their distinct function as frontier guards. Only the Szeklers managed to perpetuate both their military role and their juridical autonomy, based on a clan structure.

III. Migration toward the Szeklerland

Having galloped across the distant Steppes from east to west, to Pannonia alongside the Hungarians and other Kavars, let us now join the Szeklers on a new migration, this time from west to east in medieval Hungary. Let us start by accompanying them, battle by battle, to the west and the south of Transylvania and observe them settling, within the framework of Transylvania's institutions, in the region that was to become the Szeklerland. This three-stage migration seems to conform to the persistent 'rule of three', possibly a coincidence, not yet axiomatic.

A. From Moson to the Altland, Stopover at Telegd

During the twelfth century, the Illuminated Chronicle[57] recalls, the Szeklers fought as the vanguard of the Hungarian army on the western front: on the shores of the Oltsava river in Silesia in 1116 and near the river Leitha (the border between Hungary and Austria) in 1146. In 1258,[58] they are mentioned again near Pozsony (Bratislava: Pressburg) in a charter confirming a donation. In 1260,[59] the king of Bohemia, Ottokar II, refers to them among the auxiliary peoples of the Hungarian army in his account of his victory over King Béla IV. In spite of this defeat or maybe before,[60] the same king, Béla IV, confirms the privileges of the Szeklers. A charter dated 1314,[61] confirming the donation of the village of Parendorf (near Moson, the village of Parendorf today is in Lower Austria), mentions that Szeklers had previously lived in the vicinity. What became of these Szeklers? Were they posted to serve on other military fronts like the Pechenegs, were they assimilated in the local Hungarian structures? If we go by linguistic research,[62] there is evidence that at least part of them moved to Transylvania, but without any indication of who, when or how.

Map 4. Szekler Migrations and Establishment in the Szeklerland

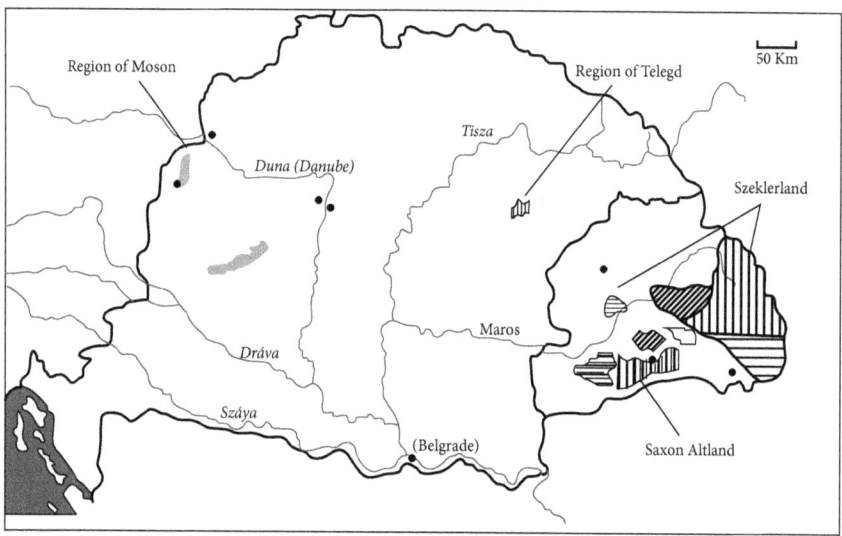

Earlier settlements	Initial Saxon seats	Assumed time of displacement	Definitive Szekler Seat
'Szeklers of Telegd' (vertical hatching)	*Altland*	before 1190	Udvarhely Csík
(horizontal hatching)	Szászsebes	before 1224	Sepsi
	Szászorbó	before 1224	Orbai
	Segesvár (Szászkézd)	before 1224	Kézdi
	Segesvár (Szászkézd)	before 1239	Aranyos
By linguistics: Moson dialect (oblique hatching)	Medgyes	after 1240	Maros

Szeklers are encountered in Transylvania during the first half of the thirteenth century. Initially in the south from 1213[63] onwards, judging by documentation concerning the brief sojourn of the Teutonic Knights (1211–1225). Installed in Transylvania by King Andrew II to protect the southeastern frontier and manifest royal authority in the face of intrigues by the Hungarian nobles, the Teutonic Knights finally exasperated the king by their claims to be answerable to the Pope only and by establishing a state within the State. He expelled them *manu militaris* in 1225;[64] they are mentioned again in connection with the privileges accorded the Saxon settlers (a charter known as the *Andreanum*, 1224).[65] The Szeklers participated in the Bulgarian campaign before 1235.[66]

In 1235,[67] the Archdeaconry of Telegd is mentioned as part of the diocese of Transylvania – even though the region of Telegd was not part of Transylvania – but the first mention of the so-called 'Szeklers of Telegd' does not occur until 1270[68] in a document that already refers to their privileges as ancestral.

What is behind the mention of these 'Szeklers of Telegd'? Telegd is situated in the county of Bihar (today in Romania), west of Transylvania, and some place names in the vicinity attest to a Szekler presence (e.g. Székelyhíd, 'Szekler Bridge'). The *Gesta* of the notary Anonymus recounts that it is here that the Szeklers joined up with Árpád. Without lingering on the – instructive – anachronisms of this chronicle, it seems reasonable to assume that the Szeklers were present in this region around 1200.[69] They may have been posted here by King Stephen I in his campaign against the chiefs of the tribal confederations at the east of the kingdom, Gyula (defeated in 1003) and Ajtony (several campaigns between 1008 or 1015 and 1028), who had waxed more partisan to Oriental Christianity than to the sovereignty of the king. The 'Szeklers of Telegd' appear to have stayed in the region long enough to have been so called and were no doubt converted to Christianity here, for it is the Church that was the most attached to this appellation, which it perpetuated with the creation of an Archdeaconry of Telegd in the Szeklerland.

When did they move on to Transylvania proper? Late enough for the Szeklers of Parendorf to have joined them initially at Telegd?

Did the Szeklers of Telegd participate in the campaign of Bulgaria? And in the course of this did they camp in the southwest of Transylvania and then settle there, in what was to become the *Altland*, the first settlement of the Saxons? In any case, the southwest was the first stop of the Szeklers in Transylvania, the point of departure for their third and definitive migration and settlement in the east, the Szeklerland.

But before setting out on this last and much more amply documented migration within Transylvania, an evocation of the institutional context within Transylvania is in order, as the regional particularism there favoured the perpetuation of the Szekler community's juridical autonomy. Similarly, a word about the place of the Saxon community and the institutional absence of the Romanians is appropriate at this juncture.

B. The Transylvanian Particularism

Throughout the Hungarian Middle Ages, Transylvania was part of the realm. The heart of the Szapolyai kingdom after 1526, Transylvania did not become a principality (with the western territories of the *Partium* attached) until after the treaty of Speyer in 1570. Nevertheless, this province already had its specific traits in its medieval institutions: a voivode, two autonomous territories with a privileged status distinct from that of its structure of counties and a provincial diet.

1. The Voivode of Transylvania The aim of King Stephen I to centralize state authority met with determined resistance by his uncle, Gyula, who commanded the tribes then established in Transylvania. Confident in his backing by Byzantium and his rights as elder of the Árpád kindred, Gyula posed a serious threat to his nephew's authority. His uncle's considerable military strength, hardly in tune with the Carolingian principles espoused by Stephen I, but also his choice of the Greek Orthodox faith, finally decided the king to re-establish his authority over Transylvania (1003–1028).

As a result of this period of effective separation, or precisely because of the need to organize the defence of the eastern frontier, an instance of intermediary authority between the counties' governors (*comites*) and the king was installed in Transylvania. This was the voivode (*vajda*), first mentioned in 1199.[70] The reorganization of the confiscated territory into seven counties dates back at least to 1105. In the course of this reorganization, special powers and titles were accorded the *comes* of the county of Fehér. It is in 1105 that the institution of *ban* of Croatia was created and some historians believe that the title of 'Voivode' must have been created at the same time. Others believe that the institution of the voivodate is a good deal older, for it would have been unwise to leave the eastern frontier without a local military commander during the time intervening since the deposition of Gyula. This said, the prerogatives accorded to the *comes* of the Transylvanian county of Fehér might well have satisfied the exigencies of a local defence force.

Comites and voivodes were royal agents, their offices were not hereditary. At the outset of the thirteenth century, there was a rapid succession of voivodes. Their responsibilities were essentially military, consequently fiscal (for the collection of taxes to finance campaigns), and judiciary (for the maintenance of public order and cohesion in the ranks of the armed forces facing an exterior enemy). The voivode and the *comites* represented the authority of the King over the royal domains – in Transylvania as in most of Hungary – essentially the forests and confiscated lands.

In two instances, under the reigns of Andrew II (1205–1235) and Béla IV (1235–1270), the heirs apparent Béla (regent of Transylvania from 1226 to 1235) and Stephen (prince of Transylvania from 1257 to 1270), sometimes referred to as 'junior kings' (*iunior rex, ifjabb király*) were administrating the eastern part of the realm. The effect was the weakening of the king's authority in cases of disagreement between him, his heirs and junior kings, both sides multiplying donations with the aim of creating ties of loyalty with partisans of their own.

Whilst in Hungary the general trend was to break up tribal structures in favour of a territorial reorganization founded on private property granted by the King in the counties, in Transylvania two territories were institutionalized in the middle of the thirteenth century, the inhabitants of each of which enjoyed collective privileges. These two Lands (*Terra Saxonorum, Terra Siculorum*) were subdivided into 'seats' (*sedes*), where the laws and customs specific to their communities applied with royal consent. But while this autonomy was confirmed in all matters relating to their internal affairs, the structural framework of these lands was subject, like the adjoining royal counties, to the authority of *comites*.

In addition to a representative of the Crown as an intermediary between the central authority and the *comites*, and its two territories enjoying specific, defined privileges, Transylvania's institutional structure included a provincial diet, known as the 'Assembly of the Three Nations'.

2. The Assembly of the Three Nations In place since the latter half of the thirteenth century, the provincial assembly of Transylvania had a role and 'house rules' that situated it somewhere between those of the Hungarian county assemblies and the Hungarian Diet of the fifteenth century. Whereas the counties of Hungary proper sent their delegates directly to the Diet, in Transylvania it was the provincial assembly, itself composed of the delegates of the nobles of the seven Transylvanian counties and those of the Szekler and Saxon Lands that chose the delegates to attend the Diet. The Transylvanian Assembly was composed of fourteen representatives of the counties, fourteen of the Szekler community and fourteen of the Saxon community.[71] With no legislative power of its own, the Transylvanian assembly was endowed with a statutory mission to assist the voivode in matters concerning the province and relations between its privileged groups, the nobles of the Transylvanian counties, the Szeklers and the Saxons.

The Absence of the Romanians from the Institutions

One of the points of contention in the history of Transylvania and its institutions is the absence of Romanian representation from the Assembly.

In 1291, King Andrew III, the last of the Árpád dynasty, convened a provincial assembly (*generalis congregatio*) where the Hungarian nobles of Transylvania, the Szeklers, the Saxons and the Romanians (Vlachs) were all represented. Thereafter, the latter no longer appeared as a representative group. There is no further reference to a provincial assembly until 1437 in either published historiography or the archives consulted, and by then only the Saxons and Szeklers appear alongside the nobles from the counties. In 1342 and 1408, assemblies are recorded that were attended only by the Hungarian nobles of Transylvania, under the authority of the voivode.

The disappearance of Romanian representation is interpreted differently by Hungarian and Romanian historians. To this day, the 'Transylvanian question' always comes up in historical research and in political interpretations that consider it logical – or not.

The Vlachs appear in documents throughout the thirteenth century alongside the Saxons and the Szeklers: around 1210,[72] the *comes* of Szeben was at the head of an army composed of Saxon, Vlach, Szekler and Pecheneg soldiers; in 1222, or possibly in 1231,[73] a royal charter exempted the Teutonic Knights from the payment of duties for crossing Szekler or Vlach lands (*terra Siculorum aut Blacorum*).

Two factors appear to be at the root of Romanian non-representation in the Transylvanian institutions starting in the fourteenth century, in spite of their incontestable presence: the political-religious question for one, and the internal organization of Romanian society for the other.

The conversion to Roman Christianity instituted by King Stephen I was long and difficult to carry through. The East–West schism was brought home to Hungary by the passage of the crusaders and it is not unreasonable to see the adherence of the Vlachs to the Orthodox Church as a serious impediment to their membership in the institutions of a realm that had made its choice in favour of the Church of Rome. During the thirteenth century, the question lost pertinence due to the Mongol invasions: Cumans and Pechenegs, still pagans then, and Vlachs, seen as schismatic, were all welcome allies. The situation changed under the reign of the Anjou dynasty. The Vlach and Moldavian states were organized as vanguards against the Mongols and subsequently revolted against the King of Hungary. C. Durandin recalls that – in the view of Romanian historiography – 'this double, Vlach and Moldavian, uprising is seen as the origin of the independent medieval states of Romania.'[74]

According to I.-A. Pop, the uprising made King Louis I decide to toughen his policy toward the Romanian 'infidels'. He goes on to point out that it was at the insistence of the Franciscans that the king decreed that 'only Catholics can become, and be considered as, nobles'.[75] In another article, he summarizes the situation at the end of the fourteenth century: 'The Romanians did not adhere to the faith of Rome, they were "inferior" even to the Cumans, who had formally converted to Christianity and the Roman rite, and this represented a most serious motive for not accepting them as a privileged group.'[76]

He points out that the only possibility for social advancement open to the Romanian elite was to integrate into the ranks of Hungarian nobility in Transylvania as individuals. A well-known example of such individual advancement is that of the family of Voicu, pointed out among others, by G. Castellan:

> The most famous case is that of the *knez* Voicu, ennobled in 1409 by King Sigismund of Luxemburg, receiving as donation for himself and his successors the fortress of Hunyad and twenty-five villages in the vicinity; he thus founded the fortune of the Hunyady-Hunedoara family; John, the son of the *knez* Voicu, was to become Voivode of Transylvania and hero of the wars against the Ottomans and the grandson, Matthias, known as "Corvinus", king of Hungary from 1458 to 1490.[77]

For L. Makkai,[78] the explanation for the absence of a Romanian *Nation* is the promotion of former Romanian military chiefs (voivode of Máramaros and *kenéz*) within the Hungarian nobility and consequently the descent into servitude of the Romanians living on their lands, newly acquiring the status of nobles' estates. Thus, the Romanian society of Transylvania is seen to have followed the same pattern of integration into Hungarian structures as those of the Pechenegs and Cumans (albeit maintaining its language).

In spite of its later name of 'Assembly of the Three *Nations*', the assembly of Transylvania was not composed of ethnic groups, but of privileged social groups, the equivalent of Estates in Hungary.

Within each group, delegates were elected annually to assist the representatives of the Crown. They sat in the councils of the *comites* and the voivodes. They were an integral part of the assembly of judges (*sedes judiciaria*), they passed sentence and assured that these were executed. In 1437, following a peasant uprising,[79] the Three Nations met in assembly and concluded an agreement of mutual aid in suppressing the uprising,[80] to defend their privileges against the rebelling serfs. In 1467, they federated again, but this time against the king, complaining of the unrest in Transylvania and the oppression of liberties.[81] The plot was quickly crushed and its instigators severely punished, especially the voivode, to whom the assembly had granted full power. For some historians, this rebellion marks the beginning of a collective sense of Transylvanian identity and aspirations for independence.

3. *The Saxon Community* The Saxon and Szekler communities were neighbours and their relations with royal authority were similar. Their relations with each other were not without points of friction (essentially concerning the definition of the borders between the two lands and rivalries between royal free towns). The internal organization of the Saxon community did not follow the same pattern as that of the Szeklers. They – like the Szeklers – did manage to stay well clear of the seigniorial system of governance evolving in Hungary, but their privileges were soon adapted to their proclivity as craftsmen and merchants, rather than soldiers. The Saxon community itself distinguished between – privileged – burghers and peasants living in villages; the latter, without being legally in the royal free cities' servitude, became dependent in the economic sense at least.

In addition to the Germans who had been arriving since the late eleventh century, in 1211 King Andrew II invited the Knights of the Teutonic Order to defend the eastern frontier, only to expel them *manu militari* in 1225, when they insisted on owing allegiance to the Pope only.

The year before, a charter of privilege (called the *Diploma Andreanum*) had been granted to the *Nation* referred to as 'Saxon'. This designation was perpetuated even though the German settlers were not all Saxons; the first royal charters concerning them mention *Theutonici, Flandrenses* or *Saxones,* but the privileges they were granted were based on what they called 'Saxon Custom'. To accommodate the desire of these settlers to consolidate their privileges in a unified territory and comply with the Crown's insistence on both a juridical structure (one territory, one legal system) and contiguous military organization, the Szeklers were moved to the east of Transylvania. Henceforth, the royal

Table 1. Establishment of Saxon Seats – German (Hungarian) Names

Around 1190:	in the separate German provostship (*Altland*)
Before 1224:	*Hermannstadt* (Szeben)
	Leschkirch (Újegyház)
	Großschenk (Nagysink)
	Broos (Szászváros)
	Mühlbach (Szászsebes)
	Reußmarkt (Szerdahely)
	Reps (Kőhalom).

The first charter, dated 1224, lists the above seven Seats.

The same privileges were granted to:

	Kronstadt (Brassó) 1225, after the expulsion of the Teutonic Knights
	Großschelken (Nagyselyk)
	Mediasch (Medgyes)
	Schässburg (Segesvár) – early fourteenth century
	Bistritz (Bestercze) – charter dated 1366.

counties of Transylvania were joined by the Szeklerland and the *Sachsenland*, both of them divided into Seats.

The administration in the Saxon territories was organized around seven jurisdictions, which did not precisely coincide with the seven Seats, because the settlers arriving after 1224 were assigned to the existing jurisdictions, while new Seats continued to be established. The Saxon community paid taxes on its commercial transactions, but was nevertheless obliged to provide a military contingent, under the orders of an official called *geréb*, a function that rapidly became hereditary. In recognition of their services, these military commanders received royal donations of land beyond the borders of the Sachsenland. They organized these estates like the lands of the Hungarian nobles, with bondsmen-peasants, and subsequently tried to impose this system on their properties within the Sachsenland itself. From late in the thirteenth century, the non-military Saxon community increasingly resisted such tactics, the *geréb* finally abandoned their properties situated in the Sachsenland to the community, and assimilated themselves with the Hungarian nobility of Transylvania.

Thus, rid of the *geréb* and largely relieved of their obligation of personal military service, the Saxons turned to commerce and developed an organization headed by the royal free towns, which exercised the exclusive right to hold markets and dominated the neighbouring villages. Within the towns, guilds of merchants and craftsmen were organized. The predominant role of the Saxon towns (Brassó/Kronstadt, Beszterce/Bistritz and Nagyszeben/Hermannstadt) in all of Transylvania was maintained throughout the Middle Ages; Kolozsvár/Klausenburg owed its economic development largely to the Saxons who settled there.

These dominant urban communities soon started impeding the development of adjoining large villages, threatening the principle of Saxon equality of rights between urban burghers and village peasants. Each Saxon jurisdiction elected a supreme judge and, from the fifteenth century, the entire Saxon community was under the orders of the burgomaster of Nagyszeben/Hermannstadt, who bore the title of *comes* of the Saxons. Inequality between urban and rural areas was manifest in the distribution of the tax burden, owed by the community to the Crown.

It is in the context of this Transylvanian particularism that the history of the Szeklers was to evolve from the thirteenth century onwards. No doubt, the fact of being settled in remote Transylvania helped the Szeklers maintain their privileges. Here the existence of autonomous territories detrimental to the power of magnates and, occasionally, that of the voivode were of little concern to the Crown. Moreover, the military exigencies remained compelling on the southeastern frontier and hence the Crown's need to assure itself of a loyal and efficacious warrior community had priority.

C. From the Altland to the Szeklerland

The presence of the Szeklers in Transylvania is established by references in the early thirteenth century, in the charters granted the Teutonic Knights and in the *Andreanum*, while the grant and confirmation of privileges for the Saxons shed light on their move to the Szeklerland (*Székelyföld, Terra Siculorum, 'Regnum'* in the Werbőczy text), the administrative borders of which remained stable well into the nineteenth century. According to Pál Engel, the territory measures 12,710 km^2 (plus 345 km^2 for the Seat of Aranyos).[82] The Hungarian-speaking population has maintained its presence there to this day.

Prior to studying the Szeklers as a unified community in their own land, we must deal with the fact that in the documentation we encounter different groups of Szeklers, each of which seems to have followed its own itinerary.

A trace of this diversity is evidenced by the *tres genera Siculorum*, so regularly evoked. Did they preserve their differentiation on the same criteria – whatever these were – after settling in their Szeklerland?

The Szeklers' itineraries, linguistics, ecclesiastic organization, military command structures – all these confront us regularly with ternary distinctions within the Szekler community that merit consideration as we go along.

For the moment let us recall that eventually the Szeklerland, like that of the Saxons, was divided into Seats (*sedes, szék, Stuhl*) rather than counties, as in the rest of Transylvania and Hungary. There were seven Seats and, apart from the Seat of Aranyos isolated in the midst of the counties, the Szeklerland was a compact area comprising, to its northwest, the Seats of Udvarhely, Maros and Csík and to the southeast those of Sepsi, Orbai and Kézdi. These Seats represented both military and judiciary circumscriptions.

1. The Three Stages of Settlement If we include the last and definitive move from the *Altland* and the Sachsenland to what was to become the Szeklerland, keeping in mind differences of interpretation, we can distinguish three stages in the migration of the Szeklers within the Hungarian realm.

For one, the so-called 'Szeklers of Telegd' must have left the region of Szeben (*Altland*) before 1190 – in 1190, when the provostship of the *Altland* was established, the charters state that the region was '*desertum*', i.e. uninhabited[83] – to settle in the former royal domain of Udvarhely (lit. 'place of the Court'). From there, one group of Szeklers is considered to have moved to the Seat of Csík. In the documentation, this group is referred to as the 'Szeklers of Telegd', a term that is not applied to the Szeklers of any of the three southeastern Seats.

A second group, which moved somewhat later, no doubt before 1224, comprises the Szeklers of Sepsi, Kézdi and Orbai, who left their toponymic imprint in the southwest region of Transylvania, from which they must have set out and which became Saxon as they moved to the eastern border regions. Thus, we can deduce that the group from Sebes (Szeben) moved east to establish the Seat of Sepsi, while that from Orbó settled in the Seat that came to be known as Orbai.

The same toponymic correlations permit us to assume that another group within that of the above, the Szeklers of the Seat of Kézdi, hailed from the territory called Kézd, which became the Saxon Seat of Segesvár/Schässburg, with its village of Szászkézd (Saxon Kézd). There is no unanimous agreement on the precise date of this move. For some, it took place around 1225–1230,[84] for others, in 1288.[85] There is reason to believe, however that the foundation of the Seat of Kézdi was concomitant with those of Sepsi and Orbai, i.e. anterior to 1224. There is a writ from the chancellery of Pope Innocent III dated 1199,[86] confirming the Archdeaconry of Kézdi, which Zs. Jakó correctly identifies as the archdeaconry of a new Szekler Seat of Kézdi; such a papal confirmation appears logical enough for such a new institution. Moreover, when the three seats of Sepsi, Kézdi and Orbai were unified into the Seat of Háromszék (Three Seats) much later, in 1504,[87] without supplanting the denomination of the three seats, there was a uniformity of institutions that must be considered of earlier origin. Moreover, there was a correspondence of their new geographic localization with respect to the placement of their points of origin, that cannot but suggest that the arrival of the Szeklers of Kézdi coincided with those of Sepsi and Orbai.

Table 2. Displacement and Settlement in the Seats of Kézdi, Sepsi and Orbai

Sachsenland		Szeklerland
	Segesvár (Szászkézd) (North-east)	Kézdi (North-east)
Szászsebes (West)		Sepsi (West)
	Szerdahely (Szászorbó) (South-east)	Orbai (South-east)

King Stephen V donated 'the lands called "Aranyos" of the castle of Torda'[88] to the so-called 'Szeklers of Kézd' between 1270 and 1272, and their feats of arms against the retreating Mongols at the foot of the castle of Toroczkó (west of the Seat of Aranyos) are recalled in 1289,[89] which means that they must have been in the region in 1241–1242. There are many references to 'the Szeklers of Kézd living on the lands of Aranyos'. Although it is not possible to establish unequivocally whether this is in evocation of Szászkézd, from which they moved, or their destination, the Seat of Kézdi, it is safe to assume the former, since the Seat of Kézdi was the eastern-most Seat of Transylvania, far from Aranyos.[90]

Finally, the third group, that of the Szeklers from the region of Medgyes/ Mediasch, appear to have settled the Seat of Maros in the second half of the thirteenth century.

Thus we have the following breakdown, with the point of departure in the Sachsenland and the dates of settlement in the final Szekler Seats:

Table 3. Szekler Migrations to their Permanent Seats

Seat	Original Saxon region	Settlement date
Udvarhely	Szeben	Before 1190
Csík	–	from Udvarhely
Sepsi	Sebes	Before 1224
Orbai	Orbó	Before 1224
Kézdi	Kézd	Before 1224
Aranyos	Kézd	Before 1239
Maros	Medgyes	After 1224

2. The Three Ecclesiastic Circumscriptions In the ecclesiastic organization, the Szeklerland had two archdeaconries of its own (Telegd and Kézdi) and two circumscriptions (deaconries) that were part of county archdeaconries (that of Fehérvár, which also covered part of the Sachsenland and the county of Fehér and that of Torda). The delimitations of the deaconries coincide with those of the Seats.

Is it possible to reconstruct a reasoned pattern in this organization? If we accept that the Seat of Csík emerged directly from the Seat of Udvarhely, that the populations of the Seats of Aranyos and Kézdi both originated from around Szászkézd, and that the migration of the latter two took place before 1224 along with that of the Szeklers of Sepsi and Orbai, we are in the presence of three Saxon territories abandoned by the Szeklers.

The evidence points to the logic of dividing the Archdeaconry of Telegd into two groups, that of Udvarhely/Csík on the one the hand and that of Maros on the other. The date and point of departure from the Saxon lands, but also linguistics – which discerns similarities between the language of the Szeklers of the Seat of Maros and the population of the region of Moson – distinguish the Szeklers of the Archdeaconry of Telegd. One can postulate that the Szeklers of the Seat of Maros are not 'Szeklers of Telegd'. They may well have arrived at Telegd from western Hungary, the region of Moson, where a Szekler presence is attested in the twelfth to thirteenth centuries and with which there are linguistic similarities. However, the Church might also have integrated them in the Archdeaconry of Telegd for no more profound reason than geographic proximity.

While the Szeklers of Udvarhely and Maros are well differentiated, the Szeklers of the three southern Seats seem to have come by another itinerary, not passing through Telegd. No cross-linking of available criteria leads to more weighty conclusions.

But why did the Church keep the Seat of Sepsi in the Archdeaconry of Fehérvár while incorporating Aranyos in that of Torda, not to mention the creation of a new archdeaconry, under Kézdi, for the seats of Kézdi and Orbai and another, under Telegd, for the Seats of Udvarhely, Csík and Maros? No doubt these apportionments are the fruit of power play between archdeaconries, rather than concern for the composition of the resident populations. Where the Archdeaconry of Torda obtained the deaconry of Aranyos at the expense of Fehérvár, the latter maintained its hold on Sepsi. The farther east we go (nearer the pagan and orthodox Orientals), the less we encounter a presence of county archdeaconries. Five of the seven Szekler Seats fall under the authority of archdeaconries that are entirely within the Szeklerland and do not cross into counties.

3. *The* tres genera Siculorum *in the Military Organization* Mentions of the *tres genera Siculorum* – first mentioned in 1339[91] – appear from the outset in the Szekler military organization and in reference to the community itself, without giving specifics. How to interpret this other ternary reference?

Faced with the uncertain definition of these *genera*, let us continue using the Latin term. In military usage throughout medieval Hungary, the title of *comes* was always associated with a geographical area. Only the *comes* of the Szeklers appears consistently titled as *comes trium generum Siculorum*. But since there was only one, unified Szeklerland, why would the title not refer to 'terra Siculorum' or, as was the usage later, starting with the fifteenth century, 'septem sedes Siculorum'?

L. Szádeczky[92] puts forward a theory that seems interesting: these 'tres genera', before the permanent settlement in the Szeklerland, refer to three different groups, which he sees as a throwback to the three Kavar tribes.

In the present author's opinion, this differentiation seems rather to have been maintained in territorial distinctions on their arrival in Transylvania, and from the thirteenth century the notion of the *genera Siculorum* started to coincide with their territories in the *Altland*. But *genus* is neither *sedes* nor *terra*. How should we interpret the usage of this term? What meaning did it convey at the time?

After 1200 (and the Chronicle of the notary Anonymus), the term *genus* was in increasingly wide use in Hungary.[93] We find '*Ladislas de genere Herman*', for example, who holds the office of *comes trium generum Siculorum* in 1339.[94] But caution is in order in equating medieval Western with early Hungarian notions of kindred. In referring to tribes and clans, Hungarian documents use the terms *genus* and *linea*, in Hungarian: *nem* and *ág*. For the Hungarian tribes of the time of the Conquest, we find the term *törzs* (*caudex, truncus,* in German *Stamm,* in English 'stock'). We will meet the terms 'tribe' (*genus, nem*) and 'clan' (*linea, ág*) in contexts referring to constituent parts *within* the Szekler community in documents of the fifteenth to sixteenth centuries. But these terms never coincide with the usage of the collective term *tres genera Siculorum*, rather, they appear to denote either a subdivision of one of these *genera* or refer to another system of classification. When associated in military titles with Saxon territories,[95] the use of genus for the Szeklers could well be a reference to the territories the Szeklers had left some decades earlier. Here, the implied notion of lineage suggests that the territorialization coincided with an earlier tribal differentiation.

Thus, using the dates of settlement and the linguistic distinctions, the Szekler ternarity would give us the following breakdown: the Szeklers of Udvarhely (and Csík), the first to be settled; next, those of the southern Seats, displaced at the time of the *Andreanum*, along with those of the Seat of Aranyos already installed at the time of the Mongol invasions; and, finally, the last to settle, those of the Seat of Maros, who hailed from the distant Moson and may never have passed through Telegd.

Table 4. The *tres genera Siculorum* and the other Ternary Divisions

Seat	Saxon region deserted	Settlement date	Archdeaconry	Tres genera ?
Udvarhely	Szeben	Before 1190	Telegd	1st
Csík	-	from Udvarhely	Telegd	1st
Sepsi	Sebes	Before 1224	Fehér county	2nd
Orbai	Orbó	Before 1224	Kézdi	2nd
Kézdi	Kézd	Before 1224	Kézdi	2nd
Aranyos	Kézd	Before 1239	Torda county	2nd
Maros	Medgyes	After 1224	Telegd	3rd

The application of this ternary reference persisted (and its significance was to evolve in the late fifteenth century) but only when the Szekler community was dealt with as a whole. Internally, the community set about organizing itself on different references: territorially (the seven Seats) and structurally (six tribes and twenty-four clans). Should these three *genera* be seen as a throwback to the confederation that once was the 'eighth tribe' of the Kavars or is it a designation of military significance, referring to the original three territories?

The documents shed no light on the question, and we cannot exclude the possibility that the ternarity had already undergone several mutations before appearing in writing.

In any event, the discontinuity between the two systems of structural reference is likely to have been due in part to definitive sedentarisation, where the Seats became the primary organic subdivision of the community, and may reflect a modification in its composition. While the underlying ternary reference was formally maintained, the new subdivision was superimposed for the attribution of military and judicial dignities that guaranteed the cohesion of the community and then served to safeguard the customs and privileges that were the essence of their particularism.

No doubt the customs of the Pechenegs and Cumans were assimilated into the laws of the realm because their communities were too homogeneous and unstructured internally (the survival of the Cuman–Iasian particularism can be seen as proof *a contrario*). The Szeklers' insistence on defining rules for their internal relations – which perpetuated their customs and, especially, the individual liberty of all – could be seen as the result of multi-ethnicity recomposed during the first centuries of the Hungarian kingdom.

Having surveyed the diversity of the Szeklers' origins, we should not neglect the importance of their settlement as a continuous, compact territory, where their role as frontier guards served the interests of the Crown – elements essential to the convergence of their structures in their Szeklerland and the maintenance of their juridical particularism.

Chapter II

THE NOBLE SZEKLER NATION: A PRIVILEGED COMMUNITY

Two factors characterize the Szeklers: their status of '*privileged nobles*' and the fact that '*their laws are so different*'.

What does it mean to be a privileged noble in medieval Hungary? First and foremost, it is to be free, to be subject directly to the king and to have no statutory obligation toward any other noble. This nobility is military in nature (the burghers of royal free towns are also freemen, but they are not referred to as nobles) and exempt from taxation.

Unlike the other military auxiliary peoples, the Szekler community maintained this collective juridical liberty. Within the statutory horizontality of its society, the community was structured around a system of revolving access to dignities based on clan membership.

The community saw its collective identity defined by the characteristics of its nobiliary status and organized its military and judiciary life, Seat by Seat, around its structure of clans.

I. 'Privileged Nobles'

A. A Collective Privilege

In reorganizing the southeast of Transylvania, the Crown's intent was to secure the frontier (through the Szeklers) and ensure economic development (through the Saxons), but also to clarify the juridical situation (*unus sit populus*) relative to these two privileged communities. The privileges were expressly granted to the Saxons (*Andreanum*), while for the Szeklers they were simply confirmed as pre-existent. There is no royal charter that first grants the status to the Szeklers of Transylvania. This status is self-evident. It applies to the entire community. The privileges, which define personal rights (and obligations), are confirmed for the community, which is recognized as a juristic person – as are the clans. A grant of privilege to the Szeklers of Vág, in Western Hungary, by Béla IV in the first half of the thirteenth century,[1] cannot be seen as applying to the Szeklers of Transylvania. In addition to the ethnic designation customary in such charters, the specific localization stated (*Siculi de Wagh*) is a constituent part of the beneficiaries' designation. Hence this author does not consider this charter to be the origin of the status applying to inhabitants of Transylvania. Moreover, the charter in turn expressly refers to an anterior status of freedom.[2]

1. The Notion of Privilege The term 'privilege' (*privilegium, kiváltság,* or *szabadság*) can be taken at its etymological source as 'private law' (*privata lex*), distinctive (*kivált* (special)) and as prerogative, recognition of freedom (*szabadság*). The charter of 1224 granting privileges to the Saxons is sometimes referred to as 'Szebenian Freedom'. Often, writs of donation imply the notion of privilege, the juridical status to be applied within the confines of the territory ceded (ecclesiastic privilege, privilege of royal free towns, of *hospites*, nobiliary privilege and so forth).

The notion of privilege ordinarily cannot be dissociated from personal status (freedom, exemption from imposts, military obligation) or from the donation of land. In the course of time and political expediency the Crown can be more or less generous or, on the contrary, it can recover its donations. Escheat and treason are the principal motives for donated land to revert to the Crown.

2. The Particularism of the Szekler Community's Privilege None of this held true for the Szekler community. The Szeklerland was donated to the community as a whole. Before 1562, whatever the individual circumstance (heirlessness or treason), Szekler soil could never revert to the Crown; instead, it reverted to the kindred or, at worst, to the community. The Crown had no rights over this land, only Szekler customary law applied, to the exclusion of all others.

Besides the privileges specific to the Szekler community, others were granted in three distinct cases: firstly, privileges associated with individual grants of royal land to a Szekler and his family starting in the thirteenth century – land thus donated remained under royal jurisdiction, was not integrated into Szekler land and always remained subject to confiscation; secondly, the privileges of the royal free towns starting in the fifteenth century; finally, the privileges accorded the 'sub-Seats', Miklósvár and Kászon.

All of these interventions by the Crown in the Szekler community are well documented, essentially because of the beneficiaries' recourse to litigation to try to have rights thus acquired respected by the Szekler community. Apparently, the attribution of a 'dog-hide' – literal translation of *kutyabőr* – was the common term for parchment used to record ennobling and privileges. Szeklers were noble by birth and did not need ennobling by the grant of a *kutyabőr* – it was seen as an offence against ancestral Szekler liberty. The donation of royal land, albeit outside the limits of the Szeklerland, brought on the temptation for the beneficiary families individually to try to also apply royal jurisdiction to their lands situated on Szekler soil, thereby menacing the freedom of Szeklers who were employed in tilling this soil, without losing their own privileged status. The privileges of the royal free towns evidently infringed on Szekler liberties, their inhabitants being statutory subjects of the Crown – and therefore freemen – without the burden of military obligation. As to the recognition of the 'sub-Seats', the Szeklers were particularly touchy when it came to interference, however administrative, with their own choice of structure.

In a case from the mid-fourteenth century contesting the 'established privilege' of a Szekler family in a village situated on royal soil (a county northwest of Transylvania, to the north of the region of Telegd), a royal finding was rendered. This decision, handed down after an in-depth investigation by the chapters of Esztergom and Eger, confirms that: 'recognized as true Szeklers (*vera eorundem Siculitate*), they are not obliged to present writs of privilege and may live wherever they please.'[3]

The true '*siculitas*' appears as an 'innate privilege' conserved in this case, regardless of the fact that prevailing conditions did not call for the accomplishment of the military obligation.

Another, older document,[4] on which Zs. Jakó expresses doubt – without saying whether he questions the date, the origin or the content – has attracted the attention of Gy. Bónis[5] by virtue of its statement on the autonomy of Szekler law. Around 1272, and again in 1279, King Stephen V, followed by his son Ladislas IV, ordered the community (*universitas*) of the so-called Szeklers of Telegd to accept in their midst and 'in accordance with the laws and statutes of all Szeklers' a certain Laurencius and his sons, together with their possessions (the villages of Szederjes and Szentkereszt). The special character of Szekler law is confirmed in the document: the Szeklers collectively have their own system of laws and rules. The document even reiterates one of the specific derogations in stating that the land concerned would consequently not be subject to the authority of the voivode. We see here, if we give credence to this document, that the Szekler privileges do not fall into the category of the nobiliary privileges commonly granted or confirmed by the Crown at a given moment, but that they are a system of laws that is theirs since times immemorial.

Not until the second half of the fifteenth century was the idea formulated that the Szekler privileges had not only been repeatedly confirmed by the Crown, but had explicitly been granted by it. Where Louis I attributed the Szekler's right of free movement to his *siculitas*, King Matthias in 1476[6] refers to a previously granted charter, a writ that K. Szabó says has never been found. This shift of perception from recognition of an ancestral right to confirmation of formally granted privilege need not necessarily be interpreted as just the Crown's wish to be seen as the sole source of privilege. It is also the manifestation of the Crown's will to bolster the sense of cohesion in the Szekler community, the customary juridical principles of which were beginning to be threatened by the impact of socio-economic disparities within the community.

Whereas the privileged status of the Noble Szekler Nation is an unwritten accord between the king and the Szekler community as a whole, and applicable to all of the Szeklerland, the military obligation binds every member of the community individually. It is organized around a higher, royal command structure, always situated outside the community, and rooted in an ancient internal structure that provides for a hierarchy indispensable to all military enterprise, but without infringing on the principle of individual equality before the law. The increasing material cost of accomplishing military obligations and the Hungarian model of a society of Estates put this legal equality at risk throughout the fifteenth century.

B. Personal Military Obligation

Hierarchical considerations manifested themselves very early in the documentation, giving a clear view of the political importance of the Szeklers as a military force in the realm. The most comprehensive data stem from the mid-fifteenth century when, following the fall of Constantinople, the Hungarian Diet voted for a reorganization of the army that closely affected the structure of the Szekler contingent and resulted in its organic restructuring by King Matthias.

1. The Szekler Military Structure If the Szeklers' military role is allotted space in a study of their customary law, it is by virtue of its structural aspects rather than strategic considerations. Where Werbőczy sees them as 'skilled in the art of war', we see them 'at rest' in this study, not in the din of battle. For the period before royal reorganization of 1473, their hierarchy and the conditions of their mobilization are our principal points of interest.

Still, a brief digression on their art of war must set the stage ...

From the very outset of their appearance in the earliest chronicles, the Szeklers were horsemen. Their gear was that of light cavalry. Their battle tactics, efficacious though they were, were portrayed by chroniclers of the thirteenth century already versed in occidental strategy, using heavily armoured cavalry: 'the vile Pechenegs and Szeklers [.../...] fled', says the Illuminated Chronicle.[7] Hungary having become the 'bastion of Christendom', the courtiers had forgotten that occidental texts at the time of the invasions – and before them those of Byzantium[8] – described in the same terms the tactics of the Hungarian army as a whole: 'they [the Hungarians] feigned flight to attract their pursuers into carefully planned ambushes'.[9]

In Transylvania, the Szeklers seem to have continued to use the tactics of a light – and rapid – cavalry, which had lost none of its effectiveness against oriental raiders: Tartars and then Ottomans. Equally, conserving the concept of lightly-armed cavalry allowed a larger number of Szeklers to accomplish their military obligation with limited means.

What is known about the Szekler military structures prior to King Matthias' reforms of 1473?

A first royal decree dated 1463[10] restating and confirming the military obligations of the Three Nations of Transylvania expressly refers to the 'ancient customs' of the Szeklers, citing their obligation to go to war: two-thirds of the Nation in the case of general mobilization. In the same decree, we learn that one-quarter of the nobles in all of the counties must report, and one-third must report in the county of Hunyad, which, like the Szeklerland, was a frontier region at high risk. The decree also deals with the procedure of mobilization. For the Szeklers, the order to mobilize is given by the *comes* of the Szeklers and a blood-stained sword is carried from village to village to relay the order. In the case of an emergency, the captain of the Seat issues a call to arms with bonfires on the hill-tops, the blowing of clarions and a beating of drums.

Comes and captain: we are now in the presence of the officers.

The title '*comes* of the Szeklers' was highly prized by the Hungarian nobility; it was an important stepping-stone in a royal officer's career. The Latin term *comes* translates to *ispán* in Hungarian (nowadays normally rendered as 'prefect' or 'intendant') when it concerns an office or function and later *gróf* (*Graf* in German, *Count* or *Earl* in English) as it became a hereditary title. John Hunyadi, for example, had the office of Szekler *comes* (*ispán*) and the title of *comes* (hereditary count) of Besztercze by virtue of his possessions there. The translation 'Count of the Szeklers' encountered occasionally is not wrong, as long as the intention is to confer a meaning of the late Roman Empire and agents of the Crown, or of the Merovingian and Carolinian era. In the timeframe that concerns us, the title had already become hereditary in the West; hence we will stay with the Latin term in this study.

Independent of the voivode of Transylvania at the outset, the *comes* was appointed directly by the king to be his personal representative to the Szeklers. He exercised authority over them in military matters and presided at the highest Szekler judiciary proceedings. In the name of the king, he was also the collector of imposts (customs duties on merchandise, taxes on mining, among others), but this responsibility of the *comes* did not involve the Szeklers as such, only merchant and mining activity on their territory (primarily by Saxons).

Under the *comes*' authority there was the function of vice-*comes*, but the documentation does not reveal whether his presence was systematic. He had the same charges as his superior, but exercised them under the latter's authority. This function is sometimes cumulated with that of commander of a royal fortress (*castellanus*) in the frontier regions, most often the Görgény or Törcs castle. This cumulation agrees with the primary responsibility of the *comes* and his men, the defence of the frontiers, less so the holding of judiciary assemblies or collecting imposts. Neither the *comites* nor the vice-*comites* were ever Szeklers.

Between 1441 and 1446, John Hunyadi personally held both the office of voivode and that of *comes* of the Szeklers and, after him, such cumulation became common practice in the hands of one man or, by nepotism, within a family; a practice that had already occurred on earlier occasions (e.g. the Lackfi and Losonczi families between 1344 and 1391). No doubt there was a purpose behind the concentration of strictly military authority, but the juridical autonomy of the Szekler Nation was not affected. In all of the documents consulted, when the voivode deals with matters involving Szeklers, he explicitly refers to his title of *comes* of the Szeklers in the preamble and never takes a decision or confirms a sentence without this reference. The combining of the dignities of voivode with that of the Szekler *comes* also occurred with those of vice-voivode and vice-*comes* of the Szeklers (1460, 1507, 1524 and 1537), except when the latter function was assumed by the commander of a royal fortress (1548).

These four dignities: voivode and vice-voivode, *comes* and vice-*comes* are frequently mentioned in the *Székely Archives*. Turns were taken at fairly short

Map 5. The Szeklerland (Seats and Royal Free Towns) and the Royal Fortresses

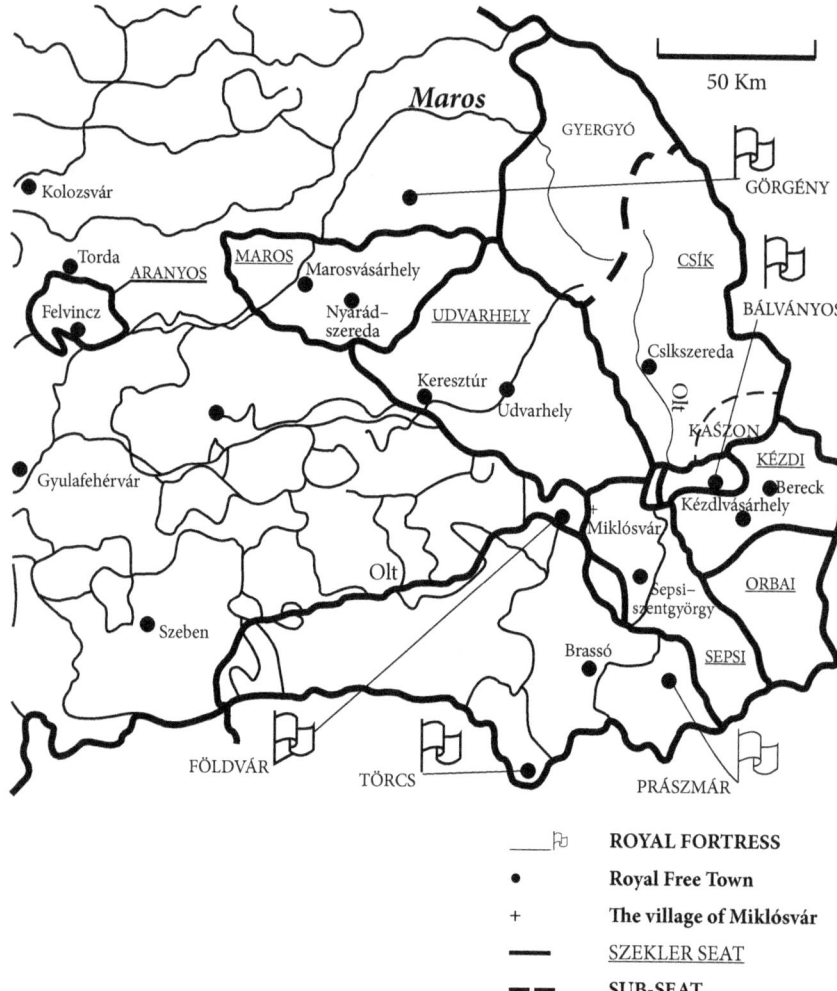

intervals in the function of Szekler *comes* (every two to a maximum of six years), somewhat less so when this office was in personal union with that of the voivode of Transylvania, but these variations were due more to political power-play at Court and developments in the history of Hungary, rather than anything to do with Szekler law.

On the next lower level, under the authority of the *comes* or his adjunct, we find the captain of the Seat; a Szekler who, like his superiors, exercised both military and judicial authority. The modus of his designation owed nothing to royal politics or manoeuvres at Court. He was designated by the Szekler community, the criterion for his selection being clan affiliation. This leaves one and all free to give the 'group of ten' (*tízes*) any reasonable interpretation: an administrative structure for the distribution of land according to some, a military or judiciary structure according to others.[11] No interpretation is in contradiction to any other. The *Székely Archives* have little to say on the subject of his military activities, his appearances are more frequent in the company of the judge in judiciary contexts. No doubt this is because the Szekler troops did not take their orders directly from this captain, they were instead organized in smaller detachments around a 'chief of ten' (*tízes*), but nothing from this echelon has reached the level at which events merited recording.

In 1499,[12] King Wladislas II Jagiello confirmed the ancestral customs of the Szeklers and consecrated the first articles of his writ to a reminder of their military obligations. The Szekler community is dealt with as a whole in this document and it is safe to assume that their obligations had not been modified by the structural reforms of 1473. All the more so since these obligations are defined along two criteria which, in this author's opinion, go back to a very ancient structure: the geographic orientation of the campaigns (in the order listed in the writ: east, south, west and north) and the command function (the king in person or one of his men).

From this geographic division it is evident that the Szeklers could be mobilized in all directions – under the king's command. Campaigns to the north or the east are not indicated when the king is not personally in command, but it is reasonable to assume that they could be called to arms in those cases as well. There is information on operations to the west and to the south, when the king was not in command: to the west only half as many men are called upon; for the south, the quota is reduced from two-thirds to one-fifth. The absence of documented details on the proportions for the north and east leads to the conclusion that the numbers are the same, whether the king was present or not: A modest contingent for the north (one in twenty, the northern frontier of Hungary has its own border guards, the Germans of Szepes) and a sizeable force for the east (two-thirds), which was the zone specifically assigned to the Szeklers.

The document lists the cardinal points (east, south, west and north) in the order of diminishing Szekler engagement. Sixty-six out of a hundred leave for the east, sixty-six or twenty for the south depending on whether the king is in command or not, ten or five to the west and five to the north.

Table 5. Szeklers Mobilized by Cardinal Point and Command

Direction	Person in Command	Szeklers Mobilized	%
East	King	2/3	66%
East	Other	–	–
South	King	2/3	66%
South	Other	1/5	20%
West	King	1/10	10%
West	Other	1/20	5%
North	King	1/20	5%
North	Other	–	–

The principal assignment of the Szeklers is the *defence* of the eastern frontier, while these articles deal with *offensive* campaigns. For defensive operations, when the danger is in the east, the document expressly states that the *comes* of the Szeklers had full authority to mobilize or exempt at his discretion.

2. The Reforms of King Matthias

An Indispensable Military Adaptation ...

Light Cavalryman in King Matthias' Time[13]

Figure 3. Light Cavalryman in King Matthias' Time, Illustration from 'Weisskunig' (Der weisse Konig – The White King), a prose chronicle of the fifteenth century, first published in 1775, in Sádvári, György and Somogyi, Győző. Nagy huszáarkönyv (*The Great Book of Hussars*), Budapest, 1999, p. 22.

Two factors affected the evolution of the Szeklers' military function in the mid-fifteenth century. Due to the Ottoman menace all available forces had to be kept at the ready, which weighed in favour of the Szeklers and their privileges, the Crown having every reason to humour this strategically placed contingent. Also, in keeping with the overall evolution of the armed forces throughout Europe, the Hungarian Diet in 1454, just after the fall of Constantinople, voted a decree[14] that imposed increasingly heavy – and expensive – armament.

This need for heavy armament left some of the Szeklers behind; they started to be referred to as 'common' and the more well-to-do disdainfully considered them arrogant in their insistence on fighting as a free contingent, when the equipment they could afford hardly measured up to that of *pedones* trailing behind the 'veritable' noble warriors. This discrepancy between the Szeklers' demands to remain free warriors and the reality of their material resources, deemed necessary for holding their place within the Hungarian army, was keenly perceived, even within the ranks of the Szekler community. The better-endowed among them were eager to assimilate the principle of Hungarian aristocracy and reserve for themselves the privileges conferred by military service. The less fortunate, as a whole, were by no means ready to renounce their role or, especially, their status.

Following the royal confirmation in 1463[15] of their collective military obligation and consequently of their privileges, the common Szeklers were comforted in their views and the conflict of interests between them and the better-placed turned into an insurrection. An assembly was held in 1466[16] in the village of Zabola to appease the situation between the notables, now referred to as *pociores* (the Latin term here used is as it appears in the *Székely Archives*) and the Szekler community. The accords reached confirmation of the freedom of the common Szeklers and forbid their being reduced to servitude. Nevertheless, in view of the recent decisions regarding heavy armour, which established onerous regulation of the gear for going to war on horseback, the better-off among the Szeklers felt justified in treating only the common horsemen as free, not the foot soldiers. The tensions persisted, and in 1473,[17] King Matthias, on a complaint by the Szekler horsemen and foot soldiers, issued a decree reorganizing the Szekler troops.

… which Confirms the Traditions of the Szekler Community

Light Cavalryman in King Matthias' Time – the curved sabre is characteristic of the light cavalry

Figure 4. Light Cavalryman in King Matthias' Time – the curved sabre is characteristic of the light cavalry.

To conserve combat effectiveness in the face of the Ottomans as a counterweight against oligarchic powers not always loyal to the Crown, King Matthias set about redefining the military dispositions regarding the Szeklers. This also allowed for the broader aim of humouring the lesser nobility who were often materially indigent – these nobles of modest economic means are often referred to 'nobles with seven prune trees'. Whilst recognizing material differences, King Matthias' decree allowed the overwhelming majority of common Szeklers to remain freemen, in spite of their modest economic means.

This royal decree reiterates the prohibition of reducing the poor to servitude and orders the *comes* to establish a general conscription of the Szeklers: the horsemen (*equites*) on the one hand and the foot soldiers (*pedites*) on the other. No-one is allowed to modify these registers, but they must be kept up-to-date under the strict supervision of the *comites*. A separate register must be kept of those among the horsemen belonging to distinguished families (*maiores progenerati*),[18] the notables (*primores*), who came to be known as *primipili* (*lófők*, pl.: 'Lófő' (*ló* = horse, *fő* = chief) is an equestrian military title in Hungarian, exclusively Szekler, the Latin translation of which shifts the accent to a notion of authority rather than that of cavalry). The horsemen and cavalrymen were formally promoted and the foot soldiers and infantrymen confirmed in their status of freemen. The Latin term *primipilus*, which King Matthias is careful to use instead of *primor*, is clearly in relation to the warrior and clan-oriented organization of the Szekler community, rather than indicative of material wealth.

This terminology establishes a hierarchy for the Szekler army consisting of two groups – horsemen and foot-soldiers – and three echelons.

1. The notables, always horsemen who, by virtue of the clan affiliation of their families, may accede to the dignities of captain or judge.
2. The common cavalrymen.
3. The common infantrymen.

This new ternarity must not, in this author's opinion, be confused with that of the *tres genera* mentioned since the early fourteenth century. Here, it refers to a pragmatic structure that reflects material realities in a military context.

The three military ranks (*ordines*) date from King Matthias' reforms (1473). Equating them to the *tres genera* found in earlier documents, as does K. Szabó[19] (and others in his wake) who interprets the first mention of the *tres genera* in 1339 as designating the three ranks established in 1473, is tenuous. For the period after 1473, a semantic shift may well have equated the three *genera* with the three ranks. This is all the more likely since we find the formulation '*tres genera septem sedium Siculorum*', an informative detail that had not been necessary before. But when the voivode, in 1519,[20] addresses notables of the three *genera* of the seven Szekler Seats, there is nothing in the context to suggest he may be referring to a military structure.

During the period when the *tres genera* were mentioned without the geographic specification of the 'seven Seats', the *comes* of the Szeklers was also *comes* of the Saxon territories (up to the beginning of the fifteenth century), before these had been granted their privileges. Here, the title is defined by reference to the territory encompassed (or its principal fortress), like those of the other *comites* in Transylvania and Hungary.[21]

No notion of military categories manifests itself. Hence it appears difficult to perceive the *comes* of the Szeklers as the *comes* of the 'Szekler notables, cavalrymen and infantrymen' – and Brassó and Besztercze – before these categories of Szeklers were even created.

Obviously, not all of the Szeklers found their place in King Matthias' conscriptions if we consider the meticulously completed register of 1614. Taking the total population of freemen and those in service, 53 per cent of the heads of family at this time are freemen, and of these 2 per cent are *primores,* and over 20 per cent are cavalrymen. Taking the repressions of the second-half of the fifteenth century into account, these proportions must be seen as a minimum for 1473,[22] but much of the pedestrian 'riff-raff' ready to go to war managed to conserve its military role and its status. Moreover, the king's decree recalls that whatever inequality may exist between Szeklers – based on clan affiliation and not material wealth – it must never lead to descent into servitude.

One of the characteristics of the nobiliary freedom recognized for the Szeklers is exemption from taxation. It was not until after the defeat at Mohács that this exemption lost much of its pertinence, with the imposition of the Szeklers' share of Transylvania's tribute to the Porte.

3. The Statutory Tax Exemption and the Gift of the Branded Oxen The Szeklers, like all noble warriors, were exempted from the various personal taxes gradually imposed by the Hungarian kingdom. They paid with their blood, but they also needed to arm and, on occasion, they shared in the cost of the campaign. A writ dated 1499,[23] points out that, in campaigns to the east or to the south, the Szeklers dispatched as vanguard were to cover their own expenses during the first fifteen days. This said, from the numerous complaints addressed to the king or the voivode by the Saxon neighbours, it is safe to conclude that a passing armed corps was seldom at a loss for finding sustenance. In 1432, for example, all of the Saxon Seats lodged complaints about the passage of the army of the Szekler *comes*. They estimate their prejudice at 7,000 florins.[24] Similar complaints are recorded in 1436, 1439, 1471 and 1521.[25]

Alongside this exemption we find the tradition of the Szeklers' gift for the king on certain occasions. This gift – which in no way impinges on the noble status and exemption from imposts – consists of oxen. The first documentary references to gifts of cattle (*pecus*) to the king date from the mid-thirteenth century.[26] Thereafter, the practice reappears relatively late in the documentation, as 'branded oxen' (i.e. oxen identified by branding with a red-hot iron, *boves signantur, ökörsütés*).[27] In Hungarian historiography, the term of 'branded oxen' always occurs with reference to the Szeklers; the term *ökörsütés* occurs only in connection with the Szeklers.[28] No doubt the practice of branding cattle as gifts was current throughout medieval Hungary, and therefore did not merit documentary mention until later (in the interval, documents originating at Court deal with the remittance of cattle, with no reference to branding). The Szeklers' gift of branded oxen aroused the curiosity of the Habsburgs on their accession, as witness their repeated queries.[29]

In 1473,[30] King Matthias recalls that that no-one may exact personal taxes from 'his faithful Szeklers who had spontaneously offered a gift of their own free will to him, as to his predecessors, on the occasion of a royal marriage and the birth of an heir to the throne', but there is no documentation from earlier on.

In 1499, a royal confirmation formalizes the tradition, and adds the coronation as the third occasion on which the gift is expected, in addition specifying the *first* marriage (and not just any wedding) and the *baptism* (and not the birth) of the first son as the two others. The collection of branded oxen from the Szeklers for the coronation of King Wladislas II Jagiello in 1490 is not mentioned until 1493,[31] and even then, the context suggests that the reason for the mention is that the voivode is suspected of having misappropriated the oxen for his own benefit. In 1501,[32] 1,800 oxen were collected for the upcoming royal marriage. The archives retrace this collection without mentioning any particular problem. Alas, in the summer of 1506 the queen gave birth to her first son and the collectors reappeared in the Szeklerland. The moment was ill-chosen, it seems. Hardly calmed after their uprising in 1505 against the corruption of their own notables, the Szeklers were not of a mind to proffer their gift again. Their defiance was put down and the success of the collection is attested to in 1508.[33] There is no mention in the *Székely Archives* of a collection for King Louis II Jagiello (1516–1526).

Not until after the defeat at Mohács is there another reference to the Szeklers' branded oxen, but conditions have changed. No more royal marriages, no births of heirs, no more presents – more or less readily offered – the situation calls for contributions to the tribute exacted by the Porte. In the Szeklers' view, this 'double taxation' was out of the question. Desertions and refusals of military service were legion. During the unsettled period of Habsburgs and Szapolyas vying for the Crown, promises, betrayals, insurrections and crackdowns follow in rapid succession until 1562.

The importance of the military function as the basis for privileges had eroded progressively since the internal conflicts preceding King Matthias' reforms. At the same time however, the Szeklers' internal, territorial structures and clan-related organiszation were affirmed and served to consolidate these very same privileges.

II. The Organization of the Szeklerland

The Szeklers were not the only privileged community in Transylvania. The Árpád kings and their successors carefully defined the territorial limits of each of the privileged communities, Saxon and Szekler, with respect to each other and those of the counties. But there were two other categories of privileged groups that could be in conflict with the community or encroach upon the Szeklerland: the Church and the royal free towns. Within their territory, the Szeklers had their own structure, their land was organized in Seats and, within these, the functioning of the institutional dignities was organized along clan lines and, interestingly enough, the villages themselves assumed the status of legal entities.

A. The Place of the Church

The archives of the ecclesiastic establishments, as *loca credibilia*, are among the principal sources for medievalists, but data on the organization of the Church tend to reveal more about its own difficulties than about the Szekler community.

Problems of Historiography During the 1990s, research resumed on the history of the Church in Hungary, but the historians engaged in this undertaking all regret the cruel absence of studies since the end of the Second World War and appreciate the effort needed to have a sufficient number of syntheses on which to base their analyses. The same is true for the Church in the Szeklerland. Gy. Kristó suggests another look at the origin of the Szeklers based on data about the ecclesiastic structure, and J. Gyöngyössi and K. Tüdős have published monographies on the fortified churches in the Szeklerland, but the juridical questions concerning the Church and the Szekler community have not been dealt with.

The *Székely Archives* reveal some points of conflict between the two privileged groups, the Church and the Szeklers, but it is not always possible to determine whether they arise from Szekler customs or whether they are the same throughout Hungary; for example, conditions for the payment of the tithe are undoubtedly similar throughout Hungary. Bequests of land in favour of the Church, on the other hand, certainly gave rise to more complications in the Szeklerland. We can deduce this from archive data and our knowledge of Szekler customs, but cannot confront it with data on the situation in other regions of Hungary.

From the limited sources available, however, it is possible to obtain insight into Szekler society from information on ecclesiastic structures, and learn about conflicts arising from land owned – or claimed – by the Church in the Szeklerland, as well as about disagreement on the juridical competence of ecclesiastic tribunals and problems with bequests of land to the Church.

1. Church History and Szekler Society

Paganism, Occidental and Oriental Christianities and Reformation   In the beginning, the conversion of the Hungarians vacillated between the Church of Byzantium and that of Rome. This ambivalence was particularly notable in Transylvania during the first half of the eleventh century. But documentation about the presence of the Szeklers in Transylvania during this period is inexistent and in their later relations with the two poles of Christianity there is no trace of a penchant toward the Oriental Church. There is no reason to doubt that, should they have started to arrive shortly before the Saxons (that is, late in the eleventh century), their conversion would have had to be already consummated in western Transylvania, by the Church of Rome.

One of the difficulties encountered by Christianity – regardless of whether Latin or Greek – in its efforts to proselytise was common to both Hungarians and Szeklers. It was the persistence, more or less covert but always present, of pagan creeds. The most obvious manifestations of this attachment are in the domain of symbolism – universal and pre-Christian – that of the sun and the moon, the emblem of the Szekler Nation in the coat of arms of Transylvania, and the use of Szekler runic writing both in the decoration of churches and on the funerary steles, where the memory of the deceased is evoked in this pre-Christian code. In the domain of Law, the ancient Ordeal of the *Bleeding Corpse (tetemre hivás, halálújítás)* continued to be forbidden time and again, well into the eighteenth century. Finally – notwithstanding the fact that the reference to latent pagan beliefs is maliciously intended – in 1515, the Szeklers are denounced as particularly violent and bloodthirsty because 'they believe that those they kill become their slaves in the nether world',[34] a belief also common among the Hungarians before their conversion.[35]

The end of the period that concerns us bears the imprint of the Reformation, and its particularly distinctive manifestations in Transylvania.[36] They range from the Hussite influence over the peasant uprising of 1437, to the Sabbatarians (*Szombatosok*, a sect the beliefs of which were close to Judaism) under the reign of Prince Gabriel Bethlen of Transylvania (1613–1629). Following the Mohács defeat and the subsequent dismembering and partition of Hungary, with the Muslim Turkish *pashalik* separating the Habsburg-dominated west from the Szapolyais' Hungary (Transylvania and the *Partium*) in the east, the new political situation had its religious repercussions. The rancour between the Szapolyai and the – very Catholic – Habsburgs in an overall political climate given to violence did nothing to curb religious divisions.[37] In 1568, the Edict of Torda accorded the status of 'recognised religions' to the Lutherans, Calvinists and Unitarians. This decision may, in the context of the rest of Europe at that time, seem like an 'edict of tolerance', but it can just as well be seen as a measure to save the Catholic Church in the face of extensive conversion or to put an end to the proliferation of new Protestant sects.

As the spirit of Reformation swept over the Szeklerland, the Unitarian (anti-Trinitarian) faith in particular found many followers among the Szeklers. Throughout, the situation in Transylvania remained an exception to the convulsions found elsewhere, the four 'recognized' religions, but also the – older but merely 'tolerated' – Orthodox, Jewish and Armenian confessions cohabited in relative peace. In the Szeklerland, there is no evidence that the religious diversity, with its potential for decomposition, had any direct influence on customary law.

All along, the Roman Catholic Church kept records and all of the information on ecclesiastic organization up to 1562 used in this study pertains to it.

Ecclesiastic Organization The earliest reference to ecclesiastic organization within the Szeklerland dates from 1199,[38] a reference to the Archdeaconry of Kézdi. Next to be mentioned is the Archdeaconry of Telegd in 1235,[39] the limits of which coincide with those of the Seats of Udvarhely, Csík and Maros.

The ecclesiastic circumscriptions cover the Szeklers in two archdeaconries of their own – Telegd for the Seats just mentioned and Kézdi for the Seats of Kézdi and Orbai – and two archdeaconries centred outside, in the counties. One at Fehérvár, which encompasses the Seat of Sepsi, and which is a throwback to the old territory of Sebes, from which Sepsi was populated, was part of the county of Fehér. The other, at Torda, paradoxically includes the Szekler Seat of Aranyos. Aranyos thus finds itself attached to the archdeaconry of its final destination and not its point of departure (like Fehérvár or Telegd); nor does it have an ecclesiastic circumscription of its own (like Kézdi). This incorporation is all the more curious since the population of Aranyos, often referred to as 'Széklers of Kézd' in the archives, appears alongside the Szeklers of the Archdeaconry of Telegd in a dispute with the Church in 1466[40] concerning the payment of tithes. Within the archdeaconries, the territorial limits of the individual Seats are represented by decanal districts bearing their names, with the exception of 'Erdőhát' ('back of the forest'), the name the Church gave to the decanal district of Udvarhely. It is worth noting that this a rare, perhaps the only, transliteration into Hungarian of the term 'Transylvania'.

There is less evidence of a decanal district of Orbai. In the Papal register of tithes for 1567, it appears as part of the Archdeaconry of Kézdi, but the register for 1332–1337 mentions no parish in this Seat. The old parish church of Gelence (in the Seat of Orbai), which is thought to have been built starting in the thirteenth century,[41] appears in a Vatican document dated 1499[42] as 'situated in the seat of Orbai, in the diocese of Transylvania'. But in 1475,[43] the Szeklers of Orbai are reprimanded by the see of Transylvania for their refusal to recognize the authority of the ecclesiastic courts of that diocese. From the document, issued by the diocese, it is not clear whether the refusal concerns all ecclesiastic authority or only that of the diocese of Transylvania. The Seat of Orbai borders on the territory of the see of Milkó, mentioned in the *Székely Archives*[44] as the Cuman diocese attached directly to the archdiocese of Esztergom. Founded around 1224, with the aim of converting the Cumans of southern Moldavia and Walachia, Milkó (or Szeret) also entertained relations with the neighbouring Szeklers but was wiped out for the first time during the Mongol invasion in 1241 and its very name disappeared from the archives in the fifteenth century.[45]

In 1567, the register of tithes does list parishes in the Seat of Orbai and hence in the diocese of Transylvania, but that does not preclude the Szeklers of Orbai having been, for a time, under the missionary diocese of Milkó.[46] The document dated 1228[47] – brought to light by J. Benkő in the eighteenth century – in which the bishop of Milkó asks the priests of the Szeklers to recognize his authority, has since been suspected of being Benkő's own creation. But another document, dated 1382,[48] refers to a Szekler of Kőröspatak (Seat of Sepsi) in the monastery of Kimpolung (*Longus Campus*, Câmpulung in Romanian) in Walachia and his ordination as subdeacon by the bishop of Szörény (in the southwest of Transylvania). The successor of this bishop is ordered by the Pope in 1439[49] to ensure the presence of clergy 'in Moldavia, the Land of the Szeklers and Walachia' until the bishopric of Milkó can resume functioning. Thus, the authority of the bishop of Transylvania over the Szeklerland appears to be neither all-encompassing nor exclusive of extraneous influences. It is also worth noting that the Saxon region of Szeben had a provostship attached directly to the archdiocese of Esztergom, and the Saxon region of Brassó (the Burzenland, *Barcaság*) was also a deaconry attached to the archdiocese.[50]

The papal register of 1332–1337 lists 165 parishes for the Szeklerland (not including the decanal district of Orbai). Gy. Kristó estimates that the density of villages having churches of their own in the early fourteenth century was around 90 per cent in the Szeklerland, while the average in Hungary for the same period was 41 per cent – an average that is corroborated by M.-M. de Cevins.[51] Gy. Kristó concludes his analysis of this exceptional density by reiterating the perpetual question of the origins of the Szeklers.

Without contradicting this analysis, open-ended as it is, two observations can help shed light on the reasons for this exceptional density of parish churches in the Szeklerland. The decision of King Stephen I imposing the erection of one church for every ten villages is seen by L. Koszta[52] as a political stratagem intended to help break up the solidarities around the clans and families, perpetuated in some measure by pagan rituals, and re-orient these ties around the parishes, the first link with the Church, the rampart of royal authority. In this perspective, we should recall that clan solidarity was, and remained, the heart of Szekler society; hence it seems possible that the Szeklers, in passing from paganism to Christianity, aimed to maintain their older structural elements even in this new, spiritual context. The erection of such a dense network of churches can consequently be seen as a manifestation of their functional autonomy: as many churches as there were clans – or nearly so.

A second observation, on reading M.-M. de Cevins' study, corroborates the notion of this aim of autonomy and freedom on the part of the Szekler clans. The author reflects on the sources that permit a census of the parish churches in Hungary to be taken, noting that numerous additional churches were erected by prominent families on their own soil; churches that may well have had the right to administer sacraments to the public for a time. Depending on whether or not these churches are counted as parish churches, the density varies and the need for erecting churches in nearby villages may have been less pressing. Here again, the situation is different in the Szeklerland. Even if some of the better-off families could have endowed churches more generously, they could never own them outright and as a result all churches counted as parish churches.

The Medieval Church of Zabola[53]
Fortification fourteenth–fifteenth-century Reconstitution

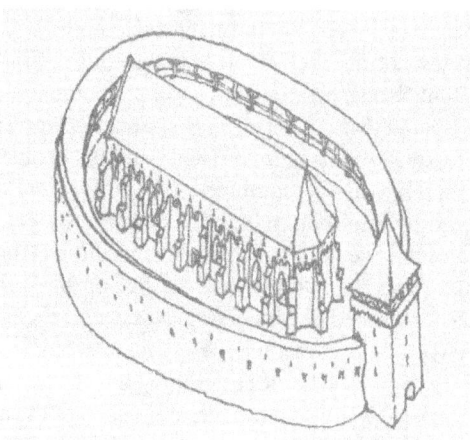

Figure 5. The Medieval Church of Zabola Fortification fourteenth to fifteenth century. Reconstitution, Gyöngyössy, János. Székely templomerődök (*Szekler Fortified Churches*), Csikszereda, 1999, p. 82.

Incidentally, this impressive density may have been a factor contributing to the fortification of churches in the Szeklerland in the course of the fourteenth to fifteenth centuries. The Szeklers (like the Saxons), with their uncompromising resistance against any form of servitude, obstinately refused the building of fortified castles. Only churches (and towns) were fortified as places of refuge in times of armed conflict, especially Tartar and later Ottoman raids, but without allowing any hereditary power to establish itself there to the detriment of the surrounding population. Much studied in history of art,[54] this phenomenon is yet again evidence of a social structure characterized by the liberty of the entire community, which could not tolerate the imposition of fortresses as an instrument of domination by the better-off. An attempt by the Voivode István Báthory to build fortresses in the Szeklerland gave rise to the Szeklers' outraged protestations to the king in 1493.[55]

2. Privileges in Conflict – Conflicting Privileges

Privileged Ecclesiastic Enclaves in the Szeklerland The presence of secular clergy, of parishes – and no doubt of associated land – has left no trace of conflict in the *Székely Archives*. It seems that each community accepted the other's privileges, particularly since the bishopric of Transylvania was respectful of Szekler custom, as we shall see shortly.

It is rather in the presence of monastic orders that the Szekler community, faced with the exorbitant prerogatives of monastic communities, was obliged to admit exceptions to its privileges.

The evolution of monastic life in Transylvania seems to have been no different from that throughout medieval Hungary. The regular clergy appears to have inspired respect in the lay population and, if the *Székely Archives* mention only a few monasteries by name, several villages conserve in their names the term '*remete*' (hermit) and hence the memory of small, reclusive, monastic communities. Other indications of monastic life can be found by cross-referencing studies of the

Table 6. Monastic Orders in the Szekler Seats of the Archdeaconry of Telegd

Seat	Village	Order	Seat	Village	Order
Maros	Mikháza	Franciscans	Udvarhely	Alsóboldogasszonyfalva	Dominicans
	Nyárád*remete*			Homorod*remete*	
	*Remete*szeg			Kereszúrfalva	Saint John
	Szentbenedek	Benedictines	Csík	Somlyó	Franciscans
	Szentkirály	Paulists		Szentdomokos	Dominicans
				Gyergyó*remete*	

principal monasteries in Hungary[56] with the data collected by L. Vofkori. With no aim to be exhaustive, we find, within the Archdeaconry of Telegd (the Seats of Udvarhely, Maros and Csík), Benedictines, Franciscans, Dominicans, Knights of the Order of Saint John and the Hungarian Order of the Paulists:

The latter Order, documented since 1250, is the hermits of St. Paul the First Hermit, at first called that of *Fratris Sanctae Crucis in Eremo*, then confirmed by Pope John XXII in 1329 as the *Ordo heremitarum Sancti Pauli primi heremitae*, often abbreviated in Hungarian to *Pálosok* and translated as Paulists. They were monks seeking the seclusion of inaccessible valleys as opposed to the so-called Augustinians (in towns or along main roads) whose rules they observed. The order had its golden age under the reign of the House of Anjou (1305–1380), counting sixty-one monasteries at the time of Mohács. One of these monasteries was situated in the Szeklerland, at Marosszentkirály. It received a bequest in the adjoining county of Torda from a Szekler family and another, situated in the Szeklerland – which was promptly bought back by the family of the bequestor.[57]

Conflicts of Jurisdictional Competence A document dated 1503,[58] a sort of concordat between the bishop of Transylvania and emissaries of the Szekler community, brings out the principal points of potential conflict between the Church and the Szeklers. Presented as a preformulated document requiring only the bishop's '*Placet*' or approval, it consists of a preamble, sixteen articles and the concluding confirmation of the episcopal accord.

The preamble points out that the agreement is accorded by the bishop at the request of the Szekler community and that therefore 'loyalty to the King and respect for the Church' are expected from the Szeklers. These pious wishes must be seen against a backdrop of abuses by the Church of Rome that were meeting with increasing opposition throughout Europe at the time.

As for the Szeklers, even if certain complaints arose in only one Seat (and hence one and the same decanal district) it was always the community as such that presented its grievances. The Szekler identity could not be carved up into ecclesiastic jurisdictions and the evocation of loyalty to the king – and not the *comes* of the Szeklers – shows the bishop's recognition that he is dealing with equals in the hierarchy of the realm.

Some of the Szekler emissaries will reappear as signatories of the conclusions of the Szekler assemblies of 1505 and 1506: András Lázár de Gyergyó (1506), Pál Nyujtódi (1505 and 1506) and János Benedekfi (1505 and 1506) (assemblies which we will deal with in Part II). Two of the members of the delegation could not be identified, but the other names show that at least the Seats of Udvarhely, Maros, Csík and Kézdi were represented; in addition, the Seat of Sepsi is explicitly mentioned by name in the articles. Taking for granted that the Seats of Aranyos and Orbai are tacitly included, represented by the Seats of Maros (with which Aranyos is frequently associated) and Kézdi respectively, we are well in the presence of the entire Szekler community.

The grievances presented fall into two categories: complaints about priests and jurisdictional conflicts. The first category (six articles) has nothing specifically Szekler to it: complaints of the clergymen's malfeasance, five articles concern abuses in the collection of alms and one article on their concubinage – when it is notorious and unrepentant.[59] The second group of articles is more closely linked to Szekler law. Three themes dominate: judicial procedure, conflicts between the jurisdiction of lay, and ecclesiastic tribunals: applicable law.

Three articles deal with points of procedure: the prohibition of legal representation before the Episcopal court, except where a layman pleads against a priest; in such a case, the latter is to plead his own cause and is not allowed to plead in writing.[60] It is safe to assume that in the early sixteenth century, familiarity with Latin and the use of writing were unevenly spread outside the Church. Hence this provision may be seen as an attempt to lessen the clergyman's advantage in a conflict. The two other articles show hints of the Szeklers' taste for bickering, a trait found in a number of other documents. These articles limit access to the Episcopal court to 'grave or atrocious' cases and cases involving significant material values.

The next theme concerns the competence of the ecclesiastic courts. These are not to judge lay matters – with no more precise definition – whereas priests must be judged only by ecclesiastic tribunals. The case of a woman accused of adultery is not necessarily for the Church to judge, whereas matters of dowry can come under ecclesiastic jurisdiction, by extension of jurisdiction over marriage.

In these two areas concerning marriage, the competence of the Church appears to be quite routinely accepted. All of the cases encountered where a dowry is in issue had been taken before the Chapter of Transylvania[61] or the Convent of Kolozsmonostor[62] – these two establishments also function as *loca credibilia*. This said, the adulterous woman, described as 'cast out, her clothes shredded as is the custom', is considered 'without merit' and is enjoined not to seek remedy at the Episcopal court, except in special cases provided for in law or custom, neither of them specified in the document. Could it be that the special case might involve adultery with a priest? The physical description of the adulteress shows that she was first judged by the community, where betrayal of a matrimonial alliance (by the woman) – endangering cohesion and solidarity in the family structure – was severely punished.

The other question concerning matrimony, the dowry, is shown in this concordat to be within the domain of the ecclesiastic courts, but the article states that the vicar has no power of enforcement, or even the right to pronounce findings regarding value or quantity, these being the domain of customary law.[63] This article enumerates the military ranks (established in 1473) within the Szekler community according to which the community determines the value of the dowry. The ecclesiastic competence is thus purely formal in this domain. It is worth noting, however, that a document dated 1431[64] shows the Church authorities exercising coercive power, the terms of a dotal contract not having been met satisfactorily: the excommunication of a widow in the Seat of Maros is lifted by the bishop of Transylvania upon payment of a disputed dowry.

Finally, three articles manifest the legal acumen of the Szekler community. One suspends all judiciary activity before the ecclesiastic courts for the duration of a military campaign, in line with the custom before lay courts in the Szeklerland. This demand is accorded only in part by the bishop, who insists on the presence of a proxy or attorney before suspending a serious case.

Finally, and most significantly, the last two articles, which attest to the inalienability of (inherited) Szekler property according the Szekler customary law, deal with the incompetence of the Church in favour of the rights of the family or, in the absence of relatives, the rights of the village, which may redeem bequests made in favour of the Church involving 'private' (acquired), as opposed to common, property.[65] This extension of family rights to acquired property is not mentioned as explicitly anywhere else in the documentation available.

This recapitulation of rules is due no doubt to the fact that their observance was not all that rigid, but it also shows the Szeklers' attachment to them and their awareness of the need to have these principles confirmed by the Church. The ecclesiastic confirmation is all the more noteworthy as the rules violate the very precepts of King Stephen's decree[66] on testamentary freedom, from which the Church had amply reaped the fruits in Hungary, but which here admits are not applicable to the Szeklers.

B. The Royal Free Towns

Beginning in the twelfth century, some localities where the Court or bishops stayed (Székesfehérvár, Esztergom, Buda) and centres of trade and crafts were accorded royal privileges, the principal characteristics of which were that they were subject directly and exclusively to the king and protected from possible exactions on the part of magnates. Moreover, these privileges gave them the right to designate their own notables, leaders (mayors) and judges. In Transylvania, after the passage of the Tartars, the Saxons were the first to engage in crafts and trade, which developed not only in the Sachsenland (Nagyszeben/Hermannstadt, Brassó/Kronstadt, Bestercze/Bistritz) but also in the counties, for instance at Kolozsvár/Klausenburg (where *hospites* are mentioned in the latter half of the thirteenth century and which is referred to as *civitas* as early as 1316[67]) and Torda.

In the Szeklerland, the appearance of free towns, chartered as such, occurs later. While merchant activity is certainly not one of the dominant characteristics of Szekler society, it would be an exaggeration to see the sole reason for this late development in the lack of the Szeklers' propensity for trade. In the present author's opinion, the reason is both statutory and concrete. The Szekler community itself was not interested in seeing enclaves with royal privileges of their own established on Szekler soil, while the Saxons, throughout the archives, show open hostility to any confirmation of Szekler royal charters for free towns that might encroach on the Saxons' monopoly of commerce.

Whereas in Hungary the royal free towns tend to be found in the vicinity of royal or episcopal seats, which in turn were normally fortresses or fortified localities, most of the Szekler royal free towns correspond to agglomerations where assemblies or tribunals were held. A policy formulated by King Sigismund in 1427[68] of 'one royal free town per Szekler Seat' is taken up in 1492:[69] 'the seven royal free towns of the seven Seats'. Documentation prior to 1427 dealing with royal free towns is sparse. K. Szabó suggests some towns that might have been behind King Sigismund's statement, all the while regretting that he had not been able to locate their charters of privilege. While the document of 1427 uses the term *civitas*[70] in connection with privileges, the term *oppidum* also occurs and can be considered to mean 'free' town. On the basis of K. Szabó's notes and the work of E. Benkő,[71] we obtain the following list.

Table 7. Royal Free Towns in the Szeklerland

Royal Free Town (Former name)	Seat	First mention as Royal Free Town (*oppidum*)	SzOkl
Kézdivásárhely (*Torjavásárhely*)	Kézdi	1427	I.CII
Marosvásárhely (*Székelyvásárhely, Novum Forum Siculorum*)	Maros	1451	I.CXXXIII
Székelykeresztúr	Udvarhely	1459	I.CLI
Sepsiszentgyörgy	Sepsi	1461	I.CLVIII
Székelyudvarhely	Udvarhely	1485	III.489
Nyárádszereda	Maros	1493	VIII.95
Bereck	Kézdi	1531	II.CCLIX
Csíkszereda	Csík	1558	II.CCCXXVII
Felvinc (*Felvincz*)	Aranyos	1558	II.CCLXXIII

The Seat of Orbai does not have a royal free town of its own, while the Seats of Kézdi, Maros and Udvarhely have two each (Kézdivásárhely and Bereck, Marosvásárhely and Nyárádszereda, Székelyudvarhely and Székelykeresztúr, respectively). Thus the elegant principle of 'one Seat, one royal free town' is not borne out by the archives. No doubt the practical reality of trade routes carried the day over mere principle.

It is difficult to derive generalizations from conflicts involving royal free towns. For Marosvásárhely, disputes tended to juxtapose the legal prerogatives of the town and those of the Seat. The interest shown by the dignitaries of the Seat to litigate disputes between townspeople no doubt arose at least in part from the desire to collect legal fees connected with rendering justice,[72] but they were certainly also motivated by the determination to keep the upper hand in all judiciary matters in the Szeklerland. The superimposition of privileges – and the irreconcilable procedural differences they entailed – is particularly well-documented for Marosvásárhely, the site of numerous assemblies, both of the Szekler community and of Transylvania as a whole. The predominance of the town of Marosvásárhely (in the Seat of Maros) over Székelyudvarhely (Seat of Udvarhely), in spite of Udvarhely's being the principal Szekler Seat, is undoubtedly due to the location of Marosvásárhely: quite close to Torda, easily accessible from the Sachsenland and less embedded in mountainous country than Székelyudvarhely. The staging of judiciary assemblies within the walls of royal free towns, or more precisely the attendant expense, gives rise to frequent recriminations on the part of the towns.

The exemption from personal military service, which allowed burghers of franchised towns to be the last to go to war, only after all the Szeklers had already left, and even then only if the campaign stayed within Transylvania, are amply evidenced by repeated confirmations and orders issued to the military dignitaries of the Szeklerland.[73]

Finally, if the attitude of the Crown, directly or through the person of the voivode, was always favourably inclined toward the rights of the royal free towns in the Szeklerland when these were challenged by the dignitaries in the Seats, the balance was not the same when two royal free towns were in dissension. The town of Sepsiszentgyörgy, for example, had its privileges confirmed when these were challenged by the Seat, but revoked upon complaints by the Saxon town of Brassó, only some fifty kilometres away. The determined protests by Brassó following the statutory elevation of Szekler towns – tardy though it was – raises doubts about the Saxons' readiness to share commerce in the Szeklerland, which had hitherto been their monopoly and was well worth defending.

Table 8. The Changes of the Status of Sepsiszentgyörgy as Royal Free Town

Year	Plaintiff	Decision	SzOkl
1492 (Sept)	Seat of Sepsi and Saxons	Status refused (1)	III.496
1492 (Oct)	Seat of Sepsi	Status accorded(a)	III.497
1510	Saxons of Brassó	Prohibition of markets (i)	V.923
1514 (Jul)	Saxons of Brassó	Prohibition of markets (ii)	III.537
1514 (Oct)	Saxons of Brassó	Prohibition of markets (iii)	III.540
1515 (Dec)	On the town's request	Status of Oct 1492 confirmed (b)	I.CCXXXVII
1519 (Sept)	Saxons of Brassó	Prohibition of markets (iv)	III.558
1520 (May)	On the town's request	Confirmation of right to hold markets	II.CCXLVI
1520 (Oct)	Saxons of Brassó	Status revoked (2), prohibition of markets (v)	III.561
1520 (Oct)	Seat of Sepsi	Status confirmed (c) – prohibition of appeal	

Year	Plaintiff	Decision	SzOkl
1525 (March)	Saxons of Brassó	Status revoked (3)	III.577
1525 (April)	Seat of Sepsi	Status confirmed (d)	II.CCLV
1528	Saxons of Brassó	Prohibition of markets (Habsburg) (vi)	III.579
1555	Saxons of Brassó	Prohibition of markets (Habsburg) (vii)	V.940

The Crown found itself in a quandary between its policy of favouring the expansion of royal free towns and the fiscal realities eagerly exploited by the Saxons, when the town of Sepsiszentgyörgy appeared less than eager to discharge its obligation of paying the tax of one-thirtieth of the merchandise traded.

Between 1492 and 1555, its status of royal free town was refused three times, accorded four times, and the holding of markets forbidden seven times upon Saxon complaints.

The clearest illustration of these contradictions occurred in 1520: in the month of May the king confirmed the town's privileges. A delegation of the Saxons of Brassó is likely to have then called to his attention that the tax of one-twentieth of the value of merchandise traded, which *they* paid regularly, was diminished as a result of competition from Sepsiszentgyörgy. Based on these fiscal considerations, the king, in October, forbade the holding of markets there, without abrogating the town's status entirely. On learning this, the dignitaries of the Seat of Sepsi, hoping to reintegrate the town entirely under their power, asked the king to revoke its status, seeing that markets would no longer be held there anyway. Exasperated, the king in October reconfirmed the town in its status, reinstated the authorization to hold markets, and strictly enjoined the Szeklers of the Seat from sending him any more emissaries with appeals in this affair of a remote, provincial locality!

A new cycle of contradictory royal decisions started in 1525. Any coherence must no doubt be sought in fiscal considerations. In the Crown's view, Sepsiszentgyörgy was a legitimate, royal free town when facing the surrounding Seat. When facing the powerful, neighbouring merchant town of Brassó, however, its right to hold markets, a characteristic of royal free towns, was regularly put in doubt. The two decisions of Ferdinand of Habsburg at the end of the period under study show that the situation had not changed.

C. *The Szeklerland, its Seats and Clans*

The land of the Szeklers is composed of seven Seats. Two complementary structures function within each of these Seats: villages, territorial delimitations; and clans, organic divisions for access to the dignities within each Seat (judge and captain) and the associated possession of land. Toward the end of the period under study, the villages extend their legal competence over clan domains, but it is always the clan structure around which Szekler customary law is exercised.

1. The Szeklerland Divided into Seats Toward the outside world, the dignitaries of the Szekler Seats generally close ranks to represent the community's interests, such as in 1493 to present grievances against the voivode or in 1503 when facing the bishop of Transylvania. Together they sit in the Assembly of the three Nations of Transylvania. But each Seat has its own 'administration': its dignitaries – the judge of the Seat and the captain of the Seat – its tribunal and, to some extent, its own customs (the value of the dowry, or monetary units such as the *oszpora*, an Ottoman denomination, in the Seat of Kézdi).

The Particularism of the Seat of Aranyos The situation of Aranyos is unique among the Szekler Seats, grouped as they are in a contiguous area of the Szeklerland. The first anomaly with which we are confronted from the archives is the succession of royal confirmations of privilege for the Szekler community of Aranyos. The first donation, by King Stephen V in 1270–1272, is followed by the confirmation of Ladislas IV in 1289, in 1291 it is Andrew III, in 1313 it is Charles I, in 1394 and 1436 Sigismund and, following the transcription of the latter by Kolozsmonostor as locus credibilis in 1468, confirmations yet again by King Matthias in 1469 (and transcription by Kolozsmonostor) and in 1484.[74] Such legal precautionary measures, not taken for the other Seats, seem to suggest that the rights of the Szeklers were frequently contested in this region. Earlier on, in 1219,[75] a part of the Seat, the area around Felvincz, had been part of a donation made in favour of the Chapter of Esztergom, which repeatedly reiterated its claims of possession, resulting only in repeated royal confirmations of the rights of the Szekler Seat.

Finally, the real autonomy of the seat of Aranyos is not always that evident, due perhaps to its isolated geographic position. From 1466 on, the Seat is often mentioned alongside the Seat of Maros, the closest one geographically and the one which shares with Aranyos the advantages – or inconveniences? – represented by its proximity to the town of Torda, the site of many of the Assemblies of Transylvania.

Another trait that is not common to all Seats is the claim of groups of villages to form sub-Seats (*fiuszékek*, subsidiary seats) of their own. This traditional designation, not found in the documents, is a reminder of the obstacles faced by these 'secessionists' in having their claims accepted.

The Sub-Seats Two essential points need to be made: the sub-Seats all owed their existence to royal grants and some owed their daily tribulations to interference by the Szekler communities in the 'parent' Seats. Obviously, their formation reduced the territory in which the dignitaries of the parent Seats could exercise their functions. While there is no word of contestation for Keresztúr and Gyergyó, the sub-Seats of Kászon and Miklósvár did not easily obtain acceptance of their autonomies, Miklósvár in fact never did.

The sub-Seats' principal demand was the right to elect their own judges and captains and thus gain independence. There are no data, however, on the underlying motives, which might well have been conflicts between clans. Some sub-Seats complain of the distance that separates their villages from the Seat tribunals. True, every one of them is situated on the territorial fringes of the principal Seat, but there is nothing in the archives to help support this explanation. A sudden demographic explosion is unlikely – there are no demographic data for the medieval period that

Table 9. Sub-Seats in the Szeklerland

Seat	Sub-Seat	First mentioned in	SzOkl
Udvarhely			
	Keresztúr	1505*	VIII.124[76]
Maros	-		
Csík			
	Gyergyó	1406	I.LXXXVII
	Kászon	1462	I.CLXIII**
Sepsi			
	Miklósvár (?)***	1404	I.LXXXI
Orbai	-		
Kézdi	-		
Aranyos	-		

*The royal free town of Keresztúr had already been mentioned in 1459.[77]
**Supposedly a confirmation of privilege granted by King Sigismund (1387–1437), since lost.
***Recognized by the Crown and historians, but never by the Szeklers of Sepsi.

could be satisfactorily validated. At the beginning of the seventeenth century, a Szekler army of about 20,000 men could be mobilized (cf. the roster of 1614). For the same period Gábor Barta estimates the population of the Szeklerland to have been 150,000, out of a total of 630,000 for all of Transylvania; the most bitter secessionist conflicts concern two Seats likely to have been more sparsely populated than those of Udvarhely or Maros. The Crown's motives in sustaining these demands are not stated either. Interfering in Szekler customary law and laying claim to the position of sole dispenser of privilege? Probably, but at the risk of working up the hot-blooded warrior community, seeing it waste its energy in internal conflict and having it become less obedient in engaging in military operations.

In spite of Gyergyó's occasional mention as a bona-fide Seat in its own right, the present author considers its status to be more likely that of a sub-Seat. Csík is mentioned as early as 1324, while the first reference to Gyergyó dates from 1406, which may be due to fragmented sources, but, more importantly, throughout the documentation Gyergyó is always mentioned alongside Csík.

Kászon appears to have had problems in asserting its independence against the dignitaries of the Seat of Csík but, in spite of its diminutive size (four villages and 230 men on the conscription roster of 1614), it is carried as autonomous in the seventeenth century registers. The determination of the inhabitants of these villages is manifest in an account from the second half of the sixteenth century relating the circumstances under which their autonomy was achieved: 'and, like all modest people, they had no better answer than that they were free Szeklers but subordinate to the Seat of Csík and only asked to live like the free Szeklers that they were, to elect their own captains and judges and not those of the Seat of Csík'.[78]

There is no evidence of such grass-roots determination for the supposed sub-Seat of Miklósvár. The royal confirmation dated 1404 is already in response to a supplication by *possessores* of the region. In 1459,[79] it appears that the Seat of Sepsi is not alone in obstructing the functioning of the tribunal of Miklósvár but, *mirabile dictu,* the inhabitants themselves (ten villages are listed) refuse to refer their cases to it, much less abide by its decisions. A detail in the two documents[80] demanding reconfirmation of the Miklósvár sub-Seat's autonomy sheds light on the reason for this lack of support. One family in particular seems very interested in the creation of the sub-Seat. This family, the Hidvég, which we will find time and again in conflict with the Szekler community, is known since the thirteenth century for its lack of respect for the Szeklers' traditional rights and customary law. The hostility of the population is probably due to the risks it sees of being reduced to servitude in a small sub-Seat detached from Sepsi and too easily influenced by a nearby, powerful family. In 1531,[81] the king renders a 'Solomonic' decision: the Seat of Miklósvár is to be independent, but its dignitaries must first be designated as dignitaries of the Seat of Sepsi and its tribunal may not pronounce a judgement that diverges from those of the seat of Sepsi. In spite of this acknowledgement by the Crown but with an autonomy devoid of meaning, the military registers continue to incorporate Miklósvár and its nine neighbouring villages into the Seat of Sepsi.

The Villages The first 'census' known is that of 1332–1337, conducted by the Church. The next, undoubtedly complete, list of Szekler villages dates from 1567 – again an ecclesiastic register of tithes. This said, with the country in the throes of Reformation and less than a year before the promulgation of the Act of Tolerance of Torda, the Roman Catholic Church is under severe pressure from conversions and the number of households having paid tithes within the villages no doubt represents only a fraction of the total population. The military census ordered by King Matthias in 1473 does not start showing results in the available documentation until 1575, and even then incompletely. The first uncontestedly complete military census dates from 1614. If the village during the period under study here is no more than a territorial entity, after 1562 it evolves into the mainstay of Szekler customs and traditions.

The 'tízes' and the Village Within the Seats, within even the villages, the root unit of the Szekler community was the '*judicatus decimalis, dészmabíróság*'[82] or *tízes* (the unit of ten, platoon of ten), a group of ten individuals – or households – and its representative. Rarely alluded to in writing, this legal entity seems to have been the basic guarantor of land allocations. As a juridical function at the local level, it can be assumed to have also dealt with the local military conscriptions as well as with the distribution of plots of soil.

Depending on the size of the village, it is possible that these *tízes* were spread into more than one village or that several *tízes* functioned within one village. The data from the roster of 1614[83] have been culled by I. Imreh.[84] One of his summary tables[85] gives an excellent overview of the density of families in Szekler villages.

In most of the 380 villages, there are less than 100 families: 340 villages (nearly 90 per cent), are home to about two-thirds of the population. It is worth noting that in the Seat of Csík (including its two sub-Seats of Gyergyó and Kászon),

Table 10. Villages in the Szeklerland by Number of Families (1614)

Seat	Villages by number of families									Totals
	1–10	10–20	20–30	30–40	40–50	50–75	75–100	100–150	150 & +	
Udvarhely	5	24	26	22	23	22	5	1	-	128
Maros	12	20	24	31	11	15	2	-	-	115
Csík	-	1	2	1	2	4	9	14	3	36
Gyergyó	-	-	1	1	-	1	2	2	1	8
Kászon	-	-	-	-	-	1	1	2	-	4
Sepsi	1	2	2	8	4	13	9	3	-	42
Kézdi	-	2	4	1	3	9	3	2	6	30
Orbai	1	3	1	-	1	5	-	1	5	17
Totals	19	52	60	64	44	70	31	25	15	**380**

situated in the most mountainous part of the Szeklerland – and nearest the eastern frontier – there are practically no small villages of less than thirty families.

From the second half of the sixteenth century, the village becomes one of the prime structural factors for the conservation of Szekler customs. As early as 1459,[86] we have a conflict concerning the delimitation of the community-owned pastures of two villages in the seat of Udvarhely. This concept of 'commons' also plays into conflicts involving land held by counties[87] or in Saxon territory.[88] The village as a legal entity now asserts itself forcefully. In the codification of 1555[89] a more detailed view appears: a village may sustain a condemnation (§ 50), which is only enforceable if it is represented by three men of its choosing (§ 51). The village tribunal is similarly composed of three men designated by it (§ 60). However, this local jurisdiction has no bearing on the dignity of the Seat judge, which is the domain of the clans, not the localities.

The growing importance of the village as a legal entity continues to develop: where before its rights were essentially limited to the administration of the common land, the village increasingly asserts its own claim in the relatives' stead when the first in line for an inheritance is not personally an inhabitant of the village where the land to be inherited is situated (§ 52). Within the village, the solidarity of common interests is anchored in the neighbourhood, which gradually replaces family and clan ties when these do not coincide with ties of residence, a deductive affirmation on the present author's part, not explicitly stated in the documentation. As early as 1503,[90] in bequests in favour of the Church, the family and the village both had the rights of buying back the bequest from the church.

The juridical role played by the village continued to gain in importance and, after 1562, it was the village that became the stronghold of Szekler custom and law. I. Imreh has found and published[91] seventy-two 'village laws' covering the period between 1581 and 1846, documents in which the village holds an assembly to formulate the rules and customs regulating daily life.

Nevertheless, being a Szekler from one village or another is not the factor determining his rights. It is clan affiliation that determines access to dignities and possession of ancestral land.

2. A Structure of Clans Studies of Szekler history generally point out that their clan structure appears very early in their evolution and often see in it a question relating to the Szeklers' origins. In the archives, on the other hand, references to the clan structure appear fairly late, in connection with observance of ancestral customs. This documentary inversion no doubt results from a preceding inversion of priorities: what is the point of wasting good parchment to write down rules, the respect of which are undisputed? In the lapse of time during which the clan organization functioned as an orally-transmitted ancestral tradition with no, or merely fragmentary, written traces until it came into view in the written records, it must have undergone the mutations inherent in this mode of transmission – itself a factor of flexibility and adaptability.

The most complete formal data concerning the clans comes to us from the Seat of Maros in the fifteenth century and will be analysed below in the context of the clans' role in determining access to dignities. At this juncture, we will only recall the principles of the clan structure as they appear from the sum of available documentation and, to some extent, historians' extrapolations.

The concepts of tribes and clans are common throughout the Szeklerland, as are the prerogatives they confer and their mode of functioning. Only members of a family belonging to a clan may be designated judge or captain. These functions are reserved to each clan in turn for one year at a time. No clan may exercise both functions at the same time. The evolution of the part played by clan-owned land in the process of access to dignities – accessory at first, later prerequisite – also appears to have been common across the Szeklerland.

The non-coincidence of the *tres genera* and the six tribes and twenty-four clans across the Szeklerland could have its origin in stratifications stemming from two different epochs. The *tres genera*, no doubt pre-existent in a confederation already homogeneous by the time the Szeklers arrived in Transylvania, had not entirely disappeared from their consciousness, but remained only as an imprint of the ancestral organization of the most ancient period of the community.

In the Seat of Maros there are six tribes, each in turn composed of four clans. The distribution of clan-owned land in this Seat with particularly complete documentation shows that not all villages have clan-owned land, while in others several clans own land. The presence of several clans in a village may either be due to an ancient decision (notably for military, strategic reasons) to concentrate dignities in one place,

Table 11. The Six Tribes and Twenty-four Clans of the Seat of Maros

Tribes	Clans	Tribes	Clans	Tribes	Clans
Ábrán	Gerő	Halom	György	Meggyes	Dudor
	Karácson		Halom		Gyáros

(Continued)

Tribes	Clans	Tribes	Clans	Tribes	Clans
	Nagy		Náznán		Kürt
	Uj		Péter		Meggyes
Adorján	Poson	Jenő	Balási	Örlöcz	Bód
	Telegd		Boroszló		Eczken
	Vácsmán		Nagy (Új)		Seprőd
	Vaja		Szomorú		Szovát

or the result of later alliances. The reason for some clans appearing more often in the documentation than others may lie in their geographic location. They are situated in the vicinity of Marosvásárhely and in the western part of the valley, in an area of lively commercial and political contact with the Sachsenland and the Transylvanian counties, where land was more likely to be the object of written transactions.

The present author is less inclined than many to extrapolate the data known for Maros to the entire Szekler territory. The total number of clans need not be exactly the same in every Seat. Moreover, the occasional nominative references to clans in the Seats of Sepsi and Kézdi do not match those of Maros. Nominative references

Table 12. Details on Clans Mentioned

Seat	Tribe	Clan	Year	SzOkl
Kézdi	Jenő	Besenyő	1548	III.615
Udvarhely	Halom	Péter	1550	VIII.160
Sepsi	Agház	Koronicza	1407	III.437
			1508	III.528
Kászon	Halom	Péter	Mid-16th c.	I.CCXIX

to clans in the whole of the territory are few and summary. Outside Maros, we find mentions of three clans, only one of which (Halom-Péter) appears also in the more exhaustive documents of the Seat of Maros. Nevertheless, historians see in village names incorporating clan-names an indication that the clan structure documented for the Seat of Maros was present in all of the Szekler territory.
It is interesting to note that in the archives there is no mention of a clan for the Seats of Orbai, Csík or Aranyos. Two names of tribes appear in the three Seats of Maros, Kászon and Kézdi, but in the latter with a clan whose name does not occur anywhere else. The two tribe and clan names mentioned for the Seat of Sepsi are to be found only there.

We have seen that the Szeklerland was settled in several waves during the first half of the thirteenth century. It is likely that the cohesion of the community is articulated around a structure, common to all of the Seats, of divisions (in the military sense of the term) organized around tribes and clans. This said, within this structure, remodelled 'top-down' by the military command, one can discern a level of local diversity of clan affiliations, imposed 'bottom-up', by the families (lineages) with which they profess to identify. As the community settles in Transylvania, ceases its migrations, and the influx of new auxiliaries stops, the clan structure becomes institutionalized and, in the sixteenth century, the list of clans from the Seat of Maros becomes the canonical norm, scrupulously repeated from document to document.[92]

One of the questions that continue to engage historians' curiosity is the origin of this system of clans. Basing his analysis on the names of the tribes and clans, Gy. Györffy[93] demonstrates that the Szeklers' clan structure existed well before their arrival in the Szeklerland. Following the linguist Gyula Nemeth, he takes up the latter's division of names into three groups: place names, names of persons and a third group which consists of only two clan names: Új (new) and Nagy (big). His analysis reposes primarily on the first two groups.

In this study centred on law and institutions, let us take a look at the two clans of the last group. Though they do not contribute much to the proto-history of the Szeklers, they reveal rather more about the vivacity and faculty of adaptation of the system of clans. The ancient origin of this structure is nowhere in doubt, but especially remarkable – whatever the names or number of clans – is that they last on and on, all the while reforming in response to ambient realities. A third clan, the Besenyő (Pechenegs), a clan of the Seat of Kézdi, presents the same characteristics of malleability of this ancient organization. Clan affiliation is a juridical fiction, an artificial notion representing a communality of interests. As soon as political reality imposes the assimilation of Pechenegs into the Szekler community and their access to Szekler dignities, a new clan emerges, bearing their name. Even more than their ancient origins, undisputed as their value may be, this capacity for remaining operational is, for the period under study here, the principal value of the Szeklers' clan organization.

The fact that towards the end of our period of study the village starts finding its place in the right of succession to clan-held lands can no doubt similarly be seen as an indication of this systemic aptitude for adaptation. When the fiction of clan affiliation, derived from consanguine family bonds, no longer coincides with the reality of a community of interests, this affiliation shifts to territorial solidarities, those of villages.

In the course of time and historical events in Hungary, the military function and clan structure no longer sufficed to guarantee the privileges of the Szekler community, in the face of internal conflicts arising from economic development, against the centrifugal force of a society of Estates and, later, against the exactions of a weakened royalty. A certain sense of identity buttressed by territorial ties and disseminated by committing the customs to writing becomes indispensable.

Part II

CUSTOMARY LAW, AS PRACTISED – AND RECORDED (FIFTEENTH–SIXTEENTH CENTURIES)

The Szeklerland is not a distant island cut off from the outside world. Confined though its societal structures were to its territory, the Szekler community evolved within the Hungarian kingdom, largely subject to the same economic constraints as the kingdom and not immune to its political upheavals. The move to put oral, customary law in writing starts in the second half of the fifteenth century, under the influence of the conditions prevailing in Hungary and Transylvania. Ignoring the growing menace posed by the Ottoman Empire, Hungarian society indulged in divisiveness and internal strife.

At the end of each reign in this elective monarchy, the very edifice of the Hungarian realm was shaken by disputes over succession. The ensuing intrigues entailed the dissipation of the Crown's patrimony among potential allies, without ensuring their fidelity. The names and the origin (heads of clans, later military leaders) of the opponents changed over the centuries, but not the state of general upheaval.

It is in the context of this elective monarchy and the resulting rivalries that in 1526 the Hungarian Crown fell to both John Szapolyai – crowned 11 November at Székesfehérvár – and Ferdinand of Habsburg, proclaimed King in Pozsony (Pressburg/Bratislava) on 16 December.

Royal Authority, Oligarchy and the Nobility

Already, in the early thirteenth century, the authority of the Crown – in spite of the occasional, energetic reign – had to struggle to assert itself over an oligarchy far from docile. The internecine feuding and rivalries of these few kindred (twenty-some families shared between them the seigniorial property rights over almost half of Hungary's soil at the beginning of the sixteenth century) did not always suffice to neutralize their forces when ranged against the Crown. Hence the king regularly relied upon the lesser nobility to counterbalance, with the help of the law, the barons' interference in the life of the realm.

This political manoeuvring prevailed within the framework of a society of Estates (prelates, barons and magnates, common nobles and, from 1405 on, the representatives of the royal free towns¹). While the offices and dignities at Court and the Royal Council were in the hands of the prelates and barons, all of the Estates had the right to sit in the Diet.

Statutorily, the principle of the society of Estates (*rendiség*) endowed a proportion – relatively large for the period – of the population with liberty and privileges of jurisdiction, but also various fiscal dispensations and the right to play a part in the political life of the realm. In reality of course, the unequal possession of land gave rise to disparities that constantly menaced the rights and privileges of the poorer.

The barons, in spite of the fundamental principle of a single and equal rank of nobility (*una eademque nobilitas*, 1351) in Hungary, were bent on reserving for themselves the right of political action as well, transforming their superior fortune into juridical domination over lesser nobles and freemen in their service.

The Noble Szekler Nation of Transylvania experienced, starting in the fifteenth century, the same trend: economic superiority endangering statutory equality. The special framework of institutions firmly anchored in this province, however, helped safeguard the privileges of, and within, the community.

The Ottoman Menace

John Hunyadi, regent of Hungary, was the hero of the struggle against the Ottomans. His son, King Matthias, succeeded in securing the southeastern frontier but he died without leaving a successor. After him, the advance of the Ottoman Empire on the European front profited from both the overall political situation prevailing in Europe and from the dissensions within Hungary between the barons and the new kings of the House of Jagiello.

At the end of the reign of King Matthias, Hungary was rich and mighty – its culture embracing and furthering the Renaissance – and the Throne powerful: reforming the judicial institutions (shown by the presence of a Royal Judge at the county assemblies) as well as the military organization (with an army of mercenaries known as 'King Matthias' black army'). Upon his death in 1490, the barons were determined to elect a less authoritarian king, Wladislas II. The barons of Hungary at the end of the fifteenth century showed disdain for the Ottoman menace and avidity only to recover privileges King Matthias had clipped. In this climate unfavourable to the lowly, the peasant revolt of 1514 erupted. Some historians link Hungary's defeat of 1526 to this uprising. Others stress the diverse alliances in the Europe of the time – in May 1526, the League of Cognac of King François I of France, Pope Clement VII, Henry VIII and the principalities of Northern Italy allied against Charles V – in which Hungary was left to its fate. The lack of authority of her young kings and the nobility's reluctance to rally – the reasons for which are still in dispute – all contributed to a defeat that turned into disaster.

On 29 August 1526, King Louis II Jagiello, who had succeeded his father, numerous barons and more than 10,000 Hungarian soldiers perished at the hands of Suleiman I's Ottoman army in the battle of Mohács. Poorly planned and poorly led, this battle, joined in precipitation, marks more than just the end of the Middle Ages; it is a hiatus from which Hungary was never to recover entirely.

The Ottoman occupation, the increasing rigidity of Hungarian society, the disdainful attitude of the House of Habsburg toward Hungary – there are ample factors from which historians may choose in explaining Hungarian history following the defeat at Mohács. All agree that this date is a dramatic turning point. In his lapidary fashion, Jenő Szűcs recapitulates the essential points made in historiographic commentaries: 'The more fortunate regions of Europe can celebrate the dawn of the Modern Age at dates of glory like 1492, the discovery of America. Less felicitous regions commemorate catastrophes like 1526, the date of the battle of Mohács and the appearance of the Habsburgs.'[2]

Hungary was cut in three (until 1711), between two rival Christian kings, Ferdinand of Habsburg in the west and John Szapolyai in the east, and a wedge subject to the Sultan following the fall of Buda, in 1541, in the middle. Secret alliances vied with outright treason to fill the decades following Mohács with war, skirmishes and brigandage. The eastern part of Hungary (Transylvania and the 'Partium') became the principality of Transylvania in 1571. Numerous studies deal with what is called the 'Golden Age' of Transylvania in the first half of the seventeenth century by virtue of the relative independence Transylvania managed to conserve, between Ottoman tutelage and Habsburg exactions.

It was during this period of upheaval in the late sixteenth century that the autonomy of Szekler customary law started being challenged by the Crown.

But also, it was in the course of this century that Szekler customary law was committed to writing, providing us with documents of eminent interest; while taking full advantage of them, however, we must not neglect the individual adjudications which most likely are closest to the spirit of customary law. Both the recorded law and the records of day-to-day decisions were the heart of the autonomy enjoyed by the Szekler community: its legal procedures and its customs regulating the possession of land.

Chapter III

THE RECORDING OF CUSTOMARY LAW

Written records of legal decisions and private acts starting in the early fourteenth century tell of some of the customary rules of the Szekler community. Not until the second half of the fifteenth century did it seem necessary to commit these rules to writing as a record of the 'general principles' of Szekler law.

The Szekler community was not the only one to resort to creating a repertory of its laws, there was a movement to codify throughout Hungary at about the same time – and for good reason: privileges were felt to be menaced and needed to be affirmed and defended.

One of the consequences of written codification was to render more rigid a code that, until then, could be interpreted appropriately to reflect both tradition and reality, in spite of repeated claims of immutable ancestrality. The written compilations had another side-effect: decided under the pressure of incipient conflict, they became the permanent rallying point for identification with privileges thus conserved for all posterity. Some historians see in this move of consolidation 'the beginning of the end' of autonomy, others, whose analysis the present author shares, see in this act the apotheosis of Szekler law.

Paradoxically enough, the difficulties Szekler customary law encountered starting in the 1490s prepared and strengthened it for the future. In spite of the challenges faced after 1562 from a central power, the Principality of Transylvania, too close and too weak to be able to resist trying to interfere in the juridical practices of its subjects, and later from an Imperial and Royal authority, too distant and indifferent for reasoned tolerance, the fact of having been recorded permitted Szekler customary law to continue to be practised and to be confirmed by a succession of sovereigns motivated by the political expediency of the moment. Within the population, common Szekler law was of daily pertinence, while in contacts with the State it was the compilation that permitted the law applied by the Szeklers to be perpetuated as an autonomous system well into the middle of the nineteenth century.

From Common Use to Codified Procedure

Any study of Szekler customary law must take care with its written traces: some of them were politically oriented rather than reflecting day-to-day practice. By its very nature, the practice of customary law is not the preserve of erudite jurists evoking obscure paragraphs. This law is everyman's business; its memory is perpetuated in public use and participation in its deliberation does not become restricted, progressively, to a smaller number until fairly late. The orality of customary law is its best safeguard against tradition entrenching itself without adaptation to changing needs. No doubt, in committing their law to writing, the Szeklers fossilized certain of its aspects. But for the most part the codified principles (as opposed to individual, oral precedents, to which there is no written reference that could become jurisprudence) deal very little with the law itself, instead establishing legal procedure – a formal framework within which the daily application of law from collective memory retained its adaptability.

During the decades of accelerating codification of customs throughout the Kingdom of Hungary, a repertory of sources sees the light that is essential to a study of Szekler law as well. This said, this writing down of customs supposedly ancestral can also be a pitfall, an optical illusion. Here and there, lines are drawn; the solemnity of the act of writing justifies rules that in fact are based essentially on political expediency and compromise. Prudence dictates scepticism before seeing a direct continuation of tradition in the codification. In the documents, innovation has its place alongside the conservation of some of the most ancient customs, as witness the 'eloquent omission' of any direct reference to clan structures in the codifications.

There are fewer than ten instances of these codifications of principle. Their chronology corresponds to three successive stages.

- At the beginning of the second half of the fifteenth century, the economic inequalities between Szeklers are institutionalized. In 1466, at the Szekler assembly of Zabola, the conflict between common and eminent Szeklers comes into the open; in 1473, the military reorganization by King Matthias into three ranks takes effect.
- At the end of the century (1493–1514), documents appear in which the Szeklers, in defence of their privileges, face down the voivode in 1493, the clergy in 1503, and finally the Crown in 1505 and 1506. The special character of the Szekler legal system was consecrated by its mention in the *Opus Tripartitum* of Werbőczy in 1514.
- After the defeat at Mohács in 1526, the dissipation of royal authority, a reduced territory in which the Szeklers were a more important component, and the economic pressure from the tribute exacted by the Sultan, revived King Sapolyai's impatience with the privileges of the Szekler Nation. These hazardous political uncertainties motivated, but also rendered possible, the detailed recording of Szekler customs (1555).

For each period we will in the following briefly recall the circumstances that led to the codifications before formally analysing their content. The concrete implications of these documents are developed in sections devoted to them, i.e.:

Codifications	of 1473 and 1499, military organization:	Part I, Chapter II
	of 1503, relations with the Church:	Part I, Chapter II
	of 1466, 1499, 1505, 1506 and 1555, process:	Part II, Chapter IV
	of 1505, 1506 and 1555, possession of land:	Part II, Chapter V.

I. Conflicts within the Community (1466–1473)

The end of King Sigismund's reign was marked by a serious peasant uprising in Transylvania, in 1437. The Szeklers, a community of statutory nobles within the Assembly of the Three Nations, ranged itself alongside the nobles, the possessors and oppressors in the counties. But the climate of tension arising from the economic conditions took hold of the community as well. The intent of Szekler *pociores* to develop their economic superiority into a difference of status created conflict. It is under these circumstances that the Szekler Assembly of Zabola convened in 1466.

A. 1466, Zabola, Confirmation of the Free Status of the Common Szeklers

This[1] is the first global confirmation of Szekler customs. The document mentions only the three southern Seats of Sepsi, Orbai and Kézdi, but the customs referred to are most probably identical to those practised throughout the Szeklerland. The assembly was presided over by the voivode of Transylvania, in his capacity as *comes* of the Szeklers. The common Szeklers having rebelled against attempted domination by the better-off, King Matthias had ordered the *comes* to have himself briefed on the customary rules of the community, put them into writing and ensure that all parties applied and respected them.

After observing protocol with a preamble of salutations, the document recapitulates the disputes giving rise to the assembly and continues with twelve articles. The first two confirm the liberty of common Szeklers who toil the land of the better-off, as well as their innate right to change 'employers' freely. This important statutory confirmation gives an insight into the economic strictures of the less fortunate. Articles 3 to 11 enter into the details of legal procedure in the Szeklerland and Article 12 concludes by prohibiting all Szeklers from engaging in sedition, brawls and disorderly conduct, under penalty of death.

Besides the ratification of the liberty enjoyed by all Szeklers, the most important information revealed by this document is the confirmation of the tradition by which, in all assemblies adjudicating legal disputes, two-thirds of the jury members had to be common Szeklers. Without question this is rooted in very ancient forms of judicial practice, with the participation of a large part of the population, even if the clan structures and the rules pertaining to them did not permit all to accede to the high dignity of presiding judge.

B. 1473, the Three Military Strata

The freedom of movement of the common Szeklers had been confirmed and reinforced in 1466, but the privilege of being a free Szekler, no matter how common, carried with it the obligation of personal military service. But correctly so, the wealthier insisted. Going to war equipped as poorly as the pedestrian rabble from the royal counties, they felt, should not entitle the common Szeklers to more rights than those of such serfs. Thus, the conflicts persisted, obliging King Matthias to redefine the military stratification of the Szekler army.

This brief royal edict,[2] drafted in the urgency created by complaints from the common Szeklers and penned in the conditions of a military encampment, is succinct and direct like a royal military order: a reminder of the juridical freedom of all Szeklers (*omnes et singuli*) as direct subjects of the King; a definition of the military rosters to be established, i.e. foot soldiers and cavalrymen, amongst the latter, the notables who, as a function of their clan affiliation – and not their economic means – are to be registered separately. Where the articles of the Zabola document of 1466 ended with a strict admonition to the common Szeklers to respect the preceding articles, the edict of 1473 ends with as severe a threat against notables who might modify or fail to respect the rosters.

The freedom of all Szeklers capable of personally going to war, even on foot and poorly equipped (hence at little expense) is yet again confirmed. The special status of some families to accede to the dignities of judge or captain is reiterated – but based on their status by clan affiliation, not wealth. Neither this statutory privilege nor superior wealth permits any act detrimental to the liberty of a Szekler duly registered. The superiority of one is not a licence to reduce another to servitude. In three sentences, King Matthias expressed the essence of the Szekler community's structure. The military rosters do not appear in the documents compiled for the *Székely Archives* until a century later. No doubt they were drawn up earlier, directly after this royal order, starting at the level of the *tízes* (group of ten, platoon), the role of which does not appear in the documents until late, however.

In 1479, István Báthory was named voivode of Transylvania and *comes* of the Szeklers. With his despotic and brutal attitude toward the Szeklers and Saxons and their privileges, he managed to attract the outraged animosity of these communities, which both lodged protests with the king. His tenure (1479–1493) may be seen as the decisive factor leading to the awareness of all Szeklers, common or eminent, of their shared interest in defending their privileges. Brawls and disorderly conduct, forbidden in the injunctions of 1466, did not disappear. But the prominent Szeklers, rather than aspiring to become 'the least' among the Hungarian nobles, now mobilized to defend the privileges of the entire community against the abusive conduct of the voivode.

II. The Affirmation of the Szekler Community (1493–1514)

A. 1493, Solidarity against the Voivode

The lengthy complaint addressed by the community to the king in 1493[3] about the offences of the voivode is not strictly speaking a codification of their customs, but István Báthory's behaviour had violated Szekler law in so many instances that their enumeration becomes *a contrario* a fairly complete repertory of their traditions.

Established jointly by the community of the seven Seats, this document is punctuated with reminders of the Szeklers' fidelity to the king and the courageous service they had rendered him in times of war. The complaints about Báthory's excesses are cleverly interspersed with accusations of that voivode's actions against the Crown's own interests. The Szeklers were quite aware that Báthory is a high official at Court (a member of the Crown Council), so the most severe accusations are circumspectly directed against his *familiares*.

The essential points of violation of Szekler customary rules by the voivode are the construction of fortresses for his private use on Szekler soil (with the Saxons and Szeklers paying the expense themselves), the confiscation of ancestral Szekler land, the violation of traditions regarding paraphernal property upon marriages arranged between his entourage and Szekler daughters and – the accusation which may have most directly offended the king – the voivode's diverting for his own profit branded oxen collected from the Szeklers as the traditional gift for the coronation of the king.

All Szeklers, prominent or common, had grievances against István Báthory and his courtiers. In this complaint they closed ranks in front of the King to indict the voivode and his henchmen. They had assembled on their own initiative to formulate their indictment. Normally their assemblies were presided over by the *comes*, but here his presence was out of the question.

István Báthory was deposed the same year both as voivode and as *comes* of the Szeklers.

B. 1499, Royal Confirmation of the Szekler Community's Privileges

This document[4] first recalls the community's obligations before evoking some points of Szekler procedure and law. In his royal indulgence, Wladislas II Jagiello grants his writ of privilege to the Szeklers at their request. The Turk is poised on the borders of the kingdom; the magnates within it are insubordinate. The insistence in this document on the military obligations leads the present author to conclude that the Szeklers had negotiated their participation in the defence of the realm in exchange for the recognition of their rights.

Thus, the first five of the seventeen articles of this writ stress the Szeklers' military obligations; the sixth recalls the conditions for the gift of branded oxen.

The next six articles elaborate on the holding of judiciary assemblies by the Szeklers and clearly owe more to Szekler insistence than to royal generosity: frequent assemblies (this will be raised again in 1505) but modest accommodations for the attending dignitaries. The last five articles reiterate the legal autonomy of the Szeklerland. The essential point is that, even in the case of high treason by a Szekler, the ownership of lands confiscated – in the name of the Crown – always remains within the community.

C. 1503, the 'Concordat' between the Diocese of Transylvania and the Szekler Community

This document[5] is not exactly a recapitulation of Szekler customs either. Owing to the misconduct of some clergymen in the villages, a Szekler delegation appeared before the bishop of Transylvania. Elsewhere in the archives, references to the clergy tend to be deferential and favourable; they appear as local notaries, the parish house a close-in *'locus credibilis'*. The clergy's perceived moral failings in the collection of alms are therefore perceived as all the more inadmissible.

Following these complaints, which take up one-third of the document, the subsequent articles deal with procedural questions and re-emphasize the autonomy of Szekler law in matters concerning dowries and inheritance. The bishop concedes the competence of Szekler custom in these matters.

The joint delegation of the Seats (i.e. deaconries) facing the bishop of Transylvania and the latter's recognition of the Szekler community as a privileged subject of the Crown are the essential points of this accord.

D. 1505 and 1506, the 'Constitutions' of Udvarhely and Agyagfalva

Twice in the space of less than a year the Szekler community met in formal assembly on its own initiative, without authorization or a representative of the Crown. The resolutions agreed at these assemblies[6] represent a solemn moment in the history of Szekler customary law. The documents were established in a near-rebellious context, the assembly of 1506 was followed by a merciless campaign of repression by Pál Thomory, better known in Hungarian history for his role in assuring defeat at the battle of Mohács. This codification, with its eclectic associations of general and political principles and pragmatic and precise 'constituent' elements of Szekler law reappears, in Hungarian, in the treatise on Szekler law and privileges published in 1818,[7] meticulously preceded by the imperial and royal confirmations of Maria-Theresia in 1717 and Francis I of Austria in 1815.

Let us return to these constitutions of the beginning of the sixteenth century for a moment. Certain elements appear as common factors in both of them. The proximity in time for one, but also the absence of a representative of the Crown, the presence of the same leaders at both assemblies and, of course, the reference made in the resolutions of 1506 to those of 1505. Common factors, that suggest dealing with these two documents together. There is, however, an essential difference between the two. The first assembly[8] took place in response to a new *internal* crisis within the community and censured once again the abuses of power by dignitaries: corruption, disdain for customs and the insufficiently frequent convocation of judiciary assemblies. In 1506,[9] on the other hand, the demand for collecting branded oxen as a gift for the birth of an heir to the throne (the future Louis II Jagiello) was an *outside* influence that enflamed the entire community. And here, besides details on the convocation of judiciary assemblies, the document openly calls for opposition to any royal emissaries found to violate traditional Szekler liberty and privileges. Attempting to exact two contributions of branded oxen within the space of five years (the first had been in 1501 for the King's marriage) was perceived as such a violation.

Rearguard Action? The conflict between prominent and common Szeklers in fact casts its shadow over both of these assemblies, suggesting 'the abandoning and neglect of ancient customs' (1506). It is in the shadowy context of this period that some historians, L. Makkai[10] among them, see 'rearguard struggles for Székely liberties'. Learned opinion to the contrary notwithstanding, the crumbling of liberties took another four centuries, as witness references in the History of Transylvania to Szekler liberty at every turn.[11]

In the present author's view Szekler custom was fragmented and crumbled so much later that the period around 1506 cannot be seen as the beginning of a decline. A society that is not expanding relentlessly is unfortunately often judged to be in decline, with no consideration for its inner vitality, typical for traditional societies, in maintaining customs rather than expanding domination.

... or Golden Age? For Gy. Bónis,[12] the end of the fifteenth and beginning of the sixteenth centuries are the 'golden age' of Szekler law. He presents the assemblies of 1505 and 1506 not as desperate attempts to maintain liberties but as evidence of growing self-confidence and awareness of a commonality of interests, respect for which had to be asserted to the outside world. According to him the privileges did not start crumbling away, one by one, until the end of the sixteenth century, in the context of the new Principality of Transylvania; he goes on to speak of a gradual 'transition toward Hungarian law, terminating in the nineteenth century'.

Golden age or rearguard action? The Constitution of 1506, like that of the preceding year, points out the urgency of 'correcting some unseemly practices' and discussing 'specific matters concerning the neglect of ancient customs'. Evidently this is in response to a situation of crisis. But the next paragraph is more political than procedural, on the dangers of discord. A call for loyalty to the king can be interpreted as a diplomatic gesture, following the disputes over the branded oxen, but also as a common entreaty on the part of all Szeklers to be subject to no other authority than that of the king. Consciousness of their ancestral unity is emphasized by the evocation of their Scythian origin.

A final formulation in this Constitution makes the document the expression of resolute autonomy: 'this also is our pleasure', an expression characteristic of legislative authority, used here to mark the supremacy of the community. In 1466 and 1499, the Szeklers had obtained by determined persistence the confirmation of their ancestral customs; in 1506, they issued a statement of principle that Werbőczy deemed worthy of calling out in a special article in his *Opus Tripartitum* and that was hence incorporated in the *Corpus Juris Hungarici*.

E. The Consecration: 1514, Opus Tripartitum, Pars III, Titulus IV

At the outset of sixteenth century, Hungary, already in conflict with an Ottoman neighbour whose army was to defeat her at the battle of Mohács in 1526, was also shaken by internal struggles around the succession to the throne following the death of King Matthias (1490). There were competing candidates to the royal succession, and contention between the higher nobility (magnates and Church hierarchy) and the lesser nobles insisting on the principle of the equality of all nobles, defying both the Hungarian oligarchy and Habsburg pretensions. In the end it was Wladislas II Jagiello, a Pole and king of Bohemia, who was elected king by the Hungarian Diet. A weak monarch, under the influence of the oligarchy, he remained passive in the face of barons and prelates bent on recovering their privileges. But, as M. Molnár observes, 'the misuse of power against the feeble is always clothed in law',[13] ancestral privileges were contested, land was confiscated and their former owners reduced to servitude, not only by brute force, but also by recourse to laws. It was in this atmosphere of juridical insecurity that the movement of codification of laws and customs was engaged in the realm.

In 1514, István Werbőczy, jurist and member of the Council of King Wladislas II Jagiello of Hungary, presented to the Diet his *Opus Tripartitum Juris Consuetudinarii Inclyti Regni Hungariae*. An outstanding jurist, seen as the defender of the lesser nobility against the abuses of the higher clergy and the barons, known to speak not only Latin and Greek but also converse *eleganter* in German, steeped in theology and philosophy, Werbőczy was presumably born around 1458 and died in Buda in 1541. He was a dominant personality in the juridical and political life of Hungary of the first half of the sixteenth century. He earned his place in the annals of Hungarian history of law more in the constitutional domain than in the codification of customary law. The *Opus Tripartitum* is composed of a long prologue (sixteen titles) and, as its name suggests, three parts (134, eighty-six and thirty-six titles, respectively). Approved by the Diet and the king, the text was never given the royal seal or promulgated as the law of the land; no doubt, as Ch. d'Eszláry points out 'due to opposition by the higher nobility, which did not share Werbőczy's view that there was no juridical difference between the higher and the lesser nobility, that nobility was one and the same (*una eademque nobilitas*)'.[14]

It is this notion of a 'nation of nobles' (or 'nobiliary nation') that divides historians of law to this day. On the one hand, the *Opus Tripartitum* is seen as the foundation stone of the Constitution of the Hungarian nation; on the other hand, this political makeup of the nation, limited to the nobles, higher and lesser, the '*Populus Werbőczianus*', is perceived – in an anachronistic criticism – as the juridical basis for a social cleavage, a rigid stratification of the population between a class of free nobles and a peasant class of serfs, a dichotomy not remedied until 1848.[15]

In spite of the fact that it was never promulgated, the *Opus Tripartitum*, first published in 1517, and translated into Hungarian (1565), Croatian (1574) and German (1599), was in constant use by the jurisprudence and incorporated into the *Corpus Juris Hungarici* in 1628. For Transylvania, the *Diploma Leopoldinum* (1690) carries it as a law in force.

If, in 1514, Werbőczy considers that a single paragraph does justice to the laws and customs '*so different*' of the Szeklers, his concise description of their customs assumes considerable importance for the Szekler community, which refers to Werbőczy's work time and again to support its fight to maintain its privileges.

Gy. Bónis[16] makes a point of noting that Werbőczy uses the term *lex* to qualify the legal system practised by the Szeklers (*Dissimili lege & consuetudine gaudentes*), a term defined in the prologue as superior even to the decisions of the Crown.

III. 1555: Codification in Detail

Life was difficult for the poor throughout Hungary. The common Szeklers, conscious as always of the statutory freedom which differentiates them from the common Hungarian peasants, suffered economic constraints that they found difficult to accept. There were uprisings in 1511 and between 1519 and 1524; pillaging raids were frequent engagements between Szeklers or, most often, against the Saxons, themselves in rebellion in 1513 and hardly inclined to come to the aid of the voivode to repress Szekler uprisings. As in the preceding century, the Szeklers did not identify themselves with the great peasant uprising (1514), but the climate was agitated. Political conditions following the disaster of Mohács did nothing to appease the situation.

Few of even the greatest Szekler families attained the level of wealth and land holdings of the rare magnates of Transylvania and the *Partium*, but the temptation to join these in the Assembly of the Three Nations was strong. The new royal authority (*à la* Szapolyai) was ready to support such ambitions. A resolution of the Assembly of the Three Nations of 1545[17] stated that the Szekler dignitaries were exempt from contributing to the tribute due the Sultan, like the nobles of the royal counties. The twists and turns in the international political situation led John II Szapolyai to resign in 1551 (at hardly ten years of age) and Ferdinand I of Habsburg appeared to take charge of Transylvania's interests. An Assembly of the Three Nations convened in 1555[18] passed a resolution calling for each of the Three Nations to commit its customs and privileges to writing and submit them for approval by the new sovereign.

It is to this resolution that we owe the hasty codification of 1555.[19] The document is both pedantic and incomplete, untidy and excessively detailed in some of its articles, incomprehensibly convoluted in places and obscurely elliptic in others; this codification no doubt gives a faithful image of the day-to-day practice of Szekler law.

It is composed of eighty-eight articles with no prologue, preamble or conclusion. In his analysis of the text, Gy. Bónis[20] sees in the phrasing shifts in tone from affirmation to supplication, suggesting awareness on the part of the Szeklers that their customs were an anachronism and the process of writing down these relics futile. In the present author's opinion, it is indeed tempting four centuries later to see this event with such melancholy foreknowledge, but another view can be opposed: we do not know precisely how these articles were prepared for recording, nor who presented them – the notables only or the notables followed by the common Szeklers – nor in what order – Seat by Seat or rank by rank. The shifts in tone, effectively perceptible and surprising, may owe more to the conditions prevailing around the process of codification than to any 'romantic' premonition the Szeklers might have had about their fate.

Having duly noted the evidently melancholy tone of Article 74:

> for as long as the Szekler people can remember, we do not know whether a
> tribe lived in this fashion on the Szekler land, for we never had a body of law;

even today, we implore Their Highnesses our Voivodes and Lords to let us live according to our laws [lit. our freedom, privilege, *szabadságunk*] and not to weigh upon us as a consequence of this.[21]

This must have struck a chord in Gy. Bónis' ears in the Transylvania of 1942, we must look beyond: the next fourteen articles are determinedly pragmatic in their affirmations. The mention in Article 83 of the *oszpora*, an Ottoman monetary unit in use only in the Seat of Kézdi, sheds further doubt on the linear continuity of the codification process. We may well hypothesize that, once the points considered most essential had been committed to writing, the representatives of Seat after Seat took their turns, with the last speakers, for want of essential new matters to bring up, being relegated to the addition of details or polite forms of address to articles already presented by other delegations.

This codification does not cover all aspects of Szekler customary law and certain silences are particularly worth noting. The omissions consist of elements that must have been so obvious to the Szeklers that they were not worth the ink. Werbőczy had already left no doubt about the noble status of the Szeklers, their military role and their clan structure. The notions of kinship are brought out in the articles concerned with the laws of succession, but no article deals with the designation of dignitaries, a process tied to the possession of clan land. Nothing on the Szekler military obligation either. If neither of these two themes, though at the core of the community's structure, was elaborated here, we must conclude that it was deemed most urgent to codify in essence the rules of procedure and some basic principles.

Procedure is a recurrent theme, in grouped sequences of Articles (1–19, 29–36, 47–55, 59–61, 66–70, 72, 75–88). The articles up to and including Article 55 give a fairly synthetic summary of procedure concerning successions (Articles 20–28), followed by criminal law (37–46) and three articles shedding light on the village as legal entity (50–51 for procedure and 52 for successions). Another theme is dealt with in a contiguous set of four articles (62–65): the personal freedom and freedom of movement of all Szeklers. Articles 56–58 and further on Articles 71–74 have nothing to do with the articles around them (that is, dealing with rules on duelling, the use of rivers as references in surveying, salt trade, and the supplication to respect the freedom of the Szekler).

To what extent do these articles describe the 'ancestral' customs? The codification informs us of the situation as it was perceived, hoped for or negotiated by the authors of the codification of 1555; but, in matters of procedure or right of property, daily practice was not always exactly as defined in the letter of these laws. The documents of the *Székely Archives* allow us to study these two essential points of Szekler law not just as codified principles but, more directly, in the light of individual decisions.

Chapter IV

THE PRACTICE OF LAW: LEGAL PROCEDURE IN THE SZEKLERLAND

The basic principles of judiciary organization in the Szeklerland are reflected in its codifications, dealt with in the previous chapter. Within the organization, procedural rules need to be understood and applied. At the heart of the conflict in 1466, subordinated to military considerations in 1499, the procedural rules were never dealt with as systematically and exhaustively as the organization was in the codifications. True, certain notions familiar in today's practice of law are not pertinent to a presentation of the judiciary organization in the Szeklerland of the Middle Ages.

Procedure and Jurisdictions

The *accusatory* process was used in all documented legal procedures between Szeklers. The only instances of *inquisitorial* process were cases involving high treason or desertion, but these were judged from the outset in the name of the Crown and not under Szekler law[1] – with the exception of judgements involving confiscations, where the special provisions of the community's law applied. There is a fairly sophisticated – but elliptically documented – intertwining between legal procedures and jurisdictional echelons. At no time do we perceive different institutions dealing with penal law and private law – as witness the fact that crimes of blood were usually settled by compensation.

Applicable Law: Territoriality versus Individuality

The jurisdictional echelons we run across in the documentation are complex, because the number of legal questions concerning the Szekler community as a whole are dealt with before the Assembly of Transylvania, as are conflicts between individuals of mixed affiliation, disputes between Szeklers and Saxons and/or nobles.

Moreover, there are circumstances under which being a Szekler was no protection against Crown law being applied. A Szekler who was also burgher of a royal free town enjoyed the terms of the town's royal privilege, such as exemption from Szekler military service (later mobilization and never going to war beyond the confines of Transylvania). These derogations were not readily accepted by the Seats, as shown by two calls to order issued against the town of Marosvásárhely, in 1484[2] and 1521, and a call to order against Sepsiszentgyörgy, in 1525. If he owned land situated on Szekler soil on the other hand, Szekler customary law was applicable,[3] his privileges as a burgher of a royal free town notwithstanding.

Land situated in a royal county, even if owned by a Szekler, was subject to royal law. In the same logic of territoriality, Szekler lands owned by non-Szekler families – acquired by matrimonial alliances or inheritance – were subject to Szekler customs. A privilege in the proper sense of the word of private law (*privata lex*), Szekler law manifests itself essentially as the law of the Szeklerland. In 1346,[4] however, a judgement recalled that a family having provided proof of their 'veritable Szeklership', all the while living in a county to the west of Transylvania, needed no further title of privilege to enjoy full freedom of movement, the essential freedom characterizing the common nobility and called out in the codification of 1555 (Articles 63 and 64).

Moreover, even if the documents dealing with the application of Szekler law are essentially limited to the Szeklerland, the royal confirmations – and even the repeal of 1562 – are addressed to the Szekler community as a whole, the privileges arising from its military obligation, the obligation of each Szekler individually to go to war.

A consequence of this personal aspect of custom was to endanger the community's cohesion, for the better-off among the Szeklers saw good reason in it to refuse to respect the freedom of the common Szeklers incapable of assuming the material burden of procuring the equipment required for armed service. It is not by chance that the two insurrectionary assemblies of 1505 and 1506 insisted on the territoriality and the broad portent of their claims: 'We the people inhabiting all of the Szeklerland, those from all Seats, without distinction of rank, make known to all concerned that which is to follow[5]' and 'We the inhabitants of the Szeklerland, all Szeklers living in this Land, be it of high position or low, make known to all concerned.'[6] It is worth noting that it is at this time that legal documents start evoking the special ethnic origins of the Szeklers, as if to overlay the functional (military) aspect of their privileges, an aspect that had a divisive effect.

An analysis of the jurisdictional structures and the areas of competence of its adjudicating actors must be reconstructed from a combination of the codified rules and the protocols of diverse legal cases: amicable settlements and judgements rendered before and contemporaneously with the codifications. Following the presentation of these jurisdictional structures, we will deal with the composition of tribunals at Szekler judiciary assemblies and the special prerequisite for access to the dignity of judge: the *Primipilate*.

I. The Echelons of Jurisdiction and the Steps of a Legal Procedure

For the most part, sources of judiciary content emanate from the highest echelons: tribunals held at Seat assemblies or assemblies of the Szekler Nation, both presided over by representatives of the Crown. The solemn character of these assemblies resulted in the recording of judgements involving individuals, so that, besides codifications and decisions of principle regarding Szekler customs, it is possible to glean information about the individual application of law from these echelons of jurisdiction. But Szekler law comes to bear above and below the level of these echelons: below, before local judges or in amicable settlements between individuals out of court before a private arbitrator; and then higher as well, for the way is open for all cases between Szeklers to be appealed to the Crown. The latter could render its own verdict or quash a verdict and order retrial. A retrial could take place before the Crown Council, before the voivode of Transylvania or the *comes* of the Szeklers. In the *Székely Archives* there are several examples of all of the above, but with no explanation for the choices of jurisdiction. The situation is all the more complex since the same person may be judge at the Crown Council, voivode of Transylvania and *comes* of the Szeklers. In the name of which office did he render his verdict? The presence of Szekler notables to assist him is mentioned sometimes, but not always. Confusing situation: the Szeklers may be seen to benefit from the recognition of their status of nobles at the highest echelons of the realm, but lose some of the uniqueness inherent in the customs farther down, within their community.

Military-Judiciary Structure One should not forget the role of the military hierarchy in the judiciary organization either. The king and his representatives were both military and judiciary authorities. The fact that a vice-*comes* – or the vice-voivode when the voivode was also *comes* of the Szeklers – might preside assemblies would suggest that a man versed in law assumed the judiciary responsibility alongside the military commander. But such a specialisation by area of competence is highly questionable. Circumstances unrelated to specifics of Szekler law were more likely to have been the reason for this division of responsibilities, as witness the interventions of commanders of the royal fortresses (*castellani*) adjoining the Szeklerland (Görgény and Törcs); they were military subordinates of the voivode-*comes* but had every right to preside over Szekler judiciary assemblies.

The Szeklers themselves accepted this relative indifference to judiciary competence, in their own structure the office of judge or captain was open to the same persons on the same criteria. There is one point, however, which reflects the diarchic tradition, shared by the Hungarians at the time of the Conquest. Tradition tells of the ritual sacrifice of the sacral chief, the *kündü* (or *künde*) Álmos around 896. At his side, the political-military authority was exercised by the *gyula*. In addition to this duality inherited from the Khazar Empire, Constantine Porphyrogenitus mentions the office of a *horka*, a personage vested with supreme judicial authority, while the *gyula* was only the military commander. Historians have not yet come to a definitive conclusion on this issue.[7] In manifesting separation between the domains of authority, the Szekler structure agrees with our modern concept of law: a person could exercise only one function at a time, judge or captain, and only for a year at a time.

Before dealing with the practice of law at a local level and the steps of a trial at the tribunal of a Szekler Seat, a succinct overview of the areas of legal competence under Szekler law and the jurisdictions with which a Szekler might find himself confronted is called for.

The following table is manifestly 'Szekler-centred', the Saxon Nation having its own judiciary system and, in the royal counties of Transylvania, the distinction made between nobles, burghers of royal free towns and non-free inhabitants being similar to the situation throughout the Hungary of the time. The column headed 'Privileges of Royal Free Towns' applies only to towns situated in the Szeklerland. The column 'Royal Law' refers to conflicts between individuals (mostly Szeklers and nobles) or involving rights disputed between communities (mostly between Szeklers and Saxons concerning the surveyed delimitations between their lands and payments due for the transport of merchandise).

Table 13. Echelons of Jurisdiction Applicable to a Szekler

Applicable Law	Szekler Custom		Privileges of Royal Free Towns	Royal Law
	Disagreement on competence: Seat or Royal Free Town *Tribunal of the Szekler Assembly*			
1st Instance	Arbitrators-mediators (often local judges or Seat Judges) If disputed value is		Town Guilds	Mixed Assemblies (Szeklers–Saxons or Szeklers– nobles of Transylvania) or Assembly of the Three Nations
	Less or	Greater than 3 Florins		
Appeal and last instance	Seat Judge			
Appeal		Seat Judge		
Appeal		Seat Tribunal		
Retrial		Tribunal of another Seat		
Appeal		Tribunal of Udvarhely	Town tribunal	Assembly of the Three Nations
Last recourse			Royal Court of Justice Final verdict or quashed for retrial	

A. Local Jurisdictions Applying Szekler Law Discreetly in evidence in documents dealing with the period under study here, local jurisdictions were to later play a significant role in the safekeeping of Szekler customs. Less in evidence to the royal authority bearing down time and again on the structures making up Szekler autonomy, they became the mainstay of peace in the villages and assured the survival of Szekler tradition, even after the repressions of 1562. Village jurisdictions also emerged increasingly in later documentation, as writing, in Hungarian instead of Latin, became more widespread.

Though mentioned only sporadically, the military-judiciary structure of the community suggests that the local authority was always present throughout the Szeklerland.

'Decarchal Jurisdictions',[8] *Village Judges and Arbitrators* In 1502,[9] at a tribunal dealing with an inheritance, the verdict mentions a *'judicatus decimalis in vulgari Desmabirosag'*.[10] This administrative entity, this microcosm of daily life in the Szeklerland, as D. Garda[11] describes it, appears as the first link in the structure of the Szeklerland, but no personage vested with this office has left a written trace. Gy. Bodor,[12] referring to citing a plea for the defence at a long trial concerning an inheritance in 1569/1571,[13] cites a lawyer presenting the associate Seat judges as competent for rendering justice in their circumscriptions (*dézsmabíróság*), but goes on to admit that there is no other reference to this judiciary echelon on record. In 1406,[14] a village quarrel is settled and the agreement is put in writing by the parish priest, alongside whose signature appears that of *'Joannes Altos, judex'*, with no further detail. In view of the insignificance of the case, it might be either an associate judge or, as in 1560,[15] a *'judex pagalis vel villanus'*. The codification of 1555 states the following:

> § 60. A judgement is rendered as follows in the Szeklerland: the village elects three true, honest men and these three men answer for the village. If they are brought someone whose misdeeds are known, they shall punish him; if he has property, they shall take from him what is his, but without touching the property of his wife and his children. If someone is brought before them on hear-say, they shall refuse to judge him.

The primary aim of the administration of justice in the Szeklerland is appeasement, the peaceful resolution of conflicts, amicable settlements that are agreeable to as many as possible. Starting in 1487,[16] we find judges elected or designated to determine the compensation due for a murder. The titles of such judges,[17] which recall the mode of designation according to Article 60 for village judges, turn up more and more often in documents in the latter half of the sixteenth century. Unlike the Seat judges, these 'mediators of justice' are never subject to royal instructions; they render their decisions on the demand of the parties that designated them. They are different also in that they do not act alone – we have only one case out of a dozen where an accord is concluded before a sole arbitrator – and their names are always mentioned in the documents, which is less the case for Seat judges. Only a vast genealogical study could come to verifiable conclusions, but just on scanning the names that do appear in the documents we note instances of arbitrators being Seat judges or parents of Seat judges.

Without necessarily being able to aspire to such a high office – the prerequisites for access to the office of judge of a Seat will be called out later – any honest man could find his place in a local career. In 1537,[18] Adorján Békés, an appropriate name for this honest Szekler (Békés means 'peaceful' and 'good-natured' in Hungarian), of Maksa appeared as *ordinator* and recorded in Latin an accord between the village of Lécsfalva and a private person about the building and operation of a watermill. This is our only document with an arbitrator acting alone and with the mention of '*ordinator*', a title of which Adorján seems to have been quite proud. Was this function of fact-finding familiarity with the rules of the established order more prevalent than the records may suggest? Were the sworn witnesses at a trial and the members of a jury at a Seat tribunal not '*ordinatores*' of a kind? Adorján Békés, more versed in procedure and Latin than is recorded for his neighbours, certainly serves as a reminder that knowledge of the customs was everyone's affair. We find him again in 1545[19] as one of the four designated arbitrators in a long, drawn-out dispute over an inheritance situated in Csernáton. Finally, his thorough familiarity with Szekler law and his respect for procedure come to light in his last will,[20] dated 1560. The renown of Adorján Békés of Maksa seems to have travelled beyond the limits of his village and the range of his activities may have covered those of a *iudicatus decimali*. Would it be reasonable to conclude that an *ordinator* was charged with such a jurisdiction?

The provisions of Article 60 of the codification of 1555 notwithstanding, a single prior arbitration (1544) bears the signatures of three elected judges. Mostly we find two or four signatories. In 1554, two documents offer a plethora of signatures: six elected judges for one, eight for the other!

One concerns a case between Szeklers about a property on county territory. The parties have carefully chosen their arbitrators, all members of eminent families, the members of which were eligible for the functions of judge or captain. One of the parties to the settlement is from the Seat of Udvarhely, the other hails from the Seat of Sepsi. Three of the judges are from Sepsi, their number satisfying the stipulations of Article 60; three others may also be grouped together, since they are all designated by the party from the Seat of Udvarhely: two of them are from this Seat; the third, no doubt a Hungarian, is from the village where the disputed property is situated. The protocol of the settlement[21] is also unlikely to have come about by chance; it lists, in the following order, the arbitrators from each of the Seats:

1. Udvarhely
2. County (in favour of Udvarhely)
3. Sepsi
4. Sepsi
5. Udvarhely
6. Sepsi

Next, the parties, from the Seats of

1. Udvarhely	
	2. Sepsi

In this enumeration there is a refrain of courtesy, a poetic sense of precedence (like a first quatrain of sequential rhymes and a second in which the rhymes alternate), an undeniable quest for balance that gives a foretaste of eventual agreement. The property in question is situated on county territory, but we are here still in the amicable phase of the disagreement and, if we assume that a Hungarian has been designated to ensure that the settlement could not be challenged under Crown law, the matter was settled between Szeklers; at least it does not come up again in the *Székely Archives*.

The second document, also dated 1554,[22] has a more bucolic charm. It concerns a dowry in the Illyés family[23] of Bölön. According to K. Szabó, the last two lines of the original document were covered over by eight little seals of green wax. Could these have been personal seals or were they emblems of office? Could every Szekler have had a sealing matrix at his disposal for use when he was called upon to officiate? More likely, it was the villages that kept them and circulated them amongst those designated. It is also possible that arbitration was an office which, even at village level, was always passed along within the same families. In the conscription registers of 1635[24] we find the family names of every one of the eight designated judges officiating in 1554, living in four villages (four of them in Bölön, the four others in nearby villages); three of the families are listed in the two higher ranks of military grade and the five others are among the 'seven sworn jurors'[25] of their villages (whose number, in fact, varies by village from three to eight). They were charged with establishing the rosters for their villages and were answerable for their veracity.

How should we interpret the coincidence between the individual designation of arbitrators and the fact that most of them were members of families from which jurors, not to say Seat judges and captains issued? Is it only by the chance survival of documents that we are deprived of more precise information about amicable agreements concluded before a few 'true and honest Szeklers' issued from the ranks of the common Szeklers? Or may we take the cases we have as reflecting reality: it would have occurred to no one to designate an arbitrator who was not a member of a family qualified for higher office? The evolution of Adorján Békés appears to be the fruit of his personal reputation. But on reading his last will we discover that he had no son and that his grandson (by his daughter), his heir, bears the same family name as one of the designated arbitrators of Bölön in 1554. The fact that Adorján went to so distant a village to find a husband for his daughter suggests a closer social proximity between the two families. While we lack details about the mode of designation for these local judges – clan affiliation, wealth, military rank? – it is clear that they represent a judicial echelon below that of the Seat. Thus, a case that could not be settled at the local level could be taken to the tribunal of the Seat.

A noteworthy omission in the codifications of 1555, which deal with higher jurisdictions, suggests that there was in fact a reserved domain for local judges. None of the dispositions, no matter how meticulously detailed, ever mentions cases of common theft. Such cases overwhelmingly being offences committed nearby, the local authorities, as 'justices of the peace', were no doubt much busier than their rare appearance in written records suggests. In this function of peace-keeping the local judges had, in fact, the fundamental responsibility for the daily exercise of the Szeklers' juridical autonomy.

B. *The Jurisdictions of the Seats* A trial before the judiciary assembly of the entire Szekler Nation is a crucial step in the application of Szekler customary law. That is where the highest Szekler judiciary dignitaries officiated: fact-finding investigation, verdict, execution of the sentence, they are present at every step. But this is also where the authority of the Crown intervened in the practice of Szekler customary law. The *comes* of the Szeklers, or his substitute the vice-*comes,* presided over the assembly, could demand additional investigation and order the sentence to be executed. As the king's emissary to the Szekler community, his role was only to oversee compliance with customary law, and for the most part he abided by this definition of his mission. John Hunyadi as voivode of Transylvania often also held the office of *comes* of the Szeklers, but he does not seem to have misused this double power. The term of István Báthory (1479–1493) is the detestable exception that confirms the generally correct handling of the office. One should not forget that the Szeklers were soldiers – and good ones, it is generally agreed – before being subjects under law and that their voivode and *comes* was above all a military commander. Peace within the community was the best assurance of having obedient and effective warriors. So what were these procedural steps incumbent upon the *comes* of the Szeklers?

C. *Procedural Steps* Here is a domain familiar to jurists, the classical steps (hearing, judgement, execution of the verdict) of judicial proceedings followed more or less identically throughout Europe in the late sixteenth century. We should recall in passing that all judiciary proceedings in the Szeklerland are 'contradictory' in nature. In examining judiciary procedure here, we will stress the aspects characterizing Szekler custom, as manifested in what we must consider as purely theoretical procedures, virtual procedures as it were, owing unfortunately to the fragmentary documentation available for an analysis based, nevertheless, on real cases. We will not follow the chronology of a trial strictly: Having called out the essential points of Szekler custom in the elements in the conduct of a trial, we will deal more in detail with the holding of a tribunal itself.

1. *Steps in the Conduct of a Trial* From three cases that were remanded for further evidence between 1484 and 1508[26] it appears that investigation is within the domain of Seat judges. The prevalent form of evidence is personal testimony. The distinction between personal, direct testimony and rumour is commonly known and recalled in Article 60 of the codification of 1555 (*nyilván való tudás*: manifest

knowledge, as opposed to *hallomás*: hearsay). In the documents we encounter cases involving one or more witnesses, without any apparent need for there to be more than one. Also, the number of witnesses was not a determinant factor: in 1470,[27] a woman appeared before the tribunal of the Seat of Sepsi, accused of adultery and, based on the testimony of twelve inhabitants of the village of Köpecz, she was convicted. On appeal, the *comes* heard the sworn testimony of twenty-four other men from the same village in favour of the unfortunate woman. As stated in the Concordat of 1503 between the Szeklers and the bishop of Transylvania, a woman found guilty of adultery is banished, after having her clothes shredded.[28] The conviction was confirmed and the twenty-four witnesses for the defence were condemned for perjury. The village of Köpecz, first mentioned in 1487, counted forty-six households in 1567:[29] the poor sinner seems to have mobilized practically all of the male population.

For witnesses, the oath seems to have been obligatory, but the parties could also be called upon to take an oath. The initiating plaintiff could not, on his own initiative, offer to swear,[30] but refusal to swear on demand of the defendant was considered an avowal, with the defendant winning his case.[31] If, however, a plaintiff thus challenged took the oath, the defendant lost the case. A litigation concluded on the basis of a plaintiff's oath could not be appealed.[32] Two of our documents tell us that witnesses testified under oath independently, one after the other, in accordance with Szekler custom[33] and that a defendant was acquitted definitively upon swearing 'in the presence of twenty-five true sons of Szeklers under the peal of church bells'.[34]

Judiciary duels were not unknown, but they were governed by the law of the realm: in the only documented case[35] in which one of the plaintiffs proposed such a duel at a Szekler trial, the Crown representative forbade it. Article 56 of the codification of 1555 confirms that duels in general cannot be tried in the Szeklerland; they fall in the royal judiciary domain. This said, it seems unreasonable to suppose that in this military society conflicts were never settled by the sword – in private. Could it be that some victims of assassinations never elucidated were losers of such duels?

The corpses of victims never avenged, their assassins unpunished, posed a problem to the villages in which they were found. With no witnesses to hear, a pestiferous atmosphere of suspicion would take hold of the village. An Ordeal of the Bleeding Corpse or 'call to the corpse' (*tetemre hivás, halálújitás* or *tetememelés*) was organized. The fact is that, like many pagan practices opposed by the Church, this kind of trial by ordalium appears in our documentation only when it is forbidden, time and again, and remarkably late.[36]

For K. Szabó, this custom is one of the distinctive characteristics of Szekler law:

> According to this custom, when the author of a murder in the Szeklerland was not identified, the relatives could demand all of the inhabitants of the village where the crime was committed to be ordered to assemble around the corpse and give the name of the assassin. If no one reacted, everyone was required to place his hand on the unburied corpse and swear that he was not the assassin

and that he did not know who it was. If anyone hesitated to swear or if during his oath the corpse started bleeding again, he was declared guilty by the judge and condemned to death, thus renewing the process of death.[37]

In 1555, Article 82 deals with this practice, not to impose restrictions, but to regulate the payment of the fees of procedure due the officiating judge: three Florins to be paid from the property of the guilty party or, if this was not possible, from the victim's. Thereafter, it is not clear whether the practice itself was condemned or the attitude of judges who – in the presence of a murder with no perpetrator designated – refused to authorize the family to bury the victim until his fee of three Florins had been paid. The prohibition of 1594 is phrased as follows:

> Among Szeklers, in the case of an assassination, the practice, incompatible with Christianity, is to leave the corpse on the ground for a long time to await what is termed a 'call to the corpse', a process of certification involving the payment of money [to the officiating judge] in what is called 'renewal of death'; all of the above is forbidden for all time to the Szeklers.[38]

Finally, as late as 1740, it is in effect this question of the fee that comes to the fore again: 'The fee for the liberation of the corpse must not be paid by the family of the deceased but by the murderer in accordance with ancestral custom or confiscated from his property.'[39]

Was the call to the corpse still practised or did the judges just try to impose a fee for the authorization of burial for victims of unsolved cases of murder? K. Szabó, who finds this trial by ordalium less brutal than others admitted by the Church, involving a red-hot iron or boiling water, sees in these repeated prohibitions proof of the continued practice of the custom, the unwavering persistence of ancestral Szekler traditions. More prosaically we could just as well discern the odour of a corpse polluting the village until the judge has been paid for authorizing its burial.

Rights of Appeal A verdict in error could be the judge's fault. In 1505 and 1506 the judges are advised not to succumb to corruption; such action could be punished by banishment and the confiscation of all property. As serious as this penalty may seem, it is mild in comparison to the fate proposed in 1466[40] for corrupt jurors: to be skinned and stuffed with straw. The codification of 1555 deals in several points (Articles 17, 76 and 81) with such problems, without explicitly calling for resulting verdicts to be quashed. In 1553,[41] the verdict of a corrupt judge had been declared null, the case sent to the tribunal of the Seat and the judge summoned before the court of the *comes*. For the most part, however, the use of the right to appeal is not exercised as a consequence of corrupt judges as far as we can tell from the records.

Litigation under Szekler law could be drawn out indefinitely. This was not due to the application of some law superior to the interests of the parties, but came about of a common accord – judges, the parties, witnesses, third parties – in conformity with the customs. In the interstice between 'in conformity with the customs' and 'of common accord' the final settlement of the case could hang in the balance for a long time. A first restriction was directed: the nearly symbolic disputed minimum value of three Florins (Article 19 of the codification of 1555). Any case involving more could, it seems, be contested several times before becoming final: one could agree to go before designated arbitrators (1), then before the Seat judge (2), still as a relatively consensual step, but from there on, a Seat judge's verdict could only be contested by taking it to the Seat Assembly (3), whence the case could be appealed to the Assembly of another Seat (4). The appeal of decision of the tribunal of a Seat Assembly could only be reconsidered by the Appeals Court of the Seat of Udvarhely (5) and from there the only way open was to the Court of the Royal Council (6), which could pronounce a final verdict or quash the previous decision and send it back for retrial before a Seat Assembly (7).

The use made of all these avenues of appeal were not always founded on law. Subtle juridical reasons given often covered up less avowable special interests with no regard for custom or equity. Nothing really exceptional in all this, other than that the procedural contortions of some of the disputes tend to show that superior power – money, nobility, royal patronage – did not normally suffice to get one's way in the Szeklerland.

Earlier on in this study we expressed regret at not having found a case that had gone through all the stages of appeal and therefore could serve as a school-book example. There was a case, however, that came close. It involved an inheritance, known as that of Péter Szép, disputed between two families: the Domokos[42] and the Angyalosi. The problem with the completeness of the case is that all of the documents stem from the Domokos family archives and certain of its incoherencies and repetitions could no doubt be clarified if decisions unfavourable to their cause had also been conserved. But even with these – probably intentional – blanks, the documents kept by the Domokos family alone give us an excellent example of procedural obstinacy.

It all seems to have started during the reign of King Matthias in 1471. A murky tale – against a background of treason, rebellion, collusion with Moldavians – that starts with the assassination of two men loyal to the king. The property of László Angyalossi, murderer and felon, was confiscated and adjudged by King Matthias to the loyal Domokos Nyujtódi. Both families registered their claim to the succession of Péter Szép, the father of said László Angyalossi. Each family asserted that it was in the right – or claimed to be. Here is the risk of orality, each party recalling only customs that suited its interests. Two generations later, the strict recital of facts had given way to the recounting of legends, the facts themselves possibly forgotten. In these circumstances, the case was brought before the *comes* of the Szeklers.

Twenty-five documents dated between 1522 and 1548 describe the episodes of an interminable procedural altercation between the Domokos on the one hand and the Angyalosi, and later the Török, on the other. Nowhere are the underlying facts clearly elucidated. Either the disputed property of Péter Szép, ancestor and legator of the Angyalosi, had been part of the property confiscated and adjudged to the ancestor of the Domokos or the confiscation had not included the Szép inheritance, devolved (or not) to the assassin before his crime. Had the Domokos in fact bought, instead of inheriting, part of the property, as an arbitration of

1497[43] seems to indicate and, if so, had they paid up? Péter Szép had three heirs, and some of his inheritance had in fact been bought, but not necessarily paid, by the Domokos. Were the beneficiaries of the adjudgment (or purchase) within their rights? The absence of judgements in favour of the Angyalosi family in the Domokos archives leaves these questions unanswered.

But from a formal point of view, this one affair shows traces of all imaginable procedural operations: the arbitration of 1497 is followed by a remand for a further investigation in 1522,[44] a first verdict[45] receives the Crown's authorization for a new hearing;[46] then the Tribunal of the Royal Council pronounces a verdict,[47] which is annulled by the king in person.[48] A new round starts with another arbitration, appealed to the *comes* of the Szeklers, who forbids the new arbitrators to reach a new agreement.[49]

After a few years of calm, the king granted another authorization for a new hearing,[50] the verdict of which was deferred for reasons of war.[51] And then a curious incident: on 30 April 1537,[52] the voivode and *comes* of the Szeklers delivers to Mózes Angyalosi the royal writ authorizing a new hearing, dated way back, in October 1534; within the week (4 May 1537)[53] the two parties were presented for judgement, which, it turns out, could not be pronounced because the royal authorization had only been valid for sixty days – an interesting procedural detail of which we learn on this occasion – and had already been null and void for some two and a half years.

What to think of a voivode who would formally deliver a royal writ and discover a week later that its validity had lapsed long before? Indifference toward a village quarrel when the Ottomans keep assailing the frontiers and two kings vie for the crown, or a prudent decision to stay out of the affair? Whatever the motive, on 4 May, the voivode decided to return the case to the Court of the Royal Council, which in turn charged him one month later with the responsibility of rendering a verdict.[54] It is not easy to determine what was at fault here, the personalities involved or the insurmountable contradiction between the rules invoked?

Soon the Angyalosi branch of the family died out and a branch by matrimonial alliance, the Török, came to the fore and the conflict flared up again and became exasperating. A judiciary duel[55] was proposed in vain. And another curious episode: the plaintiff appeared to panic because her Christian name had not been correctly registered in the complaint.[56] Not only does she rush to withdraw her complaint, but she also volunteers to pay the court fees[57] – an act uncommon elsewhere in the *Székely Archives*. The case stopped there. It is difficult to believe that this precipitate end to the affair could have been motivated by a mere error in spelling a name. There were undoubtedly other forces at work behind the development.

Let us add that these family archives contain ten more documents, concerning other disputed successions, all in the same village, with the Domokos challenging other families. One such case involves the active corruption of witnesses.[58] However, this querulous family seems not to have been excessively scrupulous about the means employed and their choice of documents to be conserved in their remarkable archives and was not likely to have been motivated by any pedantic aim of completeness.

Trying to analyse the rules of inheritance applied for divisions of property; Gy. Bónis[59] sees in this case an exception to the rules of succession under customary law applied in all other cases and regrets the confusing density of verdicts and accords. The present author does not pretend to have a clearer view of this tortuous conflict, but tends to believe that some of the devolutions – which do not make sense under Szekler law – were but reactions, political manoeuvres, to procedural perversions. They appear to be mere variations on the basis of the underlying law to try to cope with the effects of a procedure the annulment of which would have implied challenging royal institutions already badly shaken in these troubled times by the Mohács disaster. Adjudging, wrongly so under Szekler law, one part of the inheritance to another branch of the Angyalossi family could have been a ploy to restore a just balance by inflicting the effects of confiscation only on the felon – it is not clear whether his felony was murder or high treason and hence whether the confiscation was to be adjudged as *weregild* or to whom – and not those who were his descendants at the time of the crime (Codification of 1555, Articles 30 and 60).

The maddening meanders of such cases pose the question of whether certain Szeklers were particularly given to pettifoggery. In the Domokos–Angyalossi case, the incessant frequentation of legal institutions by both parties can indeed be seen as an example of such pig-headedness – occasionally neglecting fundamental rules of fair play – but it may also be the demonstration of a commonly-shared feeling that recourse to the law is everyone's everyday right.

This freedom to challenge a verdict is institutionalized in the Appeals Tribunal of Udvarhely. The first mention of a verdict on appeal pronounced at this Seat dates from 1500.[60] There are half a dozen references to judgements on appeal by the tribunal of Udvarhely between 1519 and 1555. It is worth noting that in 1550[61] a verdict rendered at Udvarhely in the first instance, was appealed directly to the Tribunal of the Royal Council.

On the pretext of avoiding legal costs and excessive delays, which in the constitution of 1505 are attributed to the rarity of juridical assemblies of Udvarhely, King John II Szapolyai in 1562 saw fit to abolish these very jurisdictions and ordered appeals to be taken directly from the Seat tribunal to the Royal Court of Justice, a simplistic economy achieved due to royal exasperation with the sheer insolence of the Szekler community's juridical autonomy.

Execution of Judgements This is one of the points stressed by the constitution of 1505: 'judgements rendered must be executed rapidly'. Like the investigative phase of a procedure, the execution of a sentence is the responsibility of the Szekler dignitaries, but usually under the supervision of a representative of the Crown. These operations fall into two categories: investiture in an adjudged property and payment of the compensation or fine decreed.

The first category, involving the delimitation by survey of land obtained by verdict and the formal investiture of the new proprietor, is the best documented. When such property is situated on county territory, the procedure is normally executed by an emissary of a *locus credibilis*, while within the Szeklerland it is the Seat judges and captains who are in charge. The Szeklers spotted such operations very early when they involved a delimitation between Szekler land and county land, but written mentions of cases situated entirely within the Szeklerland do not occur until the second half of the fifteenth century. Is this due to the loss of documents or a change in customs? Was there, in fact, individually-owned land before the fifteenth century on Szekler territory?

The first recorded investiture '*à la* Szekler', that is to say undertaken by the Seat judge and the Seat captain with no recourse to a representative of a *locus credibilis*, involved three villages jointly installed as proprietors of a fishpond.[62] But this was in the extreme western part of the Seat of Maros, very close to county territory, a region crossed by a merchant route; hence, it is likely that the application of the Crown procedure was motivated by some disagreement arising from mixed interests. Nevertheless, the process itself was in strict compliance with Szekler customs, as is pointed out with some insistence within the document. Three weeks later,[63] the first report of an individual investiture within the Szeklerland was issued, under the authority of the '*comes* of the Szeklers of the Seat of Maros' (*sic!* this title is intrinsically contradictory), the Seat captain and Seat judges.

Not until ten years later do we encounter another investiture in the Szeklerland, but again, the beneficiary is a village community[64] as a whole. The reason for this process is undoubtedly to be sought in friction with an adjoining Saxon village. Still, the operation is again conducted in strict compliance with Szekler customs. After this, another dozen reports of investitures appear in the first half of the sixteenth century, mostly in the Seat of Maros. In one of these, all of the neighbours were required to be present at the proceedings[65] in order for the operation to be valid; two other procedures required a presence from Kolozsmonostor (*locus credibilis*) alongside those of Szekler dignitaries.[66]

In each of these instances, the Crown had intervened in the legal conflict. It appears that, after King Matthias, the Jagiello and the Szapolyai kings showed less respect for Szekler customary law. Moreover, the more powerful Szekler families tried increasingly to have procedures that were applicable only to Hungarian nobles – with which the kings were familiar by virtue of their own properties situated in county territory – applied to their possessions in the Szeklerland. However, it was Szekler judges and captains of the Seat who oversaw these operations. Thus, we see the application of the prerogatives of the Szekler community evolving and spreading: in villages adjoining royal counties and Saxon territory investitures are carried out under Szekler authority and, for mixed situations, not in application of royal law. Certain families accept, demand even, that both the royal and the Szekler procedures be applied.

Conflicts were rarely settled by coercion, normally by payment of compensation or fines. There is no distinction between civil law and penal law in the documents. Articles 39 and 42 to 46 of the codification of 1555 give a list of monetary penalties imposed for crimes of blood (involuntary homicide, attempted homicide, infliction of injuries) all in favour of the victim's family. This gives the impression that only the 'civil' aspect of such acts are settled; in fact, we have no case of a crime of blood judged on a basis other than the complaint of the victim's family, 'civil plaintiffs', as it were. This said, the strictly contradictory character of the proceedings, as opposed to indictments arising from investigation by the authorities, is tempered by a detail found in some of the documents, which shows that the proceeds of the sentence were shared between the plaintiffs and the judges. It appears that, even if the legal authorities never opened a case on their own but depended on the initiative of a plaintiff, their interest in a case weighed on the penalties pronounced. To be more precise, since the fines were predetermined, the judge positioned himself between the parties and diverted part of the fine to his own benefit.

There is no mention of imprisonment anywhere, not in the codifications nor in the records of individual trials. Two reasons for this: in proceedings based on the contradictory principle, the plaintiff gains nothing from the imprisonment of the defendant; moreover, in a society organized around small entities – *tízes*, village – imprisonment places more of a burden on the village than on the convict. In addition, Article 60 of the codification of 1555 is very explicit in stating that under no circumstances may the consequences of a breach of the law be inflicted on the family of the person convicted. Imprisonment would weigh on the entire family. But also, limiting the freedom of movement of a Szekler was not so much punishment than a violation of customary law.

But especially, the community's manifest opposition to the erection of edifices representing royal authority – possibly intended for coercion – is clearly established. In 1493,[67] the seven Seats complain to King Wladislas II of the acts of injustice and cruelty committed against them by the voivode and *comes* of the Szeklers, István Báthory. The imprisonment by the voivode of a Szekler awaiting judgement is clearly forbidden in the codification of 1555 (Article 36), except in a case punishable by death. A hundred years earlier,[68] a Szekler had been locked up in a conflict with the Church (no further detail is provided in the document), leading to a verdict according him compensation for this imprisonment.

The death penalty is sometimes referred to in documents stating principles, but very rarely in concrete cases. In 1555, murder with premeditation is punished by death (Article 37), as is collective, intentional murder – apparently premeditated or not – (Article 40). In Article 68 we find another reasoning: the compelling necessity of punishment of flagrant crime, violence involving the theft of cattle or crimes of blood. The graduation is as follows: confiscation of personal property; if none, confiscation of hereditary property; and, finally, if there is really no way to inflict material punishment, the death penalty may be pronounced.

This may be what happened to the man who was hanged for having stolen a horse in 1420.[69] We are apprised of his fate by the complaint lodged with the *comes* by a respectable Szekler who felt that the fact that the thief had been strung up in front of his door was prejudicial to his interests. The document is unfortunately incomplete, not even the thief's name is known, his only stated identity is that he is another Szekler's *familiaris* and he is decidedly unlikely to have possessed anything of value. In passing, we should recall the extraordinary importance the possession of a horse represented in this military society: stealing a horse was more serious than stealing cattle; such an act could affect the social standing of a cavalryman, a crime difficult to remedy.

Werbőczy had already noted that death was a rare form of punishment in Szekler society.[70] In an order of mobilization of 1493,[71] death for possible deserters was stated as a principle. But was it ever applied? Were any executed on the spot after a summary court martial? There is nothing to suggest it. In 1500[72] a death penalty was pronounced, but in compliance with Article 36 of 1555 the accused was free to move about and he did; he fled. The *comes* was thus limited to the confiscation of the culprit's property. In 1540,[73] the same thing happened again, but with a difference: a murder had been committed by a group, the fugitive had been their leader, and we learn from the *comes'* judgement that the accomplices could not be judged or convicted in the ringleader's absence. What surprising liberalism, barring the prosecution of the henchmen in the absence of the principal instigator, respecting the hierarchy of the band of evildoers and hamstringing the judicial system.

The supreme penalty in Szekler tradition was banishment with confiscation of property. Capital punishment, not only by its nature but also by the way the verdict is rendered: the only such cases in the *Székely Archives* are sentences emanating from the sovereign Szekler community as a whole. Two cases are mentioned in the Seat of Maros, in 1498[74] and 1508,[75] one involving several instigators of an uprising in Csík and Gyergyó in 1511[76] and one case in the Seat of Sepsi in 1520.[77] We happen on these cases when the voivode-*comes* attempts conciliation; banishment appears as the supreme punishment pronounced against the most powerful, but no direct protocol of the community's judicial assemblies rendering this verdict has come down to us. The description of the conditions calling for this penalty in the constitution of 1505 concerns corrupt judges. These verdicts of ostracism, expulsions one might say, are never clearly motivated, but it appears that abuses of power are often involved. Thus, in one of the cases in the Seat of Maros, we learn from a document dated 1519[78] that, upon the departure of the banned party in 1508, Szeklers held as bondsmen (*jobbágyok*) were freed, while in 1498 the houses of the banned dignitaries were razed.

We have left the domain of legal procedure and find ourselves dealing with social conflict, with the aggressiveness of the poorer toward those they considered too powerful. These cases shed light on the internal contradictions within the Szekler society. It should be noted that the codification of 1555 does not mention banishment. We are no longer entirely in the domain of customs that have crossed the line between oral and codified law, but the terms of Article 60 still apply: banishment, too, must affect only the condemned person. The decision of 1519 reinstates a son in the property confiscated from his banished father in 1508.

This is in clear contrast with a decision of the Assembly of the Three Nations of Transylvania of 1459,[79] in which death and the confiscation of property and banishment of the *entire family* menaced all those who would violate the accord concluded. Szekler customary law is applied to the offender only. There is, however, a degree of contradiction in Szekler customary law itself, between this principle and the fact the banished individual's verdict menaces all those who might help him return to the Szeklerland with the same penalty of banishment.

It is worth noting that in a verdict dated 1382,[80] violation of the order of banishment is punishable by death. This case, the earliest judgement for voluntary homicide we have for the Szeklerland, contains a fairly complete assortment of penalties incurred: the murderer is banished – but only from his village – he is not even allowed to dismount if he crosses the village, incurs the death penalty for any attempt to contact his accomplice and he must pay compensation to the son of his victim. After this case, we must await the fifteenth century to find further instances of *weregild*.

How to interpret a curious concentration of documents involving five cases of homicide between 1477 (1476 if we include the Domokos case, where the contested *weregild* is the result of a royal judgement) and 1497? A sudden epidemic of murders, a determination to prosecute? Probably neither, more likely a modification of the compensation due. These few documented cases deal with inherited land, either just as adjudged compensation[81] or as the motive for homicide.[82] Here the written form was indispensable to ensure the passage of ownership.

And why are no further verdicts documented thereafter? The fugitive murderer of 1540[83] is also condemned to pay compensation to his victim's mother, but the document gives no further information on the nature of the compensation. It may be a coincidence, but these cases of *weregild* to be paid by relinquishing ownership of hereditary land occurred during the voivodate of István Báthory, who was notoriously disrespectful of autonomous Szekler traditions and the ceding of hereditary property is strictly contrary to Szekler customs and structures. The case of 1497[84] is somewhat different. Two Szeklers had assassinated a parish priest and profaned a cemetery. They renounced ownership of their hereditary property in favour of the diocese, in an 'amicable settlement'. But six months later,[85] we find them banished by the Szekler community, which confiscated their property (from the Church, it appears). There is no further documentation on the case to determine who ended up owning the property, the bishop or the Szekler community, but the presence of the bishop at the negotiations surrounding the 'concordate' and his acceptance of Szekler law involving hereditary property[86] suggest that the bishopric might have been careful of the risks involved in opposing the will of the community.

The lack of further such cases of *weregild* paid by transferring ownership of hereditary property can be considered as a reaction of the Szekler community to the threat of this confiscation, as is suggested by Article 68 of the codification of 1555, which distinguishes meticulously between personal property, to be confiscated first, and hereditary property, which comes into play only if there is not enough personal property to pay the penalty imposed. The payment of *weregild* had existed since times beyond recall and continued during the period under study here. It is unlikely that it applied to hereditary property for the duration of these few cases only. Challenging a traditional practice that was as advantageous to the wealthier – if not more so – as to the common Szeklers would have been a sure way to have them close ranks in defence of their privileges, as they had done in 1493.[87]

Fines are very frequently imposed, but it is not easy today to determine the values involved. We can distinguish three categories of offences punished by fines: firstly, non-compliance with judiciary decisions or arbitrations involving inheritances or the devolution of real property; next, involuntary homicide or manslaughter or bodily injuries; and finally misconduct during a judiciary assembly (calumny, violence or unexcused absence after convocation).

Fines levied on the parties for non-compliance with an agreement, judiciary or amicable, are generally high, more or less the value of disputed property. Unfortunately, we do not have documents at our disposal concerning the execution of such penalties. We could assume that they were dissuasive enough not to reappear in recorded cases.

The other two categories involve nominal, considerably lower values; the catalogue of such fines was carefully pre-established. The monetarization of the Szekler society was far from being consummated at the end of the fifteenth century when, in 1494,[88] an order of execution was worded as follows: '[order is given] to confiscate movables [.../...] up to the value of eight oxen, four cows, two heifers and two bullocks'.

In the documents under study here there is no indication of the monetary value of oxen or heifers. The only approximation possible comes through a document dated 1554,[89] which establishes a contribution of one Florin toward the tribute owed the Sultan by every Szekler who owns cattle worth six florins. Thus, if our comparison is valid, we may estimate the value of the confiscation of 1494 to be within the average recorded fines, between three and twelve Florins.

If these numbers are difficult to interpret today, it must have been not much easier at the time, due to the diversity of monetary units of account. The following table gives a sketchy overview, first relative to the diverse fines stated in the codifications and then the fines stemming from actual verdicts in the *Székely Archives*.

Table 14. Overview of Penalties Incurred

Offence	Codification of 1555 §§.	Individual Decisions	SzOkl	Date
Non-compliance with a decision about real property		100 Silver Marks	VIII.27	1427
		42 Gold Florins	III.465	1459
		40 Gold Marks	VIII.57	1462
		300 Silver Marks	VIII.61	1464
		600 Florins	I.CCI	1487
		48 Marks or 24 Gold Florins	I.CCXVI	1499
		50 Gold Florins	VIII.112	1501
		150 Marks	VIII.113	1502

Offence	Codification of 1555	§§.	Individual Decisions	SzOkl	Date
Violence with housebreaking in the house, on the field or on a cart	12 Florins	42.			
Violence with theft of cattle	6 Florins	43.			
Violence with intent to steal cattle	1 ½ Florins	43.			
Assault and battery - unarmed, throwing to ground	3 Florins	44.			
- with bloodshed, beating	12 Florins	44.			
Attempted homicide	12 Florins	45.	Condemnation, penalty not indicated	II.CCCII	1552
Broken bone, serious injury, injury by sabre	6 Florins	46.	An orchard!	II.CCCXII	1554
Light injury	½ Florin	46.			
Non-presentation at court			10 Marks	I.CCXXXI	1510
			6 Florins	II.CCXCIV	1550
			3 Marks	II.CCXCVI	1550
False accusation (triviality)	1 ½ Florins	7.	6 Marks	II.CCLIII	1524
Altercation, violence, dispute or disorderly conduct at court	12 Florins	5.			
Calumny	13 ½ Florins	32.	24 Florins	III.545	1516
			24 Marks	III.613	1548

In the *Székely Archives*, there are other mentions of fines, but with no clear indication of the offence, as well as references to compensation for injury but without the penalty, neither monetary nor in kind. In the codification of 1555, the fines are quoted in *Gyra* (monetary unit of account), but Article 9 adds that a *Gyra* is worth half a Florin in the Szeklerland. This is the basis for the calculation of fines in the table above. The real value of the Mark as a currency of account seems to have varied before and after 1526, between half a Golden Florin in 1499 and one Florin in 1559,[90] but the same document states that the value had stayed at half a Florin in the Szeklerland.

The penalties for housebreaking, serious violence with bodily harm, are all more or less on a level with fines for misconduct before a tribunal. We should note that the codification of 1555 does state the penalty for non-presentation at court, no doubt because it varied with the seriousness of the case, the authority issuing the summons, and other such considerations. If no fine is predefined for non-compliance with decisions involving real property, no doubt these penalties were dissuasive, consisting of, or equivalent in value to, the real property in dispute. Articles 42 to 46 meticulously enumerate the penalties for assault and battery.

Housebreaking, theft and violence are linked in the presentation of these articles. Violence with intrusion in a house, on a field or on a cart or armed housebreaking, or attempted homicide cost twelve Florins. If we follow the hierarchy of fines, any violence with theft of cattle is as serious as grave injury. An apparent contradiction appears in Articles 44 and 46 between violence with effusion of blood, at twelve Florins, and injury by sabre, for only six Florins. There is no indication whether the penalties may be cumulative. One might wonder about the fine for light injury (half a Florin): the opposing party might make a profit by bringing a countercharge of insufficient significance (one and a half Florins).

Finally, it may appear odd that, while the slightest altercation or injury (punishable by as little as one and a half Florins) is called out, theft without violence appears nowhere in the codification. The conclusion that suggests itself is that such infractions were dealt with by local jurisdictions, village judges or *ordinatores*.

In the case of a legal procedure without surprise, Szekler customary law requires that all operations be handled by Szekler dignitaries. There is an initial period devoted to pacification and debate, one might almost say tribal palavers – the exercise of customary law can be fastidious, sometimes fussy, all the while remaining empirical in its conception. Through the codifications and certain verdicts, we perceive the influence of personalities, be they the villainous Voivode Báthory, the calmly competent *ordinator* Békés, or some vindictive pleaders. There are some basic principles or, less consciously, some traditions, that transcend individual human interests: ownership of land does not pass from one family to another for a simple consideration like murder; the good faith of a party proven by his taking the oath closes the case; an investiture in the Szeklerland must be done by lay dignitaries from within the community; judges and captains, not by clerical agents of the Crown, the emissaries of some *locus credibilis*. Szekler law remains a reserved domain. But the judgement itself, the decision with which the parties must comply, is not left to the sole Szekler dignitaries; it is pronounced in the presence of the *comes*.

2. The Holding of Judiciary Assemblies How is a Szekler assembly held? How often do Szekler assemblies take place? Not often enough, according to the Szeklers in 1505, too often for King John II, in 1562. Where were the assemblies held, who took an active part and who would just attend? What was the cost of legal action? Answers can be found in the *Székely Archives*, though dispersed and fragmentary.

A first, quantitative assessment from the documents gives us a good idea of the frequency of Seat assemblies and assemblies of the Szekler Nation. What actually transpired in each is a matter of piecing together anecdotal fragments scattered across the archives.

The criteria for the choice between convening an assembly at Seat level or taking a case to a plenary assembly of the Szekler Nation are nowhere defined clearly. Decisions involving Szekler royal free towns were always taken at assemblies of the entire nation, but certain other decisions could well have been sought at Seat assemblies, if no convenient access to a national assembly presented itself to the pleading parties.

Judiciary Assemblies in the Székely Archives The archives contain thirty-some documents dated between 1344 and 1553 concerned with judiciary assemblies. Six assemblies are just mentioned, either by reference to their imminence (1458) or indicating decisions that they had previously taken (1498, 1514 and 1555).

Ten of these assemblies (of which four were just mentioned) are stated to be assemblies of the entire Szekler community. The Seat of Udvarhely is presented as the principal Seat of the Szeklerland and its tribunal as the court of appeals, but it was not always the venue of Szekler assemblies. One was held at Kolozsvár (1492), possibly around a Transylvanian Assembly of the Three Nations, four in Udvarhely and five in Marosvásárhely.

Two assemblies involve more than one Seat: the assembly at Kézdivásárhely in 1407[91] is presented in the document as a general assembly with the *comes* presiding. This assembly certainly involved more than just the one Seat, the case involved property situated in the Seat of Sepsi, but Kézdivásárhely seems hardly central enough for an assembly of the entire Szekler community and all the officials named are from the southern Seats. K. Szabó is undoubtedly right in supposing that this was an assembly of the three southern Seats (Sepsi, Kézdi and Orbai) as was a case in 1466 but in this author's opinion he makes anachronistic use of the term *Háromszék*, first mentioned in 1502. Another assembly, involving the Seats of Maros and Udvarhely, was held in 1460 on neutral ground, on Saxon territory.

The nine assemblies of the Seat of Maros were held at Marosvásárhely, and one, in 1500, sat in the fortress of Görgény, no doubt due to pressing military obligations that did not allow the *comes* to leave the fortress. Finally, three assemblies of the Seat of Sepsi and one of Udvarhely were held in their respective towns of Sepsiszentgyörgy and Udvarhely. The town of Marosvásárhely is on record as the site of one out of two assemblies listed, whether because the records were among those conserved or because of it geographical location (on the trade routes used by the Saxons and near the political centre, Torda).

Classing the assemblies by verdict, we find five criminal (compensation for homicide and banishment) and nineteen civil judgements (mostly concerning successions), and a further eight decisions concerning jurisdictional competence between Szekler assemblies and royal free towns (four each involving Marosvásárhely and Sepsiszentgyörgy), all taken by assemblies of the Szekler community as a whole. The decisions handed down by Szekler assemblies on this subject clearly show how reluctantly the privileges of the royal free towns – exorbitant in the face of Szekler customs – were accepted by the Szekler community.

Frequency of Assemblies In the *Székely Archives* we find twenty-some assemblies between 1448 and 1519 held fairly regularly about every five years, with the *comes* of the Szeklers presiding. The complaint expressed in 1505 that assemblies were too rare does not appear entirely justified. But with the eternal question of whether written records were always kept and conserved we can only note that a frequency of annual general assemblies in the presence of the *comes*, as called for in a rule of 1499, is not confirmed by the documents at hand. Or is there confusion between general assemblies of the Szeklerland and those of individual seats? Article 75 of 1555 takes up the requirement stated in 1466[92] that Seat assemblies be held three times a year. This might indicate that it was these less formal and more popular assemblies that were felt to be too rare.

How did a Szekler judiciary assembly proceed? Noisily, according to a near-contemporary description: 'They come to their assemblies armed, the dignitaries take their seats in front, the rest stand all around, making a lot of noise and shouting angrily when they disagree with a proposition.'[93]

No doubt, we may take him at his word. In 1555, misconduct during an assembly was discouraged by serious fines: breaking of objects, calumny, insult, lack of respect for judges. The list is long, but we do not have a record of any individual judgement imposing a fine. Such behaviour might have been dealt with on the spot, the fine going into the judges' pocket with no further formalities.

Where were the assemblies held? Nowhere is it stated whether they were held in the open or in a specific building. For the insurrectional assembly of 1506, known only from a document copied in the eighteenth century, in Hungarian, it is said they met in the *major* of Agyagfalva. In Latin, this term might give 'village' (*villa*) or farm, small holding, or manorial domain (*praedium*). The recital of the secession of the Seat of Kászon, prettily told, is live with details that do nothing to embellish the protagonist and can be taken for a factual account known by all, which helps render the details credible. We find a judge, seated on a haystack to take testimony, in a barn.[94]

In the absence of any hint at the existence of a 'consecrated' place for trials, some displacements appear all the more interesting. In 1487, on 4 and 15 February,[95] the *comes* and voivode was in judiciary assembly at Marosvásárhely. Curiously enough, in between, on 8 February,[96] he summoned the parties in a murder case to Jánosfalva, near the river Homorod, to the south of Udvarhely (a straight-line distance of about 80 kilometres southeast of Marosvásárhely; more, if he took the road south to Segesvár and followed the river to the village). Was that the place of the crime? Was there a need for settling the problem at the very scene of the crime? We are reminded of the complaint of an indignant Szekler in 1420,[97] in front of whose door a horse-thief had been hanged, and wonder about the forceful effect of the scene of the crime also being the scene of punishment. A symbolism all the more pertinent if there was no one place dedicated to the meting out of justice.

On the other hand, there were buildings that were 'consecrated' and could conceivably have served as more dignified places of assembly than marketplaces or barns. The Szeklers could have assembled in fortified churches like their Saxon neighbours. The belfries of Saxon fortified churches where assemblies were held have four smaller spires, one in each corner, to identify the building as a place of justice.

A remark in 1506 to the effect that judicial decisions rendered on Sundays were null and void would suggest that some judges, profiting for their own convenience from the fact that the faithful were assembled for Sunday mass held trials following the observances; one more indication that assemblies were, at least on occasion, held within churches and their fortifications.

In fact, the Szeklers seem to have been less concerned about where judicial assemblies were held than about how they were held. How long was an assembly to last and who was to furnish lodgings for the officiating dignitaries? These two points were codified. The latter was often a subject of discussion between Szekler officials and burghers of royal free towns – which were in principle subject to Crown law – and who showed little interest in hosting Szekler assemblies of any kind.

How long did a Szekler assembly last? According to Article 84 of the codification of 1555, judicial assemblies before the voivode (and *comes* of the Szeklers) lasted about one week, and were to be held in the period between the feast of St. George (the end of April) and Pentecost (mid-June). This period was not static, however, as the season was pleasant for meetings but also ideal for military campaigns. Article 85 states, in agreement with the resolutions of 1466 and 1499, that Seat assemblies should last two weeks. In practice, with decisions handed down every few days within an assembly, it would seem that the duration was more on the order of three weeks to one month (in 1487 between 4 and 23 February[98] for the assembly of the entire Szeklerland, in 1501 between 4 and 23 March[99] and in 1519 between 23 August and 27 September,[100] for assemblies of the Seat of Maros).

The logistical support was not so easy to ensure by decree. Over and above the classical friction between town and village, the conflicting privileges enjoyed by royal free towns and the surrounding Szeklerland gave rise to disputes when it came to holding a Szekler judiciary assembly within and at the expense of royal free towns. Marosvásárhely was particularly affected, but Sepsiszentgyörgy, Udvarhely and Kézdivásárhely also complained of abuses by officiating Szekler dignitaries. It appears clearly from the documents that the burghers' foremost objective was to avoid as much as possible footing the cost of assemblies that did not concern them. The visiting dignitaries: vice-*comites*, judges and captains, were hampered in exercising their prerogatives of a judiciary (they had no jurisdiction over these townspeople) as well as military nature (burghers were the last to be mobilized and never fought outside Transylvania), and seemed to see these 'descents'[101] on townships as an opportunity for exorbitant misconduct: gifts and provisions slyly exacted or, if not forthcoming, rounds of random requisitions. Abuse of power and looting by Szekler notables, are recorded in the towns' complaints. In 1499,[102] a call to order states that 'no provisions or services are to be exacted from royal free towns beyond the duration of assemblies'. On the occasion of the confirmation of the privileges of Sepsiszentgyörgy as a royal free town,[103] the circumstances for holding assemblies were defined: 'judges are not to descend more than once a year, only one-third of them, and they are not to exact gifts during their stay'.

In 1519,[104] the town of Marosvásárhely lodged a complaint against the judges for non-payment of labour and services exacted, for intimidating conduct and abuse of power. In 1525,[105] it is Sepsiszentgyörgy that accuses officials of covering up banditry committed within the town and, in 1558,[106] the dignitaries of the Seat of Udvarhely are reminded that they are not allowed to exact victuals and gifts from the inhabitants of the town of the same name. In the codification of 1555 (Article 85), we find the definition of the logistics support due a judicial assembly, but not who is to pay: the town or the Seat.

In addition to the attending public, often somewhat turbulent it appears, and the officiating members of the tribunal who, as we have seen, sometimes behaved abusively, there were the parties' attorneys and attending auxiliaries at the tribunal's service.

We encounter lawyers, or proxies, representing parties who may or may not be present at the debates. There are several cases of wives represented by their husbands, but as proxies, not as heads of family.

Representing a party was a serious responsibility. Written mandates within a family were not always required: in 1538,[107] a man was represented by his brother, but in 1494 a tribunal took note of the absence of a written procuration.[108] Several Szeklers, members of the most powerful families – and maybe the most avid to litigate – issued written powers of attorney. Important as legal affairs may be and requiring presence at court, the primary obligation of a Szekler was to go to war, and he had to assure his legal rear when obliged to leave the Szeklerland. One could almost follow the military movements by the powers of attorney left behind. Such mandates were most often issued by the most eminent men, and women not confident of being able to assert themselves.[109] The wording was more or less standard, whether recorded before the Convent of Kolozsmonostor (four out of six documents), before the voivode of Transylvania, or a judge of the Seat of Sepsi.[110] These procurations were limited to a term of one year and the number of attorneys thus mandated is considerable: between four principals mandating six attorneys in 1441[111] and one principal – a woman – mandating fifteen in 1514,[112] and so on.[113]

To all appearances, these *procuratores* can be held responsible for their acts. In 1461,[114] a demand for compensation was lodged by a plaintiff against the attorney (*procurator*) of the defendants. Not content with just representing his principals, this attorney had, on behalf of his clients, seized the disputed object, a watermill.

It is possibly such excessive zeal that King John II intended to discourage in 1562, when he ordered 'That there be sworn notaries in the Seats, to be paid at the plaintiffs' discretion, with the money they formerly used to pay their attorneys or others.'[115]

Besides these auxiliaries engaged by the parties, auxiliaries of the tribunal itself were in attendance from time to time. It is reasonable to assume that the *comes* of the Szeklers (often the voivode of Transylvania at the same time), by virtue of his position in the hierarchy, was attended by his own clerk or registrar. In strictly local cases, parish priests issued certificates for the sale or pawning of property.[116] Their knowledge of Latin and the presumption of moral integrity was a prerogative of these men of the Church, potentially backed up by the Convent of Kolozsmonostor or the Chapter of Gyulafehérvár as *loca credibilia* for Transylvania. For the judicial assemblies, the only evidence of registry we have is the fees charged for documents.

With writing not yet prevalent in the Szeklerland, we must assume that judiciary activity was much denser than the available documented decisions. For one, we see references to assemblies that have left no written protocols, but also, individual decisions did not always reach us in writing unless they were appealed to a Seat tribunal, the first decision remaining in force – and giving occasion to appeal – without necessarily having been committed to writing. A good example of the weight of oral testimony, of memory cited generation after generation and of statements under oath – with the increasing use of writing – appears in the case of this notable whose origins and rights are questioned:

> Mihály Láczok <u>reports to</u> Péter Bazini and Szentgyörgyi, Voivode of Transylvania and *comes* of the Szeklers that in the presence of several Szekler dignitaries he has <u>questioned under oath</u> Lázár Kövér, who confirmed that, during the term of his father Benedek Kövér as chief judge of the Seat of Sepsi, Antal Bodor had <u>presented the letters of privilege of his family</u> and that consequently his father, with the consent of the tribunal of the Seat, had confirmed him in his dignity of belonging to the tribe of Agház and in his property, receiving the judiciary fees due in the case.[117]

Writing assumes an ever-widening place in Szekler judiciary practice, but it is not mandatory. Its progress can be observed in the diverse codifications: for Werbőczy in 1514, there is a fee for translation (from spoken Hungarian to official Latin) and, in 1555 in the Szeklerland, a fee for the writing of documents.

In addition to these fees for written documentation, there were court costs: a deposit at the opening of a trial, costs for the verdict – due even if in the meantime the parties had settled their dispute amicably – cost of appeal, cost for quashing a verdict – not to forget the fee for the 'ordeal of the bleeding corpse'. All these fees, duly listed in the codification of 1555 (Articles 1, 2, 4, 8, 11, 12, 82, 83 and 86) range between one and three Florins, or one-third to one-eighth of the fines imposed. The court costs paid – and globally two-thirds to three-quarters of the fines imposed – were shared out to judges, captains and representatives of the Crown – following precise calculations (Articles 61, 78, 80 and 83 of the codification of 1555).

These costs were shared out as follows according to the few documents giving specifics:

Table 15. Penalties Incurred for Court Costs

Year	Amount of Fine	*Comes* or vice-*comes*	Judges	Plaintiff	SzOkl
1492	100 Florins	one-half	one-quarter	one-quarter	III.494
1499	24 Florins	two-thirds	-	one-third	I.CCXVI
1500	100 Florins	two-thirds	-	one-third	III.512
1524	6 Marks	two-thirds	-	one-third	II.CCLIII

An important element in this judicial organization was, of course, the composition of the tribunals of Seat assemblies in the Szeklerland. Szekler customary law applied at these tribunals, but it was a representative of the Crown who presided and handed down the decisions. It is sometimes stressed that these decisions 'respect Szekler ancestral customs' or were taken after consultation with Szekler dignitaries. There is a degree of confusion in the titles cited for the latter, with the unfortunate effect of some erroneous interpretations.

II. The Judged and the Judges

A. The Community, Juries, Seat Judges, Captains and Judges of the Crown Council: What these Terms Signify

Following a study of the active exercise of ancestral Szekler customary law, we need to deal more formally with the persons involved; its actors and participants.

The phenomenon of ternarity characterizing the Szekler community extends into the casting of participants in the legal process. Like the three ranks of military hierarchy, the three components of the title *comes trium generum Siculorum*, a Szekler judiciary assembly was also composed of three levels of participation. There are the dignitaries (one), the members of the jury (two) and the community (*universitas*) (three). Does this composition really embrace the Szekler community in its entirety? In the course of time, some terminological evolutions can be observed in the designation of the jury members and the community. As representativeness shows signs of lessening, persisting generic designations recall time and again that the Szekler community is based on the all-pervading notion of equality.

Table 16. Composition of a Judiciary Assembly in the Szeklerland

Szekler Assembly *Congregacio generalis*					
Dignitaries			Jurors *iurati Assessores*		Community *Universitas* ...
Representative of the Crown	Judge	Captain	*Seniores*	*Pociores*	... *Siculorum*
Comes or *vice-comes*				*Superiores*	... *Populorum*
Castellanus					... *Senioribus*
					... *trium generum Siculorum*

Over and above the evocation of principles in 1466 and 1499, there are eighty-eight documents dated between 1344 and 1562 with over a hundred occurrences of terms that permit us to observe closely the permutation of the juridical designations. Before dealing with the composition of the tribunal itself (representatives of the Crown, judges, captains), we will look at the terminological evolution of the

Szekler community as individual subjects of the exercise of justice and as actors in the process of jurisdiction, by sitting as jurors in the judicial assemblies, and so representing the community.

B. *'Universitas Siculorum'*

A term recurring regularly until the mid-fifteenth century, it serves as a reminder that the tribunal sits in the midst of an assembly of the Szekler community, but it is also used as the form of address for decisions or confirmations. A first, subtle nuance appears in 1453[118]: a decision is said to apply to the Szekler community *and* inhabitants[119] of a village of Szentkirály in the Seat of Maros. Szekler law applies to all, but this formulation suggests that not all of the inhabitants of the village were necessarily considered Szeklers. The term *populus* turns up again in 1487,[120] in contrast to *gentes*. The constitution of 1505 reintegrates this *populus* into the Szekler community with the terms 'royal subjects' (*regnicole terre Siculiane*, i.e. freemen) and common Szeklers (*simplices, közszékelyek*), but the quality of being Szekler is not defined as a function of the existence of a geographical territory, the Szeklerland. The significance of personal military obligation in the status of Szeklership is thus brought home.

The term 'community' is progressively abandoned (last mention in 1537) in favour of references to general assemblies of the three Szekler *genera* (*congregacio generalis trium generum Siculorum*) with all the ambiguity inherent in this expression. Finally, starting in 1541, the Crown addressed itself to the community again, but now it was the community of the elite, the most powerful.

This first diminution of the Szekler community is also manifest in the designation of jury members who take an active part in the administration of justice. The term 'notable' used in this study by reason of its neutrality to designate jury members and occasionally judges and captains is not that used in the texts. The original designations are more explicit – and more subject to interpretation.

C. *'Iurati Assessores'*

Seniores, iurati assessores, pociores, maiores, superiores are the terms most often encountered. Sometimes a single designation encompasses all jury members, but not always in the same order; not to forget the ubiquitous *ceterique*, which gives free rein to interpretations regarding the representativeness of the jury.

The earliest documents show more restraint. From 1344 to 1444, we encounter only *seniores* (twelve of them in a case in 1407).[121] They are replaced by *iurati assessores* in 1448 and 1451 (twenty-four of them in the latter case),[122] but the *seniores* reappear from 1453 to 1464. The terms intermingle in 1462,[123] with a first mention of *iurati seniores*. One can reasonably presume that the hybrid term designated the same persons, once by their function in the assembly (*iurati assessores*) and then by their intrinsic quality (*seniores*). A problem arises when we try to define the second term.

It is not until 1466, the codifying assembly of Zabola, that the expression *pociores* appears, to be taken up again starting in 1501 (thirteen occurrences). In the Zabola document we also encounter the terms *maiores* and *superiores,* but while *maiores* recurs once more in 1495,[124] there is no further mention of *superiores*. The very first references to *primores* in a judiciary and not in a military context occur in 1519[125] (three occurrences). All these qualifiers are evidently used to designate an elite, differentiating them from the common Szekler. As to the term *seniores*, is it just a variant or does it designate a distinct category?

In Ch. d'Eszláry's view,[126] the term *seniores* designates the elders (from among the common Szeklers) at least until the fourteenth century, and then the 'distinguished', as opposed to the common, starting in 1466.[127] For this same date L. Makkai[128] sees both terms, *seniores* and *pociores*, covering one and the same population – the powerful – and refers to 'elder notables'. From 1466 on, at least for the three Seats involved in the assembly of Zabola, there seems to be a clear juxtaposition between *seniores* and common Szeklers: the members of a jury must be designated either from among the *seniores*, or from among the members of the 'real community'.[129] Thus *seniores* and *pociores* are notables. L. Makkai and Ch. d'Eszláry arrive at the same ratio: one-third (*seniores*) and two-thirds (*communitas*).

Yet, the pain taken to record each of the terms in the same document, following the Zabola assembly (between 1501 and 1558), suggests favouring an interpretation where the *seniores* are not necessarily notables, all the more so since, whenever several designations are used, the order of precedence is always: the *pociores* first, then the *seniores*, or the *pociores* and then the *assessores* (with one exception in 1515,[130] where the *seniores* come before the *pociores* in the Seat of Sepsi). We note that the *primores* always precede the *pociores* when both are cited. Semantic precedence meets that of protocol.

The distinctions made in Zabola in enumerating the rules allow for the safekeeping of the common Szeklers' memory. Thereafter, it is difficult to determine whether the use of the terms *pociores ac seniores* or *seniores seu maiores* is a redundancy in deference to these notables or a subtle reminder distinguishing between those designated by tradition and those superior through the acquisition of power or wealth. The royal confirmation of 1499 is no more explicit when it calls for twelve jurors (*coassessores*) from among the *primores* and other nobles and honest men.[131] Given that all Szeklers are nobles, as Werbőczy pointed out, one can only conclude that the distinction between *primores* and the rest does not exclude the presence of common Szeklers among the jury members.

The role of the jurors was to embody the memory of ancient customs and advise the *comes* accordingly for the determination of the verdict. Normally there were twelve per Seat. The total number of jurors and the quota per Seat for general assemblies of the Szekler community are nowhere indicated. While it is true that wealth and position account for a part of a jury's composition, no criterion of clan affiliation or land ownership, determining access to the office of judge or captain, was required of jurors.

D. *The Szekler Tribunal*

According to the confirmations of principle – and in practice in the individual judgements – the tribunal is composed of the Crown Judge, the captain and the judge of the Seat. The protocols of assemblies show compliance with this harmonious presentation. There are tribunals that seem to have been convened with a sense of urgency, in the context of military operations. Between 1548 and 1550, four verdicts were recorded in the fortress of Görgény (two others in the fortified town of Szamos-Újvár in northwestern Transylvania and two in Prázsmár, in the southeast).

The vice-*comes* did not act alone; four to nine other persons are listed in the protocols. A subtle nuance is the absence of judiciary titles, only the family and Christian names appear for these persons. They are all members of Szekler families eligible to the functions of Seat judge or captain, but it is pertinent that within the walls of a fortress, which was Crown territory, the Szekler titles are not given. Other protocols always show tribunals composed of a representative of the Crown, a Szekler captain and one or more Szekler judges. Adjuncts (*vice-gerentes*) are sometimes mentioned for one or another of the officials.

There is a point of terminology which, in this author's opinion, was too quickly digested by the historians who dealt with it: the designation of 'Judge of the Crown' or Crown Judge.

1. Who Was the Crown Judge? According to the royal confirmation of 1499 the answer is clear; it is the vice-*comes* of the Szeklers: '*vicecomites, qui appellantur judices regii*'. J. Conner and L. Szádeczky both accord a few lines to the role of the Crown Judge. Their analyses present this personage as the same before and after 1562. It is appropriate, however, to point out that the term refers to different functions before and after this date.

J. Connert's[132] analysis starts in 1545. That of L. Szádeczky,[133] more amply documented, is based on two questionable anterior arguments. For one, an amalgamation between 'the king's man' and the 'king's judge'. Szádeczky thus carries back the impact of royal authority within Szekler structures to 1407[134] (the first mention of a homo *regius* in a Szekler tribunal).

The expression '*homo regius*' occurs frequently in documents involving county territory, but not in a position endowed with the authority of jurisdiction. Most often, he is witness at the execution of an investiture, normally in the company of a representative of a *locus credibilis*. The term '*homo regius*' was also extended to encompass all of the lay witnesses enumerated in the protocols issued by the *loca credibilia*.[135]

This document of 1407 concerns a transfer of ownership (a fishpond in a hamlet). True, it is within the Szeklerland; hence the transaction should have been conducted under supervision of a Seat judge or Szekler captain as well as the representative of a *locus credibilis*. It so happens, however, that one of the parties is a member of a family that owns property in an enclave under royal domain (the Apor family). For a *homo regius* to be in attendance alongside the mentioned two Seat judges does no harm to the integrity of Szekler customs and it is incorrect to interpret the term *homo regius* as applying to the Szekler judges, two of them, all the more so since all are cited by name. If we follow the logical composition of a Szekler tribunal, the 'man of the king', Málnási András, lay witness to an investiture, could well be the missing captain.

The second element from which L. Szádeczky derives his interpretation that the terms Crown judge and Seat judge designate the same person starting in the fifteenth century is the Constitution of 1505. He bases his conclusion on Volume I of the *Székely Archives*, published in 1872, which contains a copy in Hungarian from the seventeenth century. By 1934, S. Barabás had the original Latin version and published it in Volume VIII.[136] In this version, no mention of a *homo regius* is to be found. János Orbán, the notary of the seat of Udvarhely who had translated the document into Hungarian, did so for practical, not historiographic purposes. In his time the expression had a different sense and his extrapolations were quite justified. The present author considers, begging to differ with the cited opinions, that, up to 1562, the term (always in the singular during the time under study here) always designated the vice-*comes* of the Szeklers, an officer named by the king, whose judicial prerogatives were delimited by the judges of the Szeklerland.

The end of the Szapolyais' reign is marked by the drastic shrinking of the territory under their control and consequently their rapacious determination to seize any opportunity to assert sovereign authority. Any title had to appear to have been granted by the king in person: 'Our royal judges, Our Szekler Seats.' Authority is like jam: the less there is, the thinner it has to be spread. Before the royal edict of 1562 – where the term 'royal judge' is effectively used for the judges of Seats – occurrences of this term in the Szeklerland appear only in conflicts with royal free towns[137] (where Crown law applies) or in connection with military operations[138] (here the vice-*comites*, though military officers, used their judiciary titles).

Following the royal decision of 1562, the term is used only for those who had formerly been entitled judge of the Seat, as appears from a later document, where another term designates the vice-*comes*: *Officii Judicatus Regii*.[139] But if the vice-*comites* (the first-line royal judges) were effectively named by the king, the judges of the Szeklerland, now called royal judges, continued to be designated by the Szeklers until 1849. From 1562 on, those who in the period under study here were Seat Judges, were referred to as 'royal judges', which explains the translation by the notary of Udvarhely. Not to forget, however, that the term designates two different categories according to whether it is used before or after the decree of 1562.

2. The Judge of the Seat (iudex terrestris) He is at the centre of judiciary life in the Szeklerland. Like the captain, he represents the Szekler community – and he owes his office not to the king but to the traditional Szekler criteria of designation – and has an active role in the determination of justice at the Seat tribunals. It is also he who is charged with the fact-finding investigation in a case and the execution of the verdict.

He is also the principal target of criticism and recrimination in the constitution of 1505. These attacks demonstrate not only the abuses committed but also the power vested in him by the community and the importance attached to his function. The mode of designation of a judge, as of the captain, evolved during the period under study (and will be dealt with in the next section).

3. The Captain While the judge of a Seat is nowhere involved in the Szekler military organization, the captain is indispensable in its judiciary structure. Between 1407 and 1461, the nomenclature used for this military authority varies like that of the judge. Originally *primipilus*[140] or *maior exercitus* he became *capitaneus maior exercitus* from 1451 on; after 1464 he is always referred to by the sole title of 'captain'. This is the only occurrence of this curious combination of titles. We should note, incidentally, that this document exists only in a copy made by J. Benkő, a transcriber with a notoriously inventive bent. A decision of the Assembly of the Three Nations dated 1439[141] does not bother with Szekler etiquette and refers to *ductores*.

The notion of *primipilus*, which turns up again in the military reorganization of 1473, is inseparable from that of the primipilate (*primipilatus*), this plot of Szekler land that is the emblem of the function of judges and captains.

III. The Paradox of the Primipilate

Let us return once again to Werbőczy: '[Szeklers] who (following their ancient customs) share out their possessions and functions among their tribes and clans.' In the early sixteenth century, the tribal system is still in place.

A. The Principles of Eligibility to the Dignities of Judge and Captain

Jury members, we have seen, were designated from among both the common Szeklers and the more powerful. As for the designation of judges (and captains; in this section the term 'dignitary' – or 'dignity' for the office – covers both categories), the determining factor both for access to these dignities and the rights to the land associated with them, was belonging to a clan. The Latin term *judices eligerentur* and the context observed in the assemblies of 1505 and 1506 suggest that judges were elected by the populace. To avoid anachronism, it would undoubtedly be more appropriate to speak of a designation of dignitaries, for their 'election' was subject to immutable, clan-related conditions of eligibility.

A shift can be observed at the end of the fifteenth century, when the possession of clan land – the primipilate – became the determining factor for eligibility, whereas before, clan land was attributed to the elected dignitary for the duration of his mandate. The shift was undoubtedly slow and progressive, a result of the adoption of a settled lifestyle by the Szeklers. As they turned from animal husbandry to agriculture, it became less convenient to redistribute the clans' land among them annually, a practice characteristic of a pure clan structure.

Yet, even after the personal ownership of land had become a condition for eligibility, the condition itself was limited to clan-held land – the primipilates – and the principle of annual rotation remained in place, now applied to the dignity. There is no trace of a single judge or captain who did not own a primipilate. Ownership of land did not of itself qualify for eligibility. Mandates were always for one year at a time. It was a rotational system and for one dignity at a time: when it is a given clan's turn, one of its members is designated judge or captain but never for both functions, as opposed to the representative of the Crown, who had both judiciary and military authority.

There was misconduct by dignitaries, as witness the uprisings of the community and condemnation of dignitaries to banishment: in the Seat of Maros in 1498,[142] Csík in 1511,[143] and Sepsi in 1520.[144] Some individuals, aware of the constraints imposed by the Szekler system in comparison to the private justice exercised by the nobles in the neighbouring counties, started avidly collecting primipilates to multiply their chances of access to Szekler dignities – but in strict observance of Szekler customary law.

1. From Land that Comes with the Function ... Let us return to the earlier times, to the period – from which unfortunately we are not blessed with written records – when land did not yet have the value it gained in the fifteenth century, when animal husbandry dominated the Szekler economy – a characteristic that puts in context the tradition of the branded oxen. At that time land was redistributed annually to the families, a practice that did not pose as much of a problem in a cattle-raising economy as it would in a society of farmers. The plots – for a time possibly delimited by arrow-shot[145] – were not all of the same size. Upon designation, dignitaries were assigned larger plots than the others, plots of land known as 'primipilates' (*primipilatus, lófőség*).

The Szekler system of dignities was a rotating system. Rotation was annual, as a rule. We can assume that a term of office traditionally started in the spring, because a green branch (*zöld ág, arbor frondosa viva*) was affixed to the gate to identify the home of the newly designated dignitary, a custom that persisted to the end of the period under study here.[146] One may conclude that the redistribution of land also took place in the spring, logically enough in a society of cattle raisers, but not practical in an agricultural society.

2. ... to Land as a Condition for Access to the Function Let us go directly to the last century covered in this study, replete as it is with sources, abounding in references; to a clan system that was still in place, but also to these curious plots of land that constitute primipilates. The Szekler community had long settled, conditions for accomplishing military obligations had changed; the need was more for metal – armour or tinkling loads of coin – than for personal valour.

For a long time already, as tilling the soil rather than putting cattle to pasture had become the Szeklers' primary occupation, part of the land formerly owned jointly by the clan had, generation after generation, been worked by the same families. Eventually, ownership of these plots of land also passed on from generation to generation, but conditioned on membership in the clan: land previously attributed to dignitaries mandated for one year ceased to rotate with the green branches. Late in the fifteenth century, it was the ownership of such a plot of land, a primipilate, that constituted entitlement – but still always in the name of the clan – to be designated for a term of Szekler office.

But if land can be transmitted from generation to generation by inheritance, it can also be transmitted by marriage, in fact, theoretically, bought and sold. In spite of the severe restrictions governing the alienation of hereditary Szekler land (the subject of the next chapter) some non-Szekler Hungarians did succeed in acquiring primipilates and assuming dignities of judge and captain – in strict compliance with Szekler customary law, when the clan of their primipilate had its turn. We know of at least two of them: Gáspár Barcsai and Lénárt Apafi. But perhaps Lénárt Apafi is the only case. The ancestry of Gáspár Barcsai is not clear. Genealogies do present a Transylvanian family named Barcsai, but no Gáspár corresponding to the period concerned by the documentation. Two considerations lead the present author to the conclusion that it is nevertheless the same family. Firstly, that there is no Szekler village name in the family name of our Gáspár and, secondly, the frequent occurrences of this Christian name in the Transylvanian Barcsai family. What is more, Barcsai – like Apafi – owes his primipilate-related entitlements to the inheritance of his Szekler wife. This said, a true Szekler, Miklós Tóth, also obtained his entitlements by marriage.

If we follow the logic of the constitution of 1505, it appears that their entitlement to Szekler clan office was deemed lawful – even though acquired by marriage to Szekler heiresses. A point of particular interest is that they, though natives of an environment where land-owners were *de facto* and *de jure* judge and jury over all those in their service, readily accepted the rules of the Szekler community. But it was maybe precisely this difference that motivated their acquisition – by virtue of the clan rights held by their wives – of numerous primipilates. Possibly also a roundabout way of reconstituting at least part of their double prerogative (land-ownership and juridical power) on Szekler soil, but always with at least formal observance of Szekler customs.

For, while it is true that each primipilate gave access to only one of the two dignities and only for the year in which it is the clan's turn, there was nothing to prevent ownership of several primipilates, each in the name of a different clan, and thus open the way more often to the possibility of exercising power. It is true also that our two Hungarians, but also certain Szekler families, were avid collectors of primipilates.

The story of the origin of the Seat of Kászon[147] is evidence that taking several turns at holding office was well accepted by the population:

> They [the inhabitants of Kászon] were happy at the news and to a man all agreed to have confidence in Bálint Lázár and even to entrust to him the dignities, which he could exercise <u>in the name of each of their six tribes</u> [*nemek*] <u>as its turn came up</u> and at the end of each mandate he was to be received into another tribe until the Halom tribe's turn came up again, when he would assume in the name of Halom, but that he safeguard their liberty and protect them against all abuses of authority […/…] And Bálint Lázár started assuming the functions, as the people had promised, but he died before he had exercised them in the name of each of the six and his son András Lázár assumed them after him. When all the tribes had had their turn, the people said:
> 'Sir, come and join the tribe of Halom.'
> And the members of the tribe of Halom said:

'It is not just for us to keep him to ourselves and deprive the other tribes, for Bálint Lázár fought for us all.'

Finally they agreed that the successors of Bálint Lázár should be judges one year, the second year neither judge nor captain and in the third year captain again.

The situation was less harmonious in the Seat of Csík.[148] There, an uprising in 1511 may have been motivated by the dignitaries' stance favouring Kászon's independence, rather than their misconduct in office.

3. The Number of Dignitaries by Seat Throughout the documentation we find two or three dignitaries present at a tribunal held within a Seat assembly. From the royal free towns' recriminations[149] in 1492 we learn that 'only one-third of the judges' were invited to attend tribunals held within the towns. True, at the assembly of 1505 seventeen judges were elected for just the Seat of Udvarhely (with a mention of the sub-Seat of Keresztúr), but this is the only documented example of such an election and the context in which the assembly was held suggests that the designation of such a large number of judges was exceptional, rather than the traditional rule.

The decisions of judiciary assemblies practically never mention the names of judges and captains in office, so caution is in order for the definitive assertions to follow, but we maintain our view that 1505 was an anomaly. Can it be that this election was really in keeping with tradition or is it more likely to have been a determined and thorough reshuffling of the dignitaries?

It is the only document which describes the procedure (presentation of candidates to office before the assembly, election of the dignitaries by the population, followed by their swearing-in) and gives the names of the dignitaries elected. Many of them can be found in the genealogies and in the *Székely Archives* and they are, true to tradition, members of families belonging to clans. But was the sequential order of rotation in office respected or are we dealing here with a faction of notables acting in protest against the corrupt judges mentioned at the outset of the assembly's minutes? Was this designation of seventeen judges organized to redefine mandates for several years or was it for one year only, but more than one per office?

There are two arguments in favour of a reshuffling: the rebellious context of the assembly and the signatories' apparent determination to record the names of the new judges. And yet, only seven of the Udvarhely judges reappear in 1506, when a new constitution is voted for by all of the seats.

The distribution of dignitaries by seat is shown in Table 17.

This distribution shows a measure of regularity, but also some curious adaptations have taken place to achieve it. We have our sacrosanct number of seven Seats, but the aligning of the Seats Csík and Kézdi together is a first. If we include the sub-Seats, we get the breakdown in Table 18.

The Practice of Law: Legal Procedure in the Szeklerland

Table 17. Dignitaries per Seat (1506)

Seat	Dignitaries	Note
Udvarhely	7	Incl. the president
Maros & Aranyos	7	
Csík & Kézdi	10	
Sepsi & Orbai	7	

Table 18. Breakdown of Dignitaries by Seat and Sub-Seat

Seat	Sub-Seat	Dignitaries	Totals (1506)
Udvarhely		5	
	Keresztúr	2	7
Maros		5	
Aranyos		2	7
Csík		3	
	Gyergyó	2	
	Kászon	2	
Kézdi		3	10
Sepsi		3	
	Miklósvár ?	2	
Orbai		2	7

It is, of course, a purely theoretical breakdown, but it has the advantage of giving a number by Seat of dignitaries signing the constitution of 1506 in proportions that agree with the rest of the documentation of the archives. It gives one captain and one or two judges (and two adjuncts?) each for Udvarhely and Maros), but only if the structure officially accepted the existence of sub-Seats, which is not expressly admitted in the constitution. On the other hand, it is worth mentioning in this context that the constitution of 1505 does mention both Udvarhely and Keresztúr.

Another interpretation is also possible, however: the entitlements of one and the same clan could have been shared out between several individuals in the course of successions. Then the distribution would not be by Seat and sub-Seat, but by identifying several signatories with one and the same dignity. Such groupings, resulting from matrimonial alliances, are difficult to trace through the sparse genealogical data available for the signatories' families in that period of time.

There are nevertheless indications supporting this interpretation: a pair of brothers (Benedekfi) are cited for the Seat of Udvarhely; for the other Seats, there are names that we find associated with the same clan entitlements (Gyalakuti and Barcsai, Tóth and Alárd for the Seat of Maros; Lázár and Betz, Apor and Baláskó for the Seats of Csík and Kézdi; Kálnoki and Mikó for the Seat of Sepsi). Thus a partial breakdown with this interpretation could be as follows:

Table 19. Distribution of Dignities by Seat and Family

Seat	Dignities	Dignitaries	Totals (1506)
Udvarhely	4	The president Nyujtódi & Kacsai Two brothers: Benedekfi	7
Maros & Aranyos	5	Gyalakuti & Barcsai Tóth & Alárd	7
Csík & Kézdi	8	Lázár & Betz Apor & Baláskó	10
Sepsi & Orbai	6	Kálnoki & Mikó	7

The grouping of the Seats of Csík and Kézdi could thus be explained by an alliance between the Lázár and Betz families. But more genealogical data would be needed to prove this hypothesis for the distribution of dignities.

Lack of precise sources prevents us pursuing our verification of the practical application of documented principles in all of the Szeklerland. But in the attempt to reconstruct for 1506 the manner in which the dignities were shared out we have seen that a clan structure can be articulated around the distribution of functions in each Seat or around family alliances across several Seats.

The Seat of Maros is the only one to have bequeathed us fairly complete data and several documents of sale or succession to permit an analysis of the distribution of primipilates: by clan, by family and by village.

B. The Case of the Seat of Maros in the Early Sixteenth Century

We have three registers with the sequence of clan entitlements for the Seat of Maros from the first half of the sixteenth century.[150] The same six tribes and the same twenty-four clans appear in all three of these documents:

Table A. The Six Tribes and Twenty-four Clans of the Seat of Maros (in alphabetical order)

Tribes	Clans	Tribes	Clans	Tribes	Clans
Ábrán	Gerő	Halom	György	Meggyes	Dudor
	Karácson		Halom		Gyáros

The Practice of Law: Legal Procedure in the Szeklerland

Tribes	Clans	Tribes	Clans	Tribes	Clans
	Nagy		Náznán		Kürt
	Uj		Péter		Meggyes
Adorján	Poson	Jenő	Balási	Örlöcz	Bod
	Telegd		Boroszló		Eczken
	Vácsmán		Nagy (Uj)		Seprőd
	Vaja		Szomorú		Szovát

Two of these registers[151] give a detailed account of the sequence of rotation in each of the dignities in exactly the same order. The most recent (1557) adds the names of the families vested in the dignities during the period from 1491 to 1514.

Table B. The Sequential Order of Rotation for the Dignities of Captain and Judge. Seat of Maros, 1491 to 1514 (In parentheses): tribe and clan reintegrated by K. Szabó into the list of the manuscript.

CAPTAIN Tribes	Clans	Years	JUDGE Tribes	Clans
Örlöcz	Bod	**1491**	Jenő	Boroszló
Jenő	Szomorú	**1492**	Adorján	Poson
Meggyes	Meggyes	**1493**	Ábrán	Nagy
Adorján	Telegd	**1494**	Örlöcz	Bod
Ábrán	Nagy	**1495**	(Halom	György)
(Halom	György)	**1496**	Meggyes	Kürt
Örlöcz	Szovát	**1497**	Jenő	Balási
Jenő	Nagy (Uj)	**1498**	Adorján	Váczmán
Meggyes	Dudor	**1499**	Ábrán	Uj
Adorján	Poson	**1500**	Örlöcz	Eczken
Ábrán	Gerő	**1501**	Halom	Péter
Halom	Halom	**1502**	Meggyes	Dudor
Örlöcz	Seprőd	**1503**	Jenő	Szomorú
Jenő	Boroszló	**1504**	Adorján	Vaja

CAPTAIN Tribes	Clans	Years	JUDGE Tribes	Clans
Meggyes	Kürt	1505	Ábrán	Karácson
Adorján	Vácsmán	1506	Örlöcz	Seprőd
Ábrán	Uj	1507	Halom	Halom
Halom	Náznán	1508	Meggyes	Gyáros
Örlöcz	Eczken	1509	Jenő	Waij (Wij)
Jenő	Balási	1510	Adorján	Telegd
Meggyes	Gyáros	1511	Ábrán	Gerő
Adorján	Vaja	1512	Örlöcz	Szovát
Ábrán	Karácson	1513	Halom	Náznán
Halom	Péter	1514	Meggyes	Meggyes

Table C. The Families Occupying the Dignities in the Seat of Maros from 1491 to 1514

Captains	Tribes	Clans	Years	Tribes	Clans	Judges
BARCSAI GYALAKUTI	Örlöcz	Bod	1491	Jenő	Boroszló	TÓTH Szentgyörgyi
BARCSAI APAFI	Jenő	Szomorú	1492	Adorján	Poson	TÓTH
BARCSAI	Meggyes	Meggyes	1493	Ábrán	Nagy	*Zancijali*
BICSAK *Pijnkolccij*	Adorján	Telegd	1494	Örlöcz	Bod	BARCSAI GYALAKUTI
BICSAK de Szentpál	Ábrán	Nagy	1495	(Halom	György)	(–)
(–)	(Halom	György)	1496	Meggyes	Kürt	GYALAKUTI *Cijanij*
KERELŐI Jánossi	Örlöcz	Szovát	1497	Jenő	Balási	BICSAK
TÓTH Szentgyörgyi	Jenő	Nagy (Uj)	1498	Adorján	Váczmán	GYALAKUTI
APAFI	Meggyes	Dudor	1499	Ábrán	Uj	KERELŐI
TÓTH	Adorján	Poson	1500	Örlöcz	Eczken	BICSAK
KERELŐI Márton	Ábrán	Gerő	1501	Halom	Péter	BICSAK TÓTFALVI

The Practice of Law: Legal Procedure in the Szeklerland

Captains	Tribes	Clans	Years	Tribes	Clans	Judges
BARCSAI GYALAKUTI	Halom	Halom	1502	Meggyes	Dudor	BICSAK GYALAKUTI *Pijnkolccij*
–	Örlöcz	Seprőd	1503	Jenő	Szomorú	– [Barcsai ?] [Apafi ?]
TÓTH	Jenő	Boroszló	1504	Adorján	Vaja	–
BARCSAI GYALAKUTI	Meggyes	Kürt	1505	Ábrán	Karácson	APAFI
GYALAKUTI	Adorján	Vácsmán	1506	Örlöcz	Seprőd	Balassi
KERELŐI	Ábrán	Uj	1507	Halom	Halom	BARCSAI GYALAKUTI
Lázár	Halom	Náznán	1508	Meggyes	Gyáros	APAFI Márton
BICSAK	Örlöcz	Eczken	1509	Jenő	Waij (Wij)	– [Tóth ?]
BICSAK GYALAKUTI	Jenő	Balási	1510	Adorján	Telegd	BICSAK
APAFI	Meggyes	Gyáros	1511	Ábrán	Gerő	BARCSAI GYALAKUTI
–	Adorján	Vaja	1512	Örlöcz	Szovát	Mikó
APAFI	Ábrán	Karácson	1513	Halom	Náznán	Lázár BICSAK
–	Halom	Péter	1514	Meggyes	Meggyes	BARCSAI

CAPITAL LETTERS: family names recurring three times or more.
Lower case: family names listed once or twice.
Italics: family names not identifiable in the manuscript.
(in parentheses): tribes and clans reintegrated by K. Szabó into the list of the manuscript.
[in square brackets?]: families holding the other function in the name of the same clan/tribe,
? possibly holders of undivided entitlements.

1. The Sharing out of Dignities between the Clans The dignities seem to have been spread widely, each clan taking its turn only every twenty-four years in each dignity (Table B). The sequential order in which turns are taken by the tribes (and within the tribes, the clans) is not the same for each dignity. If we assign numbers to the tribes holding the captaincy by chronological sequence (1, 2, 3, 4, 5, 6), the same tribes (the same numbers) turn up in a different order for the judgeship (2, 4, 5, 1, 6, 3). The same can be observed with the clans; if we number the turns at the captaincy sequentially, we find the clans acceding to the judgeship in six different combinations (1, 4, 3, 2), (3, 4, 1, 2), (3, 2, 4, 1), (2, 3, 4, 1), then (1, 3, 4, 2) and (1, 4, 2, 3). Which suggests either a well-trained memory or the existence of a register copied several times over.

2. Sharing in, and Concentration of, Clan Rights by Families All the while, we find fewer families than clans: seventeen names of families, perhaps eighteen (the eighteenth name, Semjén, could be a Christian name; if so, it would go with the Gyalakuti family). Within these families, six share twenty-eight of the forty-eight mandates (twenty-four clans times two mandates, captaincy and judgeship, Table C).

On the other hand, all the entitlements of a clan were not necessarily held by the same family. It appears that they could be divided into two-halves, one-half and two-quarters, or four-quarters (Table D). This is confirmed by sales records involving halves and quarters of properties.[152] There are other situations in which the rights are held by a family but the dignities – and probably in particular the revenues that accrue from them – are shared by two heirs. This is the case of the clans of Jenő-Nagy and Jenő-Boroszló, shared by Miklós Tóth and György Szentgyörgyi, his uncle by marriage (the circumstances of this particularly contested division are dealt with in the following chapter). It is possible that the four instances of association between the Barcsai and Gyalakuti families (Örlöcz-Bod, Ábrán-Gerő, Halom-Halom and Meggyes-Kürt) were similarly due to matrimonial alliances.

Clan entitlements can be shared by halves between the dignities and each dignity can be held by two families or two individuals of the same family (the original documents list certain family names in the plural; no doubt these are brothers who together bear one-quarter of a clan entitlement). It is not clear whether there is a sequential order in the sharing of dignities or whether it varies according to whether the division is the result of a sale (division by two, each in turn divided into quarters) or a succession (division in two-halves of each of the two dignities of judge and captain).

The entitlements of the Adorján-Telegd clan are held by two families for the dignity of judge, while for that of captain only one family is mentioned. The same is true for the entitlements of the Örlöcz-Szovát clan. The sharing of the Meggyes-Kürt clan's rights involves three families, but the family holding one-half of the rights in fact has one-quarter of the rights to the judgeship and one-quarter of the captaincy rights. In the cases just discussed, on the other hand, the dignity of judge was entirely held by one family.

Table D. Clan Rights to Dignities Borne by Families (C: Captain; J: Judge)

Tribes Clans	APA	BAR	BIC	GYA	KER	TÓT	Other families	No. of families Parts
Örlöcz Bod		C J		C J				2 (¼ + ¼) - (¼ + ¼)
Jenő Szomorú	C [J?]	C [J?]						2 or more ½ ? - ½ ?
Meggyes Meggyes		C J						1
Adorján Telegd			C J				C *Pijnkolccij*	3 (½ + ¼) - ¼
Ábrán Nagy			C -				C de Szentpál J *Zancijali*	3 ¼ - ¼ - ½
(Halom György)							(–) (–)	–
Örlöcz Szovát					C -		C Jánossi J Mikó	3 ¼ - ¼ - ½
Jenő Nagy (Uj)						C [J?]	C Szentgyörgyi	1 ou 2 (¼ + ½ ?) - ¼
Meggyes Dudor	C -		- J	- J			J *Pinkolccij*	3 ou 4 ½ - (¼ - ¼) - ½
Adorján Poson						C J		1
Ábrán Gerő		- J		- J	C -		C Márton	4 ¼ - ¼ - ¼ - ¼
Halom Halom		C J		C J				2 (¼ + ¼) - (¼ + ¼)

Tribes Clans	APA	BAR	BIC	GYA	KER	TÓT	Other families	No. of families Parts
Örlöcz Sepröd							C – J Balassi	1 or more ½ - ?
Jenő Boroszló						CJ	J Szentgyörgyi	1 ou 2
Meggyes Kürt		C –		CJ			J Cijanij	3 ¼ - (¼ + ¼) - ¼
Adorján Vácsmán				CJ				1
Ábrán Uj				CJ				1
Halom Náznán			– J				C Lázár J Lázár	2 ¼ - (½ + ¼)
Örlöcz Eczken			CJ					1
Jenő Balási			CJ	C –				2 or more (¼ + ¼)- ¼ - ?
Meggyes Gyáros	CJ						J Márton	2 ou plus (¼ + ¼)- ¼ - ?
Adorján Vaja							C – J –	–
Ábrán Karácson	CJ							1
Halom Péter			– J				C – J Tóthfalvi	2 or more ¼ - ¼ - ?

Read: **APA**FI, **BAR**CSAI, **BIC**SAK, **GYA**LAKUTI, **KERELŐI**, **TÓTH**

The Ábrán-Gerő clan's rights are shared between four families. We cannot be sure about the rights of the Meggyes-Dudor clan. Either we admit that the two families jointly hold, by succession, one-quarter of the rights to the judgeship (or the Bicsak and Gyalakuti families, who also share rights of the Jenő-Balási clan; or the Bicsak and *Pijnkolccij* families who share between them the entitlements of the Adorján-Telegd clan), or we assume that the halves of dignities can in turn be divided by thirds. If we accept the latter hypothesis, we find the same situation if we consider Semjén to be a family name. The dignity of captain, held in the name of the Ábrán-Gerő and Halom-Halom clans, would also be seen to be divided into thirds.

It is worth noting that each of the six families most often exercising the dignities detains the totality of the undivided entitlements of a clan – and only one clan:

Table E. The Six Principal Families Bearing Dignities in the Seat of Maros (1499–1514)

Family	Tribe-Clan
Apafi	Ábrán-Karácson
Barcsai	Meggyes-Meggyes
Bicsak	Örlöcz-Eczken
Gyalakuti	Adorján-Vácsmán
Kerelői	Ábrán-Uj
Tóth	Adorján-Poson

To the detriment of symmetry, the six families are not spread across six different tribes.

Whereas within a clan one can observe that the two mandates are assumed at irregular intervals (Table F) within the period of twenty-four years, the above six families return to office more frequently (Table G and G.1) by accumulation and assumption of partial dignities, hoarding the dignities without interruption.

In all, through concentration and division, and to different degrees in the different clans, the six families turn up forty-five times in twenty-four years. Which leads the present author to be sceptical concerning attempts to estimate the number of primipilates on the basis of the twenty-four clans. The numbers developed by Gy. Bodor[153] make for stimulating reading but are, in this author's opinion, quite hypothetical.

Table F: Rotation of Dignities (C: captain; J: judge)

Tribes Clans	1491	1492	1493	1494	1495	1496	1497	1498	1499	1500	1501	1502	1503	1504	1505	1506	1507	1508	1509	1510	1511	1512	1513	1514	1515
Örlöcz Bod	C																								
Jenő Szomorú		C		J																					
Meggyes Meggyes			C																						J
Adorján Telegd				C												J									
Ábrán Nagy			J		C																				
(Halom György)						J	C																		
Örlöcz Szovát								C													J				
Jenő Nagy (Uj)									C								J								
Meggyes Dudor													C	C	J										
Adorján Poson	J										C		C												
Ábrán Gerő												C										J			

The Practice of Law: Legal Procedure in the Szeklerland

Tribes	Clans	1491	1492	1493	1494	1495	1496	1497	1498	1499	1500	1501	1502	1503	1504	1505	1506	1507	1508	1509	1510	1511	1512	1513	1514
Halom	Halom												C												
Örlöcz	Seprőd													C			J								
Jenő	Boroszló	J													C										
Meggyes	Kürt						J									C									
Adorján	Vácsmán								J								C								
Ábrán	Uj									J								C							
Halom	Náznán												J						C						
Örlöcz	Eczken															J				C					
Jenő	Balási																	J			C				
Meggyes	Gyáros																				J	C			
Adorján	Vaja															J							C		
Ábrán	Karácson																J							C	
Halom	Péter										J														C

Table G. Rotation of Dignities within the Six Most Frequently Cited Families (C: captain; J: judge)

Families	1491	1492	1493	1494	1495	1496	1497	1498	1499	1500	1501	1502	1503	1504	1505	1506	1507	1508	1509	1510	1511	1512	1513	1514
Apafi	C								C	J?			J							C		C		
Barcsai	C	C	C	J						C	J?		C				J							J
Bicsak				C	C		J			J	J	J			C	C	J					J		
Gyalakuti	C			J			J			C J				C	C	J				C	J			
Kerelői							C			J		C				C								
Tóth	J	J										C			C	C			J?					

The Practice of Law: Legal Procedure in the Szeklerland 129

Table G.1 Rotation of Dignities within Families, by Clan (C: captain; J: judge)

Families	Tribes Clans	Captain	Judge
Apafi	Jenő Szomorú	1492	1503 ?
	Meggyes Dudor	1499	
	Meggyes Gyáros	1511	1508
	Ábrán Karácson	1513	1505
Barcsai	Örlöcz Bod	1491	1494
	Jenő Szomorú	1492	1503 ?
	Meggyes Meggyes	1493	1514
	Ábrán Gerő		1511
	Halom Halom	1502	1507
	Meggyes Kürt	1505	
Bicsak	Adorján Telegd	1494	1510
	Ábrán Nagy	1495	
	Meggyes Dudor		1502
	Halom Náznán		1513
	Örlöcz Eczken	1509	1500
	Jenő Balási	1510	1497
	Halom Péter		1501
Gyalakuti	Örlöcz Bod	1491	1494
	Meggyes Dudor		1502
	Ábrán Gerő		1511
	Halom Halom	1502	1507
	Meggyes Kürt	1505	1496
	Adorján Vácsmán	1506	1498
	Jenő Balási	1510	
Kerelői	Örlöcz Szovát	1497	
	Ábrán Gerő	1501	
	Ábrán Uj	1507	1499
Tóth	Jenő Nagy (Uj)	1498	1509 ?
	Adorján Poson	1500	1492
	Jenő Boroszló	1504	1491

3. Presence of Clans and Primipilates in the Villages These registers dating from the end of the period under study deal only with clans; they say nothing that would permit us to localize the associated primipilates. But by the early sixteenth century it is possible to locate these clan entitlements by analysing the sales and conflicts of succession involving primipilates. In the *Székely Archives*, we find information on sixteen primipilates of seven clans in fourteen villages in the Seat of Maros in twelve documents dated between 1485 and 1517.

To this documented list of primipilates (see legend beneath Map of the Seat of Maros) we have added the six villages, the names of which correspond to the names of clans. The *Székely Archives* contain other documents dealing with the inheritance or sale of primipilates, but they lack two elements of information: clan references and rights to dignities. These incomplete primipilates are subject to the same, restrictive conditions concerning alienation as the clan primipilates with associated dignities, but it seems that the term (in Hungarian in *lófőség*) in this case designates Szekler family land (sometimes called *siculicalium* in Latin) and not clan land; Gy. Bodor refers to them as 'common primipilates' and includes them in his calculations. Such siculicates have not been included in the map.

The borders of the territory circumscribe the Seat (the open space at the eastern end of the Seat represents a thinly populated, mountainous area between the Maros valley and the plateau of Gyergyó). A line drawn to connect the outermost villages with primipilates shows that these form a parallel to the borders of the Seat (the dotted line on the map). Most likely these emplacements are of ancient origin, they present characteristics of military positioning (the dignities are placed along the periphery) and occupation of a territory.

Map 6. Twenty Villages of the Seat of Maros with Primipilates (Late Fifteenth Century)

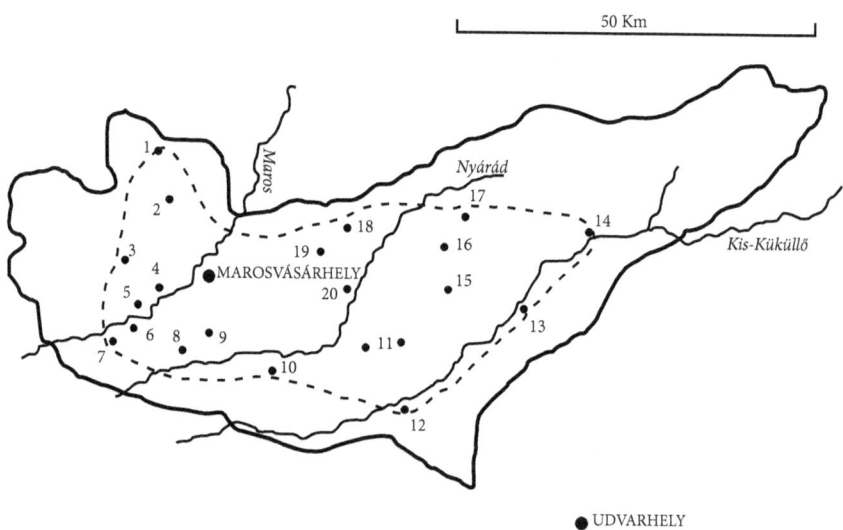

Solid line: Seat border
Dotted line: Villages with the outermost primipilates

N°	Village	Tribe-Clan	Families	Sources (Year, SzOkl)
1	Mezömajos	–	Apafi	1496, III.503
2	Bánd	Meggyes-Meggyes	Barcsai	1501, III.518
3	Panit	Ábran-Új	Alárd vs Frátai	1524, II.CCLIII
4	Kisfalud	Meggyes-Dudor Meggyes-Kürt Halom-Náznan	Lázár vs Tóth	1508, I.CCXXIX
5	Meggyesfalva	Meggyes- –	–	Toponymie
6	Nyárádtö	–	Apafi	1485, III.488
7	Lörinczfalva	Halom-Péter	Tóth vs Bicsak	1502, VIII.113
8	Szentmiklós	–	Márton de Szentbenedek	1497, III.505
9	Nyárádkarácson	Ábrán-Karácson	–	Toponymie
10	Székelyvaja	Adorján-Vaja	–	Toponymie
11	Kis- & NagyAdorján	Adorján- –	–	Toponymie
12	Havadtö	Meggyes-Meggyes	Barcsai	1501, VIII.112
13	Kibéd	Örlöcz-Szováth	Barcsai	1499, I.CCXVI
14	Szováta	Örlöcz-Szováth	–	Toponymie
15	Kendö	Halom-Náznan	Boncza	1509, VIII.133
16	Maja	Meggyes-Meggyes	Boncza	1509, VIII.133
17	Seprőd	Örlöcz-Seprőd	–	Topon.
18	Nyárádszentmárton	–	Káli	1498, VIII.110
19	Kisszentlörincz	Örlöcz-Szováth	Barcsai	1499, I.CCXVI
20	Sárd	Ábrán-Új	Bicsak	1517, VIII.147

The Szekler dignities are tied to the clan structure, even when the latter passes from transmission by succession to being tied to the possession of clan lands, dignities of captain and judge are always granted on behalf of the clans. Not even the entry of Hungarian nobles late in the fifteenth century brought any change to this structure. The conditions of land ownership remained an essential aspect of Szekler customary law.

Chapter V

LAND OWNERSHIP

Land. From the earliest times and documents, Szekler society was essentially structured around the occupancy and use of land. We have seen that the judiciary and military dignities, closely tied to clan membership, gradually became linked to plots of land, the ownership of which had become the very expression of clan law. Land – its ownership and the rules governing its alienation – has a dominant place in the documents from the mid-fifteenth century on.

Military valour and the chancy material fortunes of booty or animal husbandry lost significance as the hardy Szekler society settled. Booty-hunting started taking on new forms: dowry-chasing, inheritance-grabbing. All through the records of the Convent of Kolozsmonostor we see some families consolidating their fortunes, while others appear only for an instant, to mortgage or sell property. There is a first group of Szeklers who have left us traces of vicissitudes involving land ownership: families receiving royal donations. The documents dealing with these cases shed light on how contrary this form of private ownership of Crown land was to Szekler custom. Later, as alienations multiplied, we perceive compromises, accommodations in customary law, even as it was being fixed in writing, no longer impermeable to influences of the society of Estates. And yet, in glimpses of out-of-court settlements, in debates at legal procedures before Szekler Assemblies, we find the ancient clan rules perpetuated in daily practice.

The Szeklerland as a whole had a privileged status and was not subject to Crown law. This juridical autonomy did not tolerate donation or confiscation of land by the Crown within the Szeklerland. It engendered a sophisticated system of succession in which, in the case of escheat of a family in its broadest sense, succession passed to the village or the Seat[1] which redistributes the property, never to the Crown. But there were distinctions of status between different plots of Szekler land: some were subject to customs that closely resemble the rules of civil law as we know it, but special plots, which we shall call 'hereditary Szekler property' ('Szekler heritage', 'Siculicate', *Siculicalium* in the documents), though individually owned, were subject to rules of alienation restricted by rights reflecting clan afiliations. Within this category of hereditary land, some property had more value than others; these were the so-called 'primipilates' (*Primipilatum, vulgo lofewsegh* (lófőség) in the documents), ownership of which was the condition for access to the dignities of judge and captain. A Szekler could own land outside the Szeklerland, and a non-

Szekler was not hermetically excluded from acquiring hereditary Szekler property, but the latter created situations when gaining access to hereditary land entailed lengthy disputes concerning the choice of applicable law – Szekler or royal – to the enthusiastic joy of present-day historians of law.

In the following we will see a few, unsuccessful attempts in the thirteenth to fourteenth centuries to modify the borders of the Szeklerland (the integration of Hungarian families and their land in the Szeklerland and royal donation of adjoining county land to Szekler families), the rules governing the alienation of hereditary Szekler land, the rules of succession and, finally, some attempts – also unsuccessful – to confiscate Szekler land prior to the royal decrees of 1562.

I. Prohibition of Royal Donations and Confiscations in the Szeklerland

In 1456, a royal donation bordering Szekler and Saxon land explicitly states that the property rights it confers are limited by those of the adjoining land, the Crown's own, 'the royal fortresses', as well as Saxon and Szekler land.[2] Szekler land could neither be donated nor confiscated. While in the course of centuries its precise borders are sometimes difficult to define, it appears nevertheless that it could not be reduced by as much as a hide, nor could it be added to.

A. Hungarian Families and Szekler Land

The case of the family of Laurencius (between 1270 and 1280)[3] shows the Crown powerless to impose its will in the face of refusal by the Szekler community: less than a generation after the devastating passage of the Mongols, a time when the bravery of the Szeklers was common knowledge, King Stephen V established a writ asking the Szekler community of Telegd, with explicit mention of its rights,[4] to accept in their midst one Laurencius and his sons and especially his land, adjoining theirs, which he removed from the authority of the voivode. The writ adds that the Szekler community should thus extend their protection to the newcomers. In *Erdélyi okmánytár*[5] it is noted that this original document on vellum, with fragments of a pendant seal, conserved in the manuscript collection of the Hungarian Academy of Science[6] can be considered suspect due to spelling and linguistic errors. There is no suggestion of an alternative origin or dating, however.

This donation was reiterated by King Ladislas IV in 1279, no doubt because it had never been successfully carried through. The document states that the land in question would no longer be under the authority of the voivode, but says nothing about the status of its inhabitants. It is precisely this question of the personal status of the inhabitants – not necessarily free men – that may have been the reason for the Szeklers' refusal to accept integration of the two villages in question. A document dated 1478[7] mentions one of the villages – still situated in county territory.

At about the same time and similarly affected by the passage of the Mongols, the situation of the Toroczkay family was somewhat different. The Szeklers had valiantly fought the Mongols at the base of the fortress of Toroczkó[8] and in the following years,[9] between 1252 and 1272, the family gave the Szeklers of Aranyos and their descendants the right to use their family's lands on condition that they stay in place and ensure the family's armed protection.

The document states that the Toroczkay family conserved all rights of seigniorial ownership to the castle.[10] The situation seems to have lasted and it is not until 1464[11] that the Convent of Kolozsmonostor is called in to resolve contention with a survey of the boundary between the Toroczkay family's property and that of the Szekler community.

Apart from this question of boundaries, there is no further evidence of legal conflict in this case. It did not involve integration of (un-free) Hungarian families and their possessions into the Szeklerland. This would not have been possible, because it would have opened a breach for the intrusion of Crown rights, or at least the appearance of a population within these villages having an inferior personal status irreconcilable with that of the free Szeklers.

In the course of the ensuing centuries, Hungarian families did integrate the Szeklerland, but it was Szekler law that was applied in all cases involving the Szekler land that they owned. It appears clearly that applicable law in matters of land ownership was that of possession, not that of the possessor.

B. Szekler Families and Royal Donations of Land Adjoining the Szeklerland

The statutory integrity of the Szeklerland was immutable, but a Szekler's personal status did not prevent him owning land subject to Crown law. Some Szekler families did receive royal donations bordering Szekler land; a proximity that did not fail to complicate the choice of applicable law in cases of succession or alienation. Two families, the Apor and the Hidvég, though Szeklers themselves, were repeatedly involved in confrontations with the Szeklers in defence of their rights to property that they considered 'private'.

In 1324,[12] the king ordered, for the third time, the Chapter of Transylvania to proceed with the investiture of the Apor family in a property in the Lokkászon valley, near the fortress of Bálványos, a royal enclave in the Seat of Kézdi. For a successful investiture, the assent of the Szeklers of Csík would have been necessary, but they did not show up and the donation did not become effective.

In 1349,[13] the Apor received a donation of land inside two villages less than fifteen kilometres from Bálványos. The donation was reiterated in 1360[14] and the investiture was successfully carried out a few weeks later:[15] a subtle interlacing of royal law and Szekler law in these surroundings, not in the open country but inside the boundaries of villages.

In a donation dated 1497 by King Wladislas II of properties in another village belonging to the royal fortress, we read that the donation is valid only if in fact the land is under royal law.[16] In the two donations in the fourteenth century cited above, it was expressly stated that they could only be realized if there was no opposition,[17] a period of time is given during which opposition may be expressed, a procedure that the Szeklers of Csík did not even deign to acknowledge. The status of Szekler land was recognized.

Such a condition was not stated in the donation of 1252,[18] by King Béla IV to Vincze, son of the Szekler Akadás, of the lands called 'Zék', devastated by the passage of the Mongols and said to be uninhabited. The notion given here of land that is desolate, emptied of its inhabitants, is undoubtedly more juridical than real. It means that there is no longer a landowner recognized by the Crown, but there were certainly some peasants left who had escaped the massacre. The document specifies that the Zék land is situated between that of the Vlachs of *Kircz*,[19] the Saxons of Brassó and the Szeklers of Sepsi. This mention distinguishing 'Zék' from the three surrounding territories is accompanied by geographical references fraught with opportunity for contradictory interpretations. An elevation (*monte nomine Vecul*), the identification of which is much disputed between archivists, and the course of the river Olt, known for its frequent shifting, gave rise to boundary disputes between Szeklers and Saxons in 1519[20] and in 1546-1547. The Szekler community never accepted the applicability of this donation to certain villages it considered to be part of the Seat of Sepsi (Hidvég, Árapatak and Bölön among others, along the eastern shore of the river Olt).

In 1342,[21] there is a first indication of Szekler opposition to this donation: premeditated violence and destruction were committed in this area.[22] In 1349,[23] a survey report confirms the hostile climate: in the course of their survey mission, emissaries of the Chapter of Transylvania encounter representatives of the Seat of Sepsi, who express their opposition to the boundary survey and regret not having learned of it early enough to be able to prevent it.[24]

Ten years later,[25] the Szeklers used force and occupied, pillaged and put the torch to the properties.[26] The Nemes and Mikó de Hidvég families, Szeklers and descendants of our Vincze, inherited some more Szekler land not far away at Málnás and Oltszem. To add to the confusion, we have a royal intervention in 1366[27] ordering the re-investiture of these Szekler families in their Szekler possessions, previously occupied by the Szekler community. Such combinations of Szekler land and adjoining land under Crown law within one and the same family have served to enrich the *Székely Archives*. More than sixty documents concern the Hidvég family (and its Nemes and Mikó branches). With a few exceptions (perjury in a case involving adultery, conflicts with the Saxons of Brassó, etc.) they are conflicts about these possessions, cases of violence, surveys, successions – and assassinations!

We will deal here with one conflict of succession that brings another Szekler family into the contention over this same land. In spite of a royal confirmation of donation dated 1448[28] – included in the writ is an order to the Szeklers to stop harassing the Hidvég family – in 1475,[29] the five sons of Simon Forró turned to the voivode to again challenge a Hidvég's right of succession to certain lands on which the the Forró had rights of priority according to Szekler customary laws of succession. On the rejection of their case, they turned to the Court of Justice of King Matthias, whence the matter was sent back in 1479[30] to the voivode, who carefully examined the documents presented by the parties. This included another decision, dated 1427, concerning the payment of a dowry which, according to Szekler law, excluded the Forró from the line of succession, demonstrating for our purposes that Szekler law of inheritance was applied to this dispute at least once.

Finally, the applicability of Crown law to the donation of 1252 was confirmed, but challenges continued well beyond the period under study here.

In the minds of the Szeklers, the donation was null from the outset, since the land had been Szekler land well before the donation of 1252, even if they did not have a written document to put up against a donation confirmed in writing many times over. Three centuries after the donation, the Crown admitted the legality of the appeal and the validity of a plea based on the oral tradition of Szekler customary law.

In addition to these conflicts arising from mixed legal situations, there is abundant documentation on alienation of land ownership. There were Szeklers who owned – without the restriction of applicable clan rights – property in the royal counties, which they sold in accordance with the laws of the realm. But when it was Szekler land that was to be alienated, different conditions were claimed to prevail that made such operations much more difficult to carry through successfully. The weight of this procedure – undoubtedly difficult to assume in some individual situations – under which any cession of property was subject to the assertion of clan rights, made many Szeklers give up trying to sell property and emigrate – during our period but especially later. But this association of land with clans was instrumental in maintaining cohesion within the community.

II. Alienation of Land Property

Documents dealing with the sale of Szekler land, from the earliest dated 1280,[31] consistently refer to kinship rights. From the fourteenth to the mid-fifteenth centuries, only 'perpetual' sales are known, mortgaging does not appear until 1471.[32] The specifically Szekler rules do not apply to all land ownership, only to hereditary Szekler land.

A. The Categories of Szekler Land: Acquest and Inheritance

The distinction is always clearly drawn between hereditary and acquired (*lelemény, inventum, sollertia*; the first occurrence of the term dates from 1560[33] and stems from a Szekler, Adorján Békés) property. The latter is not further characterized. It seems the term covers essentially movable belongings and chattels: booty brought home from a campaign, purchases, compensatory payment received for an assassination; certain purchased plots of ground can also be considered as acquests. Everything that is not classed as hereditary is personal property over which the owner has undivided rights. The only restriction mentioned is the right open to relatives or, in their absence, to the village to buy back acquests bequeathed to the Church.[34]

In the documentation we find two kinds of Szekler hereditary property: the primipilates – clan land the possession of which gives access to the dignities of judge and captain – and the siculicates, ancestral land the alienation of which is subject to the same preferential conditions concerning kinship as the primipilates, but they are never mentioned in association with a clan or tribe and apparently did not open access to dignities. Less precisely designated than the primipilates, the siculicates are more difficult to track through the *Székely Archives*. The modest social status they confer may not have diminished the intensity of legal actions, but these must not have been seen to be important enough to be taken before Seat tribunals and recorded. Across the documentation we see cases of Szekler hereditary lands being sold, but it seems that following a sale they lost nothing of their hereditary status, the restrictions attached to them passing to the purchaser,[35] at least for the primipilates.

Another restriction conditioning the alienation of a primipilate weighs upon the potential acquirer. All records dealing with the sale or mortgaging of primipilates show that these transactions take place between Szeklers already owning primipilates. Lénárt Apafi, a Hungarian married to a Szekler heiress of land, for example, did not start buying up primipilates until after his marriage. Such a rule is nowhere to be found in writing, but consistency of practice across more than twenty documents covering a period of over thirty years can hardly be due to the random luck of the conservation of sources. It was not enough to be able and willing to pay the price; to acquire a primipilate, one had to already own one.

This restrictive condition was a factor of differentiation within the Szekler community (a purchased primipilate did not give access to a dignity) but no more so than clan-affiliation, which had always been a condition for such an entitlement. At the same time, it had a cohesive effect in restricting access to dignities. Matrimonial alliance alone opened the way into the inner circle of families possessing a primipilate.

B. The Types of Alienation: Mortgaging and Sale in Perpetuity (perpetua proprietas)

The codifications of Szekler customary law do not take up the subject of the alienation of non-hereditary land, which appears to have largely followed the rules of customary law in the rest of the Hungarian realm. Article 25 of the codification of 1555, formulated along the lines of the *Tripartitum*, specifies that claims arising from a mortgage are not subject to prescription; Article 27 evokes 'all forms of alienation' and Article 28 'sale', without any further elaboration in either.

It appears that the difference between sale and mortgage as legal transactions was not always clearly understood. In 1539,[36] the voivode reminded the creditor of a lien on land that he must return the property as the debt had been paid. It seems that in this case the land given in pledge was appropriated by the lender and resembles more a sale with option to repurchase. This said, mortgaging was not always seen as alienation, but at most a legal transaction with a risk of being dispossessed. In 1555, a pledge is bought back by the son of the debtor with the explanation[37] that the debtor's youth – and the fraudulent manoeuvres against him – when the property was pledged, appear as a stronger argument for this repurchase than the gravity of the act itself. There is no evidence of opposition by relatives in a case where land is given in pledge.

Between 1505 and 1508, a curious case mixes mortgaging with outright sale of property and sale of the lien.

In February 1505,[38] Ferencz Székely d'Esztergom pledged his three primipilates situated at Kisfalud to a Bernát Székely for a sum of 150 Florins. In June[39] the same Ferencz sold the same property to Miklós Erdő de Csávás for a sum of 626 Florins, with no reference to the lien on it. One month later, in July,[40] our Ferencz, who normally had no rights to the property, pledged it for 200 Florins to Miklós Erdő, who had just bought the land! A year passed and, in May 1506,[41] Miklós proceeded to sell, not his property, but his mortgage claim to Miklós Tóth de Szentanna for the 200 Florins due from Ferencz. Finally – at least as far as the principles of mortgaging and selling property are concerned – in March of 1508,[42] Ferencz sold his land yet again to András Lázár,[43] for 1,000 Florins.

What part is played by skulduggery and what episodes may be missing in the documentation can no longer be established for sure: was the first sale between Ferencz Székely and Miklós Erdő annulled, reimbursed and replaced by the mortgage in July 1505? If so, the transactions of 1506 and 1508 would appear to be coherent, leaving only the mortgage due Miklós Tóth. Whatever the case, these transactions smack of a real confusion between the notion of loan, which involves only an obligation of repayment, and mortgage – and sale with a right to repurchase – which involves risk.

C. Conditions for Alienation of Inheritances: Kinship Rights

Ownership, characterized by the right to dispose freely over property, is personal. For property not classed as Szekler heritage – property situated in the counties or that acquired in Szekler territory – there was complete freedom of ownership; no-one could interfere with its alienation. As for hereditary property, which we find being sold more and more often starting in the fifteenth century, the kindred did not have direct ownership rights, but they could exercise pre-emption for an acquisition and veto a sale. This ancestral right to intervene, protective of the kinship's cohesion, represented a risk factor for any acquirer. In 1451,[44] the Assembly of the Seat of Maros established a period of thirty-two years during which any sale of Szekler hereditary property could be challenged. This period[45] is used throughout Hungary for the nobility. This article also mentions the period applicable to Crown property: 100 years and for Church property: forty years. This time-limit, which transformed the kinship's right of opposition into a kind of prescription in favour of the purchaser once the time had expired, was clearly intended to ensure the legal security of transactions:

'We decree that absolutely no person, not having acquired a hereditary property of any kind prior to a period of thirty-two years, may not by any legal action or prohibition validly acquire or claim said property, but that he must forever hold his peace.'[46]

In 1555, Article 24 of the codification reiterates this prescription of thirty-two years, after which the owner – whether heir or buyer – need no longer fear any action by remote relatives:

§ 24. 'If thirty-two years pass in a Szekler inheritance without anyone having taken any action, the other party is not obliged to give a response.'

A subtle nuance is introduced by Article 25, which reiterates the terms of the *Tripartitum*.[47] The creditor of a pledge made on a Szekler inheritance has priority over a buyer of the same property and his claim does not lapse even after thirty-two years; unfortunately, nothing is said about whether or not he can file a complaint to recover the lien from a purchaser, or whether his claim against the person selling the pledged property is not subject to prescription:

§ 25. 'There is no prescription for mortgaged property.'

In the following, the codification turns to the relatives:

§ 26. 'If a man has ties of blood to a succession, there is no prescription since, as is stated in the *Decretum*, there cannot be prescription between relatives.'

(The *Decretum* is Werbőczy's *Opus Tripartitum*. Gy. Bónis[48] observes that it was the Szeklers who first referred to this work as the *Decretum generale*, in 1535.)[49]

§ 27. 'A relative cannot alienate or give in whatever fashion property against the will of his relatives; if he has alienated such property and if opposition was expressed within the thirty-two years, those with ties of blood may buy it back, unless they had been given another inheritance in place of this one.'

Thus Article 26 reinstates the imprescriptibility of blood relatives' rights, referring to Werbőczy's *Opus Tripartitum*. This affirmation of principle in favour of the clan stated, the very next articles are more technical and concrete, and once more limits are put on these rights. In Article 27, the thirty-two-year period from 1451 for taking action or filing opposition is restated. Buying back seems possible even beyond this time-limit, provided there is a blood-tie with the succession and notice of opposition had been given within the thirty-two years following the sale.

But a new refinement then appears: a sale that violates the principle of the preservation of clan patrimony can be validated by compensating the clan with the attribution of other hereditary property. The decision of 1451 and the first part of Article 27 give the impression of strong personal links between the clan and the hereditary property. True, the property must be recovered by paying for it, the relative not having had rights of succession, but it seems that we are within a tightly-defined clan entity encompassing the persons and the property.

In this author's view the substitutive compensation admitted in the second part of Article 27 represents a loosening of clan ties by blood in favour of a broader admissibility of alienation. But, let us not forget, in all documented cases in which primipilates are ceded, the new owners are already integrated into the Szekler clan structure that governs access to dignities. What seems to count is not so much that a family remain tied to its soil but rather that the family retain the equivalent value of its rights, even if it is on different land. The upholding of the structure requires this – unwritten – condition involving the person of the acquirer.

The diminution of the rights of clan relations continues in the following article:

> §28. 'If someone sells an inheritance without having proposed it to the (relatives) concerned, and if a relative concerned voices opposition, he should be given up to fifteen days to buy it back and if he cannot pay for it or he has not voiced opposition when it was offered to him, the property must go to the one who has paid for it and the relatives must never again start a procedure to recover it.'

From thirty-two years we go to fifteen days! The formulation is ambiguous; most likely we should read 'without having proposed in priority', and we should note that here the relatives concerned by the hereditary property had been informed of the intention to sell, which was not necessarily the case in Article 27. Here the family has been consulted in advance, which makes the short notice somewhat less shocking. But again, the price that can be charged for the property, its material value, is more important than maintaining it within the lineage.

We encounter the subject of family relations and Szekler hereditary property again, further on in the codification:

> § 54. 'If someone wants to take legal action concerning a Szekler hereditary property, the plaintiff is assumed to act in the name of all relatives, he must therefore certify that none have taken legal action against him.'

The most interesting litigations take place between relatives. The relatives may take legal action, but they must speak with one voice; internal dissention shuts down access to any recourse. Finally, one more article evokes the thirty-two years for taking action against alienation of a Szekler hereditary property:

> § 52. 'If a notable or a *lófő* (i.e. a *primipilus*, a dignitary) possesses a hereditary property in a village and has no heirs among the population of the village, he cannot install an heir (from another village) without their consent; if he does so anyway, they can redeem it during thirty-two years.'

We move from the lineage to the village. The fact that this article deals only with notables can undoubtedly be attributed to the near-complete silence of the documentation on the subject of 'small hereditary properties'. Blood relations and the village always coincide for these 'siculicates', but apparently less so for the hereditary property of dignitaries by the time of this codification. We are at the middle of the sixteenth century, the Hungarian realm is dismembered, Transylvania in turmoil, and the codification, all the while recalling the most ancient customs, takes into account new socio-economic developments. Priority is given here to village solidarity over the interests of a legitimate heir no longer residing in the village.

The clan structure, the capacity for adaptation, which was already manifest in the shift from blood ties to membership in the 'class' of dignitaries, here takes another step in its evolution, in favour of the notion of legal entity for the Szekler village.

The right of blood-relatives to oppose the cession of a property is clearly in evidence in documents well before 1451. In the archives we find sales of hereditary property in 1280[50] and 1307,[51] where the problem is not the time period but precautions against intervention by blood relations, peremptorily in 1280[52] and by taking care to record the consent of the relations in 1307.[53]

In 1455,[54] Lucia, née Szilágyi, was formally prohibited by her sister's husband in his own name and that of his spouse and their children from selling an inheritance she had just won in a legal dispute. These relatives were not mentioned in the document on the legal dispute in which she acquired the property, more precisely its usufruct, which had been as heatedly contested as its holding in fee simple, but they felt concerned by its sale. They cite Crown law in the quest for this Szekler hereditary property. There is no risk in interpreting this invocation of Crown law as a reference to the common custom, throughout the realm, of imprescriptibility between blood relatives.

We have no document mentioning a sale the proceeds of which were shared out to branches of the seller's family; there is no evidence of a right of *abusus* for another family branch, or of holding in fee simple or bare or joint ownership with rights of usufruct for another branch in a succession. If a sale is accepted, its proceeds accrue to the sole heir and proprietor. But besides this strictly material aspect of a sale, the lineage's rights of assuring conservation of clan patrimony put Szekler hereditary propriety in a class apart.

The ceding of primipilates shows the evolution of the Szekler clan structure, which assents to the passing of such property between Szeklers already holding title to the rights of primipilates, and the ascension of the village, which obtains a right of opposition – within thirty-two years – to heirs by blood ties. An analysis of the law of succession puts in evidence the aim to conserve traditions within related lineages and, here again, the adaptability of the structure to account for unforeseeable demographic changes and the possible absence of male heirs.

III. Rules of Inheritance

In addition to isolated documents in which Szekler inheritances appear for an instant with no further data on possible later developments, the *Székely Archives* contain some cases of litigation 'long and very tangled',[55] to quote K. Szabó, that is to say rich in instructive legal detail. We make the acquaintance of entire families, the personalities of delightful 'dowry hunters' emerge and take shape from document to document. We are taken with compassion for the unfortunate fate of orphaned heiresses pursued by these gluttons. We must nod with approval when one of the unfortunate, orphaned girls reappears a few decades later as a wily and combative widow: justice is done!

It is not easy to escape the fascination of evolving family sagas, as complex as they are engaging, and step back to analyse the legal context with academic rigour. How can we tell whether the expression or application of a rule presented as customary – but carefully committed to writing – is not in fact a dictate of circumstance, an 'amicable settlement' under the weight of one of the personalities involved or the influence of a particular family? Keeping in mind this background of customary law pragmatically exercised, we can draw enough material from the documented evidence to propose an outline of the principal rules of the law of succession from the early fifteenth to the mid-sixteenth centuries.

The first distinction to be drawn is the validity of testamentary dispositions in situations involving Szekler inheritance. Then, the specific provisions of Szekler law of succession concerning rules of sharing an inheritance and the rights and obligations of the heirs and their kin, which includes the obligation to provide a dowry and, finally the evolution that takes place during our period in the order of successoral devolution: the priority of direct descendants over collaterals, the priority of male heirs over their sisters, the fate of inheritances accruing in the absence of male heirs, a situation which, under Szekler law – precludes defaulting to the Crown in the case of escheat – gives rise to the process termed 'daughters deemed sons'. In Hungarian successoral law, this notion is termed 'prefection' (*praefectio*). It involved fathers without male heirs petitioning the king to make their daughters into sons, which, if granted, was equivalent to a 'new donation'.[56] Any interventions by the king being excluded in Szekler successions, this convenient term could not be applied in our context without the risk of misleading interpretations; hence the down-to-earth transliteration of the Szekler term '*fiúsított leány*', daughter deemed son, and appropriate variations were preferred here.

A. The Testament

The testamentary route is not unknown among Szeklers. Put in place among the laws decreed by King St. Stephen, testamentary freedom was one of the essential measures of his policy in favour of the Church, but it also aimed at breaking the grip of clan ties as expressed in joint ownership of land, a system rooted in pre-Conquest tradition but hampering the exercise of central authority by the Crown. Formulated in Article 6 of King Stephen's first book of laws, the principle of testamentary freedom and of private property was reiterated and expanded in the provisions of the second book of laws (II. § 2).

However, where hereditary Szekler property was concerned, these provisions were in contradiction with customary Szekler law, which restricted individual freedom to dispose over property of this kind in favour of the rights of relatives in the broadest sense. In the *Székely Archives* we find dozens of testamentary dispositions, but few of them involve the possession of real estate situated within the Szeklerland.

The first mention dates from the beginning of the fourteenth century. In 1311,[57] with confirmation by the Chapter of Transylvania in 1320,[58] a member of the Apor family established a will in favour of his son and nephews, with some bequests to the Church, but none of the property was Szekler; all was situated in a Fehér county enclave in the heart of the Szeklerland, constituted by the royal fortress of Bálványos and its surroundings. What is more, the authenticity of this document, the first known testament, has been put in question as it was published in AOkl, because it is amongst forgeries made by József Kemény; there is no further comment on what part of the documents is false, nor what font of documents the eighteenth-century compiler might have wished to enrich.

In 1364,[59] a Szekler of Aranyos and his family were the beneficiaries of a bequest; but the property was situated in the county of Csanád, well away from the Szeklerland. The will of András Toldalagi, certified in 1471,[60] in favour of the monks of the Order of St. Paul the First Hermit at Szentkirály was later contested by his family and continued to occupy the tribunals, but the bequeathed property, along the boundary of the Seat of Maros, was stated to be situated in the county of Torda. The same is true of the property bequeathed to the same monastery by Dorottya, widow of György Pisky de Szentiván, though this donation was challenged in turn in 1529.[61]

In 1536,[62] the widow of Benedek Csakó, a Szekler of Csík, obtained the Crown's intervention with two notables of the Seat (Ferenc Lázár and Miklós Kornis), designated by her late husband as executors of his will, to remind them of their duties of assistance to the legatee. The ensuing royal inquest indicated that her rights were indeed threatened. This case is situated in the Szeklerland, but there is no mention of hereditary Szekler property.

In 1556,[63] Adorján Békés (whose legal competence we have already encountered), a Szekler from the Seat of Kézdi, and his wife Katalin concluded a mutual donation of a number of real properties; here again, the fact of committing the transaction to writing appears as a means of safeguarding the rights of the beneficiaries. The husband states that the will is made to prevent his brothers' opposition to the rights of his wife. One has the impression that this is a will of survivorship. Four years later,[64] Adorján, undoubtedly widowed in the meantime, donates the same property to his grandson, cited by name, reserving for himself a life annuity and the obligation for the heir to care for him in his lifetime. The particular significance of these two documents lies in the care taken by their author to insist that the bequeathed properties are acquests (*lelemények*), not inherited property, giving details of when they were acquired and at what price, that the property had been proposed to the relatives and that all had been in his possession for over thirty-two years. All of the rules of the codification of 1555 are here formally respected, which permitted Békés to conclude that he could freely dispose over this property.

Meticulous attention to detail – or wary precaution? – is manifest in these documents. Adorján Békés had called upon the Seat judge, two captains and three witnesses to countersign his testament. Benedek Csakó had designated two notables as executors of his bequest to his widow, but she was still obliged to appeal to the Crown to intervene. In 1484,[65] the auxiliary archdeacon of the Seat of Maros opened an investigation into the authenticity of the testament of Miklós Madarasi and his wife, at the request of the voivode of Transylvania. The inquest concluded that the testament was authentic – upon the testimony of a priest, with seal and the oath of five notables.

Unfortunately, we know nothing more of this document and its content. The only daughter of Miklós Madarasi, Dorottya, one of the heiresses, the future wife of Lénárt Apafi, is destined to occupy the tribunals time and again with their matrimonial muddles and it would have been interesting to know whether Miklós Madarasi had designated his daughter as his sole heir – as was the case with judge Benkő and his daughter in the Seat of Kézdi in 1500[66] – or whether, fearing for the future of his primipilates in the hands of a young girl, he had tried to designate an heir. This is precisely what János Káli did in 1499[67] at the expense of his sole daughter Magdolna, in designating an heir charged with ensuring the education and upkeep of the young lady or, as is perceptible in reading between the lines, marrying her when she came of age. The mother and an uncle of the girl voiced their opposition to this disposition and the testament was never executed.

There are two other testaments that deal with Szekler hereditary property. The first is just a mention of a sale in a confirmation. In 1498,[68] the mother of Jakab Káli, a Szekler of Maros, bought back a primipilate that had been bequeathed by her late son to the Order of St. Paul the First Hermit. It is surprising to learn that a primipilate had been bequeathed, primipilates constituting the very essence of property, the private alienation of which is strictly limited by Szekler customary law. The beneficiary's 'person' is just as astonishing: though not all primipilates provide access to the dignities of judge and captain, all do carry with them the obligation of personal military service. This may be the consideration that motivated the reverend members of the Order to relinquish the property. As so often, there is unfortunately insufficient information in this document for a better reconstruction of the circumstances.

Was it the mother, aware of the absurdity of this bequest, who initiated its recovery? Did the monks realize that the military obligation, irreconcilable with their own rules, bore the risk of conflict with the Szekler community? Nothing is said, not even the price of the buy-back or the name of the primipilate, nor does any other document refer to this case, singular in every sense of the term. In Nagyernye, the village from which this family hails, the military rosters of the early seventeenth century lists its members as having title to a primipilate: János Káli[69] in 1602; György Káli[70] in 1604; and, in 1635,[71] Pál Káli, son of János Káli the elder, and János Káli, son of György and his sons Mihály and György.[72] Unable to follow an uninterrupted line between the two periods, we may nevertheless suppose that the primipilate so carelessly bequeathed stayed in the family after its recovery in 1498. We only know that the pious monks showed more intransigence about holding on to bequests when a bequest was situated in the royal counties.

The other testament involving a Szekler hereditary property is, happily, very detailed! In 1549,[73] János Lázár was owner of numerous properties in the Seats of Maros and Csík. He was well-versed in the complexities of Szekler law, involved as he had been for years in a tortuous litigation over three primipilates in Kisfalud, in the Seat of Maros, acquired by his father. His testament was in strictest compliance with the codification of 1555. In those times of torment, between the Ottoman menace and the rivalry between Habsburg and Szapolyai, vying with each other to intervene in the affairs of Transylvania, János Lázár had suffered the consequences of his political choices. He had experienced the tribulations stemming from two attempted confiscations. The first time he was condemned for treason was in 1521, following an uprising by the Szeklers in 1519 against the Voivode John Szpolyai.[74] The next time, by the same John Szapolyai, now king, was in 1529, for conspiracy in favour of Ferdinand of Habsburg.[75] In the end his property was restituted in 1538, by the same John Szapolyai.[76]

By his testament, he might also have wanted to ensure application of customary law and give his children more effective means of defence against attempts at intrusion by the Crown than just the reciting of orally-transmitted custom. The document organizes the distribution of his property among his sons, entrusts to them the payment of their sisters' dowries, gives precise instructions on the payment of annuities to religious orders, and meticulously disposes of his silverware and other objects of any value. An interminable inventory of the family patrimony, this testament may have spared his heirs the disputes over successions that abound in the *Székely Archives*, to the joy of researchers. This said, the copy of the testament conserved for posterity stems from a legal altercation in 1607.

These documents show that testamentary freedom had its limits where it encountered customary law governing Szekler hereditary property. As Werbőczy observed, the devolution of such property was governed by customary law.

B. Custom: Division and Orderly Succession

Why do we have no document on partition – judiciary or by amicable settlement – prior to 1408? We can exclude the hypothesis of chance in the conservation of sources. Szekler hereditary property, as long as its monetarization remained rare, no doubt remained undivided in practice, even when the rights to it were shared. The legal record of 1408 is evidence of shared inheritance,[77] jointly owned property in today's terms; the first references to appear are in the context of large sums of money. In these documents we also find the names of non-Szekler families, reason enough for recourse to writing.

It is more than likely that recourse to writing started with the first violations of customary rules, successions in which all heirs were familiar with their rights, not needing the intervention of a tribunal or *locus credibilis* and thus not leaving a written trace. The rules appear before our eyes as their observance encounters problems, initially through litigation and legal decisions, later more comprehensively through the dispositions taken by the Assembly of 1451 and the codification of 1555. Still, there are blind spots in these precious sources, certain points of law alluded to briefly elsewhere or suggested by common sense are clearly absent.

In amicable settlements there are glimpses of widows' usufruct, but nothing is said on this subject in the codification of 1555. Should we assume that widows' rights were so rarely questioned that it did not occur to the codifiers to mention the subject, or had it already lapsed and hence lost pertinence?

Successions with no male heirs went to the daughters and the brothers and sisters of the deceased, but such collateral successions are not mentioned in the codification either. Nevertheless, the question of their rights is pertinent. We see them evolve across the judicial decisions. Had their rights lessened further by this time or were they sufficiently stabilized not to require elaboration in writing?

Were we to follow the logic that rules systematically respected did not deserve written mention, we would end up doubting the force of those that were written down. This is not a purely theoretical question founded on the unlikely hypothesis of a rigorously systematic preparation of this written codification. Rather, alone the disorder in which subjects come up would suggest a lively assembly and it is easy to imagine that subjects on which the text is silent had simply not come up.

As for the articles that do define the rules of succession, we might suppose that, in the light of the 100 years of jurisprudence preceding the codification, where they exclude others in the presence of male heirs, they were relatively recent and hence in need of meticulous codification. Some pleas in earlier cases seem to imply that, as long as joint ownership was in practice, the rights of all heirs, sons and daughters and, perhaps to a lesser extent, collaterals had been shared.

1. Codified Rules of Division

In 1451, at an assembly of the Seat of Maros, and in 1555 at the Assembly of the Szekler Nation at Udvarhely, the customary rules concerning the division of inheritances were recorded.

In 1451:[78] 'And also always when two brothers had, in ancient times, divided their Szekler inheritances between them, then their heirs, inheriting these same Szekler inheritances, must possess and hold them the same way.'

Over 100 years later this disposition was refined in the codification of 1555:[79]

§ 20. 'If a man has a son and a daughter, the son inherits, but in assuring the dowry of the daughter in accordance with the customs of each Seat.'

§ 21. 'If a man has two sons, one of whom has a son and the other a daughter, the daughter inherits from her father like the son from his.'

§22. 'If a man has two daughters and no son, they both inherit, but in such a way that the younger may have first choice within the inheritance with a worth comparable to that of the older; if, on the other hand, the younger cannot be give an equivalent part to the older, the inheritance must be divided into equal parts.'

§ 23. 'If a man has two daughters and one of them has a son and the other a daughter, the daughter inherits from her father like the son from his, but if the [grand]daughter [later] has a son and a daughter, the son must provide the dowry of the daughter.'

Of the eighty-eight articles making up the codification of 1555, ten (20 to 28 and 52) deal with Szekler inheritance and the rules that apply to it. Only Articles 20 to 23 deal with devolution and in a casual manner present the rules that apply if there are descendants. The expressions 'two sons' and 'two daughters' represent plurality; one should read 'two or more'. Articles 20 and 21 apply just as well if there are several sons and several daughters, the use of the singular serves only to stress the dichotomy between male and female descendants. Inappropriate as it may seem when applied to humans, it is the partitive form that would best express the legal distinction between heirs by their sex: 'a man having any son' or 'a man having some daughter'.

The situation defined in 1451, 'if a man has two sons, they share the inheritance', is not reiterated in the 1555 codification. As for daughters, the division between heiresses gives priority to the youngest – the justification of this privilege may lie in the assumption that she is the most likely to procreate and have an heir – all the while imposing a certain balance of shares in the division (comparable, if not equal). Is there the same right of the elder or of the younger between sons? There is nothing to indicate it, not in the codification, nor in the cases adjudicated either. In 1555, only the descendants' rights are dealt with, but concrete cases that came before tribunals give us a view of the rights of widows and collateral relatives, and on the obligation to provide a dowry which weighs on inheritances.

The Status of the Widow We have already met widows, designated as legatees by their late husbands. In two cases, the widow is legatee for the personal belongings of the deceased. Fifty more documents tell of sales, purchases and claims against inheritances, in which widows are involved. To what extent do they have the right to intervene in these questions of patrimony? The codification of 1555 is remarkably silent on this subject; only in Article 60 do we find, parenthetically, that wives and children may possess belongings of their own:

> **§ 60.** A verdict is determined as follows in the Szeklerland: the village elects three true and honest men and these three answer for the village. If they are brought someone whose misdeeds are known, they shall punish him; if he has property they shall take from him what is his, but <u>without touching the property of his wife and children</u>.[80] But if someone is brought before them on hearsay, they shall refuse to judge him.

The terms do not allow us to determine whether the property in question consists of private, personal belongings or hereditary Szekler property. Women may well possess, sometimes a lot, but never Szekler hereditary property. Across the numerous documents we encounter widows organizing the sale of their possessions, but most turn out to be situated in counties and Szekler hereditary property is nowhere involved.

As to the question of whether a widow may exercise rights over Szekler inheritances, the answer depends on the presence of children. If she has children and until they are of age, the widow appears to have rights of usufruct and claim in her role as trustee.

In 1455,[81] we find Katalin, widow of Péter, son of Dénes Szentmihályfalvi, involved in a dispute over a Szekler inheritance, at the side of her sons. Three years later,[82] remarried, she and only one of her sons (did the other die in the meantime or come of age? He never shows up again in the documents) entrust the management of their property to her new husband.

In 1498, Ilona, née Szengyeli, widow of one János Káli, concludes an agreement[83] with Miklós Tóth de Szentanna, father of a minor who is to marry her daughter Magdolna, also a minor, and the only descendant of János Káli. According to the terms of this agreement, all Szekler property and property in the counties was to revert to Magdolna, not under the suspensive condition of the future marriage of the two children, but under the executory condition of the widow's own remarriage. In that case the Szekler inheritance was to pass immediately to her daughter's future husband. Surprise at first reading: why would a widow renounce either the security of a new marriage or the benefits of usufruct on her late husband's property? The possibility of remarriage does not seem to have been hypothetical: early in 1499[84] we find the same cast of characters arrayed before the tribunal of the Seat of Maros, and Ilona is remarried, with a certain János Andrássy.

The verdict is in the latter's favour; he obtains adjudication of the usufruct on the property until Magdolna, Ilona's daughter, still a minor, would marry. The initial disposition of the widow's renunciation remains illogical, and the verdict seems to indicate that it had in fact been contrary to customary law from the outset. A widow's usufruct was not a life annuity, it ended the moment the heirs married, but it could not be interrupted before, nor could it be nullified by, the remarriage of the widow.

This rapacious step-father, Miklós Tóth de Szentanna crops up time and again in the *Székely Archives*. Not that he is completely unsavoury but he was in fact involved in a murder in 1494[85] – his acquisitive interpretations of Szekler customs are a gold-mine for historians of law – but he does appear always on the hunt for personal gain and insatiably avid to lay his hands on Szekler hereditary property. His son's marriage to Magdolna is presented as the wish of the widow and her brother, who neglect the deceased's own testamentary dispositions to establish an alliance differently. One can readily suppose that Miklós Tóth de Szentanna took advantage of the situation in concocting the accord of 1498 so as not to have to await the coming-of-age of his son and the conclusion of the marriage before reaping the fruit of the inheritance. Were we a bit more sceptical about his integrity, we might even suspect that he was informed of the widow's impending remarriage, reason enough to impose the executory clause and thus hasten his access to the inheritance. However, he had underestimated Ilona's new husband, who quickly mastered the situation and obtained the reversal of Miklós Tóth de Szentanna's fortunes and clauses.

In a third case, in 1507, a widow was confronted with the demands of her late husband's brother.[86] Ilona, widow of Gergely Békési, had no children from her first marriage. She had been remarried for several years and already had two children by her second husband when she concluded an agreement with Pál, the brother of her first husband Gergely, giving him a sum of money in exchange for his abandoning all claim to his brother's inheritance. Unfortunately, we have only this one document, which does nothing to shed light on the custom that might have justified such an agreement. It seems the widow had had a right of usufruct on the inheritance of her late husband since his death. According to the stipulations of 1451, the collateral relatives inherit in the absence of descendants. With no mention of a testament for his personal belongings, it is likely that all of the deceased's patrimony was involved. The agreement covers the entire inheritance: real estate in the Szeklerland and the royal counties, movables and cash. The transaction is estimated to be worth 371 Florins, payable to the brother, 'to his entire satisfaction'. As long as he was within the thirty-two-year prescription period, the brother had every right to claim the inheritance or, as was the case here, to sell it for cash.

One last case sheds light on the order of hereditary succession, in particular a widows' right of usufruct in the presence of minor collateral relatives, in this instance unmarried girls. In 1463,[87] the widow of Mihály Barlabássi de Szentpál had promised to return all of the inheritance of her father-in-law, previously deceased, to her two sisters-in-law, the daughters of the deceased. This promise – of which we learn because it had not been kept – was in fact made to the prospective husbands of the girls and on condition that they marry. It is safe to conclude therefore, that a widow continued to have usufruct rights until the minor collaterals came of age, in other words: got married.

The widow herself has no right of outright ownership to a Szekler inheritance. She may only act as fiduciary tutor of children who are not of age. What becomes of her thereafter? A dependent mother-in-law? Nothing appears in writing on the subject, but tradition, in practice to this day, suggests that she shared the family's domicile and the daily life of the younger generations.

The Rights of Collaterals When we find brothers acting jointly in the *Székely Archives*, it is not in cases involving Szekler inheritance: we find brothers who commit murder, calumny, looting 'as one man'; we even encounter betrothals set up for one man, where his brother ends up marrying the girl in question. In June 1485, Dorottya Madarasi is engaged to Ferenc Apafi[88] and in August to his brother Lénárt[89] whom she ends up marrying, as described in a document from sometime before 1496.[90] The latter document in which we find Dorottya already married to Lénárt, also shows that Ferenc is still alive. We also find brothers sharing the revenues of a Szekler dignity. This sort of 'fraternal nepotism' was common throughout Hungary; it is not just in Transylvania where brothers were voivode and vice-voivode, voivode and bishop and so forth. As for land ownership, royal donations were made to brothers and their descendants, land surveys were carried out at the behest of brothers. In the Szeklerland, the right of brothers to inherit is clear: they share the inheritance – but, in legal terms, as co-sons rather than brothers.[91]

What of the brothers of a deceased? First in line within the kindred, they have the right to oppose the alienation and, as we have seen in their litigation against widows, they succeeded in an inheritance in the absence of descendants. In 1514, Werbőczy noted that in the Szeklerland 'A man, even if convicted and sentenced, cannot lose his hereditary property, it reverts to his descendants and his brothers.'[92]

From 1451 on, priority was given to the descending line, be it female. As to the deceased's sisters, not mentioned in the codification of 1555, they inherited with their nieces in 1451[93] and 1463,[94] in complete contravention of the principles enounced in 1451[95] and the codification of 1555. In these cases we find no brothers of the deceased; hence we cannot tell whether their presence might have excluded the sisters. Without delving into anachronistic notions of the immediate family as opposed to more distant relations, we can conclude that, for as much as the kindred, 'the clan horizontality', conserves an important right of clan pre-emption on an inheritance, or the right of *veto* against outsiders' access to it, the descending line within a kindred, 'family verticality' as it were, always had precedence in the successoral devolution, even if there were only girls.

Before broaching the subject of the dowry and its place in a Szekler inheritance, we should note a few documents that deal with a deceased's ascendants. In 1485, a grandmother organizes the engagement of her granddaughter (it is once again Dorottya Madarasi, and her engagement to Ferenc Apafi), reserving for herself an annuity on certain properties.[96] This annuity applies to property distinct from the primipilates owned by her deceased son, Miklós Madarasi. The latter had made a testament the dispositions of which we do not know. His mother's personal belongings may have been a bequest, or they may have come from her dowry. In a document dated 1453,[97] the mother of a Szekler abroad on military service conserves the trusteeship over his Szekler hereditary property during his absence. In 1538,[98] the father of a deceased Szekler captain retains the right of trustee over a Szekler inheritance in the name of his minor grandchildren. Aside from these cases of tutors, who act in the name of heirs, ascendants do not figure in the successoral devolution.

The Question of the Dowry Laconically dismissed in Article 20 of 1555 as a matter to be dealt with according to the customs of each Seat, the question of the dowry regularly complicates Szekler successions. At a time when Hungarian law had a defined 'daughters' quarter of the inheritance'[99] (*Leánynegyed, quarta puellaris*), i.e. the part due to daughters (no matter how many they are) from their father's inheritance, it was instituted in the Golden Bull (1222) under the influence of Roman law introduced by the Church. Starting in the reign of King Louis the Great, it is given in the form of money or movable goods. Szekler law seems hesitant about the value, the nature and the origin of the dowry. Whether inheritance or dowry, both are within the domain of the 'family's rights of patrimony', but the lines seem blurred. Daughters' and sisters' rights of succession in the absence of male descendants seem to be in a state of suspension, conditional on both their marriage and the demise of the ascendant or brother. This period of contingency, consubstantial with the inheritance, seems on occasion to be applied to the transfer of dowries. Both conditions had to be met in a case in 1485,[100] the betrothed of an orphan (yet again Dorottya Madarasi, this time betrothed to Lénárt Apafi) – whose status of orphan met one of the conditions – demanded the transfer of the clan's gift (*nemrész*, the part of the clan) without waiting for her to be married (to him, of course); but we do not have the Szekler Assembly's response to his request.

In the absence of generally applied rules, what can we learn from individual cases? A first factor limiting the available answers: the handful of cases all stem from the Seat of Maros with the exception of one, from the Seat of Aranyos. Were the rules substantially different from Seat to Seat? We do not know. The second limit is not geographical but social. We can assume that the rules codified in 1555 applied to all members of the Szekler community. As for the conventions – or legal cases – we have, they all concern well-off Szekler families entering into alliances with Hungarian families. The two Seats (Maros and Aranyos) are effectively those most concerned by such incursions by Hungarian families. It is conceivable that here the Hungarian rule of 'the daughters' quarter' corrupted more ancient Szekler customs, at least in mixed alliances. So what happened in families of more modest means? We might deduce a glimpse from the pleas in a documented case or two, where arguments present a logic quite different from the exactions of the Hungarians.

What is a dowry? Who owes it? To the second question there is an answer in the codification of 1555, which states that this burden is borne by the brothers, the heirs. But does this mean that no dowry is forthcoming as long as the father is alive? The precipitate crowding around orphaned girls would seem to indicate that that is so. And yet, in some successoral cases, mention is made of a dowry already provided. What does a dowry consist of? Movables or real estate? In the latter case are we dealing with only the revenues from the property or its outright ownership? Can a dowry include hereditary Szekler property? A lot of questions to which the perusal of the documents gives a sampling of answers, some inconsistent, some contradictory.

A first hint comes from a document dated 1409[101] about the succession of Péter, son of Arnold, in which the Assembly of the Seat of Maros decides that, if a dowry stems from maternal property, a girl thus endowed has rights to her part of the father's inheritance as well, while a dowry from the father's property exhausts her rights of inheritance from him. It seems that in this particular case, which in the end was amicably settled, one of the girls had her dowry from paternal property, so that her heirs are excluded from succession, while the heirs of another daughter, endowed from maternal property, has a right to half of the paternal inheritance, the same as the heirs of the son. We are nowhere near the dispositions of Article 20, perhaps because at this early time the alleged division involved only the revenues, not outright ownership.

Not until the last quarter of the fifteenth century do we find more information about a dowry; in 1473,[102] a dowry is put together by an entire family: the sister, her husband and their children, the son of one of her two deceased brothers and even the half-sister, all are called upon to contribute, but there is no indication on what the dowry constitutes. In 1485, the term 'the clan's part' turns up again in connection with a dowry that consists of movables;[103] in this case it is cattle, but this case involves a sole heiress, so that the part of the clan is in addition to the totality of the paternal inheritance. Had there been brothers, they might have had to provide a dowry in the form of real property in addition to the clan's part. In 1496,[104] we find a sizeable dowry consisting of real property situated both in the

Szeklerland and in county territory, but we also learn that the future husband had been obliged to pay back the 1,000 Florins of lien on this property. It is difficult to discern a clear pattern of customary law from these few cases. The burden of a dowry clearly exists, but we have few certitudes on its nature, on who must provide it, or the moment when it comes due.

The findings of 1409, adjudicating equal shares to sons and daughters if the dowry had not come from paternal property, is in apparent contradiction with the provisions of the codification of 1555. However, other circumstances intervene to complicate interpretations of this decision: the female branch is faced with a male branch with no heirs in the following generation. We may ask whether the problem is the dowry or whether we are here witnesses to a devolution through 'women's rights'.

2. Successoral Order: 'Women's Rights' and the Kindred The situation is clear if there are male heirs: they inherit to the exclusion of all others. Things are just as simple if there is no direct heir: the collaterals inherit. Where things get a bit complicated is when there is a male heir but there are also females. Articles 22 and 23 of the 1555 codification seem clear enough: if a man has two daughters but no sons, they (the daughters) inherit. Collaterals are not even mentioned. Earlier, in 1451, it had already been stated that male descendants exclude females and that the latter in turn exclude collaterals (see genealogical tables of successoral orders):

> As long as male heirs survive in the closest line, females cannot claim any right of inheritance to the detriment of males, nor can they intervene in the ownership of such property (Szekler hereditary property) held by male survivors
> and (if) there are no male heirs of this kind and some female heirs survive, as long as they survive no male heirs of another line of kinship may rightly claim parts of such an inheritance put in the succession
> and (if) there are no heirs of either sex, then finally the above inheritances must devolve in another, natural line of kinship.

Successions by Women The uncertainties on the role of the dowry and the contradictions between the decisions of the early fifteenth century and the rules of succession in the codification of 1555 undoubtedly have their origin in the evolution of customary law following the episode of a succession with no male heirs, and the risk of the dispersal of property beyond the clan kinship occasioned by marriage of heiresses.

In the kingdom of Hungary, ever since the Angevin kings,[105] the absence of male heirs caused collateral devolution only to the fourth degree, beyond which the property defaulted to the Crown. For a female to inherit, a special act of royal favour was needed, which to all intents and purposes amounted to a new, royal donation. In contrast to this, the Szekler community considered the same situation as settled by customary law and we have a number of cases of 'daughters deemed sons', 'masculinized women' (*fiúsitott leány, fiúleány, puella tamquam filius*).

Is this really juridical reasoning aimed at safeguarding the cohesion of the clan? Cited everywhere as a specifically Szekler procedure, it nevertheless favours the vertical line in a succession, to the exclusion of the broader family, which in its horizontality is more representative of the clan.

This apparent priority given to the descendants, male or female, appears, inversely, to exclude females in the presence of males. The affirmation that girls inherit if there are no sons excludes them in all other cases, with the effect that the interests of the lineage are preserved.

From the early fifteenth to the mid-sixteenth centuries, a dozen cases of daughters-deemed-sons appear in the archives; from amicable settlements to formal verdicts, rules emerge, finally to be defined and consigned to articles of successoral procedure in the codification of 1555. But before the formal emergence of these rules favouring female descendants, day-to-day practice in the Szekler community developed a sort of code of women's rights under which all female relatives, daughters and sisters, in fact all potential bearers of a male heir in the lineage, received their part of an inheritance. The exclusion of collateral branches by the descending branch does not appear until the 1450s and even then the principle does not appear to have been systematically applied.

In the interest of protecting the integrity of kinships within the clans and avoidance of the risk of matrimonial alliances beyond the confines of the the Szekler community – one of the reproaches made against the Voivode István Báthory in 1493 – the community took another step in adapting its customs to circumstance. In effect, there is no known instance of a transfer of clan rights by women except in the case of sole, universal heiresses (daughters deemed sons).

In 1409,[106] we see the succession of Péter (Genealogical Table 2, The Madarasi Succession), son of Arnold, being shared between the heirs of his son János and those of his daughter, spouse of Szengyel. Apparently another daughter, married Sólyom, and her descendants have no further rights by reason of the dowry she had received. But it is not obvious that there was true division between the heirs in the male and female lines. János had no son and the lineage was thus threatened. Barnabás and Jakab Madarasi, grandsons of János, owed their rights to women: to Orsolya, their mother and János' daughter, and Tamás Szengyel to his mother, also a daughter of János. The division of the Gyerőfi succession was settled the same way in 1408,[107] as confirmed in 1451 (Genealogical Table 1, The Gyerőfi Succession).[108]

Also in 1451,[109] the succession of Semjén Szentkirályi (Genealogical Table 3, The Szentkirályi Succession) is divided between his daughters and his sister. Here the notables took pains to justify their reasoning: male heirs would have had precedence over any female line, but in their absence the inheritance devolved to the women's side, in this case the sister and the daughters.[110] This principle of women's rights, non-exclusive of collateral branches, was also applied in 1463,[111] in the Barlabássi succession (Genealogical Table 4, The Succession of Barlabássi, Szentgyörgyi and Káli) and confirmed in this same succession in 1502.[112] The widow of Mihály Barlabássi de Szentpál, who had not kept her promise to transfer the inheritance to her sisters-in-law upon their marriage in 1463, in fact had a daughter of her own, whose daughters claimed half of the succession of their grandfather from the heiresses of the deceased's sister in 1502. The verdict of 1502, which dispossessed Miklós Tóth of the half of the succession of his wife's uncle that he had taken by force, did not question the other half, which his wife had obtained through her mother, the sister of the deceased.

The subject of women's rights to inherit appears in another dispute in 1479;[113] the term of women's rights is reiterated three times in the Forró family's plea against the Hidvég family.

Though contrary to the dispositions of 1451 and the codification of 1555, here the ruling is nevertheless closer to the logic favouring the lineage: any female, with her potential for procreation within the kinship, is entitled to her share, commensurate with her role in the preservation of the lineage; an essential consideration, which we find defended by the disposition in Article 22 of 1555, favouring the younger daughter. All the while, the risk of undesirable matrimonial alliances by the sisters is not to be ignored.

This may be what motivated the decision of the Assembly of the Seat of Maros in 1409 to 1410,[114] in the Gyerőfi succession (Genealogical Table 1 hereinafter, The Gyerőfi Succession) to attribute the entire inheritance to the deceased's daughter. The text of the decision itself has not been conserved, only a reference to it in an order issued by King Sigismund in 1410 to apply division according to a verdict of 1408 and not the decision of the Assembly of Maros, which excluded inheritance through the sister. The situation is the same as in the Szentkirályi, Madarasi or Barlabássi successions: allowing an equal share of the succession to the sister and the daughter of the deceased would give the Somkereki family access to the Seat's Szekler dignities. It so happens that in 1409[115] the Seat is in conflict with this family over their acquisition of a forest adjoining the villages of Sáromberke and Gernyeszeg, on the border between the Seat of Maros and the county of Torda.

This succession is difficult to interpret, given the personalities of the heirs by the sister – the Somkereki and a former vice-voivode of Transylvania – and the heavy-handed intervention of King Sigismund, which cast a shadow of doubt over compliance with Szekler customary law. What is more, these heirs by the sister of the deceased had redeemed the lien of the Szekler branch for a considerable sum. This raises the question whether, conscious of the weakness of their legal position, they had not simply bought up their rights. Thus, the Seat's decision, against which the king intervened, could well be the strict expression of customary law as enounced in 1451 and 1555: the descending line excluding all collaterals, irrespective of whether the Seat's decision was taken with a lurking idea of revenge for the Sáromberke conflict, provisionally resolved – these conflicts concerning the surveys to determine the limits between Somkereki properties and the Szeklerland would drag on until 1464[116] – in which the king had also intervened.

This rule of priority for the descending line was applied in 1486 in the Szentgyörgyi succession (Genealogical Table 4, The Barlabássi, Szentgyörgyi and Káli Succession), in which two daughters-deemed-sons, appearing in the name of their deceased father, came into their grandfather's inheritance, sharing it half-and-half with their uncle. The Latin text is somewhat murky, confused between the succession of Balázs (the father) and that of Barnabás (the grandfather). This said, we know that the father was dead by 1476[117] when, ten years after that, the tribunal faults the uncle for having, one year earlier, taken over the grandfather's entire primipilates, to the detriment of his nieces. We can therefore assume that the conflict was over the succession of the grandfather, who had died the year before. The father having died ten years before, the uncle considered himself the sole heir, but the tribunal had him share the inheritance with his nieces. This done, the cousins and their children, who had associated themselves to the complaint, were reminded that they would have no rights as long as the male and 'masculinized' lines were not extinct.

If we took the inheritance to be that of the daughters-deemed-sons' father, the line of succession would be reversed in admitting a division between the daughters and the collateral male line and the degree of relationship on which the cousins based their claim would have been more remote. From the division based on 'women's rights' between daughters and sisters we might in fact conclude a division between *daughters and sons*, but then it would no longer truly involve 'rights through women'. It seems that a brother cannot bring a branch threatened in its male line back to life, that such a brother, though part of the same lineage, represents a distinct stock, the lineage of which could not have precedence over the direct descendants of the deceased.

Whether daughters or sisters, what are the limits of the rights of these 'girls-deemed-boys'? Faced with her bellicose spouse Miklós Tóth, Anna, née Szentgyörgyi, does not intervene personally except when her grandfather's succession is in dispute. The husband's role as trustee is not explicitly mentioned, it appears that he manages the property, but on his death the 'woman-deemed-man', now widowed, acquires full legal majority, even if she remarries. In the course of my research on widows' rights, I have come across some cases that dispel the impression of unfailing consistency in the right of usufruct exercised by women trustees. Cases in which widows sell not only property situated in counties – we had come to accept such situations – but they sell primipilates as well!

The rich documentation of the *Székely Archives* permits us to reconstruct the origin of such exorbitant cases from the mass of documented sales. Three of these widows – Anna Bolyai, born Szentpáli,[118] Margit Jánosi, born Szentkirályi[119] and Martha Czirjék, widow of Lőrincz Mikó, born Szentgyörgyi[120] – are not unknown: Margit had become a daughter-deemed-son in 1451,[121] Martha in 1486,[122] Anna, grand-cousin by marriage of the mother of Martha[123] is also sole heiress (for Martha and Anna, see Genealogical Table 4, The Barlabássi, Szentgyörgyi and Káli Succession). For another widow, Orsolya Czikó, née Bogáti, we have not been able to establish the genealogy. A document[124] dated 1505 evokes the accord of brothers and/or blood relatives as a group[125] without further information of how she had come to inherit. Finally, in 1517, in the Seat of Aranyos, Orsolya Szabó, another widow, sells her Szekler hereditary property and a primipilate she had got from her father, Mihály Szemes. The document[126] designates her as heiress, but without specifying the absence of male heirs. In the Seat of Aranyos, the widow Lucia, daughter-deemed-son of András Szilágyi, obtained restitution of the inheritance of Ábrahám Felsőszentmihályfalvi – in contention with another widow, by the way – but met with the relatives' opposition when she tried to sell the property. Assuming that we are not misled by a coincidence in the conservation of documents, we may conclude that, where widows' rights to an inheritance are limited to its usufruct until her children come of age, a daughter-deemed-son does not lose her rights over the inheritance, even after marriage.

Unfortunately, the *Székely Archives* do not offer us the case of a daughter-deemed-son's widowed husband. Thus, we will never know whether he obtains just the usufruct of a property as its trustee, or whether he is in turn 'feminized' by virtue of his deceased spouse's status.

3. Rules Deduced from Practice
The codification of 1555 appears as an effort to systematize the customary laws and serves as an extremely useful source for historians of law, but, as György Bónis pointed out regretfully, it is incomplete. A belated addendum to this codification, no doubt a sacrilege because it was formulated at a desk and not in a boisterous Szekler Assembly, might read something like the following.

- If a man has no children but a brother, his widow has no rights to the inheritance, which passes directly to the deceased's brother (1507, Békési succession).
- If a man has minor children, his widow has the usufruct of the inheritance until her son comes of age (1458, Katalin Szentpáli, widowed Szentmihályfalvi) or her daughter marries (1498, Káli succession).
- If a man has two daughters and two sisters, the latter also inherit (1409, Madarasi succession; 1451 Szentkirályi succession and 1463–1502, Barlabássi succession) [women's rights in actual practice, in contradiction with Article 22 of the 1555 codification].
- If the women's rights are applied and the sisters are not of age [unmarried], the widow has the usufruct of the inheritance until the marriage of her sisters-in-law (1463, Barlabássi succession).
- A widow can only dispose over her property if she inherited it by absence of male heirs (1493, Bolyai sale and 1495, Jánosy sale), but then even if she remarries (1495, Czirjék sale).

The notion of extended kinship (horizontal) evolved in favour of the descendants (vertical) by strictly circumscribing women's rights to the sole rights of daughters-deemed-sons. This rule, reiterated in 1555, though its application is far from systematic, was a response to the risks illustrated by the Gyerőfi succession and the misdeeds (not documented as cases) of the Voivode Báthory.

Assimilation of the principle of priority to descendants and the will to conserve clan rights within a lineage, beyond this contradiction the rights of women – daughters – serve only one purpose: avoiding escheat.

IV. The Right of Confiscation before 1562

In the kingdom of Hungary, there were two ways for the Crown to recover land held by the nobility: escheat and confiscation. We have seen that escheat was not possible in the Szeklerland; in fact there were provisions for property to devolve to the village or the Seat in the case of a family's total extinction. High treason, which in Hungary resulted in confiscation, was not unknown among the Szeklers. But it was not until 1562 that the principle of confiscation was imposed for Szekler hereditary property in the name of the Crown. Some attempts had been made before that, but in vain. The documents dealing with these attempts also shed light on Szekler customary law in this domain.

A. The Underlying Principles

The principle of confiscation was not unknown in the Szekler community, it accompanied the banishment of a convict. Where it differed from the rule in the kingdom was in the fact that the confiscation could never be in favour of the Crown at the expense of the community (royal confirmation in 1499). High treason was not the only possible reason for confiscation. In 1505, faced with a situation considered inadmissible – betrayal of Szekler customary law by corrupt judges – the Szekler community, sitting in assembly at Udvarhely, condemned the judges to confiscation of all, including hereditary, property without specifying who – within the community – would be the beneficiary: '(the corrupt judge) … must be condemned on the spot to perpetual banishment with confiscation of all his property, movable as well as hereditary (*tam mobilia quam etiam hereditaria*).'[127]

In 1506, the very notion of high treason having been redefined by the Szeklers – rebellion against an authority considered unjust does not constitute treason – the principle of confiscation was accepted, but in favour of the heirs of the traitor, the latter incurring banishment: '(in a case of treason) all his property shall be adjudged to his veritable heirs and equitably distributed among them.'[128]

This principle was summarized by Werbőczy in 1514. According to his *Tripartitum*, the death penalty existed in certain cases, but in fact the assemblies of 1505 and 1506 mention only banishment. According to Werbőczy:

> § 3. 'A man, even if judged and condemned, cannot lose his hereditary property, which reverts to his descendants and his brothers; nor does one cut off his head, except in cases of high treason or the most serious crimes.'[129]

In 1555, these two situations are treated separately, Article 30 deals with high treason and it does provide for decapitation for treason, but it asserts that the inheritance reverts to the kindred. One can lose one's life for political reasons, but the family must not suffer the consequences by losing their patrimony:

§ 30. 'A Szekler may not lose his inheritance under any condition, even beheaded for treason; his hereditary property reverts to his family.'[130]

Article 68 deals with common crimes. Caught *in flagrante delicto*, the criminal first risks losing his personal belongings, then possibly his inheritance, and only as a last resort his life. Atonement for such cases involves compensation before punishment. If the perpetrator has enough personal belongings adequately to compensate his victims without prejudice to his family, that is the atonement chosen. If that is not possible, his hereditary property is next in line before capital punishment:

§ 68 'A Szekler cannot be held captive before his trial unless he was caught with blood on his hands or [stolen] cattle in his possession; if he is caught, one cannot touch his inheritance as long as he has cattle of his own, if he has neither inheritance nor cattle, one may take his head.'

This codification has only been conserved in Hungarian. The term used is '*marha*' – cattle. The notion of movable property seems indistinguishable from that of cattle. This terminology may have resulted from the fact that the value of movable personal property was often expressed in the equivalent heads of cattle.

To deprive a lineage of its possessions in favour of another seems conceivable in 1555; doing so in favour of higher authority for political reasons, on the other hand, is inadmissible.

B. The Practice

We can see these principles applied in some rare cases of confiscation to be found in the *Székely Archives*. In 1326, a Szekler had his property confiscated for having assassinated the king's treasurer (*tavernicus*). The document cites *res et bona*, without further specifics. The circumstances of the Angyalosi-Domokos case in 1473 are not clear: there is a possibility of confusion between confiscation and compensation by *weregild*. Between 1481 and 1555, four Szeklers were condemned for high treason.

The first, Balázs Meggyes de Erdőszentgyörgy, in 1481, was condemned by King Matthias, whose confiscation order clearly states that it does not apply to Szekler hereditary property.[131] The Voivode Báthory, holder of property confiscated in the counties, tried in vain to also get his hands on the Szekler property of a traitor, against the fierce and finally victorious opposition from Zsofia Meggyes de Erdőszentgyörgy, who later married Gáspár Barcsai, a daughter-deemed-son, the heiress of the traitor, whose Szekler hereditary property was preserved.[132]

In 1521, two confiscations were pronounced against leaders of a Szekler uprising. One,[133] affecting the Balaskó family, involved only property situated on county territory, while the other,[134] pronounced against János Lázár and his brother, involved Szekler primipilates. It was a complicated case. It did involve

Szekler property, but this property had only been in the Lázár family for some ten years; the family had other hereditary Szekler properties, which were not concerned by the confiscation; could it be that the voivode did not consider the too recently acquired lands as hereditary?

In these two cases the voivode immediately attributed the confiscated land to two other Szekler families, who had had previous ties to these properties. The Balaskó property in county territory was given to the Apor family, the previous owners, who had pledged them to the Balaskó as security against a loan. Three primipilates at Kisfalud were attributed to the Tóth, a family holding a lien on this property from Ferencz Székely d'Esztergom, who had sold the land to the Lázár family. Thus, the Balaskó confiscation does not conflict with the principles of Szekler custom; in fact the attribution to another Szekler family serves the interest of the community as a whole.

The second confiscation, while leaving the primipilates within the community, does represent interference by the Crown in the distribution of Szekler lands, in violation of customary law. Was the confiscation really carried through? In 1529,[135] the same János Lázár was once more condemned by the same John Szapolyai, now king, for high treason in supporting Ferdinand of Habsburg. The same property is confiscated as before, and once again attributed to the Tóth family. Such repetition sheds doubt on the effective execution of the first confiscation. We run into the Tóth and the Lázár families again, in 1535,[136] before the tribunal of the Voivode István Majlád, who prudently pointed out to the king that, according to the Transylvanian Diet, 'the law and justice are on the side of the Lázár family'. In 1538, the king finally returned the properties to János Lázár and his order of investiture was executed, without opposition, the same year.[137]

In 1555, Balázs Pókai committed particularly dishonourable, aggravated treason: as standard-bearer of the army of the Transylvanian nobility he deserted to the Ottoman enemy – the standard in hand. That year he figured in two documents: his condemnation for high treason and desertion and the confiscation of his property in a Szekler village – in a document[138] not stating the day and month of the condemnation – and he is also cited in a suit involving succession to a Szekler hereditary property situated in the same village, a case he lost on 4 October 1555.[139]

Here the confiscated property is, in this author's opinion, unlikely to have been Szekler hereditary property. Either the confiscation and banishment were pronounced prior to 4 October, then Balázs Pókai could not go to court to recover his property, or the confiscation was pronounced after this date, then it was not possible to confiscate property he no longer owned. What is more, both documents are signed by the same voivodes and the choice of terminology for the confiscation indicates that only acquests were involved, not the Szekler inheritance mentioned in the case dated 4 October. The two cases are probably concomitant. According to the verdict of the voivodes, the litigation over the inheritance had already been judged by the Assembly of the Seat of Maros in the first instance and appealed to the Seat of Udvarhely in Balázs Pókai's disfavour. The voivodes are respectful of Szekler customs: all the deserter's private property (*vniuersa bona*) is confiscated and the two judgements of the Seats concerning the Szekler inheritance (*hereditatum Siculicalium*) in favour of the appealing party are finally confirmed.

Throughout the documentation studied, the notion of hereditary Szekler property is always meticulously distinct. Thus, one cannot well take the expression 'all property' to include Szekler hereditary properties. The case involving inheritance, which – fortunately – is judged during the very same weeks as the confiscation lends weight to this interpretation.

We could ask ourselves what would have happened, had the verdicts handed down by the Szekler Assemblies been in the traitor's favour. In 1553,[140] at Balázs Pókai's request, the voivodes had ordered a new hearing and returned the case to the Seat of Maros. The tone of the document clearly gives the impression that the judge who adjudged the inheritance to the adverse party had been guilty of favouritism and the voivodes seem to be leaning toward the – still glorious – standard-bearer of the army. The two voivodes were familiar with Szekler customs, having in the same year of 1555 presided at the codifying assembly; this author believes that they sincerely and willingly respected the decisions of 1553 and 1555 concerning the inheritance. Even in the presence of as heinous a felony as that of Balázs Pókai, the customary rules of the Szekler community remained untouched.

C. The Decision of 1562

The principle of non-confiscation of Szekler hereditary property was so strictly respected that King John II Szapolyai, reigning over a severely diminished realm, was powerless against the demands of the Szeklers, proportionally having grown in importance within the remaining kingdom. The very first 'whereas' of his decision of 1562 leaves no doubt about his irritation at this situation:

> Whereas the Szeklers, relying on their ancestral privileges of not losing their hereditary property, have rebelled [.../...] We have decided that if ever in the future they commit acts qualified in the Szeklerland as treason, they too, like the nobles and other faithful subjects of Our Realm, shall incur the punishment of traitors and shall each of them lose their possessions and hereditary property.[141]

From the first assembly in Zabola in 1466 to the codification of 1555, with the intervening royal confirmation of 1499 and the *Tripartitum*, in spite of occasionally violent uprisings, the 'diplomatic' relations between the Szekler community and the state – the king or voivode – always evolved in an atmosphere of respect for the Szeklers' ancestral customs by the authorities. The kingdom cruelly shrunk and weakened after the disaster of Mohács in 1526, the decision of 1562 represents the first overt transgression by the Crown into the sphere of Szekler law and rights.

Diagrams of the Rules of Successoral Devolution

Legend		Male, heir	▲
Devolution the inheritance	↙↓↘	Female, heiress (daughter-deemed-son)	●
Transfer of dowry	→	Female, excluded from succession	○
Extinction of the line	–	Female, heiress (sister-deemed-male)	◉

The rights of women:

'... *eo modo quod* <u>si</u> *idem Semyen semen masculinum post se reliquisset, extunc bona et haereditates eiusdem Semyen* <u>ante</u> *alias feminas in sexum virilem devolvi debuissent. Verum ex quo in virili sexu et semine defecisset, igitur iuxta consuetudinem siculorum huismodi bona et haereditates* <u>ad ius femineum</u> *in praefatas scilicet dominam Annam* <u>sororem</u> *carnalem* <u>et</u> *tres* <u>filias</u> *ipsius Semyen devolutae essent.*' (1451)[142]

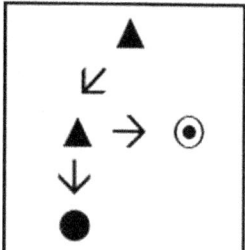

If a man has two sons:

a): '... *Et quamdocumque eciam duo fratres olim antiquis temporibus in eorum hereditatibus siculicabus ab inuicem fuerunt diuisi et sequestrati, tum eorum successores easdem hereditates siculicales, sibi inuicem succedantes, taliter possidere et tenere debeant.*' (1451)[143]

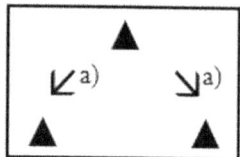

And the order of succession:

b): '... *Quod quamdiu in aliqua eorum proximitatis linea heredes masculini sexus superuixerint, heredes femini sexus, in preiudicium heredum masculini sexus, eisdem heredibus masculini sexus superuiuentibus, in dominium huiusmodi hereditatum se intromittere non valeant,*'

c): '*deficientibusque huiusmodi heredibus masculinis et aliquibus feminei sexus heredibus superuiuentibus, de prescripta alia linea proximitatis heredes masculini sexus, quamdiu superuixerint, in huiusmodi hereditatis partes in illam partem successas se iniungere non valeant,*'

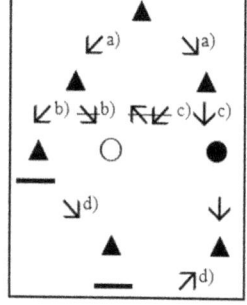

d): '*deficientibusque utriusque sexus heredibus, tandem in aliam lineam proximitatis naturalem succedere debeant hereditates antedicte.*' (1451)[144]

If a man has a son and a daughter, the inheritance goes to his son, but the son must provide a dowry for the daughter in accordance with the laws of the Seat. (1555, § 20)[145] 'Valamely embernek fia, leány vagyon, az örökség a fiat illeti: de ugy hogy a fia a leányt, kiki a maga székének törvénye szerént, kiházasitsa'.

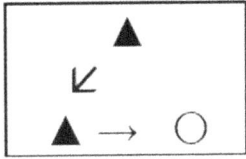

If a man has two sons and one of them has a son, the other a daughter: the daughter inherits from her father like the son from his. (1555, § 21)[146] 'Ha két férfiu egy ember gyermeke, egyiknek fia, a másiknak leánya vagyon, a leány olyan örökös az atyja örökségében mint a fia'.

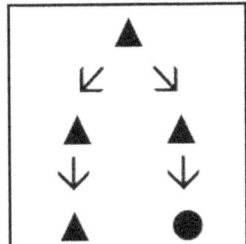

If a man has two daughters and no son, they both inherit, but in such a way that the younger may choose within the house an inheritance comparable to that of the other; if, on the other hand, the younger cannot give a comparable part to the older, the inheritance must be divided into equal parts. (1555, § 22)[147] 'Valamely embernek két leánya vagyon, fia nincsen, atyjokról maradott örökségek egyaránt illetik őket, de ugy, hogy a kissebbik válaszhasson a lakó helyben, de ugy hogy a másiknak hozzája hasonló légyen, egyaránt örökösködhessenek benne; ha pedig a kissebbik a nagyobbiknak hasonlót nem adhatna, tehát az örökség két felé osztassék'.

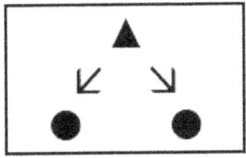

If a man has two daughters and one of them has a son, the other a daughter, the daughter inherits from her father like the son from his, but if the [grand]daughter [later] has a son and a daughter, her son must provide the dowry of the daughter. (1555, § 23)[148] 'Valamely embernek két leánya vagyon, egyik leánynak fia, a másiknak leánya vagyon, a leány is olyan örökös az atyja jószágában, mint a fiu: de ha a leánynak fia és leánya lészen, a fiu a leányt kiházasitja belőle'.

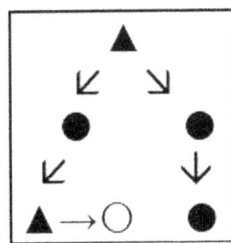

Genealogical Table N° 1

❖ The Gyerőfi Succession
(1408-1410 / 1451)

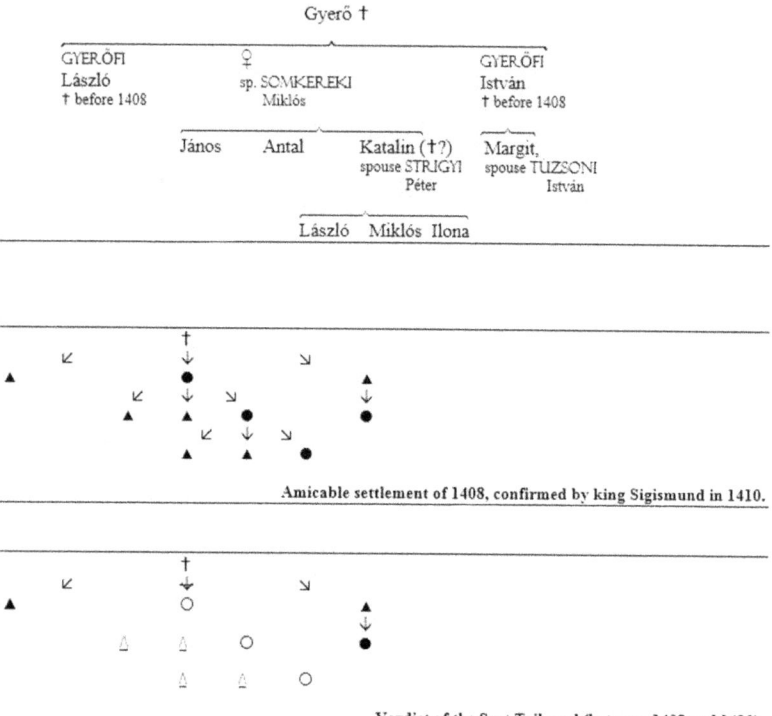

Amicable settlement of 1408, confirmed by king Sigismund in 1410.

Verdict of the Seat Tribunal (between 1408 and 1410).

Land Ownership

Genealogical Table n° 2

❖ **The Madarasi Successions**
(1409 / 1484)

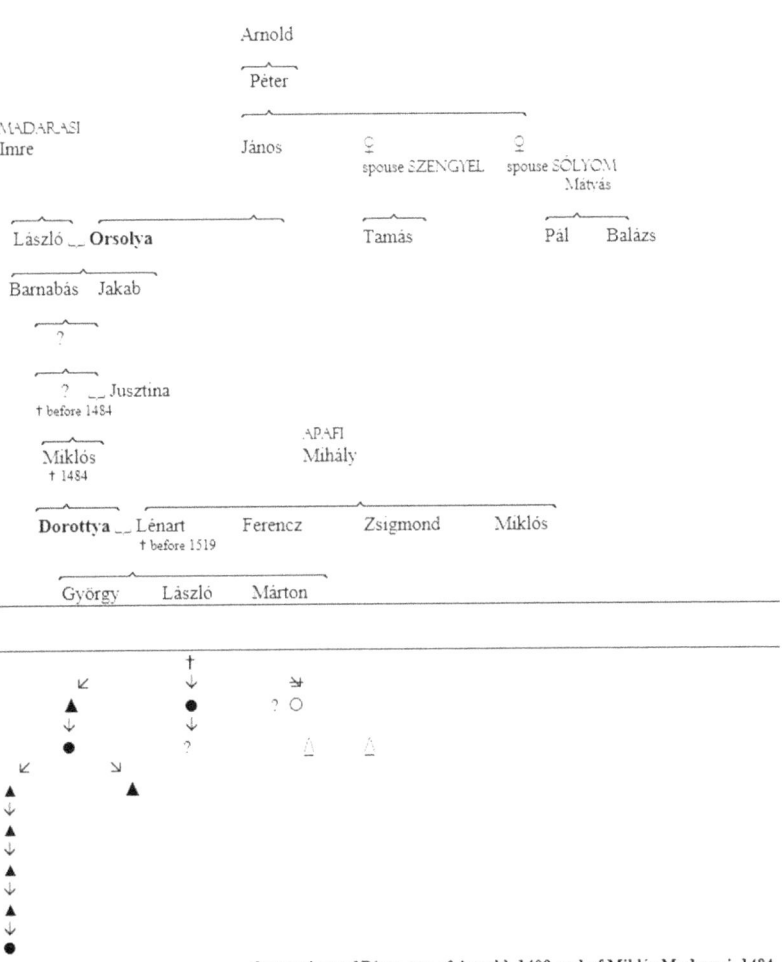

Successions of Péter, son of Arnold, 1409 and of Miklós Madarasi, 1484.

Genealogical Table N°3

❖ **The Szentkirályi Succession**
(1451)

István
├── Semjén
│   ├── Margit — spouse: JÁNOSY György † before 1495
│   ├── Anna
│   └── Ilona
└── Anna — spouse: GYULAKUTI Péter

Succession of Semjén Szentkirályi, 1451

Genealogical Table N° 4

❖ **The Successions of Barlabássi, Szentgyörgyi and Káli**
(1463-1502, 1486 and 1498)

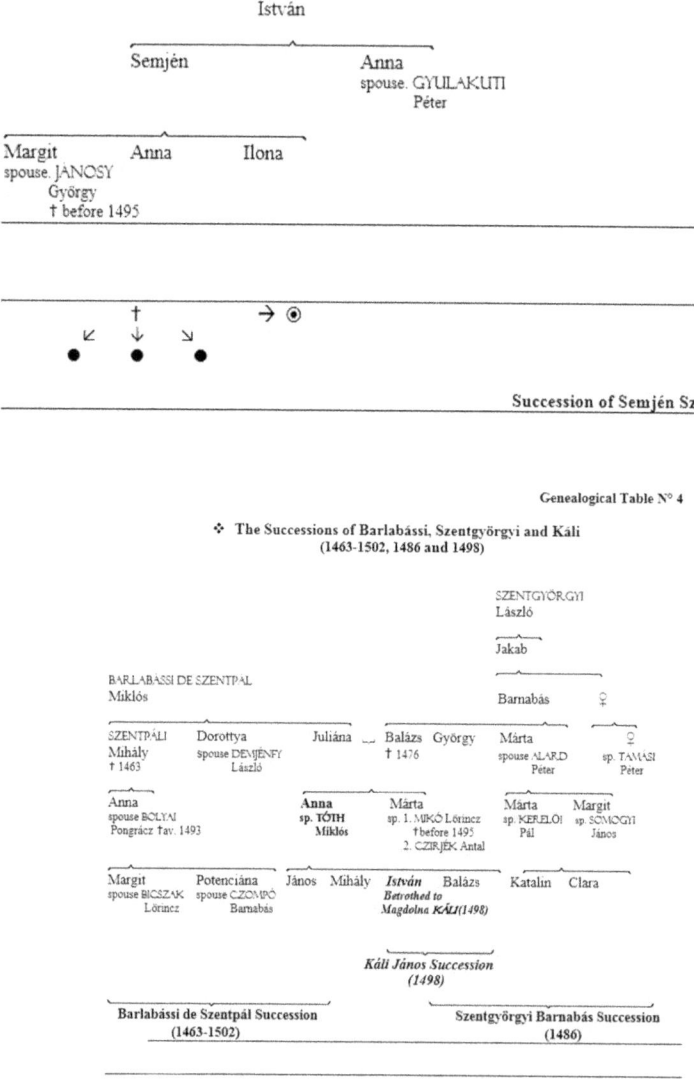

Káli János Succession (1498)

Barlabássi de Szentpál Succession (1463-1502) ‖ Szentgyörgyi Barnabás Succession (1486)

BY WAY OF CONCLUSION

This study ends with the royal decision of 1562. The particularism of Szekler law, however, did not end with this decision, royal or not.

A study of the history of law must take certain strictly historical episodes into account, even if there is nothing really juridical about them. The defeat at Mohács of 1526 finally had its effect on Szekler customary law some forty years later. Following the death of John I Szapolyai and the fall of Buda to the Ottomans (1540–1541), Transylvania became the scene of unceasing battles. As alliances succeeded betrayals, the armies of the Sultan and those of the Habsburgs criss-crossed the country. Looting, destruction and acts of retaliation weigh on the population at least as much as the tribute to be paid to the Sublime Porte. The Habsburg faction arrived on the abdication of John II Szapolyai who, on his return, was accompanied by the Sultan's armies.

In the spring of 1562, part of the nobles went over to the Habsburgs, betraying King John, who had the Sultan's favour. The common Szeklers, resenting the obligation to contribute to the tribute demanded by the Turks while also being held to their military service, rose up against their notables, who were not willing – or able – to safeguard their community's liberties in a weakened Assembly of the Three Nations. But they also rose against King John II Szapolyai, the protégé of the Sublime Porte. The rebellion was violent and determined the king's retribution, which was no more clement.

Before returning to the domain of law, let us turn to Matthias Miles (1639–1686), a Transylvanian Saxon who gave an account of these events a century later, with cruel attention to detail.[1] The Saxon's account vividly reminds us of the Szeklers' attachment to their liberty and the price they paid for it, but especially of the terror that accompanied the imposition of the royal decree.

When this [a noble Hungarian's going over to the Habsburgs] *had happened outside Transylvania, and many towns, markets and villages were put to the torch, many folk taken away and their land laid waste and war was spreading its flames everywhere, then inside Transylvania the Szeklers rose up (they are a very ancient tribe of the Huns or Scythians led here and left behind by Attila). They were angry at the King and took up arms because on the counsel of some evil, envious and greedy men he had taken away their ancient freedom and burdened them with heavy taxes and they wanted to practise their rights and customs again and not live almost like bound serfs.*

When they saw that the enemy was besetting the King outside the country, they ordered each other to take arms, every one of them, young and old: They were egged on by Gábor Majláth of Fogaras and the Despot just elected to the voivodate of Moldavia, who promised to come to the aid of the poor exploited neighbours and help them in any adversity: Thereupon the [Szekler] Captains issued a strict order that all who did not join the uprising with enough fervour should be hung before their doors and their houses, wives and children put to waste. They sent their emissaries to the Saxon towns, asking them for help in defending their cherished freedom, all the while trying to arouse the riff-raff by saying that they, too, would be so oppressed and lose their freedom if they stood by and did nothing against the excesses of the Hungarians, who would throw the worthy Saxons in the same boat of injustice as the Szeklers: For they, the Saxons, had all the means, fortified towns, much money and ammunition, only courage was needed, which they should show in the manly defence of their fatherland, then good fortune would be on their side to assure the outcome.

When the Szeklers were asked in whose name and under whose command and captainship they went into battle, they said that they were taking arms in God's name to defend and practise their freedom under His protection or, if it was His will, die with honour. To which the honourable burghers of Medwisch/Scheßburg and Kronstadt replied: We ourselves cannot give an opinion of our own on this because it is a matter for all the Saxon community, of which we are only members. Hermannstadt is our capital and we must wait to learn what they decide and deem advisable, which will guide our own doing. What they decide they will let us know by messenger and that is what we will do. With these good words they wanted only to appease the Szeklers to gain time and wait out the events avoiding a true, negative reply, which might enrage the Szeklers, who might take revenge in doing great harm in the bordering villages.

The Szeklers assembled everywhere without waiting, young ones who had but a club, old men who could hardly put one foot before the other, all rose and assembled at Kézd [Szászkézd], moved from there to establish camp near Scheßburg at Ebesfalva (near the ancestral estate and castle of our Gracious Lord and Prince Gergely Apaffi) whereupon the lord Apaffi was in great danger there. From here they moved to Bonyha and Maros Vásárhely; there to meet up with the Szeklers camped between the rivers Maros and Nyárád and passed by Szász-Régen, spreading destruction among the Saxon tenant-peasants in the region. But before the two camps could join up, a speedy messenger reached them and told them how Gábor Mayláth had burst into their country laying it to waste, burning their villages and houses cutting down all he met, women and children, to finish with the Szeklers once and for all.

Then the men on horseback veered around and stormed back to save their families and tear from the enemy's hands any prisoners who might have survived. Now when Mayláth in turn was advised to flee the vengeance of the enraged warriors, he veered around quickly, but he was met head-on by the furious Szeklers. Arriving in complete disorder, they fell upon the enemy without battle order, captains or strategies, each guided only by his frenzy to save his family, hurled himself forward with his long pike, firing his musket, with death and destruction on both sides; then the Szeklers on foot arrived to join in and with their long scythes sweeping, they cut in half even knights in armour and they raged like wild animals, one of them piercing Mayláth's horse so the lord fell, bleeding from an ear, hardly able to clamber unaided on a horse brought alongside by a faithful servant and he turned around and fled with the rest of his men.

Upon which the Szeklers took up the pursuit of the fleeing soldiers with all the more determination and cut them all down with a fury such that the roads and paths were covered with corpses and blood and none of Mayláth's men would have escaped alive, had night not fallen on this day of the Szeklers' frightful vengeance.

Among the brave men fallen in battle there was Balázs Boyér, a good soldier worthy of taking with him the honour of a faithful servant, for it was he who had saved Mayláth from among the swords, muskets and scythes, jumping from his horse to help Mayláth mount it, thus he later fell, fighting on foot. Among the captains killed was István Velenczei, a handsome young man without equal in all the camp for his force, his manliness and skill, wherefore he stood fast to face an elephantine Szekler smith whom he had seen decapitating eleven worthy nobles before himself becoming the twelfth.

Later, Mayláth often told of this battle, saying he would never have imagined such blood-thirst from human beings, or such courage from the Szeklers. And from then on he believed that they were descendants of the Scythians and the Scourge of God, for they had fought like true men.

Following this battle, the other Szeklers, who had stayed as a forward guard near Vásárhely, started savouring the victory, celebrating day and night and feasting on wine brought from the nearby noble estates and villages and they set about spreading havoc in the countryside thinking that there was no more danger and that the debacle had sapped the king's power. The king, for his part, reflecting how he could punish them for their insolence and bring them under his power again, started raising the people in all the land, advisedly in secret. And when he learned that the Szeklers, returning home, laid the countryside to waste and that their two camps had not yet joined up, he despatched five hundred horsemen with foot soldiers, just to reconnoitre what the Szeklers were doing, what arms and munitions they had, how many there were, what battle-dispositions they had taken and how one could approach them or disperse them, while King John himself stayed with his other army at Torda to await the report of his scouts and take action at the appropriate moment.

When the king's scouts approached and saw the Szeklers' state of inebriation and feeling of security, they fell upon them with great clamour during the morning meal on June 22nd by surprise, so startling them that none defended themselves and all were killed or captured, and few of them escaped, perhaps only those who were absent pillaging. The victors sent the tied-up captives and their standards to the king with noisy derision and ridicule, but the king granted pardon to most of them and let them go home peacefully. But before, he made them swear that they would forever be his faithful and obedient subjects and would never go to war or rise up against their king. And he had their hair clipped like those of monks and their clothes cut just under the belt to expose them to mockery end ridicule. Three of them had their hands cut off, the ring-leaders' ears were cut off and others' nostrils were mutilated as a sign of everlasting shame.

After these events (when all was thought to be forgotten) the king and his large court made a ceremonious entry at Segesvár, the town closest to the Szeklerland, there to hold an assembly to which the most prominent Szekler dignitaries were convoked under a strong escort and when they were all assembled in the lower church the chancellor of the time, István Csáki, suddenly entered with a list, from which he read the names of the leaders of those who had provoked the uprising. He ordered their immediate arrest and fettering and had them taken to different prisons where they were heavily guarded so that no-one could approach them. Every day the king had some of them tortured and executed by various means after their public confessions.

One of the last to be dealt with was a very massive and strong Szekler who was therefore called György Nagy [big, bulky in Hungarian] and the executioner dragged him all around the town and tore him with red-hot tongues, rammed a glowing iron crown onto his head, forced a red-hot sceptre into his hand and finally spread him on the ground and impaled him in such a way as not to touch any vital organs and thus prolong his agony. Thus he lived for three days, howling with pain and shrieking horribly from unimaginable torment, when he implored passers-by to put an end to his torture and an unknown took pity and lifted him to ram him down further, but the pain and screams were even worse until someone finally put him out of his misery with a musket-shot.

The other Szeklers were forced to erect with their own labour and means a fortress in their land where the king placed a strong garrison to prevent further uprisings, with orders to keep them docile and oppress them and as an eternal reminder he gave the fortress the name 'Székely-Támadt', which in the language of the Szeklers means 'Szekler rose up'. And this is how this uprising came to a horrible end.

It was in these circumstances that King John II Szapolyai held his assembly of 1562 at Segesvár, where he issued his edict concerning the Szeklers. It was by no means the first Szekler uprising, no more than it was the first time one was quelled. Nor would it be the last. But, in 1562, it was the first time that a sovereign's decision curtailed the Szeklers' privileges and liberty.

The royal edict of 1562, in article after article, shatters the principles constituting the juridical autonomy of the Szekler community. In its protocol and sixteen articles, it pursues two principal aims: the will to divide the community and reduce its juridical autonomy.

On the first point, the king's intent appears to be the most subtle: assure himself of the Szekler notables' favour in equating them with the nobles of the Transylvanian counties (exemption from taxes against armed service on horseback exclusively, reserving for them alone the access to salt produced in Transylvania).

It is not entirely unreasonable to presume sincerity on his part when he expresses sympathy for the common Szeklers' complaints. But after the spring rebellion and in the context of the moment, some scepticism is in order. The king's protective stance in certain articles appears rather condescending. In his formulations there is no allusion to the noble status or the liberty of the common Szekler. Nonetheless, this decision does not reduce the common Szeklers to a status comparable to the servitude weighing on peasants in the rest of Transylvania: 'the common Szeklers shall be free under Our authority'. The perversity of the formulation consists in its institutionalizing the *de facto* economic cleavage within the community. A narrow margin of liberty under such a king, but this division prevented the more powerful Szeklers to be quite on a level with the nobles in the counties, who lorded it over the populations living on their lands.

Some essential points of Szekler legal procedure were nevertheless abrogated: the juries – always composed of twelve members – had henceforth to consist exclusively of notables, verdicts were to be reached in closed session 'excluding all from the place of deliberation so they could judge in the calm, according to the justice of God and their good conscience'. The king intended to put an end to the noisy assemblies of free Szeklers so vividly described by A. Verancsics.

Similarly, under the pretext of protecting the common Szeklers against their notables, the king intervened in the juridical autonomy of the community. Did a common Szekler have a complaint against a notable? Let him submit it – in writing – to the judge of his Seat, henceforth called 'Judge Royal'. Was a Szekler unhappy with the verdict of a tribunal? Let him lodge his appeal directly with the Tribunal of the Royal Court. Finished were the appeals to the court at Udvarhely, together with the elaborate Szekler procedures which, according to a king 'concerned about the misery of the Szeklers', had caused so much delay in the settling of an issue, whereas – as we have seen – it was in fact against the rareness of assemblies that the Szeklers had protested in 1505.

But the notables also had their prerogatives curtailed – with no benefit for the common Szeklers. Put on a level with the county nobles in matters of fiscal privilege and armed service – they also shared the latter's fate in the case of treason: capital punishment and confiscation of their property, which, of course, fell to the Crown, as stated in the very first Article and reiterated in Article 10. The shortening of the appeals procedure served to smooth the way for cases between Szeklers to come more quickly under royal jurisdiction, but it also deprived the notables of their functional autonomy.

This latter aspect, the curtailment of the Szekler dignitaries' power and hence the diminishing of their statutory prestige, motivated them to take up the struggle again for the community's autonomy, with the support of the common Szeklers, as early as 1571 and many times thereafter, whenever political circumstances allowed.

Paradoxically enough, the more the juridical customs of the Szeklers came under pressure, starting in the second half of the fifteenth century, the more the community was intent to protect them by consignment to writing. Certain historians see this as the 'beginning of the end' of Szekler autonomy, but in fact the fixing of formerly oral traditions in writing served to accentuate the community's consciousness of its particularism. Not until the last quarter of the nineteenth century (in 1876, Law XXXIII merged the Szekler and Saxon Seats with the counties), again some while after the upheavals of 1848–1849 and the nationalistic waves that swept away particularisms that had not found their berth in nation-states, was when all expression of Szekler juridical specificity ended, but not the collective memory and individual sense of identity.

There is one part of the community's structure that this royal decision could not undermine: the village. Halfway through the nineteenth century, the community's traditions and the spirit of statutory equality were alive – nurtured by the conscience of common identity acquired at the turn of the sixteenth century – village by Szekler village. In spite of the ups and downs in the conservation of the community's privileges against the pressures of the central authority (in its diverse manifestations) the sense of its right to common liberty was perpetuated in village assemblies – out of reach of the reigning powers – and this collective memory continued to come to the fore at the community level on every occasion.

I. Imreh collected these 'village laws' in a volume, with numerous laws voted in assembly and including an occasional village poet's work, whose memorized, ingenuous verses would assure recall. Recalling one of these at the end of this study, I would like to remind the reader that the sense of right and justice was not struck down by the edict of 1562:[2]

> Like our fathers, brave and just:
> In law and justice we will trust.
> The village must by laws abide,
> Our every action they must guide.
>
> The law is there for all to heed,
> The just, the rogue; the brave, the meek,
> The heir, or upstart; rich and poor,
> The learned, dunce, the wise or boor.
>
> Laws and justice find what's true,
> Foil false claims and grant what's due;
> Let the righteous have their way
> And force the rogues their sins to pay.
>
> Pasture, forest, fields and streets,
> Fencing, orchards, land and fields,
> The rules are written in this book:
> The village judge knows where to look.

GLOSSARY

Admonitions of St. Stephen (*Libellus de institutione morum*) A text written around 1010-1020 (the author or authors have not been definitively identified), modelled after the 'Mirror for Princes' of the Carolinian era. Its particular pertinence derives from the role it assigns to the nobility and the status it confers on the Crown, superior to that of the king's person.

Altland (region in Transylvania) Name of the territory where the Saxon colonists were first settled (late twelfth c.) The toponymy indicates that the region had been formerly settled by Szeklers.

Árpádians Dynasty of the first reigning sovereigns of Hungary, descendants of Árpád, who was the military chieftain at the time of the Conquest (*q.v.*) in 896. The last king of this dynasty died in 1301.

Assembly of the Three Nations Transylvanian provincial assembly (while Hungary had County Assemblies), seating the representatives of the nobility of its (seven) Hungarian counties and those of the two privileged Nations, Saxon and Szekler. As in Hungary, the peasantry of the counties (Hungarian or Vlach) was not represented.

Barons, magnates (*barones et magnates*) Members of the 'higher nobility' (in theory all nobles were equal). Second tier of the society of Estates.

Bohemia Between the end of the Árpádian dynasty (1301) and the defeat at Mohács (1526), the crowns of Hungary, Bohemia and Poland were periodically borne by the same sovereign:
1387-1437, Sigismund of Luxemburg (recognized King of Bohemia in 1436)
1437-1439, Albert of Habsburg (crowned King of Bohemia in 1438)
1444-1457, Ladislas V of Habsburg (Ladislas I as King of Bohemia, 1440-1457)
1490-1516, Wladislas II Jagiello (Wladislas II, King of Bohemia, 1471-1516)
Louis II Jagiello (crowned King of Bohemia in 1509)

Clans (society of) Society structured on membership (real or imaginary) *in one and the same* 'family', with 'blood ties'. A status of freedom is derived from clan membership. Clans may be politically united in tribes, where a dominant clan could impose (or imprint) its 'genealogy' on the others. The next higher level, the federation of tribes, was rarely long-lasting. This type of social structure, which was that of the Hungarians up to the Conquest, remained a driving force in the Szekler community.

Colonists (*hospites*) From the eleventh c. the Hungarian kingdom's policy of hospitality benefited Western colonists, who enjoyed charters of privilege and were often instrumental in developing market and mining towns.

Comes A royal officer, military and judiciary head of a county or, in Transylvania, of a privileged community (*comes Saxonorum* and *comes Siculorum*). *Ispán* in Hungarian (intendant or, in modern times, prefect). The English translation of 'Count' would bear the risk of confounding this function with the hereditary title (*gróf* in Hungarian, in German *Graf*).

Conquest The arrival of the Hungarians in the Carpathian basin, referred to in Hungarian as '*Honfoglalás*' or 'land-taking'. Western historiography customarily recalls it less as an act of 'conquest' than as the subsequent series of raids west of the river Leitha. In this study, the term 'Conquest' refers to what in Hungarian history is treated as an event: *Honfoglalás*, or 'land-taking'. Although in the English language 'Conquest' has come to be associated with 1066, it is applied here to the Hungarians' appropriation of a territory that was to remain theirs. An analogous semantic situation exists with the Vikings, whose permanent settling of Iceland and the islands from the Faeroes to the Hebrides was the great 'taking up of the land', the *Landnáma*, while the appearance of the Vikings in southern Europe was seen there as 'raids'.

County Territorial entity of the Hungarian kingdom. Modelled after the Carolinian concept, the system was put in place in the eleventh c. While their geographical limits (drawn around a fortress) remained stable, land ownership within the counties shifted, starting in the thirteenth century, from Crown domains to seigniorial properties owned by the magnates.

Croatia Personal union of the crowns of Croatia and Hungary (*Pacta Conventa* of 1102). Following the assassination of Zvonimir, King of Croatia, in 1089, his widow Ilona, sister of the Hungarian King Ladislas I, called on her brother to help in the quarrels over succession. The conflicts were settled by King Coloman, with the assent of the Croatian nobles, by the establishment of a personal union for the two crowns. While the territory thus became a domain of the Holy Crown, its institutions (the office of *ban* of Croatia and the provincial Diet) remained in place.

Estates (**society of**) (*Status et Ordines Regni Hungariae ex quatuor conditionis Regnicolis, nemque Praelatis, Baronibus et Magnatibus, Nobilibus et Iberis Civitatibus constent*) The society of Estates is founded on status (birth and land ownership), not on wealth. Failure to be recognized as a member of the Estates implied loss of juridical freedom and subjection to the justice not of the king but of a prelate or noble. In actual practice, while the lower and middle nobility and the citizens of Royal Free Towns enjoyed juridical freedom, only the two primary Estates carried a certain degree of political weight in front of the King.

Feudal society vs. *familiaritas* In its general acceptance, the term, as defined by Marc Bloch[1]: 'In present-day usage, "feudalism" and "feudal society" cover a whole complex of ideas in which the fief properly so called no longer occupies the foreground', can conceivably be applied to the kingdom of Hungary, inasmuch as we encounter a progressive shift from royal authority to that of a nobility with the right to mete out justice over a non-free population. And yet, as Gy. Bónis[2] points out, the most striking characteristic of feudal society, the feudo-vassalic relation, did not exist in Hungary. Hence, rather than risking the use of this term, he prefers to use '*familiaritas*'. On the basis of Max Weber's analyses, he does perceive personal ties between the king and his entourage, the *familiaritas*, and a replication of this system around magnates; he also notes the existence of land donations. But, in the context of the eleventh to twelfth c., he points out that: 'The Hungarian state of the initial period does not bear the characteristics of a feudal society. It is the King's family which is spread throughout the country and its members in turn are surrounded by groups of faithful of their own.' For the following period (thirteenth to fifteenth c.), he adds, setting apart the situation of the clergy: 'For us, vassality and reward developed separately.' Finally, stressing the nature of vassalic relations, he asks: 'Is this feudalism? Certainly not, if we refer to semantics of sociology. It lacks the contractual definition of service, the balance between service and reward, the reciprocity of loyal attachment.'

Finno-Ugrian languages   A group of non-Indo-European languages, a sub-group of the Uralo-Altaic languages. Finnish and Hungarian are its principal representatives. The Szeklers, using a form of runic writing probably of Turcophonic origin, are thought to have acquired the Hungarian language shortly before the Conquest. Linguistic arguments are legion in the argumentation of the different theories on the origin of the Szeklers.

Fortress   (*castrum, vár*) The first fortresses were essentially made of hard earth and wood. Stone structures developed after the Mongol invasion (1241). Initially Crown property, centres of power over the counties, the fortresses lost their hold gradually after the thirteenth c. In the Szeklerland, several enclaves of Crown land remained in place around royal fortresses.

Golden Bull   (1222) Often compared to the *Magna Carta* of England, the G.B. was promulgated by King Andrew II under pressure from the Hungarian nobles, confirming the rights they had gradually secured at the expense of the royal estate. More, the Bull recognizes their right to share collectively in the affairs of the state and to disobey the king. Revised and confirmed several times, the Bull is the document founding the Hungarian society of Estates.

Gyula   In the Hungarian structure of the ninth to tenth c. (inspired by the diarchic system of the Khazar empire), the *gyula* was a politico-military dignitary at the head of the federation of tribes. Árpád is held to have been *gyula*, while his father Álmos is believed to have been the sacral dignitary (*kende*), executed in 895. The two dignities later combined.

Holy Crown   An abstract political concept first expressed during the reign of St. Stephen (in his Admonitions) later reinforced, more or less consciously, by the nobility through the Golden Bull, whose Article 31 concedes their right to disobey the person of the king. The Crown, in the interest of cohesion, is placed higher than the person of the king. It finds its most refined expression is in the *Opus Tripartitum* of István Werbőczy.

Horka   (or *karkhas*) Mentioned by Constantine Porphyrogenitus, this term is not uniformly accepted in Hungarian historiography as pertinent to its history. It is nevertheless referred to occasionally as a third dignity (that of judge) alongside the *gyula* and the *kende*.

Jobbágyok   (Latinized form: *jobbagiones*) Difficult to translate, this term originally referred to the (free) servants of the royal domains and fortresses (*iobbagiones castri*). From the thirteenth c. *jobbágyok* were 'given' to magnates along with the domains where they served, and the term comes to denote a non-free state. Nevertheless, the reality of the population thus referred to is variable: with or without tenure, corvée work and personal rights – marriage, private succession – factors that never quite correspond to Occidental realities (just as variable). In documentation relating to the Szekler community, the term appears much later (early sixteenth c.).

Kende   (or *kündü*) In the Hungarian organization of the ninth to tenth c. (modelled after the diarchic organization of the Khazar empire), the *k*. was a sacral dignitary responsible for relations with the 'nether world'. Álmos, father of Árpád, is thought to have been the last *k.*, his execution in 895 a consequence of the attack by the Pechenegs that caused the Hungarians to flee all the way to the Carpathian basin. The dignity of kende then merged with that of *gyula*.

Liberty, nobility, privilege   From the Middle Ages to the nineteenth c. the population of the kingdom of Hungary was divided into two categories: the society of Estates (the free, the privileged) and the rest. Beyond this cursory, binary division, the structures in Hungary were complex and diverged significantly from those known in the West, particularly as concerns the distinctions existing within the free and non-free elements.[3] Hungarian historiography sometimes blames István Werbőczy for having institutionalized this dual distinction in his oeuvre (*Opus Tripartitum*) which, while it consolidated national unity (of the nobles) around the doctrine of the Holy Crown, deepened the statutory gulf between the privileged (the *populus werbőczyanus*) and the non-free.

Partium regni Hungariae   Following the defeat at Mohács (1526) and the taking of Buda by the Ottomans (1540), the term designates the territories situated between the pashalik of Buda and the medieval Province of Transylvania. These territories were incorporated into the Principality of Transylvania upon its creation in 1570. The access of magnates from this region to the Diet of Transylvania was a factor of destabilization to the detriment of the privileged Saxon and Szekler communities.

Poland   From the end of the Árpád dynasty (1301) to the defeat at Mohács (1526), the crowns of Hungary, Poland (and Bohemia) were sometimes borne in personal union: 1342–1382, Louis I of Anjou (Louis I of Poland, 1370–1382); 1440–1444, Wladislas I Jagiello (Wladislas III Jagiello of Poland, 1334–1344). The first Prince of Transylvania, István Báthory (1571–1575) entrusted the government of Transylvania to his brother when he became king of Poland (1475–1586).

Royal domains   The Crown lands in Hungary declined from the thirteenth c. in favour of the seigniorial properties of the magnates and it was the concept of the Holy Crown that assured the cohesion of the kingdom in spite of difficult periods of dismantlement of Crown lands, principally on the occasion of successions to the throne.

Szekler vs. *Székely, Siculus*   Given the scarcity of historiographic references in the West to the community analysed in this study, the translator was faced with a terminological choice between the German, Hungarian and Latin designations. The Hungarian term '*Székely*' appears rarely and invariably gives rise to unfortunate attempts at pronunciation; the Latin '*Siculus*' seems convenient but it is taken. Lexicography carries it as the name of the ancient inhabitants of Sicily. The German term Szekler is used in this study for its linguistic convenience, but also because it is the term most frequently encountered. The abundant German-language historiography on the Saxon community of Transylvania invariably deals also with its neighbour, the Szekler.

Una eademque nobilitas   In 1351, Louis I of Anjou confirmed the Golden Bull, but introduced the concept of the equality of all nobles. This enabled the Crown to rely on support by the lower and middle nobility, the status of which was thus shielded against encroachments by the wealthier and more powerful, and which was often less disloyal than the magnates. The Szeklers were direct beneficiaries of this juridical equality.

Voivode of Transylvania   (*vajda*, a term of Slavic origin) Royal officer, intermediary between the Crown and the *comites* of Transylvania, probably following the model of the *ban* of Croatia. Charged with judiciary and, especially, military responsibilities in the border province, the voivode was almost always also *comes Siculorum* from the time John Hunyadi held both offices.

DOCUMENTS

The Szekler Constitution of Udvarhely (1505)[4]

We the inhabitants of all the Szeklerland, assembled from all Seats with no distinction of rank, let it be known to all concerned that we have decided that which follows in this document:

That we have convened and assembled in the year one thousand five hundred and five, on the fifth day after the feast of Queen St. Elisabeth [23 November] in the town of Udvarhely to settle, according to the ancient customs of our people, some urgent matters and correct some undue practices; not the least of the urgent matters needing to be settled stem from the fact that our [Szekler] national assemblies have become so rare that delays in our legal procedures on appeal have become interminable and disputes concerning our common people are constantly reopened, causing them serious prejudice and privation; but we are aware also that complacency, animosity and discord and the pursuit of personal interest in our Szekler land stand in the way of our judges' and legislatures' rendering justice.

To ensure that complaints are heard within reasonable delays and that the judges conduct themselves correctly, we have decided and herewith order in the perpetual best interest of the inhabitants of our land that the Szeklers* of [the Seats of] Udvarhely and Keresztúr elect four of their *primores* and thirteen of their *primipili* as judges in accordance with the ancient powers and authorizations** in our Szekler land to administer justice to all Szeklers with no distinction of rank in every Seat and land, pursuant to our present order.

These judges, having sworn before God that they will not yield to favour or supplication, nor to their own interests, but only to God, will render justice in His name.

If in a dispute between two parties they put all this into practice, only good can come of it. If however, God preserve us, one of them forgot his [oath before] God, and put his own salvation at risk, strayed from the path in yielding to supplications, gifts or his own interests, he must be condemned on the spot to perpetual banishment, confiscation of all his property*** and consequently he may never again inhabit the Szeklerland, given his doubtful morals and bad reputation. But also, anyone found helping or trying to help such dishonest outcasts to return to live or just to sojourn [in our country] shall in turn be condemned and suffer the same punishment.

* *Székely atyafiak*: sons of Szekler fathers.

** Reference to the confirmations of 1466 and 1499.

*** '*ingo bingo*' common expression in which *ingo* stands for movables and *bingo* for real property.

Moreover, we order the judges thus elected and sworn in to apply the law without fail in rendering judgements and verdicts without delay and also to see to it that the sentences are executed rapidly, justice being administered by the Royal Judges**** or by the captains. If by misfortune one of these judges died during his mandate, the inhabitants of the same Seat shall elect his replacement from the same ranks, in accordance with the ancient powers and authorizations in our Szekler land so that the number of seventeen judges of our own land may never lessen or diminish.

To ensure that the ordinances and conclusions written down above be put in force correctly, we charge the worthy Péter Patakfalvi with the task of making them known to everyone here at the assembly and to convey our ordinances and conclusions everywhere in terms all can understand. Also, to conclude the election of the above judges here and now by the above-mentioned Szeklers of Udvarhely and Keresztúr, we propose to the assembly as judges the following distinguished *primipili* [In Hungarian *lófejek (lófök)*]: Pál Nyujtódi, Antal Kontzai, Jánod and Péter Lokodi, Ferentz Kedei, Gergely Szombatfalvi, Imre Vágási, Kelemen Patakfalvi, Mihály Márkos, Balázs Bíró, Boldizsár Lengyelfalvi, Balás Fantali, Mihály Akadátz, Lukáts Pálfalvi; these persons have now been elected in our presence to put our conclusions and ordinances into effect and have taken the oath before our plenary assembly in accordance with our customs.

Consequently we all, with no distinction of rank, *primores*, *primipili* and common [Szeklers], raise our right hands and swear on our faith that we will respect these ordinances with all our energy and that we will be watchful that others respect them also. In witness of which we issue this writing and affix our seal as proof. Given at Udvarhely on the day indicated at the outset.

János Bögözi, captain-in-chief
Bögözi

The above has been translated into Hungarian word for word as it appears in the manuscript with the seal of János Orbán de Lengyelfalva, sworn-in notary of the Seat of Udvarhely.

Szekler Constitution of Agyagfalva (1506)[5]

We, the inhabitants of the Szeklerland, all Szeklers living in this land, of high position or low, call the following to the attention of whomever it may concern: that this one thousand five hundred sixth year after the birth of our Lord, we have assembled this fifth day of the fourth season* in this estate of Agyagfalva to deliberate matters concerning the degradation and the abandon of our ancient customs.

**** The cited text is a translation into Hungarian from the seventeenth century, when 'Royal Judge' was used for the office that, until 1562, was referred to as Seat Judge.

* K. Szabó does not propose a more precise date. Assuming that this assembly followed the demand for the payment of branded cattle due on the birth of the king's son – which occurred 1 July 1506 – one can estimate that the assembly was held on 30 September or 1 October, depending on whether the season starts on 25 December or the day after.

It is indispensable to remind all that quarrel, jealousy, pride, all obstacles to harmonious life, lead to the destruction of all great lands, gnawing even the most ancient foundations. In rightful consideration of the protection of our common interest and to prevent the dangers of discord, we herewith order and admonish all inhabitants of the Szekler land, be they of high dignity, cavalrymen, entrusted with an office, or simple inhabitants of good repute, to obey our resolutions unconditionally, in particular as regards the reverence and loyalty due our sovereign Wladislas, by the grace of God king of Hungary and of Bohemia, our gracious lord and his emissaries, obedience toward the voivode of Transylvania and the *comes* of the Szeklers; to forswear all harming of our land and conspiring to do so, or recruiting of accomplices and that no-one join [such] an uprising or convene an assembly or claim for himself a dignity or authority under which to assemble some imbeciles and so commit pillage, robbery and oppression of others, harassing, killing, attacking, starting quarrels; vengeance, destruction, arson, abandoning of dwellings, forming gangs and marauding, brigandage, or any other disturbance of public order such as have occurred in the past, so that all misdeeds may come to a definite end in our country, that all depravity or germination of treason be dried out and eradicated forever and that all incitement to rebellion be condemned, so that no-one show disrespect for our holy king or cause harm to his emissaries.

But also, if the above-mentioned royal emissaries commit offences in contravention of our laws, and if, collectively or individually, they commit acts prejudicial to the rights and liberties of our country, like the transgressions committed by insurgents, then [those afflicted] must rise up against them, else we will assemble and, of a common accord, come to the aid of those who will have come to harm by such acts, be they isolated or wide-spread, all the while keeping faith with our king by informing and consulting him so that in concert we may better resist; for while we are far from the source [of the royal authority], it behoves for his majesty our king and the Hungarian nation, of which we are part, to heed our plaints and come to our aid, so that the loyalty we have preserved without stain ever since [the time of] the great Scythia may remain invincible in the face of all unrest and conspiracy.

On the other hand, every one of us – notable, cavalryman, or invested with an office – all those mentioned hereinbefore, who ventured to rebel, plot in assembly, or sow discord shall immediately be expelled from our community, one who demeaned or dignity or betrayed our people shall lose all rights and honour, he may never again conclude a civil contract or assume public office or even dwell in our country and (in case of treason) no-one but the Sovereign may accord pardon, unless it be the entire Szekler people, all of a common accord. All that he owns shall be adjudged to his heirs and equitably distributed amongst them, his property, his cattle, his acquests, everything.

If in such a case of high treason the convicted perpetrator is poor, his belongings shall be distributed in the same manner, as booty and no-one but the Sovereign may accord a pardon, unless it is the entire Szekler people of a common accord. To ensure that these ordinances and decisions be firmly obeyed, we all, *primores*, notables invested with an office, cavalrymen and the entire community raise our right hand and vow that we will comply with every point of these articles without ever changing anything and swear reverence for God, loyalty to our king, and to safeguard and perpetuate our unity.

Furthermore, we confirm the decisions taken at the assembly held at Udvarhely in the year one thousand five hundred and five, of which we have full knowledge; we order all to comply fully and conclude the following amendment: that as of this day no dignitary, no-one vested with an office shall render a judgement on a holiday established by the Church. Any judgement pronounced on such a holiday by judges the community has named shall be null and void. Moreover, such judges shall be punished with a fine of two oxen, the execution of this penalty being controlled by the military captain or, if it is the captain who has committed the offence, by the Royal Judge.

Finally, it is also our pleasure and among the laws concluded by this assembly that judges shall render judgements in keeping with God's true justice, but we see everywhere that little is accomplished; we do not see matters being brought to their conclusion. Hence this assembly orders that all judges in our country having verified the facts and rendered judgement [must ensure that] the losing party shall pay the winning party from his property within fifteen days. If on the contrary he cannot or is not willing to do so, he shall seek the arbitration of the captain or dignitary of his seat and pay the fine to the judge or the winning party if the sentence is confirmed on arbitration.

However, the situation of the poor or feeble of mind must never be worsened by such arbitrage.

These conclusions were made at the place, the year and day mentioned above, András Lázár de Gyergyó presiding the assembly, the seat of Udvarhely being represented by the *primores* János Bögözi, Pál Nyujtódi, Antal Katzai, János and Péter Benedekfi de Bethlenfalva and János Gergely, the seats of Maros and Aranyos by Lénárt Apaffi, Mihály Gyalakuti, Gáspár Bartsai, Miklós Tót, Ferentz Alárd, Gergely Tatár, András Dénes, the seats of Csík and Kézdi by Balás Lázár, János Bláskó, Sándor Györffy, Imre Betz, János Csákó, Dimjén Urbán, Bernád Czirják, Antal Kun, István Apor and László Csomortán, the seats of Sepsi and Orbai by Bálint Kálnoki, Mihály Latzok, Balás Czirják, Péter Daczó, Mihály Mikó, István Mihályfi and Miklós Bíró – as well as a vast multitude of inhabitants of our Szekler land, all prepared to die for our country and all loyal to the Holy Crown.

Valeant.

A note dated 1769 certifies the conformity of this copy with the original.**

** In an annotation K. Szabó states: 'It is evident that the original of this constitution, like that of 1505, was in Latin, translated into Hungarian by János Orbán, notary of the seat of Udvarhely in the seventeenth century'. A certified copy was made by the Udvarhely notary Ferencz Tibád in 1769, replicated in 1777 and 1815.

CHRONOLOGY

Sovereigns of Hungary and voivodes of Transylvania

From the arrival of the Árpádians in Pannonia to the Principality of Transylvania (886–1575)

Sovereigns of Hungary			Voivodes of Transylvania
House of Árpád 886–1301			
Árpád, prince	c.886–907		
Zoltán, prince	907–946		
Falicsi, prince	948–v.955		
Taksony, prince	955–v.972		
Géza, Grand Prince	972–997		
Stephen I (St.) (*Szent István*)			
- prince	997–1000		
- king	1000–1038		
Peter (1st rule)	1038–1041		
Samuel Aba	1041–1044		
Peter (2nd rule)	1044–1046		
Andrew I	1046–1060		
Béla I	1060–1063		
Salomon	1063–1074		
Géza I	1074–1077		
Ladislas I (*Szent László*)	1077–1095		
Coloman the Learned	1095–1116	1095 1111 1113	*de genere* (*dg*) Koppán, Mercurius
Stephen II	1116–1131		
Béla II the Blind	1131–1141		
Géza II	1141–1162		
Stephen III	1162–1172		
- Ladislas II	1162–1163		

Sovereigns of Hungary		Voivodes of Transylvania	
- Stephen IV	1163–1165		
Béla III	1172–1196	1177	Gaulus (?)
Imre	1196–1204	1199–1200	Legfor
		1200	Écs
		1201	Gyula
Ladislas III	1204–1205	1203 1205–1206	Benedek, son of Korlat (Konrad)
Andrew II	1205–1235	1206–1207	Zsámboki Smaragd
		1208–1209	Benedek, son of Korlát
		1209–1212	*dg* Kácsik Mihály
		1212–1213	Mérani Bertold
		1213	Miklós
		1214	*dg* Kán Gyula
		1215	*dg* Kácsik Simon
		1216–1217	Ipoly
		1217–1218	Rafael
		1219–1221	Neuka
		1221–1222	Pál, son of Péter
		1222	Ipoly
		1226–1229	Pósa, son of Sólom
		1229–1233	*dg* Rátot Gyula
		1233–1234	*dg* Tomaj (or *dg* Türje ?) Dénes

Sovereigns of Hungary		Voivodes of Transylvania	
Béla IV	1235–1270	1235	András, son of Serafil
		1235–1241	Pósa, son of Sólom
		1241	*Vacancy ?*
		1242–1252	Lörinc
		1252–1260	Ernye Ákos
		1263–1265	Kán László jr.
		1265–1270	Geregyei Miklós
Stephen V	1270–1272	1270–1272	Csák Máté
Ladislas IV (the Cuman)	1272–1290	1272–1273	Geregyei Miklós
		1273	János
		1274	Csák Máté

Sovereigns of Hungary		Voivodes of Transylvania	
		1274	Geregyei Miklós
		1274–1275	Csák Máté
		1275	Kán László
		1276	Csák Ugrin
		1276–1277	Csák Máté
		1277–1278	Pok Miklós
		1278–1279	Aba Finta
		1279–1280	István, son of Tekes
		1282	Borsa Loránt
		1282–1283	Pécz Apor
		1284–1286	Borsa Loránt
		1286–1288	Moja (Mozes)
Andrew III	1290–1301	1288–1294	Borsa Loránt
Other Houses		1294–1301	Kán László
Venceslas of Bohemia	1301–1305		
Otto of Bavaria	1305–1307		
Charles I (Robert) of Anjou	1307–1342	1307–1313	Kán László
		1315–1316	Meggyesi Pok Miklós
		1318–1321	Debreceni Dózsa
		1321–1342	Szécsényi Tamás
Louis I of Anjou (Louis the Great)	1342–1382	1342–1344	Sirokai Miklós
		1344–1350	Lackfi István
		1351	Gönyüi Tamás
		1351–1356	Raholcai Kont Miklós
		1356–1359	Lackfi András
		1359–1366	Lackfi Dénes
		1367–1368	Lackfi Miklós
		1369–1372	Lackfi Imre
		1373–1376	Lackfi István jr.
		1376–1385	Losonczi László
Marie of Anjou	1382–1385		
Charles II de Durazzo	1385–1386	1385	Lackfi István
Sigismund of Luxembourg	1387–1437	1386–1391	Losonczi László
		1392–1393	Bebek Imre
		1393–1395	Szécsényi Frank
		1395–1401	Stiboriczi Stibor

Sovereigns of Hungary		Voivodes of Transylvania	
		1401	Szécsényi Simon
		1401–1402	Csáki Miklós & Marczali Miklós
		1403–1409	Tamási János & Szántai Lackfi Jakab
		1409–1414	Stiboriczi Stibor
		1414	*vacancy*
		1415–1426	Csáki Miklós
		1426	*vacancy*
		1427–1436	Csáki László
		1436–1437	Csáki László & Lévai Cseh Péter
Sovereigns of Hungary		**Voivodes of Transylvania**	
Albert of Habsburg	1437–1439	1437–1438	Lévai Cseh Péter
		1438–1439	Losonczi Dezsö
Wladislas I Jagiello	1440–1444	1440	Csáki László
		1441	Kusalyi Jacks László & Ujlaki Miklós
		1441	Losonci Dezsö
		1441–1446	Hunyadi János & Ujlaki Miklós
Ladislas V of Habsburg (the Posthumous)	1444–1457	1444	Lépes Loránd (*gub.*)
Interreign	1444–1446	1445	Lépes Loránd & Vingárti Gereb János (*gub.*)
Jean Hunyadi	1446–1453	1446–1448	Bebek Imre
governor		1450–1457	Ujlaki Miklós & Rozsgonyi János
Matthias I Corvinus	1458–1490	1458–1460	Rozsgonyi Sebestyén & Rozsgony János
		1460	Rozsgonyi Sebestyén & Kanizsai László
		1460	Rozsgonyi Sebestyén & Ujlaki Miklós
		1460–1461	Szilágyi Mihály
		1462–1465	Ujlaki Miklós & Pongrác János
		1465–1467	Szentgyörgyi János & Ellerbach Bertold

Sovereigns of Hungary		Voivodes of Transylvania	
		1468–1472	Pongrác János & Csupor Miklós
		1473–1475	Magyar Balázs
		1476	Pongrác János
		1478–1479	Geréb Péter
		1479–1493	Báthori István
Wladislas II Jagiello	1490–1516	1493–1495	Losonczi László & Drágfi Bertalan
		1495–1499	Drágfi Bertalan
		1499–1519	Bazini and Szentgyörgyi Péter
Louis II Jagiello	1516–1526	1520–1526	Szapolyai János
Partition Szapolyai/Habsbourg			
John I Szapolyai	1526–1540	1526–1529	Perényi Péter
Ferdinand I	1526–1564	1529–1533	Báthori István ifj.
(of Habsburg)		1534–1540	Majlát István
		1539–1540	Majlát István & Balassa Imre
John II (–Sigismund)	1540–1571	1540–1542	Bornemissza Baltazar *Chief General*
Szapolyai		1542–1552	*vacancy*
		1552–1553	Báthori András
		1553–1556	Kendi Ferencz & Dobó István
		1556–1572	*vacancy*
Maximilien	1564–1576		
(of Habsburg)		1572–1575	Báthori István, then Prince of Transylvania

Sources:
Engel, Pál. *Magyarország világi archontológia 1301–1457* (Worldly Dignitaries of Hungary, 1301–1457), two volumes, Budapest, 1996: MTA történettudományi intézet.
Hóman, Bálint and Szekfű, Gyula. *Magyar történet* (History of Hungary), 2nd edn Budapest: Királyi Magyar Egyetem, 1936.
Makkai, László. *Histoire de Transylvanie* (History of Transylvania), Budapest-Paris: PUF (Presses Universitaires de France), 1946.

NAMES OF THE CITIES OF TRANSYLVANIA QUOTED IN THIS STUDY

Hungarian	German	Romanian
Bereck	Bretz	Brețcu
Beszterce	Bistritz	Bistrița
Brassó	Kronstadt	Brașov
Csíkszereda	Szeklerburg	Miercurea Ciuc
Felvinc	Oberwinz	Vințul de Sus
Görgény	Görgen	Gurghiu
Gyulafehérvár (Fehérvár)	Weißenburg	Alba Julia
Keresztúr	Kreutz	Crișturu Secuiesc
Kézdivásárhely	Szekler Neumarkt	Târgu Secuiesc
Kolozsvár	Klausenburg	Cluj
Marosvásárhely	Neumarkt	Târgu Mureș
Nagyszeben (Szeben)	Hermannstadt	Sibiu
Nyárádszereda	Sereda	Miercurea Nirajului
Segesvár	Schäßburg	Șighișoara
Sepsiszentgyörgy	Sankt Georgen	Sfântu Gherghe
Szászsebes	Mühlbach	Sebeș
Törcsvár	Törzburg	Bran
Torda	Thorenburg	Turda
Udvarhely	Hofmarkt	Odorhei Secuiesc

LIST OF SZEKLER VILLAGES

Taking the 1614 military register, the Papal registers of 1332–1337 and the villages mentioned in this study, listed in alphabetical order by their Hungarian names, within Seats:
- Udvarhely
- Maros
- Csík (with Kászon and Gyergyó)
- Sepsi
- Kézdi
- Orbai
- Aranyos

Sources:
   This list contains Szekler villages
- of the 1614 military roster, as established by Imreh, István. 'A székely falu gazdasági-társadalmi szerkezete a XVI. Század végén és a XVII. Század elején'

(The social and economic organization of the Szekler village at the end of the sixteenth and beginning of the seventeenth centuries), in Benkő, Samu (ed.), *Székely Felkelés* 1595–1596 (The Szekler Uprising of 1595–1596), Bucharest: Kriterion kiadó, 1979, pp. 180–190.

- of the 1332–1337 papal register listing established in Kristó, Gyula. *A székelyek eredetéről'* (On the Origins of the Szeklers), Szeged: Szegedi Középkorász Műhely, 1996, pp. 128–131.

Latin names and spelling of 'latinized' names in the 1332–1337 lists as per Kristó (1996).

The Romanian names (1332–1336 and 1614) are as per *Székely Oklevéltár, új sorozat* (Szekler Archives, New Series) volume V, Kolozsvár, 1998 and Herner, János (pres. by). *Mappa Transilvaniae et Partium Regni Hungariae repertoriumque locorum* (Map of Transylvania and Part of the Hungarian Kingdom with a Repertory of Places and Objects) *Joannes Lipszky, Pest 1806,* Szeged: József Attila Tudományegyetemi kiadó, 1987.

For the prefixed Hungarian place names posterior to the 1614 roster (separated by hyphen, e.g. 'Nyárád-Szentimre') or new Hungarian place names (since the form in 1614, separated by a comma; e.g. 'Felsőtorja, Feltorja').

For German names, Vofkori, László., *Székelyföld útikönyve I-II* (Traveller's Guide to the Szeklerland) Budapest: Cartographia kiadó, 1998 and Herner, *Mappa Transilvaniae.*

Legend:
 * Latin form no longer identifiable with a village
 ** Uncertain Latin/Hungarian correspondence
 *** Part of the deaconry of Sepsi, Archdeaconry of Fehérvár
 + Not in the 1614 roster
 ++ Not included in the 1614 roster. Disputed case of the 'Hidvég' donation and of the status of the land: Szekler or royal county
 S. *Sanctus, Santa*
 in included in

Hungarian names	German names	Romanian names	1332–1337
Seat of Udvarhely			
*			S.*Laurentius*
*			S.*Michael*
*			*villa Marie*
Abásfalva	–	Aldea	
Ábránfalva	–	Obrănești	
Agyagfalva	–	Lutița	
Alsóboldogasszonyfalva, Alsóboldogfalva-	–	Bodogoaia	*villa S.Marie*
Árvátfalva	–	Arvățeni	

Szekler Villages

Hungarian names	German names	Romanian names	1332-1337
Atyha	–	Atia	
Bágy	–	Bădeni	
Bardocfalva, Bardoc	–	Brăduț	*Bardach****
Bencéd	–	Benţid	
Bétá	–	Beta	
Betfalva	–	Beteşti	
Bethlenfalva, *in* Sz.-Udv.			
Bibarcsfalva	–	Biborţeni	*Byborch****
Bikafalva	–	Tăureni	
Bogárfalva	–	Bulgăreni	
Bögöz	Begesen	Mugeni	*Bugus*
Bordos	–	Bordoşiu	
Böződ	Basendorf	Bezid	
Böződújfalu	–	Bezidu Nou	
Cibrefalva, *in* Sz.-Udv. (Csatova)			
Csehétfalva	–	Cehețel	
Csekefalva	–	Checheşti	
Csöb	–	Cibu	
Décsfalva	–	Dejuțiu	
Ége	–	Ighiu	
Énlaka	–	Inlăceni	*Jandalaka*
Erdő-Füle	–	Filia	
Etéd	–	Atid	
Farcád	–	Forţeni	
Farkaslaka	–	Lupeni	
Felsőboldogasszonyfalva, Felsőboldogfalva	Ober Mariendorf	Feliceni	*villa S. Marie superioris*
Fenyéd	–	Brădeşti	
Fiátfalva	–	Filiaş	
Firtos-Martonos	–	Firtănuş	
Firtos-Váralja	–	Firtuşu	
Gagy	–	Goagiu	
Gyepes	–	Ghipeş	
Héjjasfalva+	Teufelsdorf	Vânători	*villa Eyanis***
Hodgya	–	Hoghia	
Homoródalmás	Almesch	Mereşti	*Almas*
Homoród-Jánosfalva	Eisdorf	Ioneşti	

Hungarian names	German names	Romanian names	1332-1337
Homoród-Karácsonfalva	Klätschendorf	Crăciunel	Karachni
Homoród-keményfalva	-	Comănești	
Homoród-Remete	-	Călugăreni	
Homoród-Szentlászló	-	Vasileni	
Homoród-Szentmárton	Sankt Merten	Mărtiniș	S.Martinus
Homoród-Szentpál	-	Sânpaul	S.Paulus
Homoród-Szentpéter	-	Petreni	
Homoródújfalu	Neudorf	Satu Nou	
Jásfalva	Jasch	Iași	
Kadicsfalva, in Sz.-Udv.			
Kányád	-	Ulieș	Kanad
Kápolnásfalu	-	Căpâlnița	
Kecset	-	Păltiniș	
Kénos	-	Chinușu	
Keresztúrfalva, in Sz.-Keresztúr			
Kisbacon	-	Bățanii Mic	
Kisfalud	-	Satu Mic	
Kisgalambfalva	-	Porumbenii Mici	
Kiskede	-	Chedia Mică	
Kissolymos	-	Șoimoșu Mic	
Kobátfalva	-	Cobătești	
Körispatak	-	Crișen	
Korond	-	Corund	Kurnud
Küküllőkeményfalva	-	Târnovița	
Küsmöd	-	Cușmed	Kusmend
Lókod	-	Locodeni	
Lövéte	Lefit	Lueta	Luce**
Magyar-Andrásfalva	-	Andreen	
Magyar-Hermány	-	Herculian	
Magyar-Hidegkút	-	Vidacut	
Magyar-Zsákod	UngarischSacken	Jacodu	
Máréfalva	-	Satu Mare	
Mátisfalva	-	Mătișeni	
Miklósfalva	-	Nicolești	S.Nicolaus
Mogyorós, Székelymagyaros	-	Aluniș	
Nagygalambfalva	-	Porumbenii Mari	Galamb

Szekler Villages

Hungarian names	German names	Romanian names	1332-1337
Nagy-Kadács	–	Cădaciu Mare	
Nagykede	–	Chedia Mare	
Nagy-Medesér	–	Medişoru Mare	
Nagysolymos	–	Şoimoşu Mare	*Solumos*
Nyikó-Malomfalva	–	Morăreni	
Ócfalva	–	Oţeni	
Oklánd	–	Ocland	
Olasztelek	–	Tălisoara	*Olazteluk****
Oroszhegy	–	Dealu	*Vricsheg*
Parajd	–	Praid	
Patakfalva	–	Văleni	*Potok*
Rava	–	Roua	
Recsenyéd	–	Rareş	
Rugonfalva	Rugendorf	Rugăneşsti	
Sándorfalva, Sándortelke	–	Alexandriţa	
Siklód	–	Şiclod	
Siménfalva	Seinegold	Şimoneşti	*S.Simon*
Sófalva, Felsősófalva Felső-Sófalva, Alsó-Sófalva appears only in 1793	–	Ocna de Sus	
Sükő	–	Cireşeni	
Székely-Dálya	–	Daia	*Daya*
Székely-Derzs	Darsch	Dârjiu	*Ers*
Székely-Dobófalva	–	Dobeni	
Székely-Fancsal	–	Fâncel	*Farchad*
Székely-Keresztúr város	Kreuz	CristuruSecuiesc	*S.Crux*
Székely-Lengyelfalva	–	Poloniţa	
Székely-Muzsna	Meschen	Mujna	
Székely-Pálfalva	–	Păuleni	
Székely-Száldobos	–	Doboşeni	*Zaldubus*
Székelyszállás	Szeklerzollest	Sălaşuri	
Székely-Szenterszébet	–	Eliseni	*villa S.Elyzabrth*
Székely-Szentkirály	–	Sâncrai	
Székely-Szentlélek	–	Bisericani	*S.Spiritus*

Hungarian names	German names	Romanian names	1332-1337
Székely-Szentmihály & Demeterfalva *in* Kobátfalva	–	Mihăileni Cobăteşti	S.Michael
Székely-Szentmiklós	–	Nicoleni	
Székely-Szenttamás	–	Tămaşu	S.Thomas
Székely-Udvarhely város	Hofmarkt or Oderhellen	OdorheiuSecuiesc	Udvorhel
Székely-Vécke	Vitzka	Veţca	
Szentábrahám	–	Avrămeşti	S.Abraam
Szentdemeter	–	Dumitreni	
Szentegyhazasfalu (Olahfalu)	Wlahitza	Vlăhiţa	
Szolokma	–	Solocma	
Szombatfalva, *in* Sz.-Udv.			
Tarcsafalva	–	Tărceşti	Tarka
Telegdibacon	–	Băţanii Mari	
Telekfalva	–	Teleac	
Tibód	–	Tibod	
Timafalva, *in* Sz.-Keresztúr			
Tordátfalva	–	Turdem	
Újszékely	–	Secuieni	
Ülke	–	Ulcani	
Vágás	–	Tăietura	Voygias
Vargyas	–	Vârghis	Wardach***
Városfalva	Diesendorf	Orăşeni	
Zetelaka	Sitelak	Zetea	Zatholaka
Seat of Maros			
*			Poruk
Ákosfalva	Achatiusdorf	Acăţari	
Atosfalva *in* Hármasfalu	–	Hoteşti - Trei Sate	
Backa-Madaras	–	Păsăreni	
Bazéd	–	Bozed	
Bede	–	Bedeni	
Berekeresztúr	–	Bâra	S.Crux? or Maroskeresztúr?
Bodzaszeg *in* Náznánfalva			
Búzaháza	–	Grâuşorul	
Csejd	–	Cotuş	
Cserefalva	–	Sterejiş	

Szekler Villages

Hungarian names	German names	Romanian names	1332-1337
Csibafalva, Csiba	–	Ciba	
Csíkfalva	–	Vărgata	
Csitt-Szentiván	–	Sântioanna de Mureș	S.Johannes
Csittfalva *in* Csitt-Szentiván			
Csókfalva *in* Hármasfalu	–	Cioc - Trei Sate	
Deményháza	–	Dămieni	
Demeterfalva or Szentdemeter. 1503 '*villa siculicalis Zenthdemether*'	–	Dumitreștii	
Egerszeg	–	Cornățel	
Ehed	–	Ihod	
Erdőszentgyörgy	–	Sângeorgiu de Pădure	S.Georgius in the deaconry of Erdőhát
Fintaháza	–	Cinta	
Folyfalva *in* Karácsonyfalva			
Galambod	–	Porumbeni	*Galambud*
Geges	–	Ghinești	
Göcs	–	Găiești	
Gyalakuta, Gyulakuta	Gielekoten	Fântânele	*Kulakuta*
Hagymás-Bodon	–	Budiu Mic	
Harasztkerék	–	Roteni	*Harchkerek*
Harcó	–	Hărțău	*Hudzov*
Havad	–	Neaua	
Havadtő	–	Viforoasa	
Ikland	–	Icland	
Ilencfalva, Lukailencfalva	–	Ilieni	
Iszló	–	Isla	
Jedd	–	Livezeni	
Jobbágyfalva	–	Valea	
Jobbágytelke	–	Sâmbriaș	
Káposztás-Szentmiklós	–	Nicolești	S.Nycolaus
Karácsonyfalva, Nyárádkarácson	–	Crăciunești	
Kebele	–	Sânișor	
Kebeleszentiván	–	Ivănești	S.Johannes
Kelementelke	–	Călimănești	

Hungarian names	German names	Romanian names	1332-1337
Kendő	–	Cându	
Kibéd	–	Chibed	
Kisfalud, Ompolykisfalud	Kleindörfel	Micești	
Kisgörgény	–	Gruişor	
Koronka	–	Corunca	*Korunka*
Lőrincfalva	–	Leordeni	
Lukafalva	–	Gheorghe Doja,	
Mája	–	Maia	
Makfalva	–	Ghindari	
Malomfalva	Mühlendorf	Morești	
Márkod	Markod	Mărculeni	
Maros-Agárd	–	Poienița	
Maros-Keresztúr	–	Cristești	*S.Crux?* or *Berekeresztúr?*
Maros-Szentanna	–	Sântana de Mureş	*S.Anna*
Marosszentgyörgy	–	Sângeorgiu de Mureş	*S.Georgius*
Maros-Szentkirály	–	Sâncraiu de Mureş	*S.Rex*
Marosvásárhely+	Neumarkt	Târgu Mureș	*Novum Forum*
Meggyesfalva+(SzOkl új IV p. 149, 1603 military roster)	–	Mureșeni	
Mező-Bánd	Bandorf	Band	*Band*
Mező-Bergenye	–	Berghia	*Bergune*
Mező-Csávás	–	Ceuașu de Câmpie	
Mező-Fele	–	Câmpenița	
Mező-Kölpény	–	Culpiu	*Kulpen*
Mezőmadaras (Fekete)Mezőmadaras includes also the parish known as *Fekete*	–	Mădăraş	*Madaras*
Mezőmajos+(SzOkl III.503, 1496)	–	Moișa	
Mező-Ménes	–	Hergelia	*Menes*
Mező-Panit	–	Pănet	*Pambus***
Mező-Sámsond	–	Şincai	*Sancsund*
Mező-Szabad+(SzOkl új IV p. 132, 1602 military roster)	–	Voiniceni	
Mezőuraj+, Uraly	–	Oroiu	*Vrey*
Mikháza	–	Călugăreni	

Szekler Villages

Hungarian names	German names	Romanian names	1332-1337
Mogyorós, Nyárádmagyaros	–	Măgherani	
Nagyadorján & Kisadorján+	–	Adrianul Mare Adrianul Mic	
Nagy-Ernye	Arn	Ernei	*Ernec*
Náznánfalva	–	Nazna	
Nyárád-Andrásfalva	–	Sântandrei	
Nyárád-Bálintfalva	–	Bolintineni	
Nyárád-Gálfalva	Gallendorf	Gălești	
Nyárád-Köszvényes	–	Mătrici	
Nyárád-Remete	–	Eremitu	
Nyárád-Selye	–	Șilea Nirajului	
Nyárád-Szentbenedek	–	Murgești	*S.Benedictus*
Nyárád-Szentimre	–	Eremieni	*S.Emericus*
Nyárád-Szentlászló	–	Sânvăsăi	*S.Ladislas*
Nyárád-Szentmárton	–	Mitrești	*S.Martinus*
Nyárád-Szentsimon	–	Sânsimion	*S.Symon*
Nyárádszereda & Nyárádszentanna Nyárádszereda: known as Szentanna parish	Sereda	Miercurea Nirajului Sântana Niraj-	*S.Anna*
Nyárádtő	–	Ungheni	*Naradyu*
Nyomát	–	Maiad	
Remeteszeg	–	Remetea	
Rigmány	–	Rigmani	
Sáromberke+(SzOkl III.427 and III.428, 1409)	Scharberg	Dumbrăvioara	–
Seprőd	–	Drojdii	
Somosd	–	Cornești	
Sóvárad	–	Sărățeni	*Varad*
Szabéd	–	Săbed	
Száltelek	–	Țiptelnic	
Székejy-Csókafalva	–	Corbești	
Székely-Abod	–	Abud	
Székely-Bere	–	Bereni	
Székely-Bő	–	Beu	*Bev*
Székely-Bós	–	Bozeni	
Székely-Hódos	–	Hodoșa	*Hudus*
Székely-Kakasd	–	Vălureni	
Székely-Kál	–	Căluşeri, MS	*Gaal*

Hungarian names	German names	Romanian names	1332-1337
Székely-Kövesd	-	Ciueşd	
Székely-Moson+ (SzOkl új IV p. 149, 1603 military roster)	-	Moşuni	
Székely-Szentistván in Hármasfalu	-	Ştefăneşti - Trei Sate	S.Stephanus
Székely-Tompa	-	Tâmpa	
Székely-Vaja	-	Vălenii	Voya
Székes	-	Săcăreni,	
Szentgerice	-	Gălăţeni	S.Gratia
Szentlőrinc, Kisszentlőrinc	-	Lăureni	S.Laurentius
Szentrontás, Szentháronság	-	Troiţa	S.Trinitas
Szováta	-	Sovata,MS	
Szövérd+	-	Suveica	Zwerd
Tófalva	-	Tofalău	
Torboszló	-	Torba	
Udvarfalva	-	Curteni	Vdorfalua
Vadad	-	Vadu	
Vadasd	-	Vădaşd	
Vece	-	Veţa	
Seat(s) of Csík (& Kászon & Gyergyó)			
Csík			
*			S.Johannes
Csatószeg	-	Cetăţuia	
Csík-Bánkfalva	-	Bancu	
Csík-Borzsova	-	Bârzava	
Csík-Csekefalva	-	Ciucani	
Csík-Csicsó	-	Ciceu	
Csík-Csomortán	-	Şoimeni	
Csík-Dánfalva	-	Dăneşti	
Csík-Delne	-	Delniţa	Delna, Dolna
Csík-Jenőfalva	-	Ineu	
Csík-Karcfalva	-	Cârţa	
Csík-Kozmás	-	Cozmeni	S.Cozma & Damyan
Csík-Madaras	-	Mădăraş	
Csík-Madéfalva	-	Siculeni	
Csík-Menaság	-	Armăşeni,HR	

Szekler Villages

Hungarian names	German names	Romanian names	1332–1337
Csík-Mindszent	–	Misentea	*Omnium Sanctorum*
Csík-Pálfalva	–	Păuleni-Ciuc	
Csík-Rákos	–	Racu	*Rakus, Batus*
Csíksomlyo	Somlyoer-Berg	Şumuleu-Ciuc	*Sumbov*
Csík-Szentdomokos	–	Sândominic	
Csík-Szentgyörgy	–	Ciucsângeorgiu	*S.Georgius*
Csík-Szentimre	–	Sântimbru	
Csík-Szentkirály	–	Sâncrăieni	*S.Rex*
Csík-Szentlélék	–	Leliceni	*S.Spiritus*
Csík-Szentmárton	–	Sânmartin,HR	*S.Martinus*
Csík-Szentmihály	–	Mihăileni	*S.Michael*
Csík-Szentmiklós	–	Nicoleşti	*S.Nycolaus*
Csík-Szentsimon	–	Sânsimion	*S.Symon*
Csík-Szenttamás	–	Tomeşti	*S.Thomas*
Csík-Szépvíz	–	Frumoasa	
Csíkszereda	Szeklerburg	Miercurea-Cuic	*Chik, Chyk*
Csík-Taploca	–	Topliţa-Ciuc	
Csík-Vacsárcsi	–	Văcăreşti	
Csík-Verebes	–	Vrabia	
Csík-Zsögöd	–	Jigodin	
Göröcsfalva	–	Satu Nou	
Lázárfalva	–	Lăzăreşti	
Tarkó-hegy	–	–	*Torku, Torkov*
Tusnád	Tuschnad	Tuşnad	
Várdótfalva, *in* Cs.-szereda	–		
Kászon			
Felsőfalva,Kászonfeltíz since 1744	–	Plăieşii de Sus	
Kászon-Imperfalva	–	Imper	
Kászon-Jakabfalva	–	Iacobeni	
Kászon-Újfalu	–	Caşinu Nou	
Nagykászon,Kászonaltíz in 1567 but Nagykászon in 1614	–	Plăieşii de Jos	*Kazun, Kasin*
Gyergyó			
Ditró	–	Ditrău	
Gyergyó-Alfalu	–	Josem	
Gyergyó-Csomafalva	–	Ciumani	

Hungarian names	German names	Romanian names	1332-1337
Gyergyó-Remete	–	Remetea	
Gyergyó-Szárhegy	–	Lăzarea	
Gyergyó-Szentmiklós	Niklasmarkt	Gheorgheni	*Gyargyo, Gorgio*
Gyergyó-Tekerőpatak	–	Valea Strâmbă	
Gyergyó-Újfalu	–	Suseni	
Seat of Sepsi			
Aldoboly	–	Dobolii de Jos	
Angyalos	–	Angheluş	*Angelus*
Árapatak++	Arndorf	Araci	*Aruapotok*
Árkos	–	Arcuş	*Arkus*
Barót	Baroth	Baraolt	*Baroch*
Bikfalva	–	Bicfalău	
Bodola++	Bodeln	Budila	*Buduli*
Bodos	–	Bodoş	
Bölön	Blumendorf	Belin	*Belen*
Egerpatak	–	Aninoasa	
Eresztévény	–	Eresteghin	
Étfalva, *in* Zoltán			
Étfalva-Zoltán	–	Zoltan	
Feldoboly	–	Dobolii de Sus	
Fotos-Martonos	–	Fotoş	
Gidófalva	–	Ghidfalău	*villa Guidonis*
Hidvég++	Fürstenberg	Hăghig	*Hydueg*
Illyefalva városa	Ligendorf	Ilieni	*Helye*
Kálnok	–	Calnic	*Kalnuk*
Kilyén	–	Chilieni	*Kylien*
Kisborosnyó	–	Boroşneu Mic	
Kökös	–	Chichiş	
Komolló	–	Comolău	
Köpec	–	Căpeni	
Középajta	–	Aita Medie	
Lisznyó	–	Lisnău	*Lizno*
Málnás	Malnasch	Malnaş	
Martonos *in* Fotos	–		
Miklósvár	–	Micloşoara	*Myclosuara*
Nagyajta	Altou	Aita Mare	*Ahch*
Nagy-Bacon	–	Băţanii Mari	*Rachan*

Szekler Villages

Hungarian names	German names	Romanian names	1332–1337
Nagyborosnyó	–	Boroşneu Mare	*Suruzno*
Oltszem	–	Olteni	*Olthzem*
Réty	–	Reci	*Reech*
Sepsi-Besenyő	Beschendorf	Pădureni	*Besenczsed*
Sepsi-Bodok	Bodoc	Bodoc	*Buduk*
Sepsi-Kőröspatak	–	Valea Crişului	*Kerruspotok*
Sepsi-Magyarós	–	Măgheruş	
Sepsi-Szentgyörgy város	Sankt Georgen	Sfântu Gheorge	*S.Georgius*
Sepsi-Szentkirály	–	Sâncraiu	*S.Rex*
Szacsva	–	Saciova	
Szárazajta	–	Aita Seacă	*Sanzahca*
Szemerja *in* S.-szentgyörgy	–		*villa S.Marie*
Szentiván(laborfalva)	–	Sântionlunca	*S.Johannes*
Szotyor	–	Coşeni	
Uzon	Usendorf	Ozun	*Vzun*
Zalán	–	Zălan	*Zalan*
Seat of Kézdi			
*			*S.Michael*
*			*Sitka*
Alsócsernáton	–	Cernatu de Jos	*Kuruacun*
Alsótorja, Altorja	Torian	Turia de Jos	*Torya Inferior*
Bélafalva	–	Belani	
Bereck város	Bretz	Breţcu	*Beze***
Bita	–	Bita	*Bycha*
Csomortán	–	Lutoasa	
Dálnok	Dayla	Dalnic	*Dalnuk*
Esztelnek	–	Estelnic	*Yskulnuk*
Felsőcsernáton	–	Csernatu de Sus	
Felsőtorja, Feltorja	Torian	Turia de Sus	*Torya Superior*
Futásfalva	–	Alungeni	
Hatolyka	–	Hătuica	*Hotolka*
Ikafalva	–	Icafalău	*Ika*
Kézdi-Albis	–	Albiş	
Kézdi-Almás	–	Mereni	
Kézdi-Márkosfalva	–	Mărcuşa	
Kézdi-Martonfalva	–	Mărtineni	
Kézdi-Martonos	–	Mărtănuş	

Hungarian names	German names	Romanian names	1332-1337
Kézdi-Oroszfalu, *in* K.-Vásár.	–	Ruseni,	
Kézdi-Polyán, K.-Szentkereszt	–	Poian	*Polyan*
Kézdi-Sárfalva	–	Tinoasa	
Kézdi-Szászfalu	–	Lunga	
Kézdi-Szentlélek	–	Sânzieni	*S.Spiritus*
Kézdivásárhely	Szekler Neumarkt	Târgu Secuiesc	
Kurtapatak	–	Valea Scurtă	
Lécfalva	–	Leţ	*Lezofalua*
Lemhény	Lennen	Lemnia	*Lehmem*
Maksa	–	Moacşa	*Moya, Moxa*
Mátisfalva *in* K.-Márkosfalva			
Nyújtód	–	Lunga	*Nachtond*
Ozsdola	–	Ojdula	*Usdula*
Peselnek+ *in* Kézdikővár		Petriceni	*Pusulnuk*
Szentkatolna	–	Catalina	*S.Katherina*
Seat of Orbai (Not in the 1332–37 papal register)			
Barátos	–	Brateş	–
Cófalva	–	Ţufalău	–
Csoma-Kőrös	–	Chiuruş	–
Damokosfalva *in* Sz.-Tamásfalva			–
Gelence	Gelentz	Ghelinţa	–
Haraly	Harayl	Harale	–
Hilib	–	Hilib	–
Imecsfalva	–	Imeni	–
Kovásna	Kowasna	Covasna	–
Orbai-Telek	–	Telechia	–
Páké	–	Pachia	–
Papolc	–	Păpăuţi	–
Páva	–	Pava	–
Székely-Petőfalva	–	Peteni	–
Székely-Tamásfalva	–	Tamăsfalău	–
Szörcse	–	Surcea	–
Zabola	–	Zăbala	–
Zágon	–	Zagon	–

Szekler Villages

Hungarian names	German names	Romanian names	1332–1337
Seat of Aranyos (Not in the fifteenth–sixteenth centuries military rosters)			
Aranyos-Mohács	–	Măhăceni	*Muhac, Michach*
Bágyon	–	Bădeni	*Ragin*
Felső-Szentmihályfalva	–	Mihai Viteazu	*S.Michael*
Felvinc(*Cf.* chapter II, The Particularism of the Seat of Aranyos)	Oberwinz	Unirea	–
Gyéres-Szentkirály			*S. Rex*
Harasztos	–	Călăraşi	*Hazartus, Harastus*
Kercsed	–	Stejeriş	*Kerchech*
Mészkő	–	Cheia	*Mezkun*
Mezőbodon			*Bakun, Budun*
Mezőszengyel	–	Sânger	*Zengyel*
Sinfalva	–	Corneşti	*Semfalua, Zemhaza*
Sósszentmárton			*S.Martinus*
Székely-Földvár	Kaltherberg	Războieni-Cetate	*Felduar*
Székely-Hidas	–	Podeni	*Hydus*
Székely-Kocsárd	–	Lunca Mureşului	*Kuchard*
Torockó-Szentgyörgy			*Aranas de S.Georgio*
Várfalva	Burgdorf	Moldoveneşti	*Warsalua*

ABBREVIATIONS

Apart from the expression *Székely Archives* for the eight volumes of Székely Oklevéltár (SzOkl), the use of abbreviations is limited to the notes.

AOkl I.-XL. Kristó, Gyula. *Anjou-kori oklevéltár* (Anjou-period Archives) I.-XL., Budapest-Szeged, 1990-2015.

EOkm I. Jakó, Zsigmond. *Erdélyi okmánytár 1023-1300* (Transylvanian Documents 1023-300), I, Budapest: Akadémiai kiadó, 1997.

H&E Csernus, Sándor and Korompay, Klára eds *Les Hongrois et l'Europe: conquête et intégration* (The Hungarians and Europe, Conquest and Integration), Paris-Szeged: Publications de l'Institut Hongrois de Paris, 1999.

HoT Köpeczi, Béla, ed. *History of Transylvania*, Budapest: Akadémiai kiadó, 1994.

Kmk I. & II. Jakó, Zsigmond. *A Kolozsmonostori konvent jegyzőkönyvei 1289-1556*, (Notary Records of the Kolozsmonostor Convent), I-II, Budapest: Akadémiai kiadó, 1990.

KMTL Kristó, Gyula, ed, *Korai Magyar történeti Lexikon, 9-14. század* (Encyclopedia of Early Hungarian History, ninth-fourteenth centuries), Budapest: Akadémiai kiadó, 1994.

NEH 1965 *Nouvelles Etudes Historiques*, I-II. Budapest: Akadémiai kiadó, 1965.

SRH Szentpétery, Imre, *Scriptores rerum Hungaricarum*, I-II, Budapest: Nap kiadó, 1938 (facsimile, 1999).

SzOkl I. Szabó, Károly. *Székely Oklevéltár 1211-1519*, I, Kolozsvár: Papp Miklós, 1872.

SzOkl II. Szabó, Károly. *Székely Oklevéltár 1520-1571*, II, Kolozsvár: Papp Miklós, 1876.

SzOkl III. Szabó, Károly. *Székely Oklevéltár 1270-1571*, III, Kolozsvár: Féjer Vilmos, 1890

SzOkl IV. Szabó, Károly and Szádeczky, Lajos. *Székely Oklevéltár 1264-1707*, IV, Kolozsvár: Ajtai K. Albert, 1895.

SzOkl V. Szádeczky, Lajos. *Székely Oklevéltár 1296-1603*, V, Kolozsvár: Ajtai K. Albert, 1896.

SzOkl VIII. Barabás, Samu. *Székely Oklevéltár 1219-1776*, VIII, Budapest: Magyar Tudományos Akadémiai kiadó, 1934.

SzOkl új IV Demény, Lajos, ed. *Székely Oklevéltár, új sorozat* (new series) IV, Kolozsvár: EME (Erdélyi Múzeum Egyesület kiadó), 1998.

Ukb V. Gündisch, Gustav. *Urkundenbuch zur Geschichte der Deutschen in Siebenbürgen* (Archives on the History of the Germans in Transylvania) V, Köln-Wien: Böhlau Verlag, 1975.

SOURCES

About Szeklers

Barabás, Samu. *Székely Oklevéltár [VIII] 1219–1776*, Budapest: Magyar Tudományos Akadémiai kiadó, 1934. Available online at: https://library.hungaricana.hu/hu/view/KozMagyOkmanytarak_szekely_okleveltar/?pg=0&layout=s

Demény, Lajos, ed. (1983–2003), *Székely Oklevéltár, új sorozat* (new series) I–VI, Kolozsvár: EME (Erdélyi Múzeum Egyesület kiadó).

Székely de Kilyén, Mihály. *A Nemes Székely Nemzet Constitutiói, Privilégiumai, 's Jószág Leszállását tárgyazó némely Törvényes Itéletek* (Constitutions and Privileges of the Noble Szekler Nation and its Rules of Devolution), Pest, 1818.

Szabó, Károly. *Székely Oklevéltár I 1211–1519*, Kolozsvár: Papp Miklós, 1872.

Szabó, Károly. *Székely Oklevéltár II 1520–1571*, Kolozsvár: Papp Miklós, 1876.

Szabó, Károly. *Székely Oklevéltár III 1270–1571*, Kolozsvár: Féjer Vilmos, 1890.

Szabó, Károly and Szádeczky, Lajos. *Székely Oklevéltár IV 1264–1707*, Kolozsvár: Ajtai K. Albert, 1895.

Szádeczky, Lajos. *Székely Oklevéltár V 1296–1603*, Kolozsvár: Ajtai K. Albert, 1896.

About Transylvania and Saxons

(1815), *Erdély országnak törvényes könyve (Corpus juris Transsilvaniae)*, Kolozsvár.

Gündisch, Gustav. *Urkundenbuch zur Geschichte der Deutschen in Siebenbürgen*, V (Archives on the History of the Germans in Transylvania), Köln-Wien: Böhlau Verlag, 1975 and Zimmermann, Franz et al., I–III, Hermanstadt, 1892–1902 and Gündisch, (1981), IV–VI.

Jakó, Zsigmond. *A Kolozsmonostori konvent jegyzőkönyvei* (Notary Records of the Kolozsmonotor, convent of (see also *locus credibilis*) Convent) *1289–1556*, I–II, Budapest: Akadémiai kiadó, 1990.

Jakó, Zsigmond. *Erdélyi okmánytár 1023-1300* (Transylvanian Documents), I, Budapest: Akadémiai kiadó, 1997.

Miles, Matthias. (1639–1686), 'Siebenbürgischer Würgengel' (The Strangling Angel of Transylvania), in Armbruster, Adolf (1984, introd.), *Schriften zur Landeskunde Siebenbürgens* (Documents on the Regional History of Transylvania), Band 8, Köln-Wien: Böhlau Verlag, 1984.

Verancsics, Antal. (1504–1573), in Szabó, László (ed.), *Erdély öröksége* (Transylvanian Heritage), Budapest, I Tündérország, 1541–1571 (Fairy Country), Franklin kiadó, 1942.

About Hungary

Corpus juris hungarici, seu decretum Opus Tripartitum generale inclyti regni hungariae artiumque eidem adnexarum - (in duos tomos distinctum), Budae, 1779. continens Opus Tripartitum Juris Consuetudinarii ejusdem Regni, Authore Stephano de Werbőcz.

Bak, János M., Banyó, Péter and Rad, y Martin, eds Stephan Werbőczy, *The Customary Law of the Renowned Kingdom of Hungary in Three Parts (1517), The Laws of Hungary*, I–5, Idyllwild, CA and Budapest: Charles Schlacks Jr, 2005.

Dercsényi, Dezső. (1968), 'introd', in *Chronicon Pictum, Chronica de Gestis Hungarorum, Wiener Bilderchronik* (Hungarian Illuminated Chronicle), Budapest: Dausien Verlag.

Dőry, Franciscus, Bónis, Georgius and Bácskai, Vera. *Publicationes archivi nationalis hungarici II. Decreta regni Hungariae 1301-1457*, Budapest: Akadémiai kiadó, 1976.

Fejérpataky, László. *Monumenta Vaticana Historiam Regni Hungariae illustrantia tomus primus, Rationes collectorum pontificorum in Hungaria 1281–1375*, Budapest: METEM (magyar Egyháztörténeti Enciklopédia Munkaközösség), 1887 (facsimilé 2000). https://library.hungaricana.hu/hu/view/KozMagyOkmanytarak_Vatikani_1_01/?pg=0&layout=s

Győrffy, György. 'introd', in *Árpád-kori oklevelek* (Archives of the Árpád Period), Budapest: Balassi kiadó, 1997.

Hegedűs, András, et al. *Monumenta Ecclesiae Strigoniensis* (Esztergom) *Ab A. 1350. Ad A. 1358*, Esztergom-Budapest: Esztergomi Prímási Levéltár, 1999.

Knauz, Ferdinandus, ed. *Monumenta Ecclesiae Strigoniensis* I–III, Esztergom: Typis descripsit Aegydius Horák, 1874–1924.

Kristó, Gyula, ed. *Anjou-kori oklevéltár* (Archives of the Anjou Period) I–XL, Budapest-Szeged, 1990–2015. https://library.hungaricana.hu/hu/collection/kozepkori_magyar_okmanytarak_anjou/

Kristó, Gyula. *A honfoglalás korának irott forásai* (Written Sources on Epoch of the Conquest), Szeged: Szegedi Középkorász Műhely, 1995.

Mályusz, Elemér (from manuscripts), Borsa, Iván, 'introd', in *Zsigmondkori oklevéltár* (Archives of the Reign of Sigismund), *1415–1420*, V–VII, Budapest, 1997–2001; Mályusz, Elemér, I-II, Budapest, 1951–1958; Mályusz-Borsa, III–IV, Budapest: Magyar Országos levéltár, 1994.

Mezey, Barna, ed. *A Magyar jogtörténet forrásai* (Sources for Hungarian History of Law), Budapest: Osiris kiadó, 2000.

Pauler, Gyula and Szilágyi, Sándor. *A magyar honfoglalás* (Sources on the Hungarian Conquest) *kútfő*, Budapest: Nap kiadó, 1900 (facsimile 2000).

Szentpétery, Imre, *Scriptores rerum Hungaricarum* I-II, Budapest: Nap kiadó, 1937 (facsimilie 1999).

Dictionaries and glossaries

Bod, Péter. *Dictionarium latino-hungaricum*, 1ère édition: Szeben, 1767, 2nd edn: Szeben-Pozsony: Sardi Samuel 1767, Füsküt & Hochman, 1801.

Eder, Jozséf. *Dictionarium ungaro-latino-germanicum*, Szeben-Pozsony, 1801 (published with the second edition of *Bod*), Füsküt & Hochman).

Herner, Jáno. 'introd.', in *Mappa Transilvaniae et Partium Regni Hungariae repertoriumque locorum objectorum, Joannes de Lipszky* (Pest, 1806) Szeged: József Attila Tudományegyetemi kiadó 1987.

Kristó, Gyula, ed. *Korai Magyar Történeti Lexikon, 9–14. század* (Encyclopedia of Early Hungarian History, Ninth–Fourteenth centuries), Budapest: Akadémiai kiadó, 1994.

Révai, Sámuel and Révai, Leó. *nagy lexikona, az ismeretek encylopédiája* (Encyclopedia Révai), 21 volumes, Budapest: Babits kiadó (reprint 1989–1996), 1911–1935.

Sauvageot, Aurélien. *Dictionnaire général français-hongrois et hongrois-français* (French-Hungarian and Hungarian-French Dictionnary), 2 volumes, Budapest: Dante kiadó, 1932–1937.

Szamota, István, ed. *Magyar Oklevél-szótár* (Hungarian Archive Dictionary), Budapest: Hornyánszky Viktor, 1901–1906 (reprint 1984).

Touati, François-Olivier, ed. *Vocabulaire historique du Moyen Âge* (Dictionnary of Historical Terms from the Middle Ages), 3rd ed., Paris: Éditions La boutique de l'histoire, 2000.

NOTES

Preamble

1 Translation from the *Corpus Juris Hungarici*, Buda, 1779, vol. I, p. 103.
2 *nobiles privilegiati, nemesek* in Hungarian.
3 '*Siculi*' in the Latin text.

Introduction

1 Hungarian Illuminated Chronicle, *Chronica de Gestis Hungarorum*, Dercsenyi, Dezsö (ed.), Budapest, 1968.
2 St. Stephen's admonition to his son, the prince Imre: '*Sicut enim ex diversis partibus et provinciis veniunt hospites, ita diversas linguas et consuitudines, diversaque documenta et arma secum ducunt, que omnia regna ornant et magnificant aulam et perterritant exterrorum arrogantiam.* **Nam unius lingue uniusque moris regnum inbecille et fragile est.**' *Libellus de institutione morum*, in SRH II, p. 625. NB. The abbreviations and the publications to which they refer in detail are appended.
3 Bloch, Marc. *Feudal Society*, Chicago: University of Chicago Press, 1961, (first edition in French, Paris, 1939), p. 21.
4 Molnár, Miklós. *Histoire de la Hongrie* (History of Hungary), Paris: Éditions Hatier, 1996, p. 144.
5 Bérenger, Jean, *Histoire de l'empire des Habsbourg 1273-1918* (History of the Habsburg Empire), Paris: Éditions Fayard, 1990, p. 11.
6 Székely de Kilyén, Mihály. *A Nemes Székely Nemzet Constitutiói, Privilégiumai, 's Jószág Leszállását tárgyazó némely Törvényes Itéletek* (Constitutions and Privileges of the Noble Szekler Nation and its Rules of Devolution), Pest, 1818.
7 Critique written in 1905 by Szádeczky, Lajos. 'Csíki székely Krónika' (The 'Szekler Chronicle' of Csík), in György, Attila (ed.), *Csíki székely krónika* (The Szekler Chronicle of Csík), Csíkszereda: Hargita kiadó (2000), pp. 49–118.
8 Györffy, György. 'La chancellerie royale de Hongrie aux XIII-XIVe siècles' (The royal chancellery of Hungary in the Thirteenth and Fourteenth Centuries) in Glassl, Horst (et al.), *Studia Hungarica 32, Forschungen über Siebenbürgen und seine Nachbarn II* (Research about Transylvania and its neighbours), München: Wissenschaftszentrum Ost- und Südosteuropa, 1988, pp. 159–176.
9 In H&E, '*Lexique*', p. 450. Details of cited publications in annexes 'Abbreviations' and Sources'.
10 Györffy, György and Borsa, Iván. 'Actes, 'Locus credibilis' et notariat dans la Hongrie médiévale' (Private writs, 'locus crediblis' and notary records in medieval Hungary) in *Notariado publico y documento privado de los origines al siglo XIV.*, Actas del VII congresso Internacional de Diplomatica (Valencia, 1986), Valencia, 1989, vol. II, pp. 941–949.

11 The references within the SzOkl point to documents by volume and page number. In the present study, references are to the volume number and the SzOkl document number followed, where appropriate, by the date.
12 Szádeczky-Kardoss, Lajos. *A székely nemzet története és alkotmanyá* (History and Constitution of the Szekler Nation), Budapest: Akadémiai kiadó,1927 (facsimile 1993.
13 Imreh, István and Egyed, Ákos, amongst others.
14 The posthumous publication of Sándorfy, Kamill. *Erdély reformkorszakának jogtörténete* (1825-1848) (History of Transylvanian Law in the Reform Era [1825-1848]), Budapest: EFO kiadó, 2000, pp. 70–100, its title notwithstanding, synthesizes Szekler law on thirty pages, of which six deal with their customary law at the end of the Middle Ages (1451–1555). The academic work of Balás, Gábor. *Erdély jókora jogtörténete* (The History of Transylvanian Law), Budapest: Budapest Füti Nyomda (print) 1977–1982, devotes seven pages to Szekler law prior to 1540.
15 Bodor, György. 'Az 1562 előtti székely nemzetségi szervezetről' (The Structure of the Szekler Nation before 1562), *in Történelmi Szemle* (Journal of History), 83/2, Budapest: Akadémiai kiadó, 1983, pp. 281–305. The exact title of the posthumous publication is 'A székely nemzetiségi szervezetről', i.e. the organization of Szekler nationality. I follow István Imreh's judicious recommendation in reading *nemzetség* = nation rather than *nemzetiség* = nationality, since the notion of *nemzetiség* = nationality would be anachronistic and devoid of sense in this study of Szekler societal structures in the Middle Ages.
16 Bónis, György. *Magyar jog - székely jog* (Hungarian Law, Szekler Law), Kolozsvár: Kolozsvári Tudományos Könyvtár, 1942.

Chapter I

1 György, György. 'Formation d'Etats au IXe siècle suivant les 'Gesta Hungarorum' du Notaire Anonymus' (The Formation of States in the Ninth Century According the 'Gesta Hungarorum' of the Notary Anonymous), in *Nouvelles Etudes Historiques*, I, Budapest: Akadémiai kiadó, 1965, pp. 27–53.
2 in SRH II. 'P. magistri, qui Anonymus dicitur, Gesta Hungarorum': *omnes Siculi qui primo erant populi Atthyl regis,* [50], p. 101.
3 in SRH I. Simonis de Keza Gesta Hungarorum: *Remanserant quoque de Hunnis [… / …] qui se sibi non Hunnos sed Zakulos vocaverunt.* [21], p. 162.
4 in SRH I. [21] p. 162 in Latin in the Illuminated Chronicle, in SRH I. [21] p. 279 or translated into German, in Dercsényi, Dezső. 'introd.', in *Chronicon Pictum, Chronica de Gestis Hungarorum, Wiener Bilderchronik* (Hungarian Illuminated Chronicle), II, Budapest: Dausien Verlag, 1968, [21] p. 104.
5 Orbán Balázs. *A Székelyföld leírása* (Description of the Szeklerland 'Szeklerland (*Székelyföld, Terra Siculorum*)') Pest: Szekszárdi Hasonmásolat (1991), Rath (1868).
6 Eszlary, Charles d'. *Histoire des institutions publiques hongroises* (History of the Public Institutions of Hungary), Paris: Éditions M. Rivière et Cie and CNRS, I (1958–1963), p. 59.
7 SzOkl I. XIII, between 1235 and 1270.
8 Le Calloc'h, Bernard. 'Qui sont les Sicules?' (Who are the Szeklers?), in *Bulletin de l'association des Anciens élèves de l'Institut National des Langues et Civilisations Orientales* (Bulletin of the Alumni of the National Institute of Oriental Languages

and Civilisations - INALCO), Paris: INALCO (Institut National des Langues et Civilisations Orientales), 1990. pp. 11-30.
9 Le Calloc'h, 'Qui sont les Sicules?', pp. 15-18.
10 Bóna, István. 'Transylvania in the Early Kingdom of Hungary', in *History of Transylvania*, pp. 154-155. The charters in question are published in Györffy, György (ed.) *Árpád-kori oklevelek* (Charters from the Age of the Árpád kings) Budapest, 1997, pp. 26-30 and p. 48.
11 Kordé, Zoltán, in his article 'Székelyek' in KMTL.
12 in SzOkl új IV, p. 199, pp. 119-135 and p. 844.
13 Le Calloc'h, 'Qui sont les Sicules?', pp. 15-18.
14 György, 'Formation d'Etats au IXe siècle suivant les 'Gesta Hungarorum' du Notaire Anonymus', p. 41.
15 Makkai, László, 'The Emergence of the Estates', in *Histoire de Transylvanie* (History of Transylvania), Budapest-Paris: PUF (Presses Universitaires de France), 1946, p. 178.
16 Cf. Vékony, Gábor of the University of Budapest ELTE, cited in the newspaper *Népszabadság* of June 25, 1999 in an article by Pekarek János 'Bizonyiték a kettös honfoglalásra?'(Proof of the Double Conquest?).
17 Constantine VII Porphyrogenitus (905-959) *De Administrando Imperio*, [39] in Pauler, Gyula and Szilágyi, Sándor. *A magyar honfoglalás* (Sources on the Hungarian Conquest) *kútfő*, Budapest: Nap kiadó, 1900 (facsimile edition 2000), p. 124.
18 Szádeczky-Kardoss, Lajos. *A székely nemzet története és alkotmanyá* (History and Constitution of the Szekler Nation), Budapest: Akadémiai kiadó, 1927 (facsimile 1993), pp. 52-53.
19 SzOkl I. XXXVII.
20 Györffy, György. 'A székelyek eredete és településük története' (The Origins of the Szeklers and History of their Settling), in Mályusz, Elemér, *Erdély és népei* (Transylvania and its Peoples), 1st edn, Budapest: Franklin kiadó 1941, Maecenas kiadó 1999, pp. 37-86.
21 György, 'Formation d'Etats au IXe siècle suivant les 'Gesta Hungarorum' du Notaire Anonymus', p. 41.
22 Eszláry, *Histoire des institutions publiques hongroises*, p. 59.
23 Makkai, *Histoire de la Transylvanie*, p. 50.
24 Kordé, Zoltán. *'Kabars, Sicules et Pechenègue: les Hongrois et les auxiliaires militaires'* ('*Kavars* (see also *Khazar Empire*)', Szeklers and Pechenegs: '*Pechenegs*' the Hungarians and the Military Auxiliaries), in Csernus, Sándor and Korompay, Klára (eds), *Les Hongrois et l'Europe : conquête et intégration* (The Hungarians and Europe, Conquest and Integration), Paris-Szeged: Publications de l'Institut Hongrois de Paris, 1999, pp. 231-243.
25 Balás, Gábor. *A székekyek nyomában* (On the Track of the Szeklers), Budapest: Franklin kiadó, 1984, p. 269.
26 Makkai, 'The Emergence of the Estates (1172-1526)', in *Histoire de Transylvanie*, p. 178.
27 Sinor, Denis, 'The Historical Attila', in Bäuml, Franz and Birnbaum, Marianna, eds. *Attila, the man and his image*, symposium of the Center for medieval and Renaissance Studies, UCLA: Corvina kiadó, 1988, published in 1993, pp. 3-15.
28 Werbőczy, István, *Opus Tripartitum Juris Consuetudinarii, Prologi, Titulus 6*, in *Corpus Juris Hungarici*, Buda, 1779, vol. I, p. 3.
29 SzOkl I. CCXXVI.
30 Cf. Kordé, *'Kabars, Sicules et Pechenègue: les Hongrois et les auxiliaires*, pp. 231-243.

31 Zimonyi, István. 'Prehistoire hongroise: méthode de recherche et vue d'ensemble' (Hungarian Prehistory: Research Methodology and Overview), in Csernus, Sándor and Korompay, Klára (eds), *Les Hongrois et l'Europe: conquête et intégration* (The Hungarians and Europe, Conquest and Integration), Paris-Szeged: Publications de l'Institut Hongrois de Paris, 1999, pp. 29–43.
32 Kristó, Gyula. 'L'an Mil: changement de régime en Hongrie' (The Year One Thousand: Change of Regime in Hungary), in Csernus, Sándor and Korompay, Klára (eds), *Les Hongrois et l'Europe : conquête et intégration* (The Hungarians and Europe, Conquest and Integration), 11–25, Paris-Szeged: Publications de l'Institut Hongrois de Paris, 1999, pp. 11–25.
33 Berta, Árpád. 'Le système des noms de tribus d'origine turke' (The System of Turkic Tribal Names), in Csernus, Sándor and Korompay, Klára (eds), *Les Hongrois et l'Europe: conquête et intégration* (The Hungarians and Europe, Conquest and Integration), Paris-Szeged: Publications de l'Institut Hongrois de Paris, 1999, pp. 121–136.
34 In France Lucien Musset, René Grousset et al.; in English, English translations of Hungarian authors and on maps of ninth–tenth century migrations.
35 Györffy, György. *Autour de l'Etat des semi-nomades: le cas de la Hongrie* (About the Semi-Nomad States: the Case of Hungary), Budapest: Akadémiai kiadó, 1975, p. 6.
36 Molnár, Miklós. *Histoire de la Hongrie* (History of Hungary), Paris: Éditions Hatier, 1996, pp. 11–22.
37 Nyék, Megyer, Kürt-Gyarmat, Tarján, Jenő, Kér, Keszi.
38 György Györffy and Charles d'Eszláry.
39 Eszláry, *Histoire des institutions publiques hongroises*, p. 58.
40 Györffy, György. *König Stephan der Heilige* (King Stephen the Saint), Budapest: Corvina kiadó, 1988, p. 154.
41 Györffy, *König Stephan der Heilige*, p. 154.
42 Bónis, György. *Magyar jog - székely jog* (Hungarian Law, Szekler Law), Kolozsvár: Kolozsvári Tudományos Könyvtár, 1942, p. 36.
43 Eszláry, *Histoire des institutions publiques hongroises*, p. 11.
44 Illuminated Chronicle, cited in EOkm I. 8, 1116–1146.
45 EOkm I, 37, around 1210 and SzOkl VIII. 4 - EOkm I. 212, 1250.
46 Musset, Lucien. *Les invasions: le second assaut contre l'Europe chrétienne (VIIe–XIe siècles)* (The Invasions – the Second Assault against Christian Europe [Seventh–Eleventh Centuries]), Paris: PUF (Presses Universitaires de France), 1965, p. 72.
47 Pálóczi Horváth, András. *Pechenegs, Cumans, Iasians, Steppe Peoples in Medieval Hungary*, Budapest: Corvina kiadó, 1989, pp. 33–38.
48 SzOkl I. XXXIX - AOkl VIII.23 and SzOkl I.XXX - VIII.6 - AOkl VIII.56, 1324.
49 SzOkl III.615, 1548.
50 SzOkl I.CXCV, 1484.
51 SzOkl I.CXLI, 1455.
52 Makkai, 'The Emergence of the Estates (1172–1526)', in *Histoire de Transylvanie*, pp. 194–195.
53 Pálóczi Horváth, *Pechenegs, Cumans, Iasians, Steppe Peoples in Medieval Hungary*, pp. 54–55.
54 Pálóczi Horváth, *Pechenegs, Cumans, Iasians, Steppe Peoples in Medieval Hungary*, p. 64.
55 Pálóczi Horváth, *Pechenegs, Cumans, Iasians, Steppe Peoples in Medieval Hungary*, pp. 62–67.

56 Horváth, Péter. *Értekezés a kúnoknak és jászoknak eredetekrül azoknak régi és mostani állapotjokrúl* (Essay on the origins and ancient and present structures of the Cumans and the Iasians), Jász-Berény: Székely Gábor (1820, facsimile 1996), pp. 68–71.
57 Cf. EOkm I.8.
58 SzOkl I.XI.
59 EOkm I.231.
60 SzOkl I.XIII (undated) (1235–1270).
61 SzOkl III.413.
62 Cf. Kordé, Zoltán, 'Székelyek' *in* KMTL.
63 SzOkl I.III - Eokm1.61, 1213; SzOkl I.IV - EOkm 1.119, 1222.
64 Cf. Bogdan, Henry. *Les Chevaliers Teutoniques* (The Teutonic Knights), Paris: Éditions Perrin, 1999, pp. 85–97: 'L'Ordre Teutonique en Hongrie: une tentative malheureuse d'implantation en Europe centrale' (The Teutonic Order in Hungary: an Unsuccessful Attempt at Settling in Central Europe).
65 SzOkl I.V - EOkm I.132, 1224.
66 SzOklI. VII.
67 EOkm I.179 and 180.
68 SzOkl III.409.
69 Cf. György, 'Formation d'Etats au IXe siècle suivant les 'Gesta Hungarorum' du Notaire Anonymus', p. 41.
70 Bóna, István, 'Transylvania in the Medieval Hungarian Kingdom (895–1526)', in, *Histoire de Transylvanie*, p. 153 and in KMTL, Kordé Zoltán, 'Vajda'.
71 Szokl I.CCCXXV, 1506.
72 EOkm I.37.
73 SzOkl I. IV. L. Makkai thinks it is a forgery established in 1231.
74 Durandin, Catherine. *Histoire des Roumains* (History of the Romanians), Paris: Éditions Fayard, 1995, p. 51.
75 Pop, Ioan-Aurel, 'Elita românească din Transilvania în secolele XIII-XIV, origine, statut, evoluție' (The Elite of Transylvania in the thirteenth–fourteenth centuries, origin, status, evolution), in Diaconescu, Marius (ed.), *Nobilimea românească din Transilvania* (Romanian Nobility in Transylvania), Satu Mare: Editura Muzeului Sătmărean, 1997, pp. 69–84, summary in French pp. 85–86.
76 Pop, 'Elita românească din Transilvania în secolele XIII-XIV, origine, statut, evoluție', in Diaconescu, (ed.), *Nobilimea românească din Transilvania*, pp. 36–54, summary in French pp. 59–63.
77 Castellan, Georges. *Histoire des Balkans, XIVe-XXe siècle* (History of the Balkans, Fourteenth–Twentieth Centuries), Paris: Éditions Fayard, 1991, p. 159.
78 Makkai, 'The Emergence of the Estates (1172–1526)', in *Histoire de Transylvanie*, pp. 212–214.
79 Cf. Pasco, Stefan. *La révolte populaire de Transylvanie des années 1437-1438* (The Popular Uprising in Transylvania in 1437-1438), Bucharest: éditions. de l'Académie de la République populaire roumaine, 1964.
80 SzOkl I. CXIII.
81 SzOkl I. CLXXI.
82 Engel, Pál. *The Realm of St. Stephen, a History of Medieval Hungary (895-1526)*, London-New York: I.B. Tauris, 2001, p. 115.
83 Cf. HoT pp. 179–180.

84 Szádeczky-Kardoss, Lajos. *A székely nemzet története és alkotmanyá* (History and Constitution of the Szekler Nation), Budapest: Akadémiai kiadó (1993), 1927 (facsimile 1993), p. 31.
85 Makkai, *Histoire de la Transylvanie*, p. 182.
86 EOkm I. 27.
87 Benkő, Elek, 'Kézdiszék', *in* KMTL and SzOkl VIII. 117: '*ad dictas Tres sedes*'.
88 EOkm I. 304.
89 SzOkl I.XVII-EOkm I.452.
90 Cf. Györffy, 'A székelyek eredete és településük története', in Mályusz, *Erdély és népei*, pp. 37–86.
91 SzOkl I. XXXVII.
92 Szádeczky-Kardoss, *A székely nemzet története és alkotmánya*, pp. 52–53.
93 György, 'Formation d'Etats au IXe siècle suivant les 'Gesta Hungarorum' du Notaire Anonymus', p. 30.
94 SzOkl I. XXXVII.
95 SzOkl I. XL: '*Nos Magister Andreas, Comes trium generum Siculorum, de Brassow et de Bistrica …*'.

Chapter II

1 SzOkl I XIII.
2 (… *quia predicti Siculi in libertate persistentes prenotate* …).
3 SzOkl I. XLI, 1346.
4 SzOkl III. 409 - EOkm I. 292, 1270–1272 and SzOkl II. 410 - EOkm I. 367, 1279.
5 Bónis, György. *Magyar jog - székely jog* (Hungarian Law, Szekler Law), Kolozsvár: Kolozsvári Tudományos Könyvtár, 1942, p. 9.
6 SzOkl I. CLXXIX.
7 Published, among others, in SRH and quoted in EOkm I, 8, for the battles of 1116 (on the shores of the Oltsava) and 1146 (along the Leitha).
8 Emperor Leo the Wise (886–912), *Taktika [XIV. 42]* describes the tactics of the Hungarians in the same terms. Cited by Györffy, György. *A Magyarok elődeiről és a honfoglalásról* (On the Ancestors of the Hungarians and the Conquest), Budapest: Gondola kiadó, 1986, pp. 108; Kristó, Gyula. *A honfoglalás korának irott forásai* (Written Sources on Epoch of the Conquest), Szeged, 1995, pp. 102 ff and (with the text in Greek) Pauler, Gyula and Szilágyi, Sándor. *A magyar Honfoglalás kútfői* (Sources on the Hungarian Conquest), Nap kiadó, 1900, (facsimile 2000), p. 9.
9 Fasoli, Gina. 'Points de vue sur les incursions hongroises en Europe au Xe siècle' (Points of View on the Hungarian Invasions in Europe during the Tenth Century), in *Cahiers de Civilisation Médiévale*, II, Poitiers: CESCM (Centre d'études supérieures de civilisation médiévale), 1959, pp. 17–36.
10 SzOkl I. CLXIV.
11 *Cf.* Vofkori, László. *Székelyföld útikönyve* (Guide to the Szeklerland), I-II, Budapest: Cartographia kiadó, 1998, pp. 82–84.
12 SzOkl III, 511.
13 Illustration from 'Weisskunig' (*Der weisse König* - The White King), a prose chronicle of the fifteenth century, first published in 1775, in Ságvári, György and Somogyi,

Győző. *Nagy huszárkönyv* (The Great Book of Hussars), Budapest: Magyar Könyv Klub kiadó, 1999, p. 22.
14 In Dőry, Franciscus, Bónis, Georgius and Bácskai, Vera. *Publicationes archivi nationalis hungarici II. Decreta regni Hungariae 1301-1457*, Budapest: Akadémiai kiadó, 1976, pp. 378-383.
15 SzOkl I. CLXIV.
16 SzOkl I.CLXX - III. 473.
17 SzOkl I. CLXXIX.
18 '*Facta per vos sine mora generali collustacione fidelium nostrorum Siculorum equites in suo statu a maioribus progeneratos in seorsiuas tabulas referatis, qui propter permansuram distincionem Primipili vocabuntur, pedites rursus in alias tabulas, quas nemo Primorum suo arbitrio alterabit, perpetuam alioquia infamiam incursus*'.
19 Cf. K. Szabó in his footnote to SzOkl I. XXXVII.
20 SzOkl III. 559: '*Judicibus primipilis primoribus, ceterisque pocioribus et senioribus trium generum septem sedium*'.
21 Cf. Engel, Pál. *Magyarország világi archontológia 1301-1457* (Worldly Dignitaries of Hungary, 1301-1457), two volumes, I-II, Budapest: MTA történettudományi intézet, 1996.
22 Cf. Imreh, István., in Benkő, Samu (ed.), *Székely Felkelés 1595-1596* (The Szekler Uprising of 1595-1596), Bucharest: Kriterion kiadó, 1979, pp. 162-163.
23 SzOkl III. 511.
24 SzOkl III. 441.
25 SzOkl III.442, I.CXVI, III.479 and III.563.
26 SzOkl I. X, 1256 and I. XII, 1263. At this time, the Vlachs were also under the obligation to offer these gifts.
27 SzOkl II. CCLXXXV, 1544: '*boves usti et stigmate signati*'.
28 Cf. Hóman, Bálint and Szekfű, Gyula. *Magyar történet* (History of Hungary), 2nd edn, Budapest: Királyi Magyar Egyetem, 1936.
29 SzOkl II. CCXCIX and II. CCCI, 1552.
30 SzOkl CLXXIX.
31 SzOkl I. CCIX.
32 zOkl III.515, VIII.121 and VIII.122.
33 SzOkl III.525.
34 SzOkl VIII 140.
35 Szegfű, László. 'Le monde spirituel des Hongrois païens' (The Spiritual World of the Pagan Hungarians), in Csernus, Sándor and Korompay, Klára (eds), *Les Hongrois et l'Europe: conquête et intégration* (The Hungarians and Europe, Conquest and Integration), 103-120, Paris-Szeged: Publications de l'Institut Hongrois de Paris, 1999, pp. 103-120.
36 Cf. Bérenger, Jean. *Tolérance ou paix de religion en Europe centrale* (1415-1792) Tolerance or Religious Peace in Central Europe), Paris: Honoré Champion, libraire-éditeur, 2000, pp. 135-147.
37 Cf. Barta, Gábor. 'L'intolérance dans un pays tolérant, la principauté de Transylvanie au XVIe siècle' (Intolerance in a Tolerant Country, the principlality of Transylvania in the Sixteenth Century), in Sauzet, Robert (ed.), *Les frontières religieuses en Europe du XVe au XVIIe siècle* (Religious Borders in the Europe of the Fifteenth to Seventeenth Centuries), Paris: Libraire-éditeur Vrin et CNRS, 1992, pp. 151-158.
38 EOkm I.27.
39 EOkm I.179 & 180.

40 SzOkl I.CLXIX.
41 Jánó, Mihály. *A Gelencei műemlektemplom* (The Church at Gelence, Historical Monument), Sepsiszentgyörgy: Baász kiadó, 1994.
42 SzOkl I.CCXVII.
43 SzOkl III.480.
44 SzOkl I. VI, 1228; I.I, 1396 and I.CXV, 1439.
45 The last references date from 1449 and 1453, Kubinyi, András. *Főpapok, egyházi intézmények és Vallásosság a középkori Magyarországon* (Prelates, Ecclesiastic Institutions and Religious Practice in Medieval Hungary), Budapest: Magyar Egyháztörténeti Enciklopédia Munkaközösség, 1999, I, p. 76.
46 Szádeczky-Kardoss, Lajos. *A székely nemzet története és alkotmanyá* (History and Constitution of the Szekler Nation), Budapest: Akadémiai kiadó (1993), 1927 (facsimile 1993), pp. 86–87 and Vofkori, László. *Székelyföld útikönyve* (Guide to the Szeklerland), I-II, Budapest: Cartographia kiadó, 1998, I, p. 76.
47 SzOkl I.VI - EOkm I. 148.
48 SzOkl I. LXIV.
49 SzOkl I. CXVII.
50 Ukb V. 2612 & 2613, 1447: '*in Cibiensi et Brassouiensi partium Transsilvuanorum iurisdictioni almae Strigoniensi subiectis*'.
51 Cevins De, Marie-Madeleine. 'Les paroisses hongroises au Moyzen Age' (Hungarian Parishes during the Middle Ages), in Csernus, Sándor and Korompay, Klára (eds), *Les Hongrois et l'Europe: conquête et intégration* (The Hungarians and Europe, Conquest and Integration), Paris-Szeged: Publications de l'Institut Hongrois de Paris, 1999, pp. 341–385.
52 Koszta, László. 'L'organisation de l'Église chrétienne en Hongrie' (The Organisation of the Church in Hungary), in Csernus, Sándor and Korompay, Klára (eds), *Les Hongrois et l'Europe: conquête et intégration* (The Hungarians and Europe, Conquest and Integration), Paris-Szeged: Publications de l'Institut Hongrois de Paris, 1999, pp. 293–312.
53 Gyöngyössy, János. *Székely templomerődök* (Szekler Fortified Churches), Csíkszereda: Pro-Print kiadó, 1999, p. 82.
54 Cf. Gyöngyössy, *Székely templomerődök*, p. 82. and Tüdős S. Kinga. *Erdélyi védőrendszerek a XV.-XVIII. században, Háromszéki templomvárak* (Transylvanian Defense Structures, the Fortified Churches in Háromszék), Budapest: Puski kiadó, 1995.
55 SzOkl I. CCIX: '*et quod peius est, et numquam auditum, in mediuo nostri Castellum erexit, de quo nos semper tuto apprimere ac spoliere possit*'.
56 Török, József and Hervay, Ferenc. 'Le réseau monastique Hongrois et l'histoire de l'ordre des Ermites de Saint-Paul en Hongrie médiévale' (The Network of Monasteries in Hungary and the History of the Order of Saint Paul the First Hermit in Medieval Hungary), in Cercor (ed.), *Naissance et fonctionnement des réseaux monastiques et canoniaux* (Origin and Functioning of the Monastic and Canonical Networks), Saint Etienne: CERCOR (Centre Européen de Recherches sur les Congrégations et Ordres Religieux), 1985, pp. 225–233; Török, József. 'La notion de prieuré en Hongrie avant l'arrivée des Turcs' (The Concept of Priories in Hungary before the Arrival of the Turks), in Lemaitre, Jean-Loup (ed.), *Prieurs et prieurés dans l'occident médiéval* (Priors and Priories in the Medieval Occident), Paris: EPHE (Ecole Pratique des Hautes Etudes), 1987, pp. 61–66 and Kiss, Gergely. 'La fondation de l'abbaye bénédictine de Somogyvár' (The Founding of the Benedictine Abby of Somogyvár),

in Csernus, Sándor and Korompay, Klára (eds), *Les Hongrois et l'Europe: conquête et intégration* (The Hungarians and Europe, Conquest and Integration), Paris-Szeged: Publications de l'Institut Hongrois de Paris, 1999, pp. 327–340.
57 SzOkl VIII.109, in 1498.
58 SzOkl III.517.
59 *Quod quandocunque palam aliquis plebanorum concubinarius repperietur, habeatque concubinam notorie, talis admoneatur, ne de cetero tale facinus perpetret.*
60 *Si vero altera parcium presbiter fuerit, extunc laicus ille contra presbiterum causam suam per procuratorem, quem elegerit, agere possit, presbiter vero solus agat et non per procuratorem, neque presbiter contra laicum per libellum procedat. Placet.*
61 SzOkl V.905, 1427.
62 SzOkl VIII.77, 1473, III.516, 1503 and VIII.125, 1505.
63 *[...] ut agnoscaturde valore et quantitate dotis ut consuetudo illius terre est.*
64 SzOkl III.440.
65 *Item quod nullus bona sua auitcia alicui durante vita vel reliquere vel etiam testamentaliter legare possit, bona vero per se aquisita cuicunque voluerit libere et relinquere et testari possit, ita tamen quod bona vel relicta vel legata fratres vel consanguinei Illius, Juxta valorem et estimacionem huiusmodi bonorum ad se reimere possint et valeant, casu vero, quo talibus propinquis sine fratribus orbatus fuerit, extunc Incole loci Illius similiter eadem bona modo premisso ad se redimere possint et valeant. Placet hoc quoque secundum antiquam consuetudinem terre Siculie.*
66 *Corpus Iuris Hungarici: S. Stephani Decretum Liber Secundus, Caput V.*
67 Benkő, Elek's article 'Kolozsvár', in KMTL.
68 SzOkl I.CII.
69 SzOkl III.496.
70 *... in qualibet Sedium Siculorum nostrorum parcium nostrarum Transsiluanarum vnam habemus* Ciuitatem *certis libertatibus insignatam ...*
71 Benkő, Elek, et al. *Középkori mezőváros a Székelyföldön* (Medieval Market Towns in the Szeklerland) (*Székelyföld, Terra Siculorum*)', Kolozsvár: EME (Erdélyi Múzeum Egyesület kiadó), 1997.
72 SzOkl I.CLXXVI, 1470.
73 SzOkl I.CXCIV, 1484 for Marosvásárhely and II.CCLV, 1525 for Sepsiszentgyörgy.
74 SzOkl I.XVIII - EOkm I.452, 1289; EOkm I.492, 1291; SzOkl I.XXV - AOkl III.567, 1313; SzOkl I.LXXIII, 1394; SzOkl I.CX, 1436; SzOkl VIII.68 - Kmk I.1828, 1468; SzOkl I.CLCCIV and SzOkl VIII.70 - Kmk I.1913, 1469; SzOkl I.CXC, 1484.
75 SzOkl VIII.1.
77 SzOkl I.CLI.
76 '*... in sedibus Wdwarhel et Keresthwur ...*'
78 SzOkl I.CCXIX, mid-sixteenth century.
79 SzOkl VIII.52.
80 SzOkl III.464 and I.CLIII, 1459.
81 SzOkl II.CCLXI.
82 SzOkl VIII.113, 1503.
83 The Scat of Aranyos, composed of twenty-some villages, was not included in this roster. The complete register appears in a document from 1614: SzOkl új IV, pp. 197–562 with over 20,000 names. The tables published by I. Imreh vary slightly (e.g. a total of 20,196 families on page 163 and 19,275 families on page 179). The essence here is to have a scale of reference.
84 Imreh., in Benkő (ed.), *Székely Felkelés 1595-1596*, pp. 146–191.

Notes

85 Imreh., in Benkő (ed.), *Székely Felkelés 1595-1596*, p. 159.
86 SzOkl I.CLI and SzOkl VIII.57, 1462.
87 SzOkl VIII.64, 1464.
88 SzOkl V.934, 935 and 936 and SzOkl V.942, 1555.
89 SzOkl II.CCCXIV, codification of Szekler customary law in eighty-eight articles.
90 SzOkl III.517.
91 Imreh, István, *A Törvényhozó székely falu* (The Szekler village as Legislator), Bucharest: Kriterion kiadó, 1983, pp. 275–503.
92 SzOkl II.CCCXC - V.937, 1548; II.CCCXXV, 1557 and II.CCXCI, which Szabó dates at the end of the first half of the sixteenth century.
93 Györffy, György. 'A székelyek eredete és településük története' (The Origins of the Szeklers and History of their Settling), in Mályusz, Elemér, *Erdély és népei* (Transylvania and its Peoples), 1st edn, Budapest: Franklin kiadó, 1941, 2nd edn, Maecenas kiadó, 1999, pp. 37–86.

Part II

1 '*Status et ordines Regni Hungariae, nempe Praelatis, Baronibus et Magnatibus, Nobilibus et Liberis Civitatibus constent*'.
2 Szűcs, Jenő. *Les trois Europes* (The three Europes), Paris: Éditions L'Harmattan, 1985, p. 67.

Chapter III

1 SzOkl I.CLXX, III.476.
2 SzOkl I.CLXXIX.
3 SzOkl I.CCIX.
4 SzOkl III.511.
5 SzOkl III.517.
6 SzOkl I.CCXXIV - VIII.124 and I.CCXXVI, for the translations, see Appendices.
7 Székely de Kilyén, Mihály. *A Nemes Székely Nemzet Constitutiói, Privilégiumai, 's Jószág Leszállását tárgyazó némely Törvényes Itéletek* (Constitutions and Privileges of the Noble Szekler Nation and its Rules of Devolution), Pest, 1818, Pest, pp. 24–33.
8 SzOkl ICCXXIV - VII.124.
9 SzOkl I.CCXXVI.
10 In Makkai, László, 'The Emergence of the Estates', in *Histoire de Transylvanie* (History of Transylvania), Budapest-Paris: PUF (Presses Universitaires de France), 1946, p. 238.
11 In *Histoire de Transylvanie*, G. Barta: p. 284 for 1562, K. Péter: p. 336 for 1658, Zs Trózsányi: p. 433 for 1763; and K. Hegyi & Gy. Tóth: p. 756, assembly of the armed Szeklers in Agyagfalva and p. 758, integration of the Szekler and Saxon Seats in the counties in 1876.
12 Bónis, György. *Magyar jog - székely jog* (Hungarian Law, Szekler Law), Kolozsvár: Kolozsvári Tudományos Könyvtár, 1942, p. 101.
13 Molnár, Miklós. *Histoire de la Hongrie* (History of Hungary), Paris: Éditions Hatier, 1996, p. 116.

14 Eszlary, Charles d'. *Histoire des institutions publiques hongroises* (History of the Public Institutions of Hungary), Paris: Éditions M. Rivière et Cie and CNRS, 1958-1963, II, p. 21.
15 Molnár, *Histoire de la Hongrie*, p. 119 and Pamlényi, Ervin, ed. *Histoire de la Hongrie des origines à nos jours* (History of Hungary from its Origins to the Present), Budapest-Roanne: Corvina-Horváth kiadó, 1974, p. 142.
16 Bónis, *Magyar jog - székely jog*, p. 8, where Gy. Bónis refers to the term *ius Siculicale*).
17 SzOkl V.933.
18 SzOkl III.628.
19 SzOkl II.CCCXIV.
20 Bónis, *Magyar jog - székely jog*, p. 26.
21 (§74) *'Székelységnek emlékezetére nem tudjuk azt, hogy sereg ilyenképpen lakott volna székely földén; mert soha törvényünk nem volt: annak okáéert most is könyörgünk vajda uraknak ő Nagyságoknak, mint kegyelmes urainknak, hogy a régi szbadságunk szerint éltessenek, és ennek utánnaazzal ne terheljenek.'*

Chapter IV

1 Two cases in 1521, SzOkl II.CCXLVIII and II.CCXLIX and one in 1555, SzOkl II.CCCXIX.
2 SzOkl I.CXCIV, 1484, SzOkl II.CCL, 1521 and SzOkl II.CCLV, 1525.
3 SzOkl II.CCLXXIII, 1538, Seat of Aranyos.
4 SzOkl I.XLI.
5 SzOkl CCXXIV (in Hungarian in the Archive, translated from Latin according to K. Szabó by János Orbán de Lengyelfalva, notary of the Seat of Udvarhely.
6 SzOkl I.CCXXVI.
7 Cf. H&E, pp. 446 and 448 and KMTL, Marton, Alfréd's articles 'Gyula', 'Horka' and 'Künde'.
8 'Decarchal' unearthed in Peter Bod's Latin Dictionary. Consider creation of term like 'tensman', since 'decarchal' tends toward 'rule by ten'.
9 SzOkl VIII.113.
10 In today's Hungarian *'Dézsmabíróság'*.
11 Garda, Dezső. *Székely Hadszervezet és faluközösség* (Szekler military structure and the village community), Gyergyószentmiklós: Mark House kiadó, 1994, pp. 18-22.
12 Bodor, György. 'Az 1562 előtti székely nemzetségi szervezetről' (The Structure of the Szekler Nation before 1562), *in Történelmi Szemle* (Journal of History), no. 83(2) (1983): 281-305.
13 SzOkl II.CCCLXXXIX.
14 SzOkl I.LXXXVII.
15 SzOkl V.943.
16 SzOkl I.CCII.
17 e.g. SzOkl I.CCI, 1487: '... *Judices electi et delegati ...*'; SzOkl III.578, 1525: *'Judices delegati sive arbitri'*; SzOkl III.587, 1532: *'Judices delegati ...'*; SzOkl III.610, 1545: '... *electi arbitri ...*'; and finally in the Hungarian of the time, SzOkl II.CCCX: *'Mi, fogot' birajk ...'*, and SzOkl V.947, 1561: *'Mi, fogott birák ...'*.
18 SzOkl IV.670.
19 SzOkl III.610.

20 SzOkl V.943.
21 SzOkl II.CCCXI.
22 SzOkl II.CCCX.
23 We find a Gáspár Illyési in the military roster of 1635, in SzOkl új, IV, p. 22.
24 SzOkl új, IV, pp. 17–18, 22–23, 28, 30 and 79.
25 SzOkl új, IV, *septem jurati*.
26 SzOkl I.CXCV, 1484; III.494, 1492 and III.528, 1508.
27 SzOkl VIII.71.
28 SzOkl III.517.
29 Vofkori, László. *Székelyföld útikönyve* (Guide to the Szeklerland), I-II, Budapest: Cartographia kiadó, 1998, II, p. 517.
30 Codification of 1555, Article 16.
31 Codification of 1555, Article 15 and SzOkl I.CCXLIII, 1519.
32 Codification of 1555; Article 66.
33 SzOkl I.CXCVIII, 1486: '… *unusquisque illorum deinceps audire et attendere voluerit et cui consuetudine Siculorum requirentre se subicere elegit*'.
34 SzOkl I.CLVII - II.467, 1460.
35 SzOkl III.612, 1547.
36 1594, 1649, 1653 and 1740.
37 Szabó, Károly. *A régi székelység, székely történelmi és jogi tanulmányok* (The Ancient Szeklers, Studies on the History and Law of the Szeklers), Kolozsvár: Stein János, 1890, pp. 196–200.
38 *Erdély országnak törvényes könyve* (*Corpus juris Transylvaniae*) Kolozsvár, edition of 1815, Approb. Pars III, Titulus 76, Articulus 9.
39 In Székely de Kilyén, Mihály. *A Nemes Székely Nemzet Constitutiói, Privilégiumai, 's Jószág Leszállását tárgyazó némely Törvényes Itéletek* (Constitutions and Privileges of the Noble Szekler Nation and its Rules of Devolution), Pest, 1818, pp. 130–135, 'Udvarhely Széknek meg erősitett Articulussai' (The Confirmed Articles of Law of the Seat of Udvarhely), Article 16.
40 SzOkl III.473: '*Si quem ex Juratis constitutis vel constituendis contra edictum et ordinacionem prescriptam laborare aut iura alicuis scienter occultare sew intellexerint, habita prius superinde veritatis inquisicione, communi regnicolarum voto dignus sit excoriacionis crimine condempnari* et *cutis eius straminibus impleri*'.
41 SzOkl II.CCCV.
42 The ancestor of this branch of the Nyujtódi family was referred to as '*dominicus*' (not capitalized), which K. Szabó takes to be a 'first name': Domokos or Dominic. In the course of the documents his descendants are referred to with this as a patronymic: '*Paulus filius dicti condam dominici Nijwthodi*' SzOkl III.507, 1497; '*Michael Damonkos de Chernaton*' SzOkl III.566 in 1522; '*Michael filius condam P uli, filij olim dominici Nikthodi de alcharnaton*' SzOkl III.568, 1523; '*Damokos*' SzOkl III.571, 1523 and finally '*Domokos*' in SzOkl III.574, 1524.
43 SzOkl III.507.
44 SzOkl III.566.
45 SzOkl III.567, 1523.
46 SzOkl III.568, 1523.
47 SzOkl III.568, 1523.
48 SzOkl III.571, 1523.
49 SzOkl III.578, 1525.
50 SzOkl III.588, 1534.

51 SzOkl III.596, 1536.
52 SzOkl III.197.
53 szOkl III. 598.
54 SzOkl III.599.
55 SzOkl III.612, 1547.
56 SzOkl III.617, 1548.
57 SzOkl III.621, 1548.
58 SzOkl III.608, 1544.
59 Bónis, György. *Magyar jog - székely jog* (Hungarian Law, Szekler Law), Kolozsvár: Kolozsvári Tudományos Könyvtár, 1942, pp. 83–85.
60 SzOkl III.512.
61 SzOkl II.CCXCIV.
62 SzOkl I.CLXXVII, 1470.
63 SzOkl III.477, 1470.
64 SzOkl I.CLXXXVIII, 1481.
65 SzOkl II.CCLXX, 1538, but also SzOkl II.CCLXXIX.
66 SzOkl III.526, 1508 and SzOkl II.CCXLV, 1520.
67 SzOkl I.CCIX, 1493. '*Et quod peius est, et nunquam auditum, in medio nostri Castellum erexit, de quo nos semper tuto opprimere ac spoliere possit.*'
68 SzOkl III.465, 1459.
69 SzOkl III.434.
70 '... *caput etiam, demptis casibus notae infidelitatis, 1 causis criminalibus; salvum praeservavit.*' *Opus Trip. Pars III, Titulus IV, Articulus 3.*
71 SzOkl I. CCVIII.
72 SzOkl III.512.
73 SzOkl II.CCLXXVII.
74 SzOkl III.508.
75 SzOkl I.CCXXVII.
76 SzOkl III.532.
77 SzOkl III.560.
78 SzOkl I.CCXLIV.
79 SzOkl V.907.
80 SzOkl VIII.18.
81 The Domokos-Angyalossi case and SzOkl VIII.106, 1487.
82 SzOkl III.482, 1477; I.CXCVIII and I.CCI, 1486–87 and I.CCII, 487.
83 SzOkl II.CCLXXVII.
84 SzOkl VIII.106.
85 SzOkl III.508.
86 SzOkl I.CCIX).
87 SzOkl I.CCIX.
88 SzOkl III.502.
89 SzOkl II.CCCVI.
90 SzOkl II.CCCXXXII.
91 SzOkl I.XXXVIII.
92 SzOkl I.CLXX and III.476.
93 Verancsics, Antal (1504–1573) of Bosnian origin, Bishop of Esztergom. His writings were published in *Monumenta hungariae historica,* Budapest, 1857–1875. The Hungarian translation cited here is from Szabó, László (ed.), *Erdély öröksége*

(Transylvanian Heritage), Budapest, I Tündérország, 1541–1571, (Fairy Country), Franklin kiadó, 1942, pp. 11–12.
94   SzOkl I.CCXIX, mid-sixteenth century.
95   SzOkl V.912 and I.CCII.
96   SzOkl I.CCI.
97   SzOkl III.434.
98   SzOkl V.912, I.CCI & I.CCII.
99   SzOkl III.513, III.514 & VIII.112.
100 SzOkl I.CCXLIII, I.CCXLIV, III.558 & III.559.
101 *'Descensus'* in the documents.
102 SzOkl III.511.
103 SzOkl I.CCVI - III.497, 1492.
104 SzOkl III.559.
105 SzOkl II.CCLVI.
106 SzOkl II.CCCXXVIII.
107 SzOkl V. 931.
108 SzOkl VIII.97: '....*sine litteris procuratoriis* ...'.
109 SzOkl III.634, 1559: '*Et quia eadem domina exponens cum ob loci distanciam tum vero mulieris sexus fragilitatem pro constitutione procuratoria Nostram in presenciam venire nequit.*'
110 The wording might be: '*Nos ... commendamus quod ... coram nobis personaliter constitutus in omnibus causis suis et earum articulis tamper ipsum contra alios quam per alios quospiam contra ipsum in quiuslibet terminis coram quovis iudice et iustitiaris regni, ecclesiastico videlicet et seculari, a date presentium per anni circulum motis vel movendis discretos et nobiles viros ... fecit, constituit et ordinavit suos veros et legitimos procuratores, ratum et firmum se promittens habiturum, quidquid per prenominatos suos procuratores simul vel divisim exhibitores seu videlicet exhibitorem presentium actum, factum, procuratumque fuerit in causis suis prenotatis. Datum ....*' From SzOkl VIII.40, 1448.
111 SzOkl VIII.33.
112 SzOkl III.538.
113 Other forms are issued by one principal for thirteen proxies in 1448 (SzOkl VIII.40), one for six in 1469 (SzOkl VIII.69), six for ten in 1471 (SzOkl VIII.73) and one for seven in 1476 (SzOkl I.CLXXXI).
114 SzOkl I.CLVII - III.467.
115 SzOkl II.CCCXXXVI.
116 SzOkl III.483, 1477; SzOkl III.570, 1423; SzOkl VIII.152, 1525 and SzOkl III.595, 1536.
117 SzOkl III.529, 1508; translation of K. Szabó's Hungarian summary of the document; present author's underlining.
118 SzOkl I.CXXXVII.
119 '... *vniuersorum Siculorum et populorum de Zentkijral* ...'.
120 SzOkl I.CCL.
121 SzOkl I.LXXXVIII.
122 SzOkl I.CXXXIII.
123 SzOkl VIII.55.
124 SzOkl VIII.95.
125 SzOkl II.CCL.

126 Eszlary, Charles d'. *Histoire des institutions publiques hongroises* (History of the Public Institutions of Hungary), Paris: Éditions M. Rivière et Cie and CNRS, 1958-1963, I, p. 338.
127 Op. cit. p. 270.
128 Makkai, Ladislas (László). *Histoire de Transylvanie* (History of Transylvania), Budapest-Paris: PUF (Presses Universitaires de France), 1946, p. 96.
129 SzOkl I.CLXX: '*quorum dualitas de Senioribus, dualitas vero ex communitate*'. The following publication, from a badly damaged original (SzOkl III.473) says: '*qu[orum ...]tas de senioribus, dualitas vero ex communitate*'.
130 SzOkl I.CCXXXVII.
131 SzOkl III.511: '*duodecim coassessores de primoribus Siculorum et aliis nobilis ac probis hominibus*'.
132 Connert, János, Dr. *A székelyek alkotmányának históriája* (History of the Székely Constitution), Székelyudvarhely: Betegh Pál, 1906, pp. 50–58.
133 Szádeczky-Kardoss, Lajos. *A székely nemzet története és alkotmanyá* (History and Constitution of the Szekler Nation), Budapest: Akadémiai kiadó (1993), 1927 (facsimile 1993), pp. 43–48.
134 SzOkl I.LXXXVIII.
135 Cf. Borsa, István and GYÖRFFY György, 'Actes privés, "locus credibilis" et notariat dans la Hongrie Médiévale' (Private instruments, 'locus credibilis' and notary acts in medieval Hungary) *in Notariado publico y documento privado de los origines al siglo XIV.*, Valencia, 1989, vol. II, p. 944.
136 SzOkl VIII.124.
137 SzOkl I.CCXXXVII, 1515; II.CCLV, 1525; II.CCCXXX, 1558 and II.CCCXXXII, 1560.
138 SzOkl III.635, 1561 and II.CCCXXXVIII.
139 SzOkl III.638.
140 '*homine Regio ... NN ... primipilo*' in 1407. SzOkl I.LXXXVIII.
141 SzOkl I.CXV.
142 SzOkl III.508.
143 SzOkl III.532.
144 SzOkl III.560.
145 SzOkl III.533, 1511.
146 SzOkl III.615, 1548. See also Szabó, Károly, *A régi székelység, székely történelmi és jogi tanulmányok* (The Ancient Szeklers, Studies on the History and Law of the Szeklers), Kolozsvár: Stein János, 1890, pp. 218–220 and Hajnik, Imre, *A magyar birósági szervezet és perjog az Árpad - és vegyes-házi királyok allatt* (Hungarian judicial Organisation and Trial Proceedings under Arpadian- and mixed Royal Houses), Budapest: Magyar Tudományos Akadémia, 1899, p. 125.
147 SzOkl I.CCXIX, mid-sixteenth century (underlinings by the present author).
148 SzOkl III.532, 1511.
149 SzOkl I.CCVI - III.497, 1492.
150 SzOkl II.CCCXC - V.937, 1548; II.CCCXXV, 1557 and II.CCXCI, dated by K. Szabó for the end of the first half of the sixteenth century; this latter document was found in the Imperial Secret Archives in Vienna.
151 SzOkl II.CCCXV - V.937, 1548; II.CCCXXV, 1557.
152 SzOkl VIII.143, 1517 and VIII.147, 1518.

153 Bodor, György. 'Az 1562 előtti székely nemzetségi szervezetről' (The Structure of the Szekler Nation before 1562), in *Történelmi Szemle* (Journal of History), no. 83(2) (1983): 281–305.

Chapter V

1   SzOkl III.533, 1511.
2   SzOkl I.CXLIV - III.458: '... *et dummodo non sit possessio regalis aut ad castra regalia aut terras Saxonum vel Siculorum non pertineat.*'
3   SzOkl III.409 - EOkm I.292, 1270–1272, text included in SzOkl III.410 - EOkm I.367, 1279.
4   '... *que possessiones* [those of Laurencius] *sunt in vicinitate Siculorum de Telegd indistincta sine meta perfui et vti secundum legem et statutumomnium Siculorum de Telegd ...*'. SzOkl III.409.
5   Under EOkm I.367.
6   N°. I, 31, MOL, DF 243677.
7   SzOkl I.CLXXXII.
8   SzOkl I.XVIII - EOkm I.452, 1289, where their exploits are related in detail.
9   SzOkl I.XVI - III.408.
10 '... *et retenta sibi proprietate et jura dominii eiusdem Castri ...*'.
11 SzOkl I.CLXVII - V.909.
12 SzOkl I.XXXI.
13 SzOkl III.420.
14 SzOkl VIII.15.
15 SzOkl III.421.
16 SzOkl III.504: '*Item totum et omne ius nostrum Regium, si quod in eadem possessione qualitercumque haberemus.*'
17 '... *si per alios non fuerit contradictum*'.
18 SzOkl I.IX.
19 Identified in EOkm I.216 as Kerc/Carţa/Kerz, which in this author's opinion is a bit too far to the west. The Hungarian place-names Körös and Keresz are fairly frequent and variously transcribed in Latin as *Kerez, Kerch, Kers, Kircz, Kyrch,* etc. The Vlach land mentioned here must surely have been closer to the Szeklerland and the region of Brassó than Kerc, located near Szeben.
20 1519: SzOkl III.555 and 1546–47: SzOkl II.CCLXXXIX, V.935 and V.936.
21 SzOkl VIII.10.
22 '... *ex precognita malitia* [... / ...] *in eisdem possessionibus* [... / ...] *omnino destruxissent ...*'.
23 SzOkl I.XLIII.
24 '... *talia eis dixissent uerba, quod si eos, ante reambulacionem, ereccionem metarumet stacionem predictarum possessionum preuenire potuissent, eosdem a premissis prohibuissent ...*'.
25 SzOkl VIII.13, 1359.
26 '... *predictas possessiones* [... / ...] *occupatas, desolatas et combustas ...*'.
27 SzOkl I.LVI for the royal order, SzOkl I.LVII for the investiture report and SzOkl VIII.17 for survey report. It is noted that all this was carried out without opposition from the Szeklers.

28 SzOkl VIII.39.
29 SzOkl VIII.80.
30 SzOkl I.CLXXXIII.
31 SzOkl I.XVII.
32 SzOkl III.478.
33 In German: *Erwerb, Errungenschaft, Akquisition*; in Latin: *inventio, inventum, sollertia*. Acording to the dictionary of medieval Hungarian, Magyar Oklevél Szótár, 1560 (SzOkl V.943).
34 SzOkl III.517, 1503.
35 SzOkl II.CCXCIII, 1549.
36 SzOkl III.603.
37 '... *dum adhuc adolescens, nondum perfecte et mature etatis fuisset [... / ...] iconsiderate et impremeditate inuitus et coactusutcunque fecisset.*' SzOkl II.CCCXV.
38 SzOkl VIII.119.
39 SzOkl VIII.120.
40 SzOkl VIII.123.
41 SzOkl III.522.
42 SzOkl VIII.123.
43 SzOkl III.526.
44 SzOkl I.CXXXIII.
45 Werbőczy, *Opus Trip*. Pars I, *Tit*. LXXVIII, *Art*. 2.
46 SzOkl I.CXXXIII: '... *iuxta laudabilem legem vniuersorum Siculorum et consuetudinem ab antiquo approbatam, [... / ...] decrevimus, ut nullus omnino hominum quascunque hereditates, quas ante triginta duorum annorum spacio per aliquas iuridicas mociones et prohibiciones non acquisit, pro amplius acquerire et suscitare non valeat, sed perpetuo silere debeat ...*'.
47 *Opus Trip*. Pars I, *Tit*. LXXVIII, *Art*. 7.
48 Bónis, György. *Magyar jog - székely jog* (Hungarian Law, Szekler Law), Kolozsvár: Kolozsvári Tudományos Könyvtár, 1942, p. 24.
49 SzOkl II.CCLXIV.
50 SzOkl I.XVII.
51 SzOkl III.412.
52 '... *si vllo vnquam tempores aliquis ipsorum cognatorum Jacobi* [the seller] *vellent reuocare et ipsis possessionibus sibi pertinebent in irritum causam vellunt incitare, facultatem non habeant incintandi.*'
53 '... *ex permissione omnium cognatorum suorum cum omnibus utilitatibus.*'
54 SzOkl VIII.49.
55 From the summary in Hungarian of SzOkl II.CCLXIV, 1535.
56 Cf. Rady, Martin. *Nobility, Land and Service in Medieval Hungary*, London: Palgrave Macmillan, 2000.
57 SzOkl I.XXIV - AOkl III.701.
58 SzOkl I.XXVIII - AOkl V.701.
59 SzOkl VIII.16.
60 SzOkl III.478, I.CLXXVIII, 1472 and VIII.78, 1473.
61 SzOkl VIII.155.
62 SzOkl II.CCLXV.
63 SzOkl III.631.
64 SzOkl V.943, 1560.
65 SzOkl I.CXCI - III.487.

66 SzOkl V.917.
67 SzOklVIII.111.
68 SzOkl VIII.109.
69 SzOkl új IV, p. 151.
70 SzOkl új IV, p. 223.
71 SzOkl új V, p. 434.
72 SzOkl új V, p. 434.
73 SzOkl II.CCXCIII.
74 SzOkl II.CCXLVIII.
75 SzOkl III.582.
76 SzOkl II.CCLXIX.
77 SzOkl III.426: '... *omnes premissas porciones possessionarias et hereditates In terra Siculorum habitas, ad ipsos, vt prefertur, communiter deuolutas, ...*' Gyerőfi succession.
78 SzOkl I.CXXXIII, 1451.
79 SzOkl CCCXIV, April 28, 1555.
80 Author's underlining.
81 SzOkl VIII.47.
82 SzOkl VIII.50.
83 SzOkl VIII.110.
84 SzOkl VIII.111.
85 SzOkl VIII.97.
86 SzOkl VIII.130.
87 SzOkl VIII.59.
88 SzOkl III.488.
89 SzOkl III.489.
90 SzOkl III.503.
91 SzOkl I.CXXXIII, 1451.
92 '*Haereditatesque, convictus & sententiatus ipse non amittit, sed ad haeredes, fratresque ejus derivantur.*'
93 SzOkl VIII.44, Szentkirályi succession.
94 SzOkl VIII.59, Barlabássi succession.
95 SzOkl I.CXXXIII, 1451.
96 SzOkl III.488.
97 SzOkl I.CXXXVII.
98 SzOkl II.CCLXVII.
99 in KMTL, Zsoldos, Attila, article entitled 'Leánynegyed', and Mezey, Barna, ed. *A Magyar jogtörténet forrásai* (Sources for Hungarian History of Law), Budapest: Osiris kiadó, 2000, p. 169.
100 SzOkl III.489.
101 SzOkl III.429.
102 SzOkl VIII.77.
103 SzOkl III.489.
104 SzOkl I.CCXII.
105 Engel, Pál. *Társadalom és politikai struktúra az Anjou-kori Magyarországon* (Society and Political Structure in Hungary during the Reign of the Anjou Dynasty), Budapest: MTA történettudományi intézet, 1988, pp. 15–16.
106 SzOkl I.XCI - III.429.
107 SzOkl III.426.
108 SzOkl I.CXXXI.

109 SzOkl VIII.44.
110 '... eo modo quod <u>si</u> idem Semyen semen masculinum post se reliquisset, extunc bona et haereditates eiusdem Semyen <u>ante</u> alias feminas in sexum virilem devolvi debuissent. Verum ex quo in virile sexu et semine defecisset, igitur iuxta consuetudinem siculorum huiusmodi bona et haereditas <u>ad ius femineum</u> in praefatas scilicet dominam Annam <u>sororem</u> carnalem <u>et</u> tres <u>filias</u> ipsius Semyen devolutae essent.' (Author's underlining)
111 SzOkl VIII.59.
112 SzOkl VIII.113.
113 SzOkl I.CLXXXIII.
114 SzOkl III.430, 1410.
115 SzOkl III.427 and III.428.
116 SzOkl VIII.22, 30, 32, 45, 46, 61 & 62.
117 SzOkl VIII.81.
118 SzOkl VIII.96, 1493.
119 SzOkl VIII.101, 1495.
120 SzOkl VIII.102, 1495.
121 SzOkl VIII.44.
122 SzOkl I.CXCIX.
123 SzOkl VIII.59, 1463.
124 SzOkl VIII.125, 1505.
125 ... cunctorum fratrum et consanguineorum suorum ...
126 SzOkl VIII.143.
127 SzOkl I.CCXXIV - VIII.124.
128 SzOkl I.CCXXVI.
129 *Opus Tripartitum, Pars* III, *Tit.* IV.
130 SzOkl II.CCCXIV.
131 '... demtis duntawat illis, que inter Siculos haberentur ...'.
132 SzOkl I.CCXI, 1495 and SzOkl VIII.112, 1501.
133 SzOkl II.CCXLIX.
134 SzOkl II.CCXLVIII.
135 SzOkl III.582.
136 SzOkl II.CCLXIV.
137 SzOkl II.CCLXIX, CCLXX and CCLXXI.
138 SzOkl II.CCCXIX.
139 SzOkl II.CCCXVII.
140 SzOkl II.CCCV.
141 SzOkl II.CCCXXXVI.
142 SzOkl VIII.44. Succession of Semjén Szentkirályi, January 10, 1451.
143 SzOkl I.CXXXIII. Decision of principle, Assembly of the Seat of Maros, 17 June 1451.
144 SzOkl I.CXXXIII. Decision of principle, Assembly of the Seat of Maros, 17 June 1451.
145 SzOkl II.CCCXIV. Codification, Szekler Assembly in Udvarhely, on 28 April 1555.
146 SzOkl II.CCCXIV. Codification, Szekler Assembly in Udvarhely, on 28 April 1555.
147 SzOkl II.CCCXIV. Codification, Szekler Assembly in Udvarhely, on 28 April 1555.
148 SzOkl II.CCCXIV. Codification, Szekler Assembly in Udvarhely, on 28 April 1555.

Conclusion

1. Matthias, Miles. (1639–1686), *Siebenbürgischer Würg-Engel* (The Strangling Angel of Transylvania), Verlegung H. Andreae Fleischers, 1670, pp. 87–91. This first historical work by a Transylvanian Saxon was published at Szeben in 1670; a facsimile of this first edition, with an introduction by Adolf Armbruster, appeared in 1984, Böhlau Verlag, Köln-Wien.

    The full title for this work published in 1670 is: Siebenbürgischer Würg-Engel oder Chronicalischer Anhang des 15. *Seculi* nach Christi Geburth aller theils in in Siebenbürgen/theils Ungern/und sonst Siebenbürgen angräntzenden Ländern fürgelauffener Geschichten. Worauss nicht nur allein die grewlichst-blutige Anschläge/Kriege/und Zeittungen/dessen vielfältige Feinde/sondern auch die geheymbste Rath-Schlüsse beyder Keyser/Könige/Fürsten: und Waywoden zu erkündigen//durch welche diess bedrängte Vatterland theils wohl regieret/theils vollends in Abgrund des Verderbens gestürtzet worden: Auch welcher Gestalt nebenst der Augsburgischer *Confession* die übrige im Lande angenommene *Religionen* drinne erwachsen seyn. Nebenst der Ober-Regenten Sachsischer Nation, bevoraus der Haupt-Hermannstadt löbligen Magistrats ordentliger Erzehlung/wie Selbige nehmlig ihre Ampts-Geschäfften vershen haben. Welches kurtz doch warhafft und ordentlig abgebildet und heraus gegeben Matthias Miles *Mediens: Jurisprudentiae cultor.*

2. Imreh, István, *A Törvényhozó székely falu* (The Szekler village as Legislator), Bucharest: Kriterion kiadó, 1983, 317: Village Laws of Alcsernáton, recorded in 1665, 1666, 1716, 1718, copied in 1793.

Glossary

1. Bloch, Marc. *Feudal Society*, Chicago: University of Chicago Press, 1961 (first edition in French, Paris, 1939), p. XVII.
2. Bónis, György. *Hűbériség és rendiség a középkori magyar jogban* (Feudalism and Society of Estates in Medieval Hungarian Law), Kolozsvár: Kolozsvári Bolyai Tudományegyetem, 1947 from the French-language summary, pp. 557–592.
3. Rady, Martyn. *Nobility, Land and Service in Medieval Hungary*, London: Palgrave Macmillan, 2000; Bónis, *Hűbériség és rendiség a középkori magyar jogban.*
4. Translation of SzOkl I. CCXXIV.
5. Translated from SzOkl I. CCXXVI.

BIBLIOGRAPHY

Balás, Gábor. *Erdély jókora jogtörténete* (The History of Transylvanian Law), Budapest: Budapest Füti Nyomda (print), 1977-1982.

Balás, Gábor. *A székekyek nyomában* (On the Track of the Szeklers), Budapest: Franklin kiadó, 1984.

Barta, Gábor. 'L'intolérance dans un pays tolérant, la principauté de Transylvanie au XVIe siècle' (Intolerance in a Tolerant Country, the principlality of Transylvania in the sixteenth Century), in Sauzet, Robert (ed.), *Les frontières religieuses en Europe du XVe au XVIIe siècle* (Religious Borders in the Europe of the Fifteenth to Seventeenth Centuries), Paris: Libraire-éditeur Vrin et CNRS, 1992.

Barta, Gábor. *La route qui mène à Istanbul 1526-1528* (The Road to Istanbul), Budapest: Akadémiai kiadó, 1994.

Bäuml, Franz and Birnbaum, Marianna, eds. *Attila, the man and his image*, symposium of the Center for medieval and Renaissance Studies, UCLA: Corvina kiadó, 1988 published in Budapest, 1993.

Benkő, Elek, et al. *Kozépkori mezőváros a Székelyföldön* (Medieval Market Towns in the Szeklerland) (*Székelyföld, Terra Siculorum*)', Kolozsvár: EME (Erdélyi Múzeum Egyesület kiadó), 1997.

Benkő, Lóránd, 'La situation linguistique des Hongrois de la conquète et ce qui en résulte' (The Linguistic Situation of the Hungarians at the Time of the Conquest and the Consequences), in Csernus, Sándor and Korompay, Klára (eds), *Les Hongrois et l'Europe : conquête et intégration* (The Hungarians and Europe, Conquest and Integration), 121-136, Paris-Szeged: Publications de l'Institut Hongrois de Paris, 1999.

Bérenger, Jean. 'Caractères originaux de l'humanisme hongrois' (Original Characteristics of Hungarian Humanism). *Journal des savants*, S. 257-288 (1973).

Bérenger, Jean. *Histoire de l'empire des Habsbourg 1273-1918* (History of the Habsburg Empire), Paris: Éditions Fayard, 1990.

Bérenger, Jean. *Tolérance ou paix de religion en Europe centrale* (1415-1792) Tolerance or Religious Peace in Central Europe), Paris: Honoré Champion, libraire-éditeur, 2000.

Berta, Árpád. 'Le système des noms de tribus d'origine turke' (The System of Turkic Tribal Names), in Csernus, Sándor and Korompay, Klára (eds), *Les Hongrois et l'Europe: conquête et intégration* (The Hungarians and Europe, Conquest and Integration), 45-60, Paris-Szeged: Publications de l'Institut Hongrois de Paris, 1999.

Bloch, Marc.*Feudal Society*, Chicago: University of Chicago Press, 1961 (first edition in French, Paris, 1939).

Bodor, György. 'Az 1562 előtti székely nemzetségi szervezetről' (The Structure of the Szekler Nation before 1562), *in Történelmi Szemle* (Journal of History), no. 83(2) (1983): 281-305.

Bogdan, Henry. *Les Chevaliers Teutoniques* (The Teutonic Knights), Paris: Éditions Perrin, 1999.

Bónis, György. *Magyar jog - székely jog* (Hungarian Law, Szekler Law), Kolozsvár: Kolozsvári Tudományos Könyvtár, 1942.

Bónis, György. *Hűbériség és rendiség a középkori magyar jogban* (Feudalism and Society of Estates in Medieval Hungarian Law), Kolozsvár: Kolozsvári Bolyai Tudományegyetem, 1947.

Castellan, Georges. *Histoire des Balkans, XIVe-XXe siècle* (History of the Balkans, Fourteenth–Twentieth Centuries), Paris: Éditions Fayard, 1991.

Cevins De, Marie-Madeleine., 'Les paroisses hongroises au Moyzen Age' (Hungarian Parishes during the Middle Ages), in Csernus, Sándor and Korompay, Klára (eds), *Les Hongrois et l'Europe: conquête et intégration* (The Hungarians and Europe, Conquest and Integration), 341–385, Paris-Szeged: Publications de l'Institut Hongrois de Paris, 1999.

Connert, János, Dr. *A székelyek alkotmányának históriája* (History of the Székely Constitution), Székelyudvarhely: Betegh Pál, 1906.

Csernus, Sándor. 'Les Hunyadi, vus par les historiens français du quinzième siècle' (The Hunyadi, as seen by French Historians of the Fifteenth Century) in Klaniczay, Tibor and Jankovics, Jázef (eds), *Matthias Corvinus and the humanism in central Europe*, Budapest: Balassi kiadó, 1994.

Csernus Sándor and Korompay, Klára eds., *Les Hongrois et l'Europe: conquête et intégration* (The Hungarians and Europe, Conquest and Integration), Paris-Szeged: Publications de l'Institut Hongrois de Paris, 1999.

Dienes, István. *Les Hongrois conquérants* (The Conquering Hungarians), Budapest: Corvina kiadó, 1972.

Durandin, Catherine. *Histoire des Roumains* (History of the Romanians), Paris: Éditions Fayards, 1995.

Engel, Pál. *Magyarország világi archontológia 1301-1457* (Worldly Dignitaries of Hungary, 1301-1457), two volumes, I-II, Budapest: MTA történettudományi intézet, 1996.

Engel, Pál. *Társadalom és politikai struktúra az Anjou-kori Magyarországon* (Society and Political Structure in Hungary during the Reign of the Anjou Dynasty), Budapest: MTA történettudományi intézet, 1988.

Engel, Pál. *The Realm of St. Stephen, a History of Medieval Hungary (895-1526)*, London-New York: I.B. Tauris, 2001.

Engel, Pál, Kristó, Gyula and Kubinyi, András. *Magyarország története 1301-1526* (History of Hungary), Budapest: Osiris kiadó, 1998.

Eszlary, Charles d'. *Histoire des institutions publiques hongroises* (History of the Public Institutions of Hungary), Paris: Éditions M. Rivière et Cie and CNRS, 1958–1963.

Fasoli, Gina. 'Points de vue sur les incursions hongroises en Europe au Xe siècle' (Points of View on the Hungarian Invasions in Europe during the Tenth Century), in *Cahiers de Civilisation Médiévale*, II, Poitiers: CESCM (Centre d'études supérieures de civilisation médiévale), 1959.

Garda, Dezső. *Székely Hadszervezet és faluközösség* (Szekler military structure and the village community), Gyergyószentmiklós: Mark House kiadó, 1994.

Grousset, René. *L'empire des steppes, Attila, Gengis-Khan, Tamerlan* (The Empire of the Steppes, Attila, Gengis Khan, Tamerlane), Paris: Éditions Payot, 1965.

Gyöngyössy, János. *Székely templomerődök* (Szekler Fortified Churches), Csíkszereda: Pro-Print kiadó, 1999.

Györffy, György. 'A székelyek eredete és településük története' (The Origins of the Szeklers and History of their Settling), in Mályusz, Elemér, *Erdély és népei* (Transylvania and its Peoples), 1st edn. Budapest: Franklin kiadó, 1941, 2nd edn. Maecenas kiadó, 1999.

Györffy, György. *A honfoglaló magyar nép élete* (The Life of the Hungarian People at the Time of the Conquest), 1944.

Györffy, György. 'Formation d'Etats au IXe siècle suivant les 'Gesta Hungarorum' du Notaire Anonymus' (The Formation of States in the Ninth Century According the 'Gesta Hungarorum' of the Notary Anonymous), in *Nouvelles Etudes Historiques*, I, Budapest: Akadémiai kiadó, 1965.

Györffy, György. *Autour de l'Etat des semi-nomades : le cas de la Hongrie* (About the Semi-Nomad States : the Case of Hungary), Budapest: Akadémiai kiadó, 1975.

Györffy, György. *A Magyarok elődeiről és a honfoglalásról* (On the Ancestors of the Hungarians and the Conquest), Budapest: Gondola kiadó, 1986.

Györffy, György. *König Stephan der Heilige* (King Stephen the Saint), Budapest: Corvina kiadó, 1988.

Györffy, György. 'La chancellerie royale de Hongrie aux XIII-XIVe siècles' (The Royal Chancellery of Hungary in the Thirteenth and Fourteenth Centuries) in Glassl, Horst (et al.), *Studia Hungarica 32, Forschungen über Siebenbürgen und seine Nachbarn II* (Research about Transylvania and its neighbours), München: Wissenschaftszentrum Ost- und Südosteuropa, 1988.

Györffy, György and Borsa, Iván. 'Actes, 'Locus credibilis' et notariat dans la Hongrie médiévale' (Private writs, 'locus crediblis' and notary records in medieval Hungary) in *Notariado publico y documento privado de los origines al siglo XIV.*, Actas del VII congresso Internacional de Diplomatica (Valencea, 1986), Valencea, 1989.

Hajnik, Imre. *A magyar birósági szervezet és perjog az Árpad - és vegyes-házi királyok allatt* (Hungarian judicial Organisation and Trial Proceedings under Arpadian- and mixed Royal Houses), Budapest: Magyar Tudományos Akadémia, 1899.

Hamza, Gábor., ed. *Saint Etienne et l'Europe* (Saint Stephen and Europe), Budapest: Muvelödési & Közoktatási Minisztérium kiadó, 1991.

Hanák, Péter, ed. *Mille ans d'histoire hongroise* (Thousand Years of Hungarian History), Budapest: Corvina kiadó, 1986.

Hóman, Bálint and Szekfű, Gyula. *Magyar történet* (History of Hungary), 2nd edn, Budapest: Királyi Magyar Egyetem, 1936.

Horváth, Péter. *Értekezés a kúnoknak és jászoknak eredetekrül azoknak régi és mostani állapotjokrúl* (Essay on the origins and ancient and present structures of the Cumans and the Iasians), Jász-Berény: Székely Gábor, 1820 (facsimile 1996).

Imreh, István. 'A székely falu gazdasági-társadalmi szerkezete a XVI. század végén és a XVII. század elején' (The Social and Economic Organisation of the Szekler Village at the End of the Sixteenth and Beginning of the Seventeenth Century), in Benkő, Samu (ed.), *Székely Felkelés 1595-1596* (The Szekler Uprising of 1595-1596), Bucharest: Kriterion kiadó, 1979.

Imreh, István, *A Törvényhozó székely falu* (The Szekler village as Legislator), Bucharest: Kriterion kiadó, 1983.

Jánó, Mihály. *A Gelencei műemlektemplom* (The Church at Gelence, Historical Monument), Sepsiszentgyörgy: Baász kiadó, 1994.

Jósa, János. *Ujabb adalékok a székelyek régi történetéhez* (New Data on the Szeklers' Ancient History), Szeged: Uj Nemzedék Lapv, 1928.

Kállay, Ferenc. *Historiai értekezés A' nemes székely eredetéről* (Historical Essay on the Origins of the Szekler People), Nagy-Enye: Fiedler Gottfried, 1829. http://mek.oszk.hu/07800/07887/

Kiss, Gergely. 'La fondation de l'abbaye bénédictine de Somogyvár' (The Founding of the Benedictine Abby of Somogyvár), in Csernus, Sándor and Korompay, Klára (eds), *Les Hongrois et l'Europe: conquête et intégration* (The Hungarians and Europe, Conquest and Integration), 327–340, Paris-Szeged: Publications de l'Institut Hongrois de Paris, 1999.

Kordé, Zoltán. *'Kabars, Sicules et Pechenègue: les Hongrois et les auxiliaires militaires'* (Kavars (see also *Khazar Empire*)', Szeklers and Pechenegs: *'Pechenegs'* the Hungarians and the Military Auxiliaries), in Csernus, Sándor and Korompay, Klára (eds), *Les Hongrois et l'Europe : conquête et intégration* (The Hungarians and Europe, Conquest and Integration), 231–243, Paris-Szeged: Publications de l'Institut Hongrois de Paris, 1999.

Köpeczi, Béla, ed. *History of Transylvania*, Akadémiai kiadó, 1994.

Koszta, László. 'L'organisation de l'Église chrétienne en Hongrie' (The Organisation of the Church in Hungary), in Csernus, Sándor and Korompay, Klára (eds), *Les Hongrois et l'Europe: conquête et intégration* (The Hungarians and Europe, Conquest and Integration), 293–312, Paris-Szeged: Publications de l'Institut Hongrois de Paris, 1999.

Kristó, Gyula. *A székelyek eredetéről* (On the Szeklers' Origins), Szeged: Szegedi Középkorász Műhely, 1996.

Kristó, Gyula. 'L'an Mil : changement de régime en Hongrie' (The Year one Thousand: Change of Regime in Hungary), in Csernus, Sándor and Korompay, Klára (eds), *Les Hongrois et l'Europe : conquête et intégration* (The Hungarians and Europe, Conquest and Integration), 11–25, Paris-Szeged: Publications de l'Institut Hongrois de Paris, 1999.

Kristó, Gyula. *Histoire de la Hongrie médiévale*, (I le temps des Árpáds) (History of Medieval Hungary, [In the Age of the Árpáds]), Rennes: Presses Universitaires de Rennes, 2000.

Kubinyi, András. *Főpapok, egyházi intézmények és Vallásosság a középkori Magyarországon* (Prelates, Ecclesiastic Institutions and Religious Practice in Medieval Hungary), Budapest: Magyar Egyháztörténeti Enciklopédia Munkaközösség, 1999.

László, Gyula. *A kettős honfoglalás* (The Double Conquest), Budapest: Magvető kiadó, 1978.

László, Gyula. *The Magyars, their Life and Civilisation*, Budapest: Corvina kiadó, 1996.

Le Calloc'h, Bernard. 'Qui sont les Sicules?' (Who are the Szeklers?), in *Bulletin de l'association des Anciens élèves de l'Institut National des Langues et Civilisations Orientales* (Bulletin of the Alumni of the National Institute of Oriental Languages and Civilisations - INALCO), Paris: INALCO (Institut National des Langues et Civilisations Orientales), 1990.

Makkai, Ladislas (László). *Histoire de Transylvanie* (History of Transylvania), Budapest-Paris: PUF (Presses Universitaires de France), 1946.

Mantran, Robert, ed. *Histoire de l'Empire ottoman* (History of the Ottoman Empire), Paris: Éditions Fayard, 1989.

Molnár, Miklós. *Histoire de la Hongrie* (History of Hungary), Paris: Éditions Hatier, 1996.

Musset, Lucien. *Les invasions: le second assaut contre l'Europe chrétienne (VIIe-XIe siècles)* (The Invasions – the Second Assault against Christian Europe [Seventh-Eleventh Centuries]), Paris: PUF (Presses Universitaires de France), 1965.

Nagy, Iván. *Magyarország családai czímerekkel és nemzékrendi táblákkal* (Hungary's Families, with Crests and Genealogical Tables) Pest 1857-1868, I-VIII, Budapest: Helikon kiadó, (facsimile, 1987).

Nemeskürty, István. *Nous, les Hongrois* (We, the Hungarians) Budapest: Akadémiai kiadó, 1994.

Orbán Balázs. *A Székelyföld leírása* (Description of the Szeklerland) Pest: Szekszárdi Hasonmásolat (1991), Rath (1868), (facsimile, 1991).

Pálóczi Horváth, András. *Pechenegs, Cumans, Iasians, Steppe Peoples in Medieval Hungary*, Budapest: Corvina kiadó, 1989.

Pamlényi, Ervin, ed. *Histoire de la Hongrie des origines à nos jours* (History of Hungary from its Origins to the Present), Budapest-Roanne: Corvina-Horváth kiadó, 1974.

Pasco, Stefan. *La révolte populaire de Transylvanie des années 1437-1438* (The Popular Uprising in Transylvania in 1437-1438), Bucharest: éditions. de l'Académie de la République populaire roumaine, 1964.

Pop, Ioan-Aurel. 'Elita românească din Transilvania în secolele XIII-XIV, origine, statut, evolutie' (The Elites of Transylvania in the Thirteenth-Fourteenth Centuries, origin, status, evolution), in Diaconescu, Marius (ed.), *Nobilimea românească din Transilvania* (Romanian Nobility in Transylvania), Satu Mare: Editura Muzeului Sătmărean, 1997.

Pop, Ioan-Aurel. 'Un privilegiu regal solemn de la 1366 si implicatiile sale' (A solemn Royal Privilege of 1366 and its implications), *in* Diaconescu, Marius (ed.), *Mediaevalia Transilvanica I*, Satu Mare: Editura Muzeului Sătmărean, 1997.

Rady, Martin. *Nobility, Land and Service in Medieval Hungary*, London: Palgrave Macmillan, 2000.

Ságvári, György and Somogyi, Győző. *Nagy huszárkönyv* (The Great Book of Hussars), Budapest: Magyar Könyv Klub kiadó, 1999.

Sándorfy, Kamill. *Erdély reformkorszakának jogtörténete (1825-1848)* (History of Transylvanian Law in the Reform Era [1825-1848]), Budapest: EFO kiadó, 2000.

Sellier, André and Sellier, Jean. *Atlas des peuples d'Europe centrale* (Atlas of the Peoples of Central Europe), 3rd edn, Paris: Éditions La Découverte, 1993.

Szabó, Károly. *A régi székelység, székely történelmi és jogi tanulmányok* (The Ancient Szeklers, Studies on the History and Law of the Szeklers), Kolozsvár: Stein János, 1890.

Szádeczky, Lajos. (in 1905), 'Csíki székely Krónika' (The 'Szekler Chronicle' of Csík), in György, Attila (ed.). *Csíki székely krónika*, (The Szekler Chronicle of Csík), Csíkszereda: Hargita kiadó, 2000.

Szádeczky-Kardoss, Lajos. *A székely nemzet története és alkotmanyá* (History and Constitution of the Szekler Nation), Budapest: Akadémiai kiadó, 1927 (facsimile 1993).

Szegfű, László. 'Le monde spirituel des Hongrois païens' (The Spiritual World of the Pagan Hungarians), in Csernus, Sándor and Korompay, Klára (eds), *Les Hongrois et l'Europe: conquête et intégration* (The Hungarians and Europe, Conquest and Integration), 103–120, Paris-Szeged: Publications de l'Institut Hongrois de Paris, 1999.

Szűcs, Jenő. *Les trois Europes* (The Three Europes), Paris: Éditions L'Harmattan, 1985.

Török, József and Hervay, Ferenc. 'Le réseau monastique Hongrois et l'histoire de l'ordre des Ermites de Saint-Paul en Hongrie médiévale' (The Network of Monasteries in Hungary and the History of the Order of Saint Paul the First Hermit in Medieval Hungary), in Cercor (ed.), *Naissance et fonctionnement des réseaux monastiques et canoniaux* (Origin and Functioning of the Monastic and Canonial Networks), Saint Etienne: CERCOR (Centre Européen de Recherches sur les Congrégations et Ordres Religieux), 1985.

Török, József. 'La notion de prieuré en Hongrie avant l'arrivée des Turcs' (The Concept of Priories in Hungary before the Arrival of the Turks), in Lemaitre, Jean-Loup (ed.), *Prieurs et prieurés dans l'occident médiéval* (Priors and Priories in the Medieval Occident), Paris: EPHE (Ecole Pratique des Hautes Etudes), 1987.

Tüdős S. Kinga. *Erdélyi védőrendszerek a XV.-XVIII. században, Háromszéki templomvárak* (Transylvanian Defense Structures, the Fortified Churches in Háromszék), Budapest: Puski kiadó, 1995.

Vofkori, László. *Székelyföld útikönyve* (Guide to the Szeklerland), I-II, Budapest: Cartographia kiadó, 1998.

Zimonyi, István. 'Préhistoire hongroise: méthode de recherche et vue d'ensemble' (Hungarian Prehistory: Research Methodology and Overview), in Csernus, Sándor and Korompay, Klára (eds), *Les Hongrois et l'Europe: conquête et intégration* (The Hungarians and Europe, Conquest and Integration), 29–43, Paris-Szeged: Publications de l'Institut Hongrois de Paris, 1999.

ENGLISH BIBLIOGRAPHY SUPPLEMENT

In addition to the different volumes used in this work and listed in the bibliography, some other books may be of interest for the English-speaking readers of this edition who wish to read more about the medieval history of Hungary and Transylvania.

Some **primary sources** are available with an English translation:

The Laws of Hungary Series I; Volumes 1-5 abbreviated as DRMH (Decreta regni mediaevalis Hungariae):

Bak, János M., Bónis, György and Ross Sweeney, James (ed. and transl.), *The Laws of the Medieval Kingdom of Hungary, Vol. 1, 1000–1301* (Decreta regni mediaevalis Hungariae Tomus I, 1000–1301), 2nd edn. Idyllwild, CA: Charles Schlacks Jr, 1999.

Bak, János M., Engel, Pál and Ross Sweeney, James (ed. and transl.), *The Laws of the Medieval Kingdom of Hungary, Vol. 2, 1301–1457* (Decreta regni mediaevalis Hungariae T. II, 1301–1457), Salt Lake City, UT: Charles Schlacks Jr, 1992.

Bak, János M., Domonkos, Leslie S. and Harvey, Paul B. Jr. (ed. and transl.), *The Laws of Medieval Kingdom of Hungary. Vol. 3, 1458–1490* (Decreta regni mediaevalis Hungariae. T. III, 1458–1490), Los Angeles, CA: Charles Schlacks Jr, 1996.

Banyó, Péter and Rady, Martyn (ed. and transl.), *The Laws of the Medieval Kingdom of Hungary, Vol. 4, 1490–1526* (Decreta regni mediaevalis Hungariae. T. IV, 1490–1526), Idyllwild, CA: Charles Schlacks Jr, 2012.

Bak, János M., Banyó, Péter and Rady, Martyn (ed. and transl.), *The Laws of the Medieval Kingdom of Hungary. Vol. 5, The Customary Law of the Renowned Kingdom of Hungary a Work in Three Parts Rendered by Stephen Werbőczy (The 'Tripartitum') 1517* (Decreta regni mediaevalis Hungariae. T. 5, Tripartitum opus iuris consuetudinarii inclyti regni Hungariae per Stephanum de Werbewcz editum), Los Angeles, CA: Charles Schlacks Jr, 2005.

This guide may be of interest:

Kurucz, György (ed.), *Guide to Documents and Manuscripts in Great Britain Relating to the Kingdom of Hungary from the Earliest Times to 1800*, London: Mansell, 1992.

Some primary sources are now available on-line, for instance on this site:

https://library.hungaricana.hu/en/collection/kozepkori_magyar_okmanytarak/

The direct links to collections of documents used in this work are mentioned in the bibliography, e.g. *Anjou-kori oklevéltár* (Archives of the Anjou Period) or *Monumenta Vaticana Historiam Regni Hungariae*.

The website of the National Library of Hungary contains more and more facsimiles and may be of help: http://mek.oszk.hu/indexeng.phtml.

These two **dictionaries** have been especially useful:

English, Arthur. *A Dictionary of Words and Phrases Used in Ancient and Modern Law*, Washington, DC: Beardbook, 1st edn 1988, reprint 2000.
Garner, Bryan A (ed.): *Black's Law Dictionary*, St Paul, MN: West Group, 2001.

The following **selected English bibliography** contains books the author found enlightening for her approach to the medieval context of her study and some recent publications of general historic interest even though the Szeklers are not the core subject.

Bak, János M. 'Tradition and Renewal in the Decretum Maius of King Matthias', in *Matthias Rex 1458–1490 Hungary at the Dawn of the Renaissance*, Budapest, 2013, unpaginated online resource.
http://renaissance.elte.hu/wp-content/uploads/2013/09/Janos-M.-Bak-Tradition-and-Renewal-in-the-Decretum-Maius-of-King-Matthias.pdf
Balázs, Mihály and Keserű, Gizella (eds) *György Enyedi and Central European Unitarianism in the 16th-17th Centuries*, Budapest: Balassi kiadó, 2000.
Bayerle, Gustav. *The Hungarian letters of Ali Pasha of Buda 1604–1616*, Budapest: Akadémiai kiadó, 1991.
Berend, Nora. *At the Gate of Christendom, Jews, Muslims and 'Pagans' in Medieval Hungary c.1000-c.1300*, Cambridge: Cambridge University Press, 2001.
Berend, Nora, Urbańczyk, Przemyslaw and Wiszewski, Przemyslaw. *Central Europe in the High Middle Ages: Bohemia, Hungary and Poland, c.900-c.1300*, Cambridge: Cambridge University Press, 2013.
Birnbaum, D. Marianna. *The Orb and the Pen: Janus Pannonius, Matthias Corvinus and the Buda Court*, Budapest: Balassi kiadó, 1996.
Font, Márta. *Koloman the Learned, King of Hungary*, Szeged: Szegedi Középkorász Műhely, 2001.
Fügedi, Erik. *The Elefánthy, The Hungarian Nobleman and His Kindred*, Budapest: CEU Press (Central Europe University), 1998.
Golden, B. Peter. *Khazar Studies, An Historico-Philological Inquiry into the Origins of the Khazars*, Budapest: Akadémiai kiadó, 1980.
Gombás, István. *Kings & Queens of Hungary - Princes of Transylvania*, Budapest: Corvina kiadó, 2000.
Klaniczay, Tibor and Jankovics József (ed.) *Matthias Corvinus and the Humanism in central Europe*, Budapest: Balassi kiadó, 1994.
Kósa, László (ed.) *A Cultural History of Hungary, from the Beginnings to the Eighteenth Century*, Budapest: Corvina kiadó, 1999.
Kosztolnyik, Zoltán. *From Coloman the Learned to Béla III (1095–1196) Hungarian Domestic Policies and Their Impact upon Foreign Affairs*, New York, NY: Columbia University Press, 1987.
Kosztolnyik, Zoltán. *Hungary in the Thirteenth Century*, New York, NY: Columbia University Press, 1996.
Kosztolnyik, Zoltán. *Hungary under the Early Árpáds, 890s to 1063*, New York, NY: Columbia University Press, 2002.
Kristó, Gyula. *Hungarian History in the Ninth Century* (transl. Novák György), Szeged: Szegedi Középkorász Műhely, 1996.

Kristó, Gyula. *Early Transylvania (895–1324)*, Budapest: Lucidus kiadó, 2003.
Lázár, István, *Transylvania, a Short History*, Budapest: Corvina kiadó, 1997.
Nemerkényi, Előd. *Latin Classics in Medieval Hungary, Eleventh Century*, Debrecen-Budapest: CEU Press (Central Europe University), 2004.
Paládi Kovács, Attila. *Ethnic Traditions, Classes and Communities in Hungary*, Budapest: Institute of Ethnology, Hungarian Academy of Sciences, 1996.
Péter, Lászlo, 'The Holy Crown of Hungary, Visible and Invisible' in *Slavonic and East European Review n° 81*, pp. 421–510, Leeds: Maney Publishing, 2003.
Rady, Martyn. *Nobility, Land and Service in Medieval Hungary*, New York, NY: Palgrave Macmillan, 2000.
Rady, Martyn. *Customary Law in Hungary, Courts, Texts, and the* Tripartitum, Oxford: Oxford University Press, 2013.
Rady, Martyn and Simon Alexandru (ed.) *Government and Law in Medieval Moldavia, Transylvania and Wallachia,* SSEES UCL (Studies in Russia and Eastern Europe 11), London: SSEES UCL, 2013.
Róna-Tas, András, *Hungarians and Europe in the Early Middle Ages*, Budapest: CEU Press (Central Europe University), 1999.
The Central European University (CEU), Budapest, is editing volumes of *Annual of medieval studies at CEU*, since 1993: link to the CEU Library https://library.ceu.edu/ and direct link to the *Annual*: http://bohunk.info/ams/.

For French readers, these recent works may be of interest:

Cevins, de, Marie-Madeleine. *Mathias Corvin, un roi pour l'Europe centrale (1458–1490)* (Matthias Corvinus, a King for Central Europe), Paris: Éditions Les Indes Savantes, 2016.
Cevins de, Marie-Madeleine, *L'Eglise dans les villes hongroises à la fin du Moyen Âge (vers 1320-vers 1490)* (The Church in Hungarian Cities at the End of Middle Ages ca1320-ca1490), Paris-Budapest-Szeged: Publications de l'Institut Hongrois de Paris, 2003.
Kálnoky, Nathalie. 'L'autonomie judiciaire du Pays sicule à la fin du Moyen Âge' (The Judicial Autonomy of the Szeklerland at the End of the Middle Ages), in Davy Gilduin and Lauranson-Rosaz Christian (eds), *Le droit autrement, mélanges offerts au Professeur Jean-Pierre Poly* (The Law, With a Difference. Compendium for Professor Jean-Pierre Poly), 161–117, Paris: Éditions Mare & Martin, 2017.
Kálnoky, Nathalie. 'Le droit coutumier de la Noble Nation Sicule de Transylvanie et la doctrine de la sainte Couronne, deux aspects d'un sens du partage du pouvoir proto-démocratique dans la Hongrie médiévale' (The Customary Law of the Noble Szekler Nation of Transylvania and the Doctrin of the Holy Crown: Two Aspects of a Proto-Democratic Conception of Shared Powera in Medieval Hungary), 191–201, in Hungarian Studies, volume 30–2, Budapest: Akadémiai kiadó, 2016.
Kálnoky, Nathalie. 'L'organisation militaire de la Nation sicule à la fin du Moyen Âge' (The Military Organisation of the Szekler Nation at the End of the Middle Ages), in Coutau-Bégarie, Hervé and Tóth, Ferenc (eds), *La pensée militaire hongroise à travers les siècles* (Hungarian Military Thinking Through the Centuries), 29–40, Paris: Éditions Economica, 2011.
Kálnoky, Nathalie. 'Peut-on parler de 'second servage' à propos des Sicules de Transylvanie?' (Can we Speak of the Second Serfdom for the Szeklers of Transylvania?), in Cevins de, Marie-Madeleine (ed.), *L'Europe centrale au seuil de la modernité, Mutations sociales, religieuses et culturelles, Autriche, Bohême, Hongrie et*

Pologne, fin du XIVe-milieu du XVIe siècle (Central Europe Aproaching Modernity, Social, Religious and Cultural Mutations, Austria, Bohemia, Hungary, from the End of the Fourteenth to the Middle of the Sixteenth Century), 129–138, Rennes: Presses Universitaires de Rennes, 2010.

Kálnoky, Nathalie. 'L'avancée des Mongols dans les steppes d'Asie centrale, chronique d'un cataclysme annoncé. Les récits de voyage de frère Julianus, dominicain de Hongrie' (The Advance of the Mongols in the Steppes of Central Asia, Chronicle of a Foretold Cataclysm. Reports of the Travels of Brother Julianus, Hungarian Dominican Friar), in Droit & Cultures hors-série 2008, *Orient et Occident, processus d'acculturation*, (special issue 2008, Orient and Occident, Acculturation Process), 71–87, Paris: Éditions L'Harmattan, 2008.

Kálnoky, Nathalie. 'Identités nationales et identités juridiques: les Sicules et les Hongrois de Transylvanie à la fin du XVe siècle' (National and Juridical Identities: The Szeklers and Hungarians of Transylvania at the End of the Fifteenth Century) in NAGY Piroska (ed.), *Identités hongroises, identités européennes du Moyen Âge à nos jours* (Hungarian Identities, European Identities from the Middle Ages to the Present), 71–86, Rouen: Presses Universitaires de Rouen, 2006.

Kálnoky, Nathalie. 'Des princes scythes aux capitaines Iasses' (From Scythian Princes to Iasian Captains) in Droit & Cultures n°52, publication des actes du colloque *Iran et Occident, hommage à Kasra Vafadari* (Publication of the Papers Presented at the Conference on Iran and the Occident, In homage of Kasra Vafadari), 65–84, Paris: Éditions L'Harmattan, 2006. http://journals.openedition.org/droitcultures/615

Kálnoky, Nathalie. 'La communauté sicule au début du XVIIIe siècle' (The Szekler Communityat the Beginning of the Eighteenth Century) in Studia Caroliensia n° 3-4, Publication des actes du colloque *Europe and Hungary in the Age of Ferenc II Rákóczi* (Publication of the Papers Presented at the Conference Europe and Hungaryin the Era of Ferencz II Rákóczi), 195–202, Budapest: Károli Gáspár Református Egyetemi kiadó, 2004.

Rossel, Hubert. *Les églises fortifiées du pays des Sicules* (Fortified Churches of Szeklerland), Cluj-Napoca: Risoprint, 2015.

And finally, after all these academic tomes, the author takes the liberty of recommending the following historical epic, *The Transylvanian Trilogy*, wonderfully translated, entertaining, lively and richly embedded in history as well as in details of day-to-day life:

Bánffy, Miklós (translated by Thursfield, Patrick and Bánffy-Jelen, Katalin), *The Transylvanian Trilogy*:

Book One: They were Counted, London: Arcadia Books Ltd, 1999,
Book Two: They Were Found Wanting, London: Arcadia Books Ltd, 2000,
Book Three: They Were Divided, London: Arcadia Books Ltd, 2001.

INDEX

Place Names
Proper Names
Topics

-A-
Agyagfalva 78, 104, 179
Ajtony 27
Akadács, Mihály 179
Alárd, Ferentz 118, 131, 181
Albert de Habsbourg 6, 173
Álmos 85, 175
Alsóboldogasszonyfalva 55
Altland 25–7, 32–4, 36, 173
Andrássy, János 149
Andrew II 27–8, 31, 175
Andrew III 29, 61
Angyalosi (or Angyalossi), Mózes 93–5, 159
Anjou dynasty, (see also Charles I and Louis I) 30, 55
Apafi, Lénárt 115, 120–1, 124–5, 128–9, 131, 138, 145, 151, 165
Apor, István 7, 111, 118, 135, 143, 160, 181
Aranyosszék (Seat) 26, 33–7, 52, 56, 58, 61–2, 66, 117–18, 135, 144, 152, 156, 181
Armenians 52
Árpád dynasty 5–6, 17, 22, 29, 50, 173
Árpád, Prince 1, 27
Attila 14–16, 18, 167
Avars 14, 16–17

-B-
Baláskó, (or Bláskó) János 118, 159–60, 181
Bálványos 135, 144
Bánd 131
Barcsai, Gáspár 115, 118, 120–2, 124–5, 128–9, 131, 155
Barlabássi, Mihály's widow 150, 154–7, 166

Báthory, István (voivode) 54, 76–7, 90, 97, 99, 102, 115, 154, 157, 159, 176
Bazini and Szentgyörgyi, Péter (voivode) 107
Békés, Adorján 88–9, 102, 137, 144
Békési, Gergely 149, 157
Béla II 15
Béla III 14
Béla IV 24, 26, 28, 39, 136
Benedekfi, János and Péter 56, 117–18, 181
Benedictine Order 55
Benkő (judge) 145
Bereck 58
Besenyőfalva 23
Beszterce 32, 43, 48
Betz, Imre 118, 181
Bicsak 120–1, 124–5, 128–9, 131
Bihar (County) 27
Bíró, Balázs 179
Bíró, Miklós 181
Bodor, Antal 107
Bögözi, János 179, 181
Bohemia 6, 8, 26, 79, 173
Bölön 89, 136
Bolyai, Anna 156–7
Boncza 131
bondsmen (jobbágyok) 98, 175
Bonyha 168
Brassó 32, 48, 53, 57, 59–60, 136
Bratislava (Pozsony, Preßburg) 15, 26, 69
Buda 24, 57, 71, 80, 167, 171
Bulgaria (campaign of, before 1235) 27
Bulgarians 13, 17, 21
Burzenland 53
Byzantine Empire 17, 22–4, 28, 51

-C-
Calvinists 51
Carpathian basin 4–5, 15–17, 20
Chapter of Transylvania (see also *locus credibilis*) 7–8, 56, 107, 135–6, 143

Charles I of Anjou (or Charles-Robert) 61
Charles V (Holy Roman Emperor) 70
Church of Rome see Roman Catholic Church
Clement VII, Pope 70
Coloman (the Learned) 22, 174
Constantine Porphyrogenitus (see also Byzantine Empire) 17, 85, 175
Constantinople 42, 46
Croatia 28, 174, 177
Csaba (see also **Attila**) 14
Csakó, Benedek 144
Csakó, János 181
Csanád (county) 144
Csernáton 88
Csíkszék (Seat) 26, 33–7, 52, 55–6, 62,-4, 66, 98, 114, 116–8, 135, 144–5, 181
Csíkszereda 58
Csomortán, László 181
Cumans 2, 15, 19, 22–5, 30–1, 38, 52
Czikó, Orsolya 156
Czirjék (or Czirják), Bernád 181
Czirjék, Martha 156–7

-D-
Daczó, Péter 181
Danube 2, 24
daughters' quarter 151–2
daughters-deemed-sons 155–7, 159, 162
Dénes, András 181
Diploma Andreanum 27, 31, 33, 37, 39
Diploma Leopoldinum 80
Dominican Order 55
Domokos 93–5, 159
double conquest (theory of the) 16–17

-E-
Ebesfalva 168
Eger 41
Erdő de Csávás, Miklós 139
Erdőhát (deaconry of) 72
Esztergom 14, 41, 52–3, 57, 61

-F-
Fehér (county) 28, 35, 37, 52, 144
Fehérvár (archdeaconry) 35–6, 52
Felsőszentmihályfalvi, Ábráhám 157
Felvinc 58
Ferdinand I of Habsburg 60, 69, 71, 81, 146, 160

Fogaras 168
Forró, Simon 136, 155
fortified churches 50, 54, 104
Francis I of Austria 78
Franciscan Order 30, 55
François I of France 70

-G-
Gelence 52
geréb 32
Gergely, János 181
Germans of Szepes 25, 45
Gernyeszeg 155
Géza, Grand Prince 22
gift of the branded oxen 49, 77–9, 114
Gog and **Magog** 14
Golden Bull 2, 151, 175–6
Görgény 43, 85, 103, 111
Gyalakuti, Mihály 118, 120–2, 124–5, 128–9, 181
Gyergyóremete 55
Gyergyószék (Seat) 61–4, 98, 117
Gyerőfi (succession) 154–5, 157, 164
gyula 21, 85, 175
Gyula 27–8
Gyulafehérvár 7–8, 107
Gyulakuti, Péter 166

-H-
Habsburg dynasty 5–6, 49–51, 71, 79, 146, 167, 173
Háromszék (Seat) 34, 103
Havadtő 131
Henry VIII, of England 70
Hidvég 63, 135–6, 155, 188
Holy Crown 6, 174–6, 181
Holy Roman Empire 6, 43
horka 21, 85, 175
Hunor and **Magor** 14
Huns 13–15, 17, 167
Hunyad (county) 42
Hunyadi, John 43, 70, 90, 117

-I-
Iasian-Cuman (Jász-kun), status 24–5, 38
Iasians 2, 24
Illuminated Chronicle 1, 14, 25, 42
Illyés 89
Innocent III, Pope 34

-J-
Jagiello (see also Wladislas I, Wladislas II and Louis II) 70, 96
Jánosfalva 104
Jánosy, Margit 157
Jews 52
John I Szapolyai 69, 71, 146, 160, 167
John II Szapolya 6, 81, 95, 102, 106, 161, 167, 169-70
John XXII, Pope 55

-K-
Kacsai (or Katzai or Kontzai), Antal 118, 179, 181
Káli, Magdolna 131, 145, 149, 154-7, 166
Kálnoki, Bálint 118, 181
Kászonszék (Seat) 40, 61-4, 66, 104, 115, 117
Kavars (see also *Khazar Empire*) 13, 16-18, 21, 23, 25, 36-7
Kedei, Ferentz 179
kende 21, 175
kenéz 30
Kerelői 120-1, 124-5, 128-9
Keresztúr (Seat) 61-2, 116-17, 178-9
Kézai, Simon 14
Kézdi (archdeaconry) 34-7, 52
Kézdiszék (Seat) 26, 33-37, 52, 56, 58, 61-2, 64, 66-7, 75, 82, 103, 116-18, 135, 144-5, 181
Kézdivásárhely 58, 103, 105
Khazar Empire (see also *Kavars*) 16, 20, 85
Kibéd 131
Kimpolung 53
Kisfalud 131, 139, 145, 160
Kőhalom 32
Kolozsmonotor, convent of (see also *locus credibilis*) 7-8, 61, 96, 106, 133, 135
Kolozsvár 32, 57, 123
Köpecz 91
Kornis, Miklós 144
Kőröspatak 53
Kövér, Benedek and Lázár 107
Kún, Antal 181
Kurszán 21

-L-
Lackfi (voivodes) 43
Laczok, Mihály 181
Ladislas I (St. Ladislas) 15, 22, 174

Ladislas IV (the Cuman) 41, 61, 134
Ladislas V of Habsburg (the Posthumous) 6, 173
Laurencius 41, 134
Lázár, András and Bálint 56, 115-15, 121, 124, 131, 139, 160, 181
Lázár, János 145-6, 159
Lécfalva (or Lécsfalva) 88
Leitha (river) 5, 26, 174
Lengyelfalvi, Boldizsár 179
locus credibilis 87, 95-6, 102, 111, 146
Lokodi, Péter 179
Lőrinczfalva 131
Losonczi (voïvodes) 43
Louis I of Anjou (Louis the Great) 2, 6, 30, 151, 176
Louis II Jagellio 6, 49, 70, 78, 173-4
Lutherans 51

-M-
Madarasi, Dorottya 144-5, 150-1, 154-5, 157; 165
Magna Carta 2, 175
Maja 131
Majláth, Gábor 168
Majláth, István (or Majlád, voivode) 160
Maksa 88
Málnás 136
Málnási, András 111
Máramaros 30
Maria-Theresia of Habsburg 78
Márkos, Mihály 179
Maros (river) 130, 168
Marosszék (Seat) 35-7, 57, 59, 61, 65-7, 96, 98, 103, 105, 109, 114, 118-20, 125, 130, 139, 144-5, 147, 149, 152, 155, 160-1
Marosszentkirály 55
Marosvásárhely 58-9, 66, 84, 103-5, 168
Márton 120-1, 123, 131
Matthias I, Corvinus 6, 46-50, 61, 63, 70, 74-6, 79, 93, 96, 136, 159
Medgyes 26, 32, 35, 37
Meggyes de Erdőszentgyörgy, Zsofia 159
Meggyesfalva 131
Mezőmajos 131
Mikháza 55
Miklósvárszék (Seat) 40, 61-3, 117
Mikó, Lőrincz 156
Mikó, Mihály 118, 121, 123, 136, 181

Milkó 52–3
Mohács (battle of, 1526) 5–6, 10, 48–9, 51, 71, 74, 78–9, 81, 95, 161, 167, 176
Moldavia 52–3, 168
Moldavians 30, 93
Mongols (see also *Tartars*) 24, 30, 37, 52
Moravia (Great Moravia) 4
Moson 25–6, 35–7

-N-
Nagyselyk 32
Nagysink 32
Normans 5
Nyárád (river) 168
Nyárádkarácson 131
Nyárádremete 55
Nyárádszentmárton 131
Nyárádszereda 58
Nyujtódi, Domokos 93
Nyujtódi, Pál 56, 118, 179, 181

-O-
Olt (river) 136
Oltsava (river) 26
Oltszem 136
Opus Tripartitum see *Tripartitum*
Orbaiszék (Seat) 26, 33–7, 52–3, 56, 58, 62, 64, 66, 75, 103, 117–18, 181
Orbán de Lengyelfalva, János 112, 179, 181
ordeal of the bleeding Corpse, (tetemre hivás) 51, 91, 107
Order of Saint John 55
Order of St. Paul the First Hermit 95, 55, 144–5
Orthodox Church of Imperial Byzantium 27–8, 30, 36, 52
Ottokar II of Bohemia 26
Ottoman Empire 4–5, 30, 42, 46–7, 69–71, 79, 94, 145; 160, 167, 176

-P-
Pálfalvi, Lukátz 179
Panit 131
Pannonia 21, 25
Parendorf 26–7
Partium regni Hungariae 5, 28, 51, 71, 81, 176
Patakfalva 23
Patakfalvi, Péter and Kelemen 179

Pechenegs 2, 15–16, 19, 22–6, 30–1, 38, 42, 67, 176
Pisky de Szentiván, György 144
Pókai, Balázs 160–1
Poland 6, 8, 176
potiores (or *pociores*) 47, 75, 108–10
Prázsmár 111
primipilate 47, 84, 113–15, 118, 125, 129–30, 133, 137–42, 145, 151, 156, 159–60, 178–9

-R-
Reformation 51–2, 63
Remeteszeg 55
Roman Catholic Church 22, 25, 30, 50–2, 55, 63
Romanians (see also *Vlachs* and *Moldavians*) 27, 29–31
royal fortress 43–4, 48, 103, 11, 134–5, 144, 170, 175
royal free towns 2, 31–2, 39–40, 44, 50, 57–60, 62, 70, 83–4, 86, 102–3, 105, 112, 116, 174

-S-
Sabbatarians 51
Sachsenland 29, 32–5, 57, 59, 64–6, 103, 134
Sárd 131
Sáromberke 155
Saxons 23, 25–7, 29–35, 37, 39–40, 47, 50, 53, 54, 55, 57, 58, 60, 61, 43, 48–51, 53–4, 57–60, 76–7, 81, 83, 86, 96, 103–4, 136, 167–8, 171, 173
Scythians 10, 13–14, 19, 79, 167–9, 180
Segesvár 26, 32, 34, 104, 170
seniores 108–10
Sepsiszék (Seat) 23, 26, 33–7, 52–3, 56, 58–60, 62–4, 66, 75,, 91, 98, 103, 106–7, 110, 114, 117–18, 136, 181
Sepsiszentgyörgy 58–60, 81, 103, 105–6
Sigismund of Luxembourg 6, 30, 58, 61–2, 75, 155
Silesia 26
Slovakia 15, 25
Society of Estates 10, 42, 67, 69–70, 133, 174
Sólyom, Mátyás 154, 165
Somkereki, Miklós 155, 164
Somogy (county) 16
Speyer (treaty of, 1570) 5, 28

Stephen I (St. Stephen) 1–2, 4, 6, 17–18, 21–2, 24, 27–8, 30, 53, 57, 143, 173, 175
Stephen V 34, 41, 61, 154
Suleiman I (the Magnificent) 71
Szabó, Orsolya 176 **Szapolyai** (see also **John I** and **John II**) 28, 51, 96
Szászkézd 26, 34, 168
Szászorbó 26, 34
Szászsebes 26, 32, 34
Szászváros 32
Szeben (or Nagyszeben) 30, 32–5, 37, 53, 57
Szederjes 41
Székely d'Esztergom, Ferencz 139, 160
Székelyhíd 27
Székelykeresztúr 58
Székelyudvarhely see Udvarhely
Székelyvaja 131
Székesfehérvár 57, 69
Szekler hereditary property (siculicate) 97, 99, 115, 133–4, 137–46, 148–53, 156, 158–61
Szengyel, Ilona 149, 154, 165
Szentbenedek 55
Szentdomokos 55
Szentgyörgyi, Anna 122, 154–6, 166
Szentkereszt 41
Szentkirályi, Semjén 154–7, 166
Szentmihályfalvi, Katalin (born Szenpáli) 149, 157
Szentmiklós 131
Szép, Péter 93–4
Szerdahely 32, 34
Szeret 52–3
Szilágyi, Lucia 142, 157
Szombatfalvi, Gergely 179
Szörény 53
Szováta 131

-T-
Tartars (see also *Mongols*) 42, 54, 57
Tatár, Gergely 181
Telegd (archdeaconry) 25–7, 34–7, 52, 55
Teutonic Knights 27, 30–3
Thomory, Pál 78
Three Nations, assembly of 29, 31, 42, 61, 75, 81, 86, 98, 103, 113, 167, 173
Tibád, Ferencz 181
Tisza (river) 2, 24
tízes 44–5, 63, 76, 97

Toldalagi, András 144
Törcs 43, 85
Torda
 (archdeaconry) 36–7, 52
 (county) 55, 144, 155
 (town) 34–5, 57, 59, 61, 103, 169
Torda, Edict of, 1568 51, 63
Toroczkay 134–5
Toroczkó 34, 134
Tóth, Miklós 115, 118, 120–2, 124–5, 128–9, 131, 139, 149, 155–6, 160, 166, 181
Tóthfalvi 124
tres genera Siculorum 16, 33, 36–7, 48, 65, 109
Tripartitum 74, 79–80, 138, 140, 158, 161, 175–6
Turkic languages 16–18, 21, 23

-U-
Udvarhelyszék
 (Seat) 23, 26, 33–7, 52, 55–6, 58–9, 62, 64, 66, 88–9, 93, 103–6, 112, 116–18, 178–9, 181
Udvarhely (or Székelyudvarhely, town) 58–9, 78, 86 93, 95, 103–5, 112, 147, 158, 171, 178–9, 18
Újegyház 32
una eademque nobilitas 2, 70, 80, 176–7
Unitarians 51–2
universitas Siculorum 41, 108–9
Urbán, Dimjén 181

-V-
Vág 15, 39
Vágási, Imre 179
Vlachs 23, 29–30, 136, 173

-W-
Walachia 52–3
Werbőczy, István 9–11, 14, 21, 33, 74, 80, 82, 98, 107, 110, 113, 140, 146, 150, 158, 175–6
weregild 95, 99, 159
Wladislas I Jagiello 6, 176
Wladislas II Jagiello 6, 45, 49, 77, 79–80, 173–4

-Z-
Zabola 47, 74–6, 109–10, 161

www.ingramcontent.com/pod-product-compliance
Lightning Source LLC
Chambersburg PA
CBHW070030010526
44117CB00011B/1771